PRAISE FOR
LIGHT FROM ALEXANDRIA

"Petroc Willey is the consummate authority on evangelization and catechesis. In his new book, *Light from Alexandria: Recovering a Vision of Christian Paideia for Education and Formation*, he creatively tells the splendid, graced-filled story of how ancient Alexandria, through its catechetical school, became the premier city for evangelization and catechesis. In so doing, Petroc himself becomes an Alexandrian, a new Clement and Origen. In our present culture—not unlike a global Alexandria, where various religions, philosophies, and polities vie with one another—Petroc fearlessly and unapologetically professes the faith that Jesus alone is the universal Savior and definitive Lord."

—**THOMAS G. WEINANDY**, OFM, Cap., former member of the Vatican's International Theological Commission

"An erudite and engaging study of the Christian School of Alexandria in the early Christian centuries, which does justice both to the city and culture of Alexandria and to the use Christian apologists, especially Clement and Origen, made of earlier philosophical traditions in service of the Incarnate Logos, Jesus. Petroc Willey presents the Christian Alexandrian synthesis as a model and resource for present-day Catholic teaching, but non-Christians will also profit from learning how important it is to read sacred scriptures with an eye to their allegorical and typological meaning."

—**STEPHEN R.L. CLARK**, Emeritus Professor of Philosophy, University of Liverpool; Honorary Research Fellow, Dept. of Theology, University of Bristol

"Jesus attributed a certain wisdom to the scribes of the kingdom who know how to bring out what is old and what is new. In this wonderfully written, thoroughly researched, and deeply illuminating book on the catechetical school of Alexandria, Petroc Willey has made the old new and the ancient relevant to us today. There is something here for everyone—those interested in history, education, culture, inculturation, and, of course, theology and catechetics. The fruit of this work is a profound sense of how a Christian culture was built and transmitted in Alexandria, and how we might do so again."

—**STEPHEN M. HILDEBRAND**, Professor of Theology, VPAA, Franciscan University of Steubenville

"In *Light from Alexandria*, Petroc Willey paints a compelling and vivid portrait of the ancient catechetical school in Alexandria, uniting history, philosophy, and theology, not in a wistful looking back but to set the context for understanding how this venture shines with relevance for us today. Throughout the work he emphasizes the need for a holistic catechumenal approach and sacramental mindset, encouraging us to look again at how the catechetical wisdom found in Alexandria can assist catechists, families, and those in educational institutions to consider an evangelizing catechesis that can offer to others a whole way of life. The light from Alexandria shines brightly."

—ANNE JAMIESON, Executive Director, Institute for Catholic Education, Ontario, Canada

"*Light from Alexandria* is a masterful study on the convergence of biblical, liturgical, patristic, catechetical, philosophical, and cultural influences that produced the once great and flourishing Catechetical School of Alexandria. But far more than just providing an engaging historical overview of the sources of the classical Christian *paideia*, the author—himself a renowned *paedagogus* of pedagogues in our own day—points the way forward for an authentic *kerygmatic renewal of catechesis and evangelization* inspired by some of the greatest oriental lights of the See of the Gospel Evangelist, St. Mark."

—FR. DANIEL G. DOZIER, Executive Chairman, God With Us Eastern Catholic Formation, USCCB Region XV

"In his work *Light from Alexandria*, Petroc Willey spotlights the ancient catechetical school of Alexandria, so that we may see the true nature of catechetical education. More than a nostalgic look into the past, Willey's rigorous research identifies the key principles of evangelization and catechesis necessary for an authentic catechetical *ressourcement*. It is not an over-exaggeration to foresee Willey's work standing among other great texts, such as Newman's *Idea of a University*. Indeed, this work will be footnoted by every serious effort to re-envision catechesis in both parishes and Catholic schools in years to come."

—SISTER MARY MICHAEL FOX, OP, Dominican Sisters of St. Cecilia (Nashville); author of *Following God's Pedagogy: Principles for Children's Catechesis*

LIGHT FROM ALEXANDRIA

LIGHT *from* ALEXANDRIA

RECOVERING A VISION OF
CHRISTIAN PAIDEIA FOR
EDUCATION AND FORMATION

PETROC WILLEY

Foreword by Bishop Franz-Peter Tebartz-van Elst

Angelico Press

© Angelico Press 2025

For information, address:
Angelico Press, Ltd.
169 Monitor St.
Brooklyn, NY 11222
www.angelicopress.com

ppr 979-8-89280-089-1
cloth 979-8-89280-090-7
ebook 979-8-89280-091-4

Book and cover design
by Michael Schrauzer

For Josh and Charis, Carly and Ben, Nicholas, David, and each and all of our grandchildren, with love.

> what we have loved,
> Others will love; and we may teach them how.
> —Wordsworth, *The Prelude*, XIII, 446-47.

CONTENTS

ACKNOWLEDGMENTS xi

FOREWORD xiii

INTRODUCTION: A Portrait xv

CHAPTER 1: The Significance of Alexandria 1
    Underway: a catechetical *ressourcement* 5
    A catechumenal model for a new evangelization 8
    Seeing from the inside 14
    Main points of discussion 24

PART I: THE CITY AND THE SCHOOL 29

CHAPTER 2: The Preparation of the City 31
    The Ptolemaic city 32
    Intellectual, cultural and religious life 37
    A universal nurse 44
    The move to Roman rule and the gathering of the heritage 56

CHAPTER 3: The School in its Christian Setting 63
    Early Christianity in Alexandria and Egypt 64
    The value of Christian histories 72
    History and reception of Mark's association
       with Alexandria 78

CHAPTER 4: The Character of the School 89
    A point of comparison: philosophical schools 90
    A pattern of ecclesial continuity and succession 97
    The life and work of the school 111

PART II: THE ALEXANDRIAN CATECHETICAL TRADITION 131

CHAPTER 5: Serving the Paideia of the Lord Jesus 133
    Greek *paideia* 133
    Jewish *paideia* 137
    The Church: the setting of the Lord's *paideia* 144
    The kerygma of God's universal education 153
    And today 160

CHAPTER 6: Friendship with the Wisdom of God   164
    Philosophical traditions in Alexandria   168
    Opening a pathway into faith   171
    Foundations for faith   176
    Wisdom and the Logos   177
    Hierarchy and participation   182
    A spirituality of doctrine   184
    And today   188

CHAPTER 7: The Good News of Christ and the Call to Conversion   194
    The lure of Gnosticism   194
    The Alexandrian *kerygma*   200
    The paideia of love   204
    The kingdom of the Logos   205
    The call of divine beauty   208
    The journey from image to likeness   212
    Crossing the threshold   214
    And today   217

CHAPTER 8: The Catechumenate:
  The Pedagogue Forms his Children   221
    The work of healing and the *disciplina arcani*   227
    Striving under grace   234
    The pedagogy of ascent   237
    The pedagogy of divine condescension   245
    And today   253

CHAPTER 9: Christ in his Mystery: Formation for Transmission   257
    Entering the Mystery   257
    Assisting Christ the Teacher   265
    The oral word   266
    The written word   274
    And today   284

CODA: Mark's Gospel as Catechumenal Icon in Miniature   291
    Structure and themes   293
    Discipleship and conversion   294
    Baptism and faith   296

POSTSCRIPT   304

WORKS CITED   307

INDEX OF NAMES AND SELECTED SUBJECTS   327

ACKNOWLEDGMENTS

THOSE WHO ARE LOVERS OF THE WORD, AS CLEMent of Alexandria reminded his catechumens, are lovers of gratitude—a kind of rent paid gladly to the Lord for the blessings of this earthly home, for creation and life; and small payment, even more, for his costly and saving love, his wise guidance, and his rescue from the ruin of sin. Thanksgiving is the true food of the Christian life.

Within the capacious debt of gratitude of which the Christian life is made, I have incurred much in the composition of this work. My thanks go in the first place to Tom and Mary Lannon, who graciously provided hospitality during my sabbatical leave, and to all those—family, friends, and colleagues—who have patiently engaged with my musings and thoughts when the conversation inevitably turned, once again, to Alexandria. Broader thanks span many decades and two continents. The source of my initial interest in Alexandria almost certainly lies in the work of my doctoral supervisor, Stephen R. L. Clark, who gave me a love for Christian Platonism as well as a conviction that I should become better acquainted with Philo. The privilege of working in England at two places of Catholic higher education—Plater College in Oxford, where I met my wife, Katherine, and Maryvale Institute in Birmingham, the original Catholic home of John Henry Newman—afforded me many opportunities for appreciating the challenges, as well as the converting power, of long-term lay formation. My own understanding of catechesis and evangelization grew immeasurably at Maryvale under the bold leadership of Msgr. Daniel McHugh and Msgr. Paul Watson and has given me some insight into many aspects of the catechetical enterprise that was underway, with such persistence and courage, in ancient Alexandria.

The Lord's mercies never come to an end, and I now live only a few short miles from the small hamlet of *New* Alexandria in Eastern Ohio, wondering about the character and commitments of the pilgrim-immigrants who brought that name here to the banks of the Ohio River. I am again deeply blessed to be surrounded by veteran workers in the field of catechesis, and at Franciscan University by friars, faculty, and staff—both in the teaching faculty of the University and in the University's Catechetical Institute—who share a profound, and often sacrificial, commitment to the Church's catechetical and evangelizing work. While I sincerely hope that I have not anachronistically read into the Alexandrian school features of the quiet, devoted work that takes place around me on a day-to-day basis, it is easy to see parallels between that ancient school and what is evident in my own environment. The library of ancient Alexandria was justly famous, and it is to be hoped that resident scholars there found in its numerous staff something of the intelligent support that I have received so unfailingly here in Franciscan's library.

My special thanks go to Bishop Dr. Franz-Peter Tebartz-van Elst, the Holy See's delegate for catechesis, for his generous foreword and shared interest in the Alexandrian catechetical heritage. I am grateful also to John Riess who, in addition to steering this work into publication, has offered thoughtful advice and support, while the text has also benefitted from anonymous reviewers who have saved me from many infelicities and errors of judgment. Sr. Jude Andrew, O. P., deserves special thanks for reviewing and discussing the MS through three progressive editions.

Projects that absorb this kind of time and energy are only made possible because of the faithful encouragement, love, and assistance of those closest at hand, and my deepest thanks of all go to my family, and especially Katherine.

Petroc Willey

FOREWORD

TO SAY IT STRAIGHT AWAY: THIS NEW STUDY BY Petroc Willey refreshingly takes us beyond the pragmatic perspectives and narrow horizons that can be so prevalent in our thinking about catechesis and evangelization, as well as makes us aware of how profoundly the two belong together and have always formed a constitutive unit in the Christian tradition.

Under the title *Light from Alexandria* he explores in depth how this urban society of antiquity gave birth to a catechetical school that opened up paths of learning for Christians to deepen their faith within a Greek-philosophical context, sometimes in contrast to surrounding patterns of thought and sometimes in complementarity to them. The fact that this could happen in Alexandria—which can be seen here as a paradigm of a highly developed ancient urban society—only as a result of a profound understanding of the philosophies and cultures of antiquity by these early Christians is made clear from Willey's comparisons and links with the Ptolemaic world and the philosophical schools of that time.

The first part of this book shows, then, how early Christians in an urban context learned to absorb an existing culture and reinterpret or further develop it. This pastoral-theological understanding of inculturation runs throughout the book as the author carefully demonstrates how the Alexandrian adaptation of Jewish and Greek traditions offers a profile of catechesis as a living relational reality. His analysis also yields many detailed proposals that often call into question common practices of evangelization and catechesis in our own time.

This Alexandrian catechetical approach, following Jesus's own pedagogy, is unfolded in the individual chapters of the second part of the book, offering the reader an introduction to the world of the Christian Logos and to an understanding of conversion as a constantly renewed response to the divine call to follow Jesus into the promise of his Word. Not a "being born again" but a "being born again *and again and again* . . ." is seen to be a distinguishing feature of Catholic-Christian catechetics—which we can contrast with an evangelical understanding of conversion.

Petroc Willey analyzes and illustrates this dynamic of ongoing conversion especially in the eighth chapter of his book, as he studies the central features of the Alexandrian catechumenate and shows how this understanding became paradigmatic for the Church's pedagogy, developed in contrast to more time-sensitive expectations and practices in the ancient world. In this sense, we can think of the "light from Alexandria" as being precisely the "enlightenment" that can be experienced in the catechumenate. The book focuses on the nature of this enlightenment, while also opening up for the reader the importance of mystagogy as the process of a deeper "escorting into the mysteries," as Maximus the Confessor describes it. The Alexandrian understanding of mystagogy, presented in the final chapter, is rightly seen as a great legacy and corrective for many self-made aporias in today's catechetical attempts and commitments. Finally, I must note with gratitude a closing section in the book on understanding the Gospel of Mark as an Alexandrian "catechumenal icon"—a special gift from the author in this year of St. Mark.

Bishop
✠ Dr. Franz-Peter Tebartz-van Elst
Delegate for Catechesis in the First Section of the Dicastery for Evangelization
Vatican City, September 8, 2024

INTRODUCTION: A PORTRAIT

LAST MAY, A FRIEND OF MINE TOLD ME OF A LITTLE-known portrait of Pope John Paul II that had been discovered. Of striking beauty, it is titled *Light from Alexandria,* and light, he reported, is indeed the dominant and most arresting feature of this small work. Dating from the early 1980s and measuring just 12 x 18 inches, it depicts John Paul seated, his right hand resting on the open pages of his recently promulgated Apostolic Exhortation, *Catechesi tradendae*. Certain lines of the text can be read if the viewer scrutinizes the portrait closely, and his fingers seem to be settled below phrases describing the Gospel of St Mark: one can read "St Mark's is the catechumen's Gospel." An open copy of Mark's Gospel lies on the desk adjacent to the pen hand. If the eye continues to the right, one sees a waist-high bookcase, with three shelves, containing the works of early Alexandrian teachers and bishops. One can just make out some of the works from the spines—among them, Clement of Alexandria's *Protrepticus*, a volume from Origen's *Commentary on John*, Didymus the Blind on Job—and one work lies at an angle on the top shelf, Clement's *Paedagogus*. An icon of Our Lady and Child hangs on the plain white wall beyond the desk, the Virgin embracing the Child and holding Him in an interior gaze. The Pope himself is looking intently up and to his left, his left hand reaching forward, hand slightly turned, as though engaging the artist, his eyes shining, sharing in the sense of vibrant light in the painting, communicating Revelation.

The moment captured in the portrait is a magisterial one: the Pope in the act of communicating a living heritage, full of light for the Church of today. The identification, in paragraph 11 of *Catechesi tradendae*, of the catechumenal character of the Gospel of St Mark is followed in that work by a comment from John Paul on the Church's title of "Mother and Teacher" and then a reference to the "remarkable works" in the post-apostolic age. A footnote in the text offers examples of these works, singling out works from the North African church of Tertullian and Cyprian, and the Alexandrians, Clement and Origen. The *Epistula Apostolorum*, a work of probable Alexandrian origin, is also noted. Tradition places St Mark as the founding apostolic figure in Alexandria and the portrait, following these few indications in the papal text, speaks to the conviction that the Gospel's catechumenal character is fittingly and convincingly uncovered and expressed in the work of the Alexandrian catechetical tradition. The icon in the portrait carries forward this same theme, reminding the viewer of the role of Alexandria, especially under the Patriarch Cyril, in the defense of the great dogmatic formulations regarding Christ through its unswerving fidelity to the title of *Theotokos*. Cyril stood centrally within the Alexandrian tradition, drawing upon the works of Origen, Didymus and others, and it seems especially fitting that John Paul chose to close his apostolic exhortation with an appeal for the prayers of the Virgin for the work of catechesis in the Church.

I have never seen this portrait myself, and so cannot vouch for its certain existence. But my imagination was fired by this report since the portrait seemed to me to represent in essentials the argument that will be developed in this book, enabling me to hold the strands of the argument in a simple act of intellectual judgment. As I pondered this question of the existence of the portrait and its possible connection to the work I was developing I turned for help to explore the little-known mid-Victorian genre of imaginary portraits and the kinds of service they can sometimes provide for a reader. In 1887, Walter Pater published his volume *Imaginary Portraits*.[1] He was following in a style of writing that had originated in Pre-Raphaelite circles in which commentaries were composed about imaginary artworks. Shortly after Pater's work was published, Oscar Wilde wrote his *The Portrait of Mr W. H.*, a complex and multi-levelled work of fiction which was a creative exploration into the possible identity of the mysterious "Mr W. H.," the "onlie begetter" lauded on the dedication page of Shakespeare's *Sonnets*. Wilde drew together allusions, obscure references and character indications from the *Sonnets* to create a single figure, with an accompanying narrative, to account for all of these. It was consciously a work of creative fiction, and yet the portrait enabled him to communicate the unity of the *Sonnets* and allowed him to draw out a rich variety of features from the collection.[2]

The portrait of John Paul offered above might play for us a similar role of speaking to the essential *unity* of what we might call the "Alexandrian catechetical tradition" and to the urgent need for a creative *reappropriation* of its catechetical contribution. The details of the institutional embodiment of this tradition, as we shall see, are a matter of much scholarly debate, but the portrait allows for a singleness of focus, inviting us to consider how we might discover a profound

---

[1] Walter Pater, *Imaginary Portraits* (London: MacMillan and Co., 1914).
[2] For a recent study of imaginary portraits in Dante and D. G. Rosetti see Fabio A. Camilletti, *The Portrait of Beatrice: Dante, D. G. Rosetti, and the Imaginary Lady* (Notre Dame: University of Notre Dame Press, 2019).

unity of catechetical thought and approach that rises above particular characters and circumstances, thereby allowing the Church today to capture what is of enduring value from this distinguished period in the catechetical and evangelizing work in the Church. Ratzinger argued in his *Principles of Catholic Theology* that the seat of the faith lies in the unifying *memoria Ecclesiae*, the memory of the Church, a memory that must be creatively retrieved and taught for each new generation.[3] Within the security and confidence of that ample unity of ecclesial memory, stretching across time and space, one finds the freedom to identify particular sustained contributions and associations, traditions of thought and life, which can be of special service to the wider Church. The one faith, inculturated in times and places very different from our own, can carry from those places a life and momentum that can rekindle our own practice and belief because it is carried within the one Subject, the living Body of the Church. One such, the portrait urges, is the Alexandrian catechetical tradition.

If this specific portrait allows us to capture in a single gaze the focus and argument of the book, the genre of portraiture also reminds us of a central theme in the book: how important is a *personal* carrying of the faith for the work of its successful transmission. In every age the close weave of doctrine and discipline, of spirituality, belief, and practice, has to be achieved by individual persons who are called to be saints so that pastoral activity and doctrinal commitments do not drift into dissociated fields but remain, under the generous work of grace, tightly and coherently bound.

Much water has flowed under Rome's many bridges since that portrait captured a vision and an intention from the pontificate of John Paul II, but the need for Alexandrian light has only intensified since that time and this work hopes to draw out both its concordance with contemporary magisterial work in evangelization and catechesis as well as its capacity to provide clear directions for future development. The light from Alexandria is not confined to the past but illumines the paths ahead of us.

---

[3] See Joseph Ratzinger, *Principles of Catholic Theology: Building Stones for a Fundamental Theology* (San Francisco: Ignatius Press, 1987), 22–24.

CHAPTER 1

The Significance of Alexandria

IN THIS OPENING CHAPTER I WILL OUTLINE THE argument underlying this study of the catechetical school of Alexandria, a school that can be traced from around the mid-second century until AD 405. The book as a whole tells the story of this school, introduces the main figures who taught in it, and outlines its character. The story of the school is without doubt a compelling one, and it is the contention of this work that the school offers contemporary catechesis and evangelization an unmatched vision for the renewal of the Church's ministerial practices. The telling of this story utilizes historical, theological, philosophical and catechetical approaches. For some readers there will be, perhaps, too *much* history, or theology, or philosophy, or catechetics; for other readers, too *little* of one or other of these elements. There will inevitably be many questions raised by the study as well as, I hope, some questions answered. This opening chapter, by providing an outline as well as a rationale for the work, is intended to enable readers to approach the work selectively if they so wish, in order to satisfy their own interests.

In first-century Alexandria there were schools of many kinds, expressive of the cultures the city contained, propagating, refining, developing and transmitting the many traditions there: schools teaching the liberal arts; rabbinic schools studying the Torah; various schools of philosophy—Stoic, Platonic, Epicurean, Pythagorean. Into this rich mix the Church placed a new *kind* of school, a "catechetical" school. This Alexandrian catechetical school is justly appreciated as the most prestigious example we have in the early Christian world. "For centuries, the so-called catechetical school in Alexandria has intrigued scholars and stimulated speculation on its origins and early practice."[1] Compared with other evangelical and catechetical ventures in this period of the Church, the knowledge we have of this school is extensive. And what distinguishes its contribution is the consciously *pedagogical* way in which the *whole* of the Christian faith was articulated—Christ came to bring to humanity a *way of formation* for participation in the life of divinity. The registers and tones of its

---

[1] Annewies van den Hoek, "The 'Catechetical' School of Early Christian Alexandria and its Philonic Heritage," *The Harvard Theological Review* 90, 1 (January 1997), 59.

presentation of the faith are pervasively redolent of this one grand scheme of grace-filled, redemptive education.

The central task of the school was to proclaim the Good News of Christ to the surrounding peoples and to prepare converts for baptism into the new Christian community in Alexandria. From the beginning it seems also to have understood itself as carrying forward a broader agenda, that of articulating and shaping the Christian culture there. It certainly did not undertake this in isolation from wider evangelizing and educating initiatives in the Church; on the contrary, its genius lay in harmonizing work that was being undertaken in Rome, in Gaul, in North Africa, and in other major settlements of the new Christian diaspora.

One of the school's distinguishing marks was a confident proclamation that a living way had been established by One who was the fulfillment of all that had come before, in the ages and cultures of humankind, so that all that preceded him was but a type and shadow of his Person. The way of life that it offered, the school claimed, was the work of God himself. It amounted to a new creation in Christ placed into the midst of the old, a new creation that healed the human person through the restoration of a holy innocence, the recovery of an identity that had long fallen into ruin. It was a way that wove fragmented truth into a unity, and which led a creation, longing for the good and the beautiful, home to the fatherly heart of God.

The fashioning of such an understanding was to prove a monumental undertaking of careful discernment and generous living which was worked out over the following centuries in Alexandria in dialogue with the cultures around it. John Henry Newman was to see the Catholic culture it helped to form as a whole Alexandrian tradition.[2] The teaching of this tradition, he wrote in his *Apologia*, "came like music to my inward ear."[3] It was a tradition "based on the mystical or sacramental principle" which cast a magnificent vision of the whole of nature and history as "but the outward manifestation to our senses of realities greater than itself." And it was a tradition that recognized God's gracious and generous leading of all nations coming together in Christ:

---

[2] For the use of language of an Alexandrian "tradition" see, for example, Frances Young, *From Nicaea to Chalcedon: A Guide to the Literature and its Background* (London: SCM, 1983), 262; Avery Dulles, "From Images to Truth: Newman on Revelation and Faith," *Theological Studies* 51 (1990), 254.

[3] John Henry Newman, *Apologia Pro Vita Sua* (Oxford: Oxford University Press, 1967), 36. For the quotations following, see 36-37.

Nature was a parable: Scripture was an allegory: pagan literature, philosophy and mythology, rightly understood, were but a preparation for the Gospel. The Greek poets and sages were in a certain sense prophets; for "thoughts beyond their thoughts were to those high bards given." There had been a directly divine dispensation granted to the Jews; but there had been in some sense a dispensation carried on in favour of the Gentiles. He who had taken the seed of Jacob for His elect people had not therefore cast the rest of mankind out of His sight. In the fulness of time both Judaism and Paganism had come to nought; the outward framework, which concealed yet suggested the Living Truth, had never been intended to last, and it was dissolving under the beams of the Sun of Justice which shone behind it and through it. The process of change had been slow; it had been done not rashly, but by rule and measure, "at sundry times and in divers manners," first one disclosure and then another, till the whole evangelical doctrine was brought into full manifestation.

Two theological giants in the early Church, Clement and Origen, were among those who led the school. Other significant figures in the school include Pantaenus—the possible founder of the school, whose life and teaching was the initial point of attraction drawing Clement to Alexandria—and Didymus the Blind, a biblical scholar and catechist of no mean repute. The See of Alexandria itself was one of the most significant Christian centers, second in status and influence only to the See of Rome, with which it shared a uniquely close relationship; with Dionysius, Athanasius, and Cyril among its episcopal leaders, and the school playing no small part in consolidating the reputation and influence of this city and episcopal see in the early Church, Alexandria enjoyed a vital role in the development of early Christian thought and theology.[4] It is from the See of Alexandria that champions rose up to save the doctrine of the Incarnation, first at Nicaea and then at Ephesus. Athanasius endured exile five times on account of his defense of Christ's unattenuated divinity and it is said that Cyril almost bankrupted Alexandria in order to preserve the doctrine of the Mother of God and the unity of the Person of

---

[4] Until AD 451 the see of Alexandria was accorded a place of honor second only to Rome. With some justice, Samuel Rubenson argues that "from the late third century until the mid-fifth century Alexandria was the most important city in early Christianity" ("From School to Patriarchate: Aspects on the Christianisation of Alexandria," in eds. G. Hinge and J. A. Krasilnikov, *Alexandria: A Cultural and Religious Melting Pot* [Aarhus: Aarhus University Press, 2009], 144). The influence of the catechetical school in the development of the importance of the Alexandrian see was a significant factor.

Christ.⁵ The combination of intellectual fervor, endurance and radical self-gift exhibited by these two bishops also characterized the witness of the catechetical school. The Alexandrian tradition had a decisive impact on the young Christian Church, leaving a scholarly legacy that profoundly impacted Christian theology, a compelling vision of the Christian life that united the best in Greek philosophy in service to the Gospel, and—most important for our purposes—a convincing instantiation of what it means to practice the craft of catechesis.

I have divided the telling of this story into two parts. In the first part of the book, I begin by presenting the Alexandrian background to the school, exhibiting and explaining the riches of Alexandria in its many dimensions and providing an outline understanding of the religious, philosophical, and cultural reality into which the school came so as to present a picture of the Alexandrian school in the reality of its original setting. The initial chapter presents the history of Alexandria under the Ptolemies, from its founding by Alexander the Great in 331 BC as a center of Hellenistic culture until the death of Cleopatra three hundred years later in 30 BC. Christianity was brought to Alexandria in the early part of the first century, and this corresponded to the early period of Roman rule in Alexandria, a rule that was to last until the Muslim conquest of Egypt and capture of Alexandria in AD 640.

The story of the school itself and of its founding, probably in the middle of the second century, together with the development of the Christian presence in Alexandria, forms the subject of the next two chapters. These chapters also outline the character of the school as a place both of catechumenal and broader intellectual formation. The school eventually moved from Alexandria to Sidon under the leadership of Rhodon at the beginning of the fifth century, two hundred years before the close of Christian imperial rule in Alexandria. We thus have a period of around three hundred years for the historical focus of our study.

A word at the outset regarding the use of the term "school": I have often found it simplest to write of "the Alexandrian catechetical school" in the singular. As we will see, it was not a monolithic institution and so writing of the school in the singular should not be seen as an attempt to cast it as a single, unchanging entity, or to diminish in any way the distinctive features of particular figures and their catechetical approaches. But it can remind us that we can usefully speak of an identifiable catechetical tradition and help us

---

⁵ See John McGuckin, *St. Cyril of Alexandria: The Christological Controversy, its History, Theology and Texts* (Leiden: E. J. Brill, 1994), 103.

to capture what Ronald Heine calls "common trajectories" running through the work of the major figures identified with the school.[6]

While the first part of the book is more historical and contextual in nature and more attentive to the distinctive features of individuals and periods, the second part of the work is topical, examining some of the more important themes with which the school was concerned. Here, in chapters five to nine, I seek to identify in a more sustained way the key elements from the tradition the retrieval of which in a contemporary form I judge to be the most important. This second part of the work, then, seeks to show something of the "light" from this catechetical heritage for us today. The major themes that we see being played out in Alexandria are, as we will see, present in the Church's guidance on catechesis today, but it can be easy to overlook some of them and I hope this study will convince readers of their pivotal importance.

UNDERWAY: A CATECHETICAL RESSOURCEMENT

This study needs to be understood within the *ressourcement* movement.[7] It was in tandem with this movement that the Second Vatican Council launched the Church into a renewed interest in mission and catechetics. The focus of the Council, described by Paul VI simply as the "great catechism of modern times,"[8] was not on any specific element in the content of the faith, the precious deposit which has been handed down, generation by generation, since the fullness of God's Revelation in Christ; rather, the interest of the Council lay primarily in questions surrounding the transmission of the faith: the situating of the Church *vis-à-vis* contemporary culture, her fitness for mission, and the aptness of her catechetical tools for the communication and deepening of the faith of the People of God.

The Second Vatican Council, then, sought to be a point of renewal for catechetics, not by breaking with what had preceded it but by following a hermeneutic of continuity and development, drawing upon the energy of the *ressourcement* movement—a return to the Fathers, a drawing upon Sacred Tradition and upon the Fathers' reading of the Scriptures—in order to harvest insights and riches that will serve the Church today. The conviction that has motivated this movement, then,

---

[6] Ronald E. Heine, *Origen: Scholarship in the Service of the Church* (Oxford: Oxford University Press, 2010), 64.
[7] Some of the key figures of the movement were Henri de Lubac, Jean Daniélou, Yves Congar, Louis Bouyer, Hans Urs von Balthasar and Claude Mondésat.
[8] *Speech to the participants in the general assembly of the Italian Episcopal Conference*, 23rd June 1966, cited in the *Catechism of the Catholic Church*, 10. [Hereafter *CCC*]

is that renewal in the Church takes place only in a deep faithfulness to Tradition, and that the riches discoverable in certain periods can therefore be points of immense inspiration and energy for us today. Henri de Lubac expresses the intention and spirit of the *ressourcement* movement towards the end of his *Theology in History*:

> Without claiming to open up new avenues of thought, I have sought rather, without any antiquarianism, to make known some of the great common areas of Catholic tradition. I wanted to make it loved, to show its ever-present fruitfulness.[9]

This investigation into the Alexandrian school can be seen, then, as part of the *ressourcement* that has been taking place in *evangelization and catechetics* from the early part of the twentieth century, alongside the broader *ressourcement* movement in theology.[10] Building on the extensive theological and historical literature re-evaluating different aspects of the Alexandrian tradition, the aim of this present work is to tell the story of the catechetical school, seeking to understand the principles, pedagogy, and practices by which it shaped and developed a Christian culture in its own time, so as to gain insights from this for the task of pastoral formation today.

Sufficient time has now elapsed since the close of the Council to be able to take stock of how the work of catechesis is faring in the Church. The study will benefit from many magisterial initiatives and assessments that have taken place since the Council, interventions and reviews that provide an increasingly clear view of the landscape and of catechetical priorities for the Church moving forward. A new Order for the reception of converts, based on the ancient catechumenate, was published shortly after the Council. Extraordinary synods associated with Paul VI's *Evangelii nuntiandi*, with John Paul II's *Catechesi tradendae*, and with the decision in 1985 to prepare a new universal *Catechism* have been accompanied by a series of catechetical directories which have provided a catechetical vision and an account of pedagogy that is increasingly comprehensive in scope. Thus the most recent *Directory for Catechesis* directs its readers to view the history of salvation as a whole—which is the history of the whole of God's creation, and not just of a single people—within an educational

---

[9] Henri de Lubac, SJ, *Theology in History* (San Francisco: Ignatius Press, 1996), 599.
[10] A relatively recent example of such catechetical *ressourcement*, in this case with reference to Augustine of Hippo, is William Harmless, *Augustine and the Catechumenate*, rev. ed. (Collegeville: Liturgical Press, 2014). Harmless offers us the intention of his work: to assist in the renewal of catechesis "by gleaning the best from ancient styles [of] and perspectives on catechesis" (20).

perspective. It reminds us to "read" all of Christian doctrine as "the great educational work of God," to read the great dogmas "through a pedagogical lens,"[11] as guiding us along a divine path of formation. This catechetical renewal, then, is concerned in part with gaining for those tasked with teaching the faith a new confidence and energy, through catching a comprehensive and exciting vision.

There is also a desire to renew the understanding of pedagogy, to articulate the faith within what John Paul II called the "pedagogy of faith."[12] John Paul II's articulation of this need in *Catechesi tradendae* was nuanced and specific and the good that such a retrieval will be for catechesis, he claimed, "cannot be overstated." By "pedagogy of faith" he was not only emphasizing the importance of finding the most suitable educational methodologies, drawing upon the human sciences for assistance in this task; but he was, above all, looking for a recovery of the understanding, held in the memory of the Church, that God himself is Teacher and Formator and that "God's Revelation in its entirety" is the point of reference for catechesis. Following this lead, the *Catechism*, promulgated in 1992, not only synthetically captures the deposit but also strives to articulate the faith in terms of the principles worked out in the conciliar and post-conciliar catechetical documents so that catechists can teach according to the faith's own distinctive pedagogy.[13]

What John Paul II was also seeking in *Catechesi tradendae*, inseparably from this rediscovery and harnessing of this original pedagogy of the faith, was a reclamation of how to proclaim the great Story of the faith, its central *kerygma*, so that a persuasive account of its content, shape and scope could be offered. The needed renewal in this case would not be achieved by a tinkering with individual elements or

---

[11] Pontifical Council for the Promotion of the New Evangelization, *Directory for Catechesis*, 157. [Hereafter DC]

[12] John Paul II, *Catechesi tradendae*, 58. [Hereafter, CT]

[13] When John Paul II, therefore, in the Apostolic Constitution introducing the *Catechism*, *Fidei Depositum*, describes the *Catechism* as "a sure norm for teaching the faith," "*firmam regulam ad fidem docendam*" (4a), he means us to understand the normative nature of the *Catechism* in *both* senses, of content and of pedagogy. The two are, naturally, inseparable. The principles governing the pedagogy by which the Church is called to transmit the faith are derived from the content of the faith. It is the fact of the distinctive *revelatory* content of the faith that leads to there being a distinct pedagogy for catechesis. The two dimensions of "content" and "pedagogy" also correspond to the two meanings of the Latin *doctrina*, or teaching, referring both to what is taught and also to the activity of teaching. For a discussion, see Petroc Willey, "The *Catechism* and the New Evangelization," in eds. P. Grogan and K. Kim, *The New Evangelization: Faith, People, Context and Practice* (London: Bloomsbury T&T Clark, 2015), 209-20.

by a simple readjusting of certain emphases. Rather, he believed, the *Whole* needed to be reclaimed, not in any "new" or "relevant" fashion, but in a way true to the biblical and liturgical heritage of the saints, as it had been articulated in the Church's perennial Tradition.[14] The publication of the *Catechism* was in part intended to enable the reader to appreciate this panorama, this worldview, to help overcome what Ratzinger was to call a "distrust of the totality,"[15] enabling the Church see the faith again as an organic whole. If we hear the Story only in fragmented form, it will have no power to move and convert us.[16]

In the light of these expressed needs for the Church's evangelizing and catechizing mission we can say that one of the benefits of engaging with the reality of the Alexandrian school is precisely the unified understanding of the person and the cosmos that it brought to catechesis, allowing the Story to be proclaimed with passion and vigor. It tells the great Story of God's pedagogical restoration of his world through the work of the eternal Son, the Logos by whom all things were made and who took flesh to restore, through the gift of the Spirit, the lost and divided world to the longing heart of the Father. Not all of the details of the Alexandrian telling were finally appropriated within the dogmatic spirituality of the Church, but the Story is there, clear and articulate, in a form that can reawaken an understanding of the *catholicus* partly because it is not awkwardly mixed into ill-fitting cultural, anthropological and metaphysical perspectives borrowed from modernism or post-modernism which can confuse and dilute the reception of the Story today.

A CATECHUMENAL MODEL FOR A NEW EVANGELIZATION

It is particularly helpful for us, at this time, to undertake a review of an ancient school for the catechumenate since, following the Second Vatican Council, there has been widespread interest in retrieving and developing what the Church describes as a "catechumenal model" for catechesis, adapted from the patristic practices of adult reception into the Church. This model has to date focused especially upon what

---

[14] For a presentation of the problem we face, cf. Alasdair MacIntyre's verdict in *After Virtue* on contemporary thought: "What we possess... are the fragments of a conceptual scheme, parts which now lack those contexts from which their significance derived" (London: Duckworth, 1985), 2.

[15] Joseph Ratzinger, "Sources and Transmission of the Faith," *Communio* X, 1 (Spring 1983), 19.

[16] Thus see *DC* 11–14 which present the basic Story, and 48–54 which place catechesis within the perspective of a universal "going forth" of the Church, reflecting the Son's going forth from his Father.

we can learn from the ministry and writings of Ambrose, Chrysostom, Theodore of Mopsuestia, Augustine and Cyril of Jerusalem. In 1972, inspired by this patristic heritage and mandated by the Second Vatican Council, the Holy See promulgated the Order of Christian Initiation of Adults.[17] This decision of the Council was based on twentieth century biblical, patristic and liturgical scholarship that had been recovering a fuller picture of how catechesis was undertaken in the early Church. The work of two Jesuits, Josef Jungmann and Jean Daniélou, on liturgy, catechesis and Scripture has been of particular importance in this recovery and renewal.[18] The recognition of the importance of the catechumenal model has been a stable feature in post-conciliar catechetical thinking, being applied now not only to how adults should be received into the Church, but also to the whole of catechesis. Thus, the *Directory for Catechesis* urges: "catechesis should be inspired by the catechumenal model."[19]

In Alexandria we see a catechetical school that prepared candidates for baptism. We know that by the end of the second century there was already in place, in different geographical areas of the Church, a well-developed catechumenal process, uniting pastoral, catechetical and liturgical elements—Hippolytus gives us detailed evidence in Rome, Tertullian and Cyprian in North Africa, and Clement and Origen witness to this in Egypt. And reminding ourselves of how this Alexandrian catechetical school undertook its catechumenal preparation of candidates from the mid-to-late second century is particularly valuable because the evidence we have from what is often described as the "great age" of the catechumenate, developing from the mid-fourth century, is largely indicative of the social and political situation following Theodosius's declaration in AD 380 that Christianity was

---

[17] The restoration was mandated in the opening document of the Council, *Sacrosanctum concilium*, 64. Elements of the catechumenate to be restored were articulated in *Sacrosanctum concilium* 64–66 and *Ad gentes* 13–14, and the importance of the restoration reinforced in *Christus Dominus* 14, *Lumen gentium* 14, and *Presbyterorum ordinis* 6.

[18] Jungmann's catechetical and scriptural work arguing for a renewal of a kerygmatic catechesis, *The Good News Yesterday and Today*, was originally published in 1936 while his *Mass of the Roman Rite: its Origins and Development* was published in 1948. Daniélou published significant works on the Alexandrian tradition, especially Philo and Origen. Most important for an understanding of liturgy and catechesis are his *The Bible and the Liturgy* and *From Shadows to Reality: Studies in the Biblical Typology of the Fathers*.

[19] *DC* 2. See also 61–65. The catechumenal model follows the earliest account we have of Christian formation, from Acts 2:24, a holistic process of doctrinal and sacramental formation, grounded in prayer and in the community life of the Church (cf. *CCC* 3).

to be considered the only official religion of the Empire.[20] It was in *that* context, of imperial approval and support, that large numbers of adults sought to be received into the Catholic Church, with the adult catechumenate the vehicle of reception in this new situation.[21]

Such a situation of political endorsement is clearly not our own: no imperial approval or social and political advancement is to be gained from receiving Christian baptism. The restoration of the catechumenate is taking place today in a vastly different set of circumstances, one which the Church describes as a context of "new evangelization"—a time marked by a renewed concern with mission in the face of globalization and secularism, rather than in an era concerned to ensure effective integration and consolidation of the Christian faith. In 1947, Pius XII already spoke to groups of "Christian Rebirth" of "the religious crisis of our time, the most grave perhaps that humanity has ever experienced since the beginning of Christianity" which requires, alongside a reasoned exposition of the faith, "a Christianity lived in its fullness with persevering constancy,"[22] and the 2020 *Directory for Catechesis* continues the note of alarm, summing up the current context of the Church's work in this way: "Over the course of the

---

[20] See *Theodosian Code* 16.1.2. Theodosius II published the Code in 438, a compilation of the general laws promulgated by the Christian Emperors from Constantine onwards. A classic work introducing the "golden age" of the catechumenate is Edward Yarnold, *The Awe-inspiring Rites of Initiation* (1994), and there is now a mature literature exploring how the practices of this period underpin the restored *Order of the Christian Initiation of Adults*. An attractive complement to Yarnold's work is Anne Field's collection from the Fathers, arranged to provide a picture of common catechetical themes: *From Darkness to Light: How one became a Christian in the Early Church* (1997). Other works to consider include Michel Dujarier's *A History of the Catechumenate: The First Six Centuries* which offers an analysis of the development of the catechumenate from apostolic times onwards, arguing for the retrieval of second and third century catechumenal models (1979); Everett Ferguson's edited volume *Conversion, Catechumenate, and Baptism in the Early Church* (1993) and his comprehensive *Baptism in the Early Church: History, Theology and Liturgy in the First Five Centuries* (2009); Thomas Finn's *The Liturgy of Baptism in the Baptismal Instructions of St John Chrysostom* (1967) and his more general conspectus, *Early Christian Baptism and the Catechumenate: Italy, North Africa, and Egypt* (1992); and William Harmless's *Augustine and the Catechumenate* (2014).

[21] The catechumenal ministry of several of the bishops only takes place subsequent to the Theodosian edict: Augustine became bishop of Hippo in 396, Chrysostom bishop of Constantinople in 398 and Theodore bishop of Mopsuestina in 392. Figures who straddle the turning point of the Theodosian Edict are Cyril of Jerusalem and Ambrose—and both of these figures sit comfortably within the period of the Constantinian settlement (311/313), the period from which a marked toleration for Christianity began. The context of the reception of converts within which these bishops presented the faith, following the catechumenal model, was primarily one of religious and political consolidation.

[22] Pius XII, Address to Groups of "Christian Rebirth" (*AAS* 39), 58.

centuries... those societies shaped by Christian culture in particular have arrived at a cultural crisis resulting from an exaggerated secularism"[23] so that there is a need for "models of catechists who have attained holiness and even martyrdom in living their ministry every day."[24] A catechumenal model to fit this current situation is needed. Evangelizing today, the *Directory* proposes, "does not mean occupying a given territory, but rather eliciting *spiritual processes* in the lives of persons so that the faith may become rooted and significant."[25]

To understand what is involved in this task of catechetical *ressourcement* it is important to clarify a little further the way in which the Church understands the ecclesial context as one of "new evangelization."[26] The phrase came to prominence in the pontificate of John Paul II on June 9, 1979—the same year that he promulgated *Catechesi tradendae*—at Nowa Huta in Poland in the context of the countries of the Soviet Socialist Republic as he called for a re-evangelization of these cultures.[27] Most of these communist countries had been shaped over many centuries by a rich Christian heritage, a heritage that was then overlaid by atheistic communism and a determined effort to expunge the Christian worldview from society. In the process the Church was affected in complex ways. For some members of the Church this was a time of intense purification of faith, a paschal journey with the suffering Christ that led these believers to even greater insights into the Christian life and an even firmer commitment to the Person of Christ and his message of merciful Good News. Other portions and members of the Church sought various degrees of accommodation with the situation, in part to allow for some limited survival of the Church in truncated form.[28] Many of the baptized simply fell away, losing confidence in the Gospel and setting off along alternative paths. During this period supporting structures of catechesis were

---

[23] DC 103.
[24] Rino Fisichella and Octavio Ruiz Arenas, "Preface," DC, and see DC 99–100.
[25] DC 43.
[26] A comprehensive understanding of what is included in this term can be gained from the *Enchiridion* of the new evangelization that was prepared by the Pontifical Council for the Promotion of the New Evangelization as a handbook of magisterial teaching judged by the Council to be particularly relevant to its work: *Enchiridion della nuova evangelizzazione* (2014).
[27] Homily during Holy Mass in the Sanctuary of the Holy Cross, Mogila (AAS 71), 864–69.
[28] These two alternatives were broadly characterized as "valour" and "discretion" by Trevor Beeson in his careful examination of the Russian and other Eastern churches during the first decades of the Cold War period (*Discretion and Valour: Religious Conditions in Russia and Eastern Europe* [London: Fount Paperbacks], 1974).

either removed altogether or were malformed while anti-Christian worldviews and conceptions of reality were systematically promoted.

John Paul II's call for a new evangelization spoke into this situation, not only by directing attention to those broad and challenging cultural situations, but especially by focusing on the Christian community itself. He was seeking in the first place the restoration of a *living Christian culture in the Church,* knowing that the shape it needed to take would involve borrowing deeply from centuries of Christian Tradition. The remaking would need to take into account the fragmentation of the minds and lives of those who lived through this brutal assault on the Church. The overall aim of the new evangelization is to bring about a society thoroughly imbued with a Christian worldview and way of living. At the heart of this renewed Christian society, however—and needing the most immediate attention—is the need for the development of authentic communities of Christian life. The challenge of the new evangelization, John Paul insisted, is to remake, to re-weave, "the Christian fabric of the *ecclesial* community" so that there might in turn be "a mending of the Christian fabric of society."[29]

John Paul's ecclesial and cultural analysis was subsequently confirmed by Pope Benedict XVI who, in 2013, assigned the responsibility, or the "competence," for catechesis to the newly-established Pontifical Council for the Promotion of the New Evangelization.[30] That competence today lies within the Dicastery for Evangelization which, continuing to develop coherence between different branches of the Church's outreach, has drawn the work of the original Pontifical Council for the Promotion of the New Evangelization into a closer relation with missionary work and initial evangelization.[31] In other words, the Church's call to engage in a new evangelization describes the conceptual position for her work of catechesis today and in the new *Directory* it prefaces its discussion of the various ways in which a catechumenal model needs to be developed.[32]

---

[29] John Paul II, *Christifidelis laici* 34. John Paul is echoing Paul VI here who had already called for the Church to examine her "constant need of being evangelized, if she wishes to retain freshness, vigour and strength in order to proclaim the Gospel" (*Evangelii nuntiandi* 15).

[30] Benedict XVI, *Fides per Doctrinum.*

[31] See Francis, *Praedicate Evangelium* 53, 2; 58, 1.

[32] For the way in which the new *Directory* has taken up this theme cf. DC 38–54. Both catechesis and proclamation (*kerygma*) sit under the overall umbrella of evangelization. That the term "evangelization" itself should always be considered the central term to describe and to orient the work of transmission of the Gospel is reinforced by the findings concerning New Testament terminology. Thus, James McDonald, in *Kerygma and Didache: The Articulation and Structure of the Earliest*

The dissonance I have indicated between the social and political context of the "great" or "golden" age of the catechumenate and that of our own day does not, of course, invalidate the choice of this model by the Fathers of the Second Vatical Council. In the first place it is natural that attention should have been placed on the evidence from the fourth and fifth centuries since the records and writings regarding catechesis during this period are fuller and more numerous. Scholarship has therefore tended to devote itself to a consideration of what can be learned from those fourth and fifth century Fathers of the Church in the field of catechesis as also in the area of dogmatic theology. In the second place, there is, naturally, an essential continuity of the catechumenal model of the golden age with the practices of the earlier centuries which are the object of study in this present work. We can say that the later, more settled centuries allow us to view the catechumenal model in a fuller flowering—in a richer, more complete state. But the earlier stages of growth should not, on that account, be ignored. All too easily the second and third centuries can be viewed as merely transitional, and we can seek to look too quickly beyond them to what we see as moments of resolution and completion. Other features of the catechetical enterprise are revealed in times of "planting," especially a planting in a culture as challenging, variegated and rich as Alexandria: foundational principles for establishing a Christian culture have to be worked out; priorities need to be put in place and ordered; and the work of formation has to be maintained and developed in an organic way, reliant on the vulnerable path of living witness and community integrity since the benefits of more settled doctrinal definitions and pastoral structures on the one hand and of a more supportive social environment on the other are not yet present. The catechetical environment and concerns of today's Church, then, point to the especial value of retrieving evidence of catechetical practice from these earlier times when Christianity was organizing itself in a minority and controverted situation, learning to remain faithful to Christ in the face of sporadic persecutions, and establishing a Christian presence and witness in the context of a wide variety of competing beliefs and practices. As Aidan Kavanagh put it, the baptismal practices were being worked out "under enormous, and

---

Christian Message, points out that Greek *euangelion* (evangelization) occurs nearly ten times as often as *kerygma* (proclamation) in the New Testament and, as well as communicating the joyfulness of the message, is in general the most representative term of how the New Testament authors saw the nature of the transmission of the Gospel (Cambridge: Cambridge University Press, 1980, 1-11).

thus memorable, pastoral stress."[33] Insofar, then, as we see this as our environment today, we can look to find inspiration, guidance and wisdom from the teaching and practices developed at the catechetical school in Alexandria in this earlier period. Again, none of this, of course, is to undervalue—and certainly not to regret—the subsequent periods of theological and pastoral development, consolidation, and clarification. But it is to highlight the value of exposing to sight *foundational* features of Christian practice and transmission.

SEEING FROM THE INSIDE

We know that in this work of *ressourcement* no facile comparisons can be made between the school in ancient Alexandria and our own situations and no easy extraction of "lessons to be learned and applied" for our own day. To head into an investigation with that thought too much at the forefront can in fact become counter-productive, reading the past with the object of "getting something out of it" for today. The danger in seeking for the essence of such "lessons" for today is that we evacuate the past of its reality. Each lesson then turns out to be somewhat lifeless and neither as attractive nor as informative as we had hoped. Each turns out to be, perhaps, just an affirmation of what we already knew, simply a confirmation of an idea to which we were already committed. Certainly, the past can speak to us, but we hear best when we listen to as much of the fullness of what is there as possible. Without that kind of listening the tendency is to grasp mere caricatures, images of the present transposed back in time.

In *Truth and Method,* Gadamer offers a helpful discussion of what is required for a conversation with the past to be fruitful. Above all, it must avoid simply making the other persons in the conversation into objects to be scrutinized and studied, objects of my enquiry. If I conceive my methodology of study in this way, aspiring towards a scientific objectivity, trying only to classify and categorize, I risk not entering into a real conversation at all, and I can end by robbing those with whom I am engaging of their humanity. On the other hand, I must also be careful to avoid falsely detaching myself from the conversation, ignoring my own personhood. This, too, can be subtly manipulative, as I seek to "give voice" to the other while pretending non-engagement from the point of view of my own reality.[34]

---

[33] Aidan Kavanagh, *The Shape of Baptism: The Rite of Christian Initiation* (Collegeville: The Liturgical Press, 1978), 116.
[34] See Hans-Georg Gadamer, *Truth and Method* (London: Sheed and Ward, 1975), 321-25. See also the discussion by Andrew Louth of Gadamer in *Discerning the Mystery: An Essay on the Nature of Theology* (Oxford: Clarendon Press, 1984), 29-43, 102-7.

For the past to enlarge, challenge, and genuinely to teach us, a certain patience is needed, a willingness to stay with the picture being assembled, allowing the details, even if at times strange, gradually to emerge, without becoming too focused on the seeking of relevance or correlation with the present. Samuel Taylor Coleridge helpfully compares the process of uncovering truth to that of a frozen drift of snow that gradually melts due to the impact of warmth from inside:

> Truth considered in itself and in the effects natural to it, may be conceived as a gentle spring or water-source, warm from the genial earth, and breathing up into the snow-drift that is piled over and around its outlet. It turns the obstacle into its own form and character, and as it makes its way increases its stream. And should it be arrested in its course by a chilling season, it suffers delay, not loss, and waits only for a change in the wind to awaken and again roll onwards.[35]

This is a beautiful description of the ways in which patient investigation becomes fruitful, allowing the landscape we are viewing to come into focus as details are filled in and we build a picture. Truth itself is the agent here and each aspect received breathes into the snow-drift before us and progressively melts it, slowly enlarging the area of water, making channels and allowing further insights. The insistent questioning of the past to yield definitive answers gives way before a broader and less impatient interest. It is with this kind of spirit that we can seek to approach a topic such as the catechetical school in Alexandria, allowing truth to make its own way of showing us how the past can be of service to the present. In this way our engagement with the past can teach and not simply confirm us, can enlarge us and help us to transcend our existing understanding. C. S. Lewis once said that in a good reading of great literature "I become a thousand men and yet remain myself . . . I see with a myriad eyes, but it is still I who see."[36] Something analogous can take place in an engagement with our Christian past. In seeking to understand how these believers handed on the faith in their concrete setting our own understanding of evangelization and catechesis is enriched. And when the eyes through which we see include those of figures such as Clement of Alexandria and Origen, the new vision gained promises to be both ample and penetrating.

---

[35] S. T. Coleridge, *The Friend* (London: Routledge and Kegan Paul, 1969), I, 65.
[36] C. S. Lewis, *An Experiment in Criticism* (Cambridge: Cambridge University Press, 1969), 141.

I was helped in this process of learning patience, during the time of writing on the Alexandrian school, by a dream I had of a sunken cathedral. I was diving and swimming around it, trying to look in, but the glass of the great windows was difficult to see through. I knew that I had to get inside the cathedral to see the interior. I had to see from the inside and began looking for ways in. The dream was interesting from the point of view of our current study of ancient Alexandria, for excavations in the Eastern harbor have recently revealed extensive ruins and artifacts dating from the Ptolemaic and Roman periods, as well as many that predate Alexander's founding of the city.[37]

As I reflected further on the dream I saw that it spoke, not just to the effort involved in a reading of the faith of the past, but also to the goal that we seek, a seeing "from the inside": we are looking, not just to know and understand information and to record this as clearly and accurately as possible, but to gain, and thereby be able share with others, a vision of things from the inside, a vision that allows the reality of the past to enter one's life and to become part of one's own way of seeing. Josef Pieper has often written of the importance of *loving* the truth: to receive a reality one has to *want* to know it, to acknowledge it. He reminds us of a sentence from Goethe, "When sympathy goes, memory goes with it."[38] For something to enter deeply into us there must be a desire for the truth that is to be received. The French philosopher, Simone Weil, wrote something similar: "Among human beings, only the existence of those we love is fully recognized."[39] Learning this seeing "from the inside" requires that we learn to love what is before us. Only then can it make others want to learn in this same way: we wish to elicit a love and a sense of responsibility for the truth we communicate.

The cathedral in the dream also speaks, I think, to the magnificence of the reality of what we are investigating here and to its sacred quality. It points to the beauty of our object, and to the centrality of the quest for the Beautiful that was at the heart of the school's understanding of what it is to seek after God. That the dream image

---

[37] For many of these findings see Jean-Yves Empereur, *Alexandria Rediscovered* (London: British Museum Press, 1988).

[38] Josef Pieper, "Corporeal Memory: The Concrete Things of History as Living Reminders," *Communio* XLVIII, 2 (Summer 2021), 419.

[39] Simone Weil, *Gravity and Grace* (New York: G. P. Putnam's Sons, 1952), 113. In *Lectures on Philosophy* she described the state of attention we should seek in order to allow one to receive the reality of a thing: it is a matter of bringing oneself into focus, with the mind and will learning not so much to do things, as attend to what is before it (London: Routledge, Keagan and Paul, 1978), 205.

was of a cathedral also reminds us that the understanding that we are seeking takes place within a shared sacred "space." We are participating in a shared *traditio*, reading the past not as something alien, but precisely across the shared space of a common Tradition. We and the Alexandrian catechists from whom we are seeking to learn, and with whom we seek to be in dialogue, are members of the same personal Subject, the Church. Louth puts the point beautifully when he says that we are "listening to what was once written, listening across a historical gulf which is not empty... but filled with the tradition that brings this piece of writing to me, and brings me not only that piece of writing but preconceptions and prejudices that enable me to pick up the resonances of the images and arguments used in whatever it is I am seeking to understand."[40] In the Church's work of catechesis, we can therefore readily understand why the *Directory* describes the catechist as in the first place "a witness of faith and keeper of the memory of God." It continues, "The faith contains the memory of God's history with humanity. Keeping this memory, reawakening it in others, and placing it at the service of the proclamation is the specific vocation of the catechist. The testimony of his life is necessary for the credibility of the mission."[41] Learning to attend to what is before us, love that which we see, and enter sympathetically into it allows us to receive "the memory of God's history with humanity." The catechist who is a "keeper" of this memory can then "reawaken" it in others through teaching and the testimony of life, becoming him or herself the vehicle by which this love is made real for others and passed on.

As we learn how to communicate this loving truth, this covenantal truth from Christian history, we are necessarily engaged in the process of "new evangelization." One way to think about the element of "newness" is that it is the second "moment" of a culture's encounter with the Gospel. The first moment contains all that was involved in the establishing of the Christian presence in that culture: the initial witness and proclamation, the catechesis and formation, the mature development of the presence in the culture, with all of the lights and shadows associated with this over the centuries. "New evangelization" speaks to what is needed for this second moment, a *re*-founding if

---

[40] Louth, *Discerning the Mystery*, 107. Louth usefully links the importance of reading across Tradition to Michael Polanyi's notion of "tacit" knowing, that we learn to see and understand things through our participation in an interpretative framework which Polanyi describes as a kind of "indwelling," which is received over time and in which we are immersed without ever being able to make it fully explicit (see 59–64).

[41] DC 113a.

you will, but not a *new* founding; rather, one that can intelligently engage with an ancient Christian culture in terms of its history and seek to re-ignite the Church's presence there through facilitating an encounter with Christ in his Church.[42] A related way to think about the new evangelization is in terms of the incompleteness of the first—the culture was insufficiently permeated with the Gospel, only half-converted. We should not think of a culture's evangelization as a version of "once saved, always saved." A culture is always saved "in hope."[43] And societies, like people, grow weary with the call to ongoing conversion, grow bored and depressed, lose the vision of the glory which must inspire hope and provide energy, and thus seek new and easier avenues. Apostasy becomes a welcome relief from the struggle.

Either way, the "new" evangelization has its newness precisely in this point: it entails the necessity of a rediscovery of one's often-forgotten past, with evangelization understood principally as an *awakening*, a recovery of a half-forgotten memory. In its discussion of the new evangelization, the *Directory* emphasizes this qualitative aspect of newness in the process: it is a matter of awakening to the new life of the Holy Spirit, of helping others to recognize Christ's enduring presence so that they find "the way to 'save their lives' (cf. Matt 16:25) and open themselves to a new horizon."[44]

In a telling turn of phrase, T. S. Eliot describes such an awakening at the end of the *Four Quartets* as walking "Through the unknown, remembered gate."[45] It is a knowing as recollection, remembrance, recognition. The entering of that gate can involve no more initially than the swipe of a library card to access a collection. Ancient Alexandria was, of course, famous, above all, for its library. And there is no doubt that the leaders of the Alexandrian school could be described, without prejudice, as bookish. It is precisely a link between libraries and evangelization that was made at the opening of Vatican II, that Council dedicated to the work of evangelization and the pastoral mission of the Church. In his speech for the solemn opening of the Council in 1962, John XXIII identified the principal task of the

---

[42] Rino Fisichella has pointed to the numerous passages in the "new" Testament in which Christ and the apostles highlight the newness of the Gospel: thus, a *new* covenant has been made, a *new* commandment given, and a *new* way of life uncovered. Those who follow this way receive a *new* name and are made sharers in the *new* Jerusalem—and indeed in the *new* heavens and *new* earth (see, for example, *Lk.* 22:20; *1 Cor.* 11:25; *Jn.* 13:34; *Rom.* 7:6; *Rev.* 2:17; 3:12; 21:2; *2 Pet.* 3:13). See the Introduction to the *Enchiridion* on the new evangelization.
[43] Cf. *Rom.* 8:24.
[44] See DC 29; 39.
[45] "Little Gidding," *The Four Quartets* (London: Faber and Faber, 1944), V, l.243.

Council as being to guard and to transmit the sacred Deposit of the Faith. And he related the Church's *capacity* to guard and transmit this Deposit to the fact of her having the "inestimable treasure" of documentation from successive Christian centuries, bound in magnificent volumes and housed in archives and in great libraries around the world.[46] The Church's written treasury of which the Pope was speaking can be linked in a particular way to Alexandria, not only because of this connection to that ancient of libraries, but also because of the date chosen for the opening of the Council—October 11th, the feast day of the Maternity of the Mother of God, defender of the faith. That title, Mother of God, was confirmed by the Council of Ephesus in AD 431, and it was this ancient Council that first saw the systematic compilation of conciliar documentation compiled and sent to Rome, thanks to the foresight of St Cyril of Alexandria.[47] And thus we find that for those past conciliar records amid the collections of beautifully bound volumes in Rome, we are particularly indebted to an Alexandrian initiative now being revisited at this significant point of the most recent ecumenical council, the animating source of the call to a new evangelization.

Crucial to the work of the new evangelization is an ability to engage with the Christian history of each culture, and with all that has been involved in the first evangelizing "moment" of each. It must be able to distinguish between the lights and the shadows of that first moment, and it must be able, above all, to point to the great lights in the Christian history of each culture as an inspiration and apologia for the refounding and re-discovery of the faith.[48] A study of the Alexandrian school can greatly assist us in this simply because Alexandria stands at the root of so much in terms of Christian history. Precisely because it was a *gathering* point of many cultures, the heritage of Christian

---

[46] John XXIII, Address for the Solemn Opening of the Second Vatican Ecumenical Council, Thursday 11 October, 1962 (*AAS* 54), 785–95.

[47] See McGuckin, *St. Cyril of Alexandria*, 76.

[48] Here we must note the crucial point that one of the main reasons the new *Catechism* is such a key work for the new evangelization is it represents the gathering of the *Tradition*, of the faith to be transmitted, across time and across cultures, *ubicumque et semper*, encapsulating in its pages the energies of the Church through the communion of all of the local Churches and through the voices of each age of the Church in Tradition. It gathers that which is common as the reference point for all particular instantiations of the faith. In *Fidei Depositum* John Paul II wrote of his "deep feeling of joy" at the "harmony of so many voices" present in the *Catechism*. The *Directory for Catechesis* asks catechists, therefore, to avail themselves of "the Christian cultural heritage" and present this "according to the thinking of its creators," in order to "mediate the internalisation of the central elements of the evangelical message" (*DC* 105).

Alexandria has also been deeply *fruitful* in both the Eastern and the Western Christian traditions after its own fall to the Arab conquest (that fruitfulness finding a path even, circuitously, through an Islamic route that eventually added its own contribution to medieval Europe). The light that was generated from this point of Christian history in Alexandria has assisted the embedding of the Gospel in many different cultures, and a rediscovery of this ancient heritage can therefore directly nourish the work of new evangelization in this third millennium.

A recent scholar who has drawn attention to the riches of the early Alexandrian tradition for a renewal of Christian communities is the American Methodist Thomas C. Oden (1931–2016). A prominent liberal theologian for much of his career, his memoir, *A Change of Heart*, offers a compelling personal testimony to the impact of a deep and sustained immersion in the patristic heritage and of how his re-discovery of the ancient Christian tradition, his personal "return to the sources," completely re-orientated his theological focus and commitments. He recalls a dream which captures this reorientation and from which, he wrote, "I woke up refreshed and relieved."[49]

> In the season of Epiphany 1971 I had a curious dream in which I was in the New Haven cemetery and accidentally stumbled upon my own tombstone with this puzzling epitaph: "He made no new contribution to theology."[50]

He explains the relief the dream brought him: his extensive engagement with the patristic heritage had enabled him to reverse his previous adulation for originality in academic theology—"What the ancient church teachers least wished for Christian teachers is that they would become focused on self-expression or become an assertion of purely private inspiration, as if those might claim to be some decisive improvement on Apostolic tradition."[51]

His studies thus led him to a re-envisioning of his own vocation as a theologian: "For once and for all, I knew my calling would be fulfilled through building bridges between the classical Christian consensus and the lost reality of the modern world."[52] And from this

---

[49] Thomas C. Oden, *A Change of Heart: A Personal and Theological Memoir* (Downers Grove: IVP Academic, 2014), 143.
[50] Ibid.
[51] Ibid. In his *Gospel Message and Hellenistic Culture* Jean Daniélou describes Clement of Alexandria in exactly this way, as "above all the man of tradition and traditions" (London: Darton, Longman and Todd, 1973), 453. The concern to defend the principle of Tradition also led Origen to compose *De Principiis*, the first systematic overview of Christian doctrine that we have.
[52] *A Change of Heart*, 144.

revised theological trajectory a series of initiatives flowed, initiatives which cohere with this present investigation into the Alexandrian school. In the first place he led the development of a multi-volume series of patristic commentaries on individual books of the Bible, the *Ancient Christian Commentary on Scripture*, sponsored by the evangelical publishing house, Inter-Varsity Press, and employing the services of Catholic, Orthodox and Protestant scholars.[53] Origen, of course, is rightly regarded as the father of patristic exegesis, of its canons and methodology. A second scholarly focus was that which eventually led him to found the research Center for Early African Christianity.[54] In the years leading up to his death, his research and publications focused more and more on this early African heritage in North Africa and Egypt.[55] He saw that for an ongoing deepening of the Christian faith on the African continent in particular, which contains such energy and hope for the universal Church, the contemporary African churches need to be able to engage with an authentically African heritage which reaches back further than the missions of the nineteenth and twentieth century, and indeed of the Portuguese missions of the fifteenth century.[56] Oden realized that for this African *ressourcement* to take lasting shape Christian scholarship needed to become convinced of the "African identity" of the first millennial Christian presence on the African continent, so that contemporary renewal could draw from these ancient springs.[57] The importance of such a retrieval is

---

[53] The project benefitted from the encouragement of Ratzinger, with whom Oden discussed the approach and vision several times and to whom he credits planting the seeds for the entire work. See *A Change of Heart*, 210–16, 224–25, 238.

[54] https://www.earlyafricanchristianity.com/.

[55] See especially *How Africa Shaped the Christian Mind* (2007), *Early Libyan Christianity* (2011), and *The Rebirth of African Orthodoxy: Return to Foundations* (2016). In fact, in 2007 Oden spoke to ordinands at the Anglican Alexandrian School of Theology, located near where tradition has placed the Catechetical school: "I spoke to those young Arabic-speaking ordinands about how the recovery of the School of Alexandria today has consequences for the whole of Africa and of global Christianity" (*A Change of Heart*, 317).

[56] For an overview of the Portuguese missions of the fifteenth and sixteenth century and the later European and American-sponsored missions see Elizabeth Isichei, *A History of Christianity in Africa* (London: Society for Promoting Christian Knowledge, 1995).

[57] Oden summarizes his argument thus: "Throughout the first millennium (in Nilotic, Berber, Pharaonic, proto-Coptic, Ethiopian and Meroe cultures) African Christian teaching had taken root in indigenous, traditional, and primitive African cultures. Inland African cultures of the Nile and Medjerda basins had been the testing grounds for showing the ability of classic Christianity to live in different cultures without changing its memory of the history of salvation. African Christianity was not merely a coastal phenomena but penetrated deep into Africa in the first millennium" (*A Change of Heart*, 378, n.37).

a conviction he shared with Ratzinger who noted that "the desired *théologie africaine*, or *African theology*, is at present more a project than a reality"[58] since such a theology is often being sought alongside a disengagement from the Western colonial inheritance which brought the Christian faith to many African countries in recent centuries. Ratzinger argues that a recapturing and development of the "classical Christian tradition" is needed since this is "much nearer to the fundamental inheritance of human religious culture in general than the later constructions of European thought."[59]

This brings us to a third point of interest for this study from Oden's research and work. The argument that Alexandria is a key point of renewal not only for Western and Eastern Christianity, but in a unique way for the African church also, is closely linked to what Oden describes as the "African memory" that the traditional founder of the church in Alexandria was St Mark, who is also identified in indigenous and oral African traditions as the founder of African Christianity as a whole.[60] This traditional acceptance of the foundational place of St Mark in the Church's original mission to Alexandria, and thus to Africa, is in fact the point from which John Paul II begins as he traces the history of evangelization in Africa in his post-synodal exhortation to the Catholic Church in Africa, *Ecclesia in Africa*. Thus, as he reflects upon "the glorious splendour of Africa's Christian past," John Paul cites the words of Paul VI: "'We think of the Christian Churches of Africa whose origins go back to the times of the Apostles and are traditionally associated with the name and teaching of Mark the Evangelist.'"[61]

Our present engagement with an Alexandrian *ressourcement* must also, therefore, take a particular interest in the place of Mark and his Gospel. It is at this point that we can remind ourselves of the interesting identification that John Paul makes, in *Catechesi tradendae*, of Mark's as a "catechumenal" Gospel. Such a description adds further weight to the notion that it is the *catechumenal* work in Alexandria, which has Mark as its proposed founder, that needs to be explored for the vitality and renewal of the Church today. In this investigation into the school I therefore take a special interest not only in the

---

[58] Joseph Ratzinger, *The Ratzinger Report: An exclusive interview on the state of the Church*, with *Vittorio Messori* (San Francisco: Ignatius Press, 1985), 193.
[59] Ibid., and see 191–96.
[60] See the discussion in Thomas C. Oden, *The African Memory of Mark: Reassessing Early Church Tradition* (Downers Grove: IVP Academic, 2011).
[61] John Paul II, *Ecclesia in Africa* 31, quoting from Paul VI, *Message Africae terrarium* 3. Paul VI's message goes on precisely to identify the early Christian missions in Egypt, North Africa, and Ethiopia as the *African* heritage.

reception of Mark's Gospel in the Church in general, but particularly in recent catechumenal characterizations of Mark's Gospel, looking for possible points of coherence with what we can know of the practices and vision of the school.

If we would like images for the inherent capacity of Christian Alexandria to support the work of the new evangelization we might look to two that would have recommended themselves to the Alexandrian school. The first is that of the Nile itself, the determining image of everything Egyptian. Alexandria stood on the coastline where the Nile finally reached the Mediterranean ocean. The Nile has multiple sources, the three main tributaries being the White Nile, the Blue Nile, and the Atbura. From its multiple, small beginnings it flows into a single stream that travels over four thousand miles north and finally fans out into the Delta where it floods and irrigates a huge region, bringing wealth and supporting life so that the area has always been a potential treasury for the nations round about. This was no mere image for the Alexandrians themselves, of course, but the living reality of their situation.[62] And it is natural to suppose that this fact of the Nile's generative capacity would have impressed itself on the minds of the Christian community in Alexandria as well and given them a vivid sense of what might be their own position within God's economy of salvation, a life-giving source for the nations.[63]

A second image, also quintessentially Alexandrian, is that of the great port and harbor with the lighthouse dominating the horizon, one of the seven wonders of the ancient world. Clement loves to depict Christ as the Divine Pilot, steering people safely to the haven of heaven. Christ is the light that has shone from heaven so that now the whole universe has become a sleepless light,[64] and he advises the

---

[62] The river metaphor came easily to the Alexandrians—thus Clement, describing how truth is fed from many sources: "There is only one way of truth, but different paths from different places join it, just like tributaries flowing into a perennial river" (*Stromateis* 1.5.29.1).

[63] Thus Oden, noting that through the work undertaken on the *Ancient Christian Commentary on Scripture* the contributors were able increasingly to confirm that "the flow of intellectual creativity in early Christianity moved from Africa to Europe" (*A Change of Heart*, 307). Interestingly, Dujarier argues that it was "the example of the African catechumenate" from a *later* period, inspired especially by Cardinal Lavigerie's work to restore the ancient catechumenal discipline, "that roused the Churches of Europe" (*A History of the Catechumenate*, 139).

[64] *Protrepticus* 11.114.2-3. Christ our divine educator is like a pilot of a ship, holding onto our ears as to a helm to steer us, not once letting go and keeping us steady so that we can reach home (*Paedagogus* I.7.54.3). The rich young man is tossing dangerously in the seas of the law and seeking the safe anchorage which can only be found with the Savior (*The Rich Man's Salvation*, 8). The safe arrival in port

newly baptized to practice the presence of God in prayer, leaning their thoughts on the power of Christ "as if in some harbor by the divine light of the Savior", at rest from all thought and action.[65] The two images can recommend themselves to us as representing both the new life that can flow from this kind of engagement, this work of *ressourcement*, and the contemplative rest which is its end.

MAIN POINTS OF DISCUSSION

What, briefly stated, are some of the rich seams for evangelization and catechesis today that we will be mining in this study? What *is* the "light from Alexandria" that John Paul is urging upon the viewer in that portrait?

In chapter five I examine the school's understanding of a *Christian paideia*. The school understood evangelization and catechesis as a participation in the divine work of *establishing Christian culture*. All evangelizing and catechetical work had to be placed at the service of the development of such a culture. Such a participation, according to the Alexandrian school, requires from the catechist both an unshakable adherence to the Person of Christ and an awareness of the richly demanding nature of this work with which Christ has tasked his Church.

The Gospel has its own culture, unfolding in accordance with the activity of God in his creation and his saving plan. This sacramental and liturgical culture was seen to have enormous implications for our understanding of natural and human realities and capacities.[66] At the same time, the Church's culture was not to be thought of as a simple replacement of any culture which it engaged; the school was profoundly attentive to the "seeds" of the Word—those anticipatory and preparatory elements in a culture whose potential can be drawn out through an engagement with the Gospel so that the seeds can be shown to have presaged unexpected points of development beyond their natural or obvious ends, goods that reflect the gratuitous synthesis made possible by Christ.[67] The Alexandrian school's confidence in God's single overarching plan that unites all things in Christ who is both the source and goal of creation enabled a generous approach to the identification of these seeds of the Gospel in culture.

---

from the dangers of the ocean is also a favorite image for Origen: in a tiny boat he steers on the vast ocean of God's mysteries and knows himself vulnerable on the "gaping waves," so begs prayers for a "favorable breeze" of the Holy Spirit to help him "enter the port of salvation" (*Homilies on Genesis*, IX.1).

[65] *To the Newly Baptized*.
[66] Cf. *DC* 397b.
[67] Cf. *DC* 397d.

In Alexandria, the school was aware of what the *Directory for Catechesis* calls the many "cultural preconditions"[68] that have to be in place for the transmission of the Gospel to occur fruitfully. The Alexandrian Greek world had its cultural foundations in *paideia*, a commitment to a substantial effort of education and formation that Western culture later described as the *trivium* and *quadrivium*. This theme of the *paideia* is crucial to our understanding here for it concerns not only a process of individual education but more broadly the initiation of a person into a tradition and the transmission of this tradition itself. The Alexandrian school drew on this tradition to learn how, in catechesis, to *speak well*, learning a form, as it were, of "divine rhetoric," one which could echo the universal saving truth of Christ into particular cultures, fully and sensitively.[69] They saw that God's economy, enacted in and through the sacraments, provided the dogmatic foundations and saving grace necessary for the establishing of a Christian culture which would provide the proper context for the understanding and ordering of all disciplines—literary, scientific, historical, and especially philosophical. It could affirm liberal education on the basis of its contribution to what John Paul calls God's own "pedagogy," a divine pedagogy that in turn provides the basis and model for "the pedagogy of faith."[70]

In each engagement with contemporary culture, therefore, the school sought to identify points of contact and connection, while not being afraid to expose dissimilarities between the Gospel and culture that called for cultural transfiguration. In the writings of the school we therefore find on the one hand a consistent reminder of the *relativity* of all merely human traditions and on the other the Gospel's tryst with each culture which transcends all particularity without releasing one from what is contingent, but rather orientates and supersedes what it touches. The point of the inculturation of the faith is to draw out each culture's potential, requiring the light of Revelation to shine in all its brightness in the engagement. The Gospel, we might say, stands over against culture as Aristotelian act to potency, drawing the culture upwards into a fuller and richer expression. And this salvific engagement with each culture is placed within a theological account of the great sweep of creation and history, viewed through the lens of a *cosmic* kerygma, as a sacramental and liturgical formation of persons and societies, a living pedagogy offered by the

---

[68] *DC* 396.
[69] Cf. Louth's remarks on this as a general need for theology (*Discerning the Mystery*, 41–43).
[70] *CT* 58.

Church which now appears as the crown of each culture, radiating Gospel intelligence and love.

In chapter six I examine the recognition of the need for the development of a *Christian philosophy* to underpin and guide this new culture. The school held that it is the Lord himself who is the first principle of knowledge and who trains us into the knowledge of the truth.[71] It knew that it was crucial to identify the main philosophical principles that are coherent with the rule of faith since only with a commitment to these can Christ's teaching enter deeply into culture.[72] The school therefore practiced a generous engagement with the philosophical schools of the time, entering into dialogue with these schools so as to ensure an embedding of the truth of Christ who offers the "royal highway" on which one may travel safely, avoiding the perils of dangerous cliffs, rivers and deep seas.[73] It found philosophical commitments coherent with the principles of the faith largely in what is called "Middle Platonism," a form of Platonism that drew widely upon truths from other philosophical traditions and in so doing, the school judged, established perennial philosophical positions needed for the proclamation and explanation of Revelation. In fact, the school found in Platonism not only teachings and truths, but also practices and pedagogical approaches that could be embraced in the young Church. As Middle Platonism itself continued to develop into the Neo-Platonism of Plotinus, so the dedicated work of the Alexandrian school was hugely influential in helping to establish the metaphysical foundations needed for Christian culture.[74] It was a work continued by Augustine in the Latin-speaking West,[75] and by the Cappadocian fathers and Dionysius in the Greek-speaking East, until we see its full flowering in Bonaventure and Aquinas in the Middle Ages.

Chapter seven examines the process of entry into the catechumenate and the character and content of the initial proclamation of the faith. The school announced the *kerygma* as something of intense beauty,

---

[71] *Stromateis* 7.16.95.6. This training is described by Clement in his two works, *Pedagogus* and *Stromateis*, as being first that of a *pedagogue* and then of a *teacher*.

[72] For Clement on the Rule of Faith in relation to philosophical enquiry see *Stromateis* 7.16.95-96. See also Eric Osborn, *The Beginning of Christian Philosophy* (Cambridge: Cambridge University Press, 1981), 268-70.

[73] See Clement, *Stromateis* 7.15.91.5.

[74] John Paul notes the importance of the contribution of both Clement and Origen in *Fides et ratio* 38-39, his encyclical on the vital necessity of understanding the interdependence of faith and reason [hereafter FR].

[75] In this work of cultural transmission in the West, we should note that Augustine could not take full advantage of the Alexandrian heritage itself due to his lack of ease with Greek: see the detailed discussion by Henri Marrou, *Saint Augustin et la fin de la culture antique*, 4th ed. (Paris: E. de Boccard, 1958), 27-46, 420-21, 631-37.

opening up a pathway to joy. At the same time, the demands of the Christian life were made clear and the entry point into the catechumenate clearly marked.[76] The concepts of *paideia*, Word, and Wisdom were incorporated into different presentations of the *kerygma*, thus establishing a continuity with what the Alexandrians saw as the natural foundations for the Christian faith: it is the same Word and Wisdom who had befriended them in their studies who now called them deeper, unveiling a trustworthy path of formation towards perfect happiness.

Chapter eight provides an overview of the nature of formation in the school's catechumenate, and concludes that the work of Christian catechesis undertaken here is a lot more like the kind of formation that one receives today on entering into a religious community than one might initially imagine (and indeed as the model for the catechumenate began to shift during the fourth and fifth centuries onwards the kind of catechumenate that we find in the school in Alexandria was effectively transferred to the monasteries and religious communities). The school considered that the divine teaching given by Christ can be received only insofar as one has first accepted him as a *formator*—or, Clement would say, a "pedagogue"—in one's life. The first task is "to improve the soul, not to teach, and to train it up to a virtuous, not to an intellectual life."[77] The necessary light of truth must be placed in a life able to receive and bear it. Only in this way can, as John Paul puts it, "the whole of a person's humanity" be "impregnated" by God's word.[78] It is the whole person who must carry the word to birth. The Deposit of Faith is to be placed and guarded in the whole of the *life* of the catechumen.

Chapter nine focuses on the importance of *mystagogy*, of a leading from the sacraments of initiation into mystery. "The further we progress in reading, the greater grows the accumulation of mysteries for us.... For all things which happen happen in mysteries."[79] Catechesis, John Paul taught, is "the communication of the living mystery of God,"[80] and the Alexandrian school believed that one accesses

---

[76] This establishment of clear expectations for potential catechumens was crucial since, as Dujarier argues, "the devaluation of the entry into the catechumenate is the source of the devaluation of the catechumenate" (*A History of the Catechumenate*, 107). In the fourth and fifth centuries, the changed position of the Church led to precisely such a devaluation. See also his *The Rites of Christian Initiation: Historical and Pastoral Reflections* (New York: Sadlier, 1979), 24–25.
[77] *Paedagogus* 1.1.1.4.
[78] *CT* 20.
[79] Origen, *Homilies on Genesis*, IX.1.
[80] *CT* 7.

spiritual truth only through an energetic and holistic work of ongoing *discovery*, under grace. Only the ardent seeker finds. The divine work of education is one in which God reveals himself in *mystery*, hiding truth in order that it may be received only as the full human powers of intellect and desire are appropriately prepared, asking of students and their mentors alike a work of education that is at once demanding and intensely personal.[81] The Alexandrian tradition ties this mystagogy into the revelation of Christ as *teacher* and the school in the post-baptismal period assists in forming teachers of the faith. In line with the consistently pedagogical vision of the faith that we find in Alexandria, the call to holiness and to Christian perfection are presented as intrinsic to the life of a *teacher*.[82] In this formation for teaching, the chapter considers the importance for the school of the unity of the written and unwritten vehicles of Revelation, so that the *personal* and the *written word mutually accompany each other*. The formation that is given will take root well only if protected and supported in long-term structures of relationship and will limp if the personal and the textual elements in this ongoing formation are disassociated.[83] The central Alexandrian theme of the unity of faith and life is reaffirmed here, with a particular examination of the crucial place of the Scriptures in the formation for those called to teach.

In the final chapter, following this detailed examination of the life and work of the school, I seek to flesh out John Paul's characterization of Mark's Gospel as "catechumenal" and make a case for reading Mark in this way as crucial for a full appreciation of the earliest Alexandrian catechetical tradition.

---

[81] The *Directory* speaks often to the need to draw out clearly the depth of the conversion, of transformation and regeneration that is both demanded and made possible by the Gospel (DC 397c). It wants to avoid any "mere juxtaposition of the Gospel with culture," any remaining satisfied with the Gospel appearing simply as "decoration"; the transformation requires an "interior maturation" (DC 398).
[82] Thus Clement writes that the word of truth is received precisely *as a teacher*, τοῦ λόγου ἡ ἀληθὴς πρὸς τοῦ ἀξιοπίστου παραλαμβάνεται διδασκάλου (*Stromateis* 7.9.52.2). For Clement, Eric Osborn emphasizes, "Christian perfection is not a private possession but a quality necessary for the teacher within the community of faith" (*Clement of Alexandria*, Cambridge: Cambridge University Press, 2005), 15.
[83] This is a theme we also find in John Paul II, who writes continually of the needs for a passion for personal transmission on the one hand and a reliance on both the inspired word and broader Christian literature. See CT 46-50, 63-71. For Clement on this point see Osborn, "Teaching and Writing in the First Chapter of the *Stromateis* of Clement of Alexandria," *Journal of Theological Studies*, New Series 10, 2 (1959) 335-43.

PART I

The City and the School

CHAPTER 2

The Preparation of the City

TO UNDERSTAND THE CATECHETICAL SCHOOL in Alexandria we need to appreciate the significance of Alexandria itself. The school, within the providential design of God, grew up in a unique setting. Our understanding and appreciation of what it meant to found and lead a catechetical school will be helped by placing it in the context of the city itself and the culture and traditions at that time.

At the time of the birth of the Church Alexandria was the point of the confluence of some of the oldest, finest, most influential and powerful cultures of the day: Egyptian, Greek and Jewish. In time, Rome was to take these up and add her own riches to this gathering.

> From the time of its foundation by Alexander the Great in 331 BC to its capture by Octavius in 30 BC it had been the capital of a great Empire, the intellectual centre, the *arbiter elegantarium* of the Hellenic world, the magnet to which all the material riches of Asia and Africa, all the intellectual resources of the Greek world, were attracted, and the power-house which transmuted this wealth and disseminated it throughout the Mediterranean. Even after the political centre of gravity in the Mediterranean world had moved westward to Rome, Alexandria was still intellectually and culturally supreme... for nearly a thousand years, Alexandria was, in one or more of its many facets, the most important city in the world. It was the world's greatest port and emporium of commerce.... In its Museum and Library it possessed the world's great centre of academic learning and scientific research.[1]

According to tradition, it was into this city that St Mark brought the fledgling Christian Church. And in this city the holy Church of God, only decades old, made the audacious claim that she was, in God's design, the intended inheritor of all that was true, good and beautiful in each of these cultures, that in fact they contained the "seeds" of the Reality she had come to proclaim. Like the kings of old bowing before the Christ Child, these ancient cultures with their wisdom and power were to recognize themselves as forerunners of One in whose glad service they would find their correction, reward, and fulfillment.

---

[1] John Marlowe, *The Golden Age of Alexandria* (London: Victor Gollancz, 1971), 13, 16.

Articulating *this* understanding and enacting *this* project in the midst of what was arguably the richest culture in the world, the city of Alexandria, was the central task of the fledgling catechetical school which settled there in the early years of the Church's history. The convictions and the life which shaped the school allowed her to regard with confidence the cultural riches of her surroundings. Affirming everything in them that was good, true and beautiful, she sought to show how these qualities were found in their fullness in Christ, integrated in the divine Person who was the beating heart of each renewed life.[2] And from this reality, her leaders taught, a new culture and a new city was being born, a city of the Spirit, a kingdom of heaven, built by grace in collaboration with the virtuous activity of each person. Such a kingdom had been in secret preparation in the midst of each of the cultures who had come together in the earthly city and their elevation and transformation was now at hand.

THE PTOLEMAIC CITY

Alexandria in Egypt was one of twelve cities that Alexander the Great founded and named after himself. Alexander had begun his campaign against the Persians in 334 BC, with his decisive victory over the Persian king Darius II at Issus in 332. Egypt had been one of the dominions under Persian rule and the Egyptians welcomed Alexander as a liberator. It was in the winter of 332-331, during his stay in Egypt, that Alexander founded Alexandria. He intended it from the outset to be an international center of learning and a seedbed of Hellenistic civilization for his empire, a center of the great civilizing momentum of Greek culture. For centuries before Alexander there had been Greek colonies in the Nile Delta and the Greek city of Naucratis had been established on the Canopic branch of the Nile;[3] but this new city, Alexandria, was to be *the* center of Hellenism, of a new civilization. Under Alexander, the idea of the *oecumene*,[4] of

---

[2] In a discussion of the Fathers' relation to culture, Pompa rightly describes a key aspect of the approach of Clement and Origen as one of having "a spirit of solidarity with regard to the surrounding culture of which they are themselves a part" (Klaas Jan Pompa, "Patristic Evaluation of Culture," *Philosophia Reformata* 38, 1973, 99). As we will see, it is a solidarity that flows directly from the metaphysics they embraced.
[3] For the details of the founding of Naucratis see Hermann Kees, *Ancient Egypt: A Cultural Topography* (Chicago: University of Chicago Press, 1962), 206-11. Although the Ptolemies continued to attend to the city and its development, "the economic importance of that city ended with the founding of Alexandria" (210), the first sea-port on Egypt's open coast.
[4] The term *oecumene* is derived from the Greek words for home (*oikos*) and management (*nemein*) and was originally indicative of the science of household

Hellenistic civilization spreading across the inhabited world as its unifying factor, came into existence. There would be a common form of civilized speech, *koine* Greek (the type of Greek in which the New Testament is written), and there would be a common system for education, the *paideia*, the arts and sciences crowned with philosophy. The focal point of this Hellenistic civilization was to be Alexandria. The Church took up this theme of a universal civilization, but placed the nations under Christ: it is Christ who is the great civilizing and unifying figure bringing the fruits of grace to all the nations of the world.[5] As Werner Jaeger put it, "The dream of Alexander when he founded the city that bears his name was now to be realized: two universal systems, Greek culture and the Christian church, were to be united in the mighty superstructure of Alexandrian theology."[6]

Following the death of Alexander, three kingdoms grew up from his empire, an empire which stretched from Greece to India. In this divided inheritance it was Ptolemy—Alexander's chief of staff—and his successors who took the area of Egypt. Theirs was to be a kingdom in which the rulers were now to be Greek, overseeing the Egyptian majority. The cult of Alexander was promoted early on in an attempt to give divine status and legitimacy to Ptolemy and his successors. After defeating another of Alexander's generals, Perdiccas, Ptolemy was confirmed ruler of Egypt and Cyrene and also gained a new

---

management. According to Diogenes Laertius (*Lives of Eminent Philosophers* II, 12), Aristotle wrote a treatise on the subject and it was a popular topic among Greek writers in the pre-Christian period. During the time of Greek expansion it was also used to describe the ideal of Greek political culture as an international aspiration, the whole of the human race dwelling together as a family. The term was to be taken up in the Christian tradition to speak of God's plan to unite all peoples as a single family in a Christian civilization. For the background to the term see John Henry Reumann, *The Use of Oikonomia and Related Terms in Greek Sources to about 100 A.D. as a Background for Patristic Applications* (Dissertation, January 1, 1957, University of Pennsylvania, http://repository.upenn.edu/dissertations/AAI0023631).

[5] Eusebius makes exactly this point in his *Praeparatio evangelica* (I.4.6-7) where he writes of Christ civilizing the barbarians. He consciously imitates Plutarch's *On the Fortune of Alexander*, written around AD 100, and whereas Plutarch presents Alexander the Great as the great civilizing figure, Eusebius places Christ in this supreme role. For a discussion of this theme see Werner Jaeger, *Early Christianity and Greek Paideia* (Oxford: Oxford University Press, 1969), 3-12, and for Eusebius's universal perspective see Raoul Mortley, *The Idea of Universal History from Hellenistic Philosophy to Early Christian Historiography* (Lewiston, Queenston and Lampeter: Edwin Mellen Press, 1996), 151-204. This conviction of a universal mission was primarily taken by the Church from Judaism, of course, which stood out among Graeco-Roman religions in having this conception.

[6] Jaeger, *Early Christianity and Greek Paideia*, 40.

surname, Soter ("Savior" in Greek), for the assistance that he gave to the inhabitants of Rhodes. In 284 BC, Ptolemy Soter's son, Philadelphus, succeeded him and continued the consolidation of Ptolemaic rule, his fleet increasingly controlling the Eastern Mediterranean.

The site chosen for the city was superb. Situated on the Mediterranean and with Lake Mareotis due south of the city, Alexandria was defined by its relation to water, and especially, of course, to the Nile. Its position gave it an attractive climate, with the sea tempering the heat, along with Etesian winds from the north, and provided an excellent harbor, sheltered from the west wind. The fertility of the area was assured by the Nile Delta with the overflowing of the Nile in the summer filling and refreshing the canals which flowed into the city.[7]

The city built there was spacious and clean in its design – from the beginning it was a *beautiful* city, "marble from birth."[8] It was a beauty enshrined in the quality of its construction and in its dominating institutions, with the palace and its grounds, together with the library and museum, covering around a quarter of the city.[9] A Greek novelist from the late third century AD has given us a description of Alexandria, of a city that had kept its beauty for many hundreds of years:

> I tried to cast my eyes down every street, but my gaze was still unsatisfied, and I could not grasp all the beauty of the spot at once... that which I actually saw kept my gaze fixed, while that which I expected to see would drag it on to the next. I explored

---

[7] The action of the Nile is the key to the prosperity of this area. The Greek historian and geographer Strabo (c.64 BC–AD 25) correctly identified the reason for this unusual summer filling of the river rather than its drying up as being due to monsoon rains in the south which came in the summer (*Geography* XVII.1.5). Strabo spent a good deal of time in Alexandria, probably from around 25–19 BC, and Book XVII of his seventeen volume *Geography* contains much valuable information on Alexandria and on Egypt in general. Apart from what can be learned from excavations of the site – and most of ancient Alexandria remains unexcavated – it is from Strabo that our principal information about Alexandria as a city at the beginning of the Christian era comes. We rely upon him and upon other literary sources for matters such as the precise locations of the buildings and sites in the city.

[8] Edward A. Parsons, *The Alexandrian Library: Glory of the Hellenic World* (London: The Elsevier Press, 1952), 58.

[9] Beauty was one of Alexandria's exports: she became the principal home of stucco sculpture, a technique which she spread to the East and the West, gypsum, the raw material for stucco, being plentifully present adjoining the city. Mosaic art, in both stone and glass, also flourished in Alexandria (see Blanche Brown, *Ptolemaic Paintings and Mosaics and the Alexandrian Style*, Cambridge, MA: Archeological Institute of America, 1957). For a broad discussion of sculpture and architecture, especially temple architecture in this period, see Ibrahim Noshy, *The Arts in Ptolemaic Egypt* (Oxford: Oxford University Press, 1937).

therefore every street, and at last, my vision unsatisfied, exclaimed in weariness, "Ah, my eyes, we are beaten."[10]

In typical Greek fashion, the streets were ordered in a rectangular fashion,[11] two broad thoroughfares intersecting the city, the Canopic Street running from east to west and the Street of the Soma running north to south. The Canopic Street was named after the most westerly branch of the Nile while the north-south street was named after Alexander's burial place, the massive Soma, which was placed at the intersection of the two roads.[12] A twelve-mile perimeter wall marked the city's boundary. A double harbor faced the Mediterranean at the north of the city, the eastern harbor containing the Royal Port close to the Palace and the barracks of the Royal Macedonian Bodyguard. The western harbor, Eunostos, or "the harbor of happy homecoming," was built by the third Ptolemy, Euergetes. A lake harbor stood to the south, on Lake Mareotis, and the north and south of the city were connected by a canal at the western end of Alexandria. This canal was the principal route used for imports and exports. Canals also connected the lake to the Canopic branch of the Nile. Thus the city was assured both of plentiful fresh water, delivered through conduits under the main streets and with underground cisterns serving the large public buildings, and also of canal networks serving trade movements.

During its thousand years of Ptolemaic and Roman rule the city enjoyed enormous wealth and prestige. Writing about Alexandria around the time of Christ, three hundred years after its founding, Strabo described the city as "the greatest emporium of the inhabited world."[13] And around a century later, Dio Chrysostom, speaking to the Alexandrian populace during the reign of Trajan, summarized the economic achievements of the city:

---

[10] The author is the Alexandrian Achilles Tatius and the extract is from his romantic novel, *Clitophon and Leucippe*, V.1 There is some evidence that Achilles eventually became a Christian and a bishop (see Gaselee's introduction to the novel in the Loeb edition).
[11] Alexandria was typical of Hellenistic cities in being laid out in a grid fashion. For comments see Christopher Haas, *Alexandria in Late Antiquity: Topography and Social Conflict* (Baltimore: John Hopkins University Press, 1997), 24.
[12] Alexander's burial in this mausoleum was not something Alexander himself requested, but was the result of a shrewd political move on the part of the Ptolemies, claiming the body of the empire's founder for Alexandria.
[13] Strabo, *Geography*, XVII.1.13. His judgement on the exalted significance of Alexandria is worth noting since he was in a position to make broad comparisons, his *Geography* covering Western and Eastern Europe, as well as the Middle East and parts of Asia and Africa.

Not only have you a monopoly of the shipping of the entire Mediterranean by reason of the beauty of your harbors, the magnitude of your fleet, and the abundance and the marketing of the products of every land, but also the waters that lie beyond are in your grasp, both the Red Sea and the Indian Ocean whose name was rarely heard in former days. The result is that the trade, not merely of islands, ports, a few straits and isthmuses, but of practically the whole world is yours. For Alexandria is situated, as it were, at the cross-roads of the whole world, of even the most remote nations thereof, as if it were a market serving a single city, a market which brings together into one place all manner of men, displaying them to one another and, as far as possible, making them a kindred people. [14]

During the Ptolemaic period Alexandria became a major center of world trade, reaching out to both the west and the east. Trade to the east ran along two main caravan routes, through Arabia and through the Euphrates Valley. By sea, trade to the east went via the Red Sea and then to the ports of Berenica, Philotera and Myos Hormos, while the lighthouse, Pharos, counted one of the wonders of the ancient world, was built under Ptolemy Philadelphus to welcome vessels into its harbor.[15] The material wealth of the city was ensured not only by her privileged location, but also by Egypt's natural wealth—which meant especially her fertile soil. From the beginning, therefore, the Ptolemies set to work improving the irrigation, draining marshland and developing the agricultural resources of the region. Alexandria became famous for its export of grain, which formed the heart of its economic wealth,[16] while minerals from the Egyptian interior also travelled through Alexandria for export—gold from Nubia, iron from the desert, granite from Aswan. Linen, glass and pottery, tapestries and carpets, were also exported and, of course, papyrus from the Nile reeds.

---

[14] *The Thirty-Second Discourse*, 38. Dio Chrysostom delivered this discourse to the people of Alexandria in the great theatre there, possibly as an emissary of the Emperor. "... as far as possible ... a kindred people" is a plea that the Alexandrians, renowned for their violence and factions, use their cosmopolitan character for the good, not for perpetuating disunity.

[15] The lighthouse, built by the architect Sostratus of Cnidus, and aided by a vast number of mathematicians working at Alexandria's museum, was one of the most impressive achievements of this period in terms of conception and execution. Built on the island of Pharos to protect boats from Alexandria's reefs, the lighthouse was unfortunately damaged by earthquakes around 1100 and finally destroyed by further earthquakes in the fourteenth century.

[16] The free supplies of bread to the citizens of Rome, and in due course to Constantinople, the new capital, were entirely dependent on Egyptian grain. At the height of the Roman period it is estimated that Alexandria exported 83,000 tons of grain a year (Hass, *Alexandria in Late Antiquity*, 42-43).

INTELLECTUAL, CULTURAL AND RELIGIOUS LIFE

The wealth enjoyed and fostered by the city was cultural and artistic as well as material and, of course, it is for this intellectual and cultural wealth that the city is principally remembered today. In its day it enjoyed the reputation of being the foremost center for Hellenistic culture, for research and for learning. The importance of Alexandria as an intellectual and cultural center was recognized throughout the whole of the Greco-Roman period, with the centers of learning enjoying the patronage and support of the Ptolemaic rulers, and later of the Roman Emperors.[17]

The main reason for Alexandria's prestige and the main home for her learning was her famous museum and library. The museum was placed in the Brucheion district, close to the palace. Constructed in white marble and stone, it contained lecture halls, galleries for paintings, and halls for statues and numerous collections. But it was not conceived simply as a repository of antiquity, or a center for the collection of artifacts. It was to be rather a place of living scholarship and was built to serve the scholars (as many as a hundred) who lived and worked there, with sleeping quarters, cloisters, refectories and study rooms.[18] This academic community was supported financially by the city, in an arrangement that created a strong scholarly infrastructure in the city. In the museum, the academics collected, preserved and edited work of their predecessors, gathering historical, geographical, philosophical and scientific literature. It was also a center for new research as well as for the compilation and preservation of the intellectual and cultural heritage.

This museum was organized originally by Demetrius of Phalarum under the first of the Ptolemies, and through his work and those of his associates Alexandria was soon recognized as a center for mathematical and scientific studies.[19] Euclid, the father of geometry,

---

[17] From the beginning it was royal patronage and interest that enabled the growth of learning. Thus, for example, the priest who had overall direction of the museum was a Ptolemaic appointment. Later, during the Roman period, the Emperor Claudius (AD 41-54) added the *Claudium* to Alexandria's existing institutions for learning, while Hadrian (AD 117-138) added the Library of Hadrian and endowed professorships in philosophy.

[18] For a useful brief listing of key scholars and scientists working in the Museum in the Hellenistic and Roman periods, see Heine, *Origen: Scholarship in the Service of the Church*, 17-18.

[19] For helpful summaries of the achievements in this area, relating the advances to the Western history of science, see Rudolf E. Langer, "Alexandria—Shrine of Mathematics," *American Mathematical Monthly* 48, 1 (February 1941) 109-25; Harold T. Davis, *Alexandria the Golden City* (Evanston: The Principia Press Illinois, 1957), II, 407-15.

arrived in Alexandria approximately ten years after its founding, and lived and worked in the museum and the tradition of mathematical discovery was to continue into the Roman era: Diophantes, the father of algebra, worked at the museum around the middle of the third century AD. A school of medicine was also established at the museum, boasting Galen as its most important figure.

The museum had its own dedicated astronomical observatory. There were no telescopes at the time, but models of the heavens were developed which yielded increasingly accurate observational models of the stars with the help of astrolabes and dioptras, and there were many achievements by the astronomers working at the observatory using the equipment they had developed there. Famously, Aristarchus from Samos promoted a heliocentric model of the solar system, antedating Copernicus by more than fifteen hundred years, while the astronomer, Ptolemy, worked at the observatory during the second century AD. It was because of the astronomical work carried out at Alexandria that Julius Caesar, at the very beginning of the Roman period, in 45 BC, was able to correct the calendar. And in due course the preeminence of Alexandria in the area of astronomy meant that the privilege of setting the date of Easter in the Church was conceded to the Alexandrian See by the universal Church.[20]

The museum and its scholars were supported by the library of Alexandria, reputed to be the greatest in the ancient world.[21] The two institutions belonged together, with the library connected to the museum by a white marble colonnade. This was the mother library in Alexandria; a smaller, daughter library, the Serapeiana, was attached to the city's main temple, the Serapeum. This smaller library was intended for public use and so housed more popular texts, while the mother library, for the use of the resident scholars, was intended to be a comprehensive collection of learning, arranged in ten halls, the contents of each related to ten branches of knowledge.

---

[20] It was Dionysius, who led the catechetical school from AD 231 and subsequently became bishop of Alexandria in 247, with the assistance of Anatolius (a mathematician who was himself to become bishop of Laodicea) who established how to calculate the date of Easter consistently as the first Sunday after the full moon following the Spring equinox.

[21] For details of its founding see Parsons, *The Alexandrian Library*, 83-105. The evidence, from Jewish, Christian and Greek sources, consistently points to the figure of Demetrius as the one who undertook the planning of the library, although whether mainly under the patronage of Ptolemy Soter or Ptolemy Philadephus is disputed.

The account we are given in *The Letter of Aristeas* of the instructions of Ptolemy to Demetrious of Phalerum in setting up the library is breathtakingly simple: to secure a copy of every book in the world for the library collection.[22] We know that an enormous amount was achieved over the Ptolemaic period and that the library included not only Greek works, but Jewish, Egyptian, Babylonian, Chaldean, and almost certainly Indian as well. The actual size of the library is a matter of some conjecture, and it varied, of course, over time, but it is likely that at the time when Callimachus, the main cataloguer of the library, who died in approximately 235 BC, established his system of classification in the main library there were approximately half a million rolls and 42,800 rolls in the daughter library, the Serapeiana.[23]

The keepers of the library, perhaps not unexpectedly, were also some of the most learned scholars of the age. Aristarchus of Samothrace, for example, developed grammatical science, distinguishing eight parts of speech and establishing the mechanics for grammatical analysis which have come down to us today.[24] He also undertook a painstaking study to make a reliable text of Homer, which appeared around 150 BC; this was a crucial work since Homer was the common "textbook" used for memorization and inspiration in elementary schools, for analysis in the schools of rhetoric, and for furnishing both content and style for political and state ceremonial functions. Indirectly, Aristarchus's work came to be highly significant for both the Jewish and Christian communities of Alexandria. Sylvie Honigman has argued convincingly that the canons and methodology put in place for the critical editing of Homer provided the exemplar for the Jewish scholars in Alexandria when they came to translate the Old Testament into Greek. This, the Septuagint translation, played a comparably central role in education for Jews, and in due course for Christians, in the Hellenistic world to that of Homer

---

[22] *The Letter of Aristeas* (London: SPCK, 1918), 9. This letter, as we have noted, is the main source for our knowledge of how the Greek translation of the Old Testament, the Septuagint, came to be written and housed in Alexandria's library.
[23] Parsons, *The Alexandrian Library*, 204. J. H. Ellens puts the number in the main library at 700,000 in 100 BC, rising to a million in the time of Caesar (*The Ancient Library of Alexandria and Early Christian Theological Development* [Claremont, CA: The Institute for Antiquity and Christianity, 1993], 8). Callimachus devised the first great library catalogue known to the west, the *Pinakes*. For the work of this pioneer of library science, see Parsons, 204-18.
[24] For the work of Aristarchus at the library, "the foremost critical scholar of antiquity," see Parsons, *The Alexandrian Library*, 266-69.

for the Greeks.[25] From the collection in the great library attached to the museum, then, arose not only systems of cataloguing but also the development of literary criticism with the study of philology, canons of literature and rules of exegesis.

It is noteworthy that an Egyptian priest, Manetho,[26] was chosen as head of the museum and this should probably be seen as more than simply a shrewd political move, a gesture, as it were, towards Egyptian culture: it is likely that the model and prototype for the Alexandrian museum with its library was found not only in Greek antecedents (as, for example, in the Lyceum) but even more in the large Eastern temple libraries which priests oversaw and in association with which they developed their teaching.[27] The combination that we find in Alexandria of a library collection, a *scriptorium*, and a center for teaching and learning, as well as for the compilation and editing of texts, all in the context of priestly oversight and closely associated with religious cult, is paralleled in the Egyptian "House of Life" which was the temple *scriptorium*.[28]

Alexandria jealously guarded its status and reputation for scholarship—and its library stock. It acquired the manuscripts for its library by both moral and immoral means: while many works were purchased, other were simply seized.[29] It saw off its main rival for fine libraries, Pergamum, using fair means and foul, at times refusing to

---

[25] See Sylvie Honigman, *The Septuagint and Homeric Scholarship in Alexandria: A Study in the Narrative of the Letter of Aristeas* (London: Routledge, 2003), 119–43; also Sebastian P. Brock, "The Phenomenon of the Septuagint," *Old Testament Studies* 17 (1972) 23–27.

[26] Manetho wrote a history of Egypt and many works on religious life in Egypt, known to us now only through fragments and quotations from Josephus and from Christian writers. For an overview of his life and writings see the introduction in the Loeb edition by William G. Waddell, *Manetho*, vii–xxviii.

[27] See the argument of Herman J. de Vleeschauwer in "Les Bibliotheques Ptolemeennes d'Alexandrie," *Mousaion* 1 (1955), 1–40 and the evidence compiled in Stephen Shubert, "The Oriental Origins of the Alexandrian Library," *Libri*. 43, 2 (1993), 142–72. Daniel Potts also draws parallels with certain Near-Eastern collections: "Before Alexandria: Libraries in the Ancient Near East," in ed. Roy MacLeod, *The Library of Alexandria: Centre of Learning in the Ancient World* (London: I. B. Tauris, 2000), 19–34.

[28] For background, see Alan H. Gardiner, "The House of Life," *Journal of Egyptian Archaeology* 24 (1938), 157–79.

[29] "At this great port, where ships came from all the known world, vessels were searched and books or manuscripts when found were confiscated. Copies were made and given to the rightful owners with some other compensations if not too much trouble was made, but the originals were retained for the library" (Parsons, *The Alexandrian Library*, 163). See Galen, *Commentary on Hippocrates' Epidemics III*, XVIIA, 606k.

export papyrus to the Kingdom of Pergamum so as to undermine its work of collecting and copying manuscripts,[30] and eventually removed the library altogether, transferring it in its entirety to Alexandria as war booty.[31]

To understand how the nature and message of the catechetical school would have been seen and received, it is vital to appreciate how complete was the integration between civic and religious life in Hellenistic culture. The cosmos of the gods populated the world of culture and the gods represented and protected all forms of social, political and communal life. In Alexandria, Dionysus was especially honored as the god from whom the Ptolemies were said to have been descended. As the god of sailors, Poseidon was also appropriately prominent in this port city, while Demeter was associated with the grain-harvest. But there was no exclusivity in these matters: the Temple of Bendis, a Phrygian goddess identified with Artemis, stood on the shore of the Eastern harbor, the Temple of Eleusis on the Canopic canal, and a Temple to Ceres and Persephone on the Eastern side of the city; the Paneum, the Park of Pan, was a sequestered area of great beauty in the city with a grotto to him; Cleopatra's monument was probably a temple to Isis, the Egyptian goddess. The museum itself was both a cultural and a *religious* institution—as the name suggests, it was a shrine to the Muses, with statues of the goddesses of literature, science and the arts there and, as we have noted, with a priest appointed as head of the museum.[32]

Most important of all as a focus for the religious life of the city was the Serapeum, the principal temple, dedicated to the cult of Serapis. The details we have concerning the political origins of the god Serapis is a vivid reminder of what worship of the gods signified. One of Soter's first acts was to provide a unique god for the city who could be worshipped by both Greeks and Egyptians and thus provide

---

[30] Alexandria was in a position to do this since Egypt controlled the paper trade from papyrus. In the ancient world, it held a monopoly on the preparation of papyrus for writing purposes: "Egypt supplied the whole Roman Empire, from Hadrian's Wall to the Euphrates and from the Danube to the First Cataract" (Colin H. Roberts, "The Greek Papyri," in ed. S. R. K. Glanville, *The Legacy of Egypt* [Oxford: The Clarendon Press, 1942], 251).
[31] The library at Pergamum probably contained around 200,000 rolls. Thus, "ruthlessly deprived of her greatest glory, the second library in all antiquity, the sun of Pergamum set" (Parsons, *The Alexandrian Library*, 31). Before this removal of its library, Pergamum had used the lack of papyrus to good effect by developing and honing the skills needed to make improved parchment to the extent that the name of the city eventually became synonymous with this product, called *pergamene*.
[32] See Strabo, *Geography* XVII.1.8.

the key bond of social unity in Alexandria. Serapis was conceived as a combination of the Greek gods Zeus and Asclepius, and of the Egyptian gods Apis and Osiris. The Egyptian goddess, Isis, was "given" to him as his consort. Ptolemy Soter enlisted the help of Timotheos the Athenian and the Egyptian Manetho to assist him in this task. Serapis, Marlowe wryly comments, was perhaps the "only example the world has ever seen of a god created by a committee."[33] The worship of Serapis was intended to provide the essential cement for civic life in Alexandria, a focus for her sense of growing importance, and the local foundation for that unity of political, social and religious life which was characteristic of Hellenism.[34] The Serapeum was to be always the visible reminder and symbol of this unity, established in the Egyptian district of the city as a special focus for this community, to assist it in identifying with Greek rule.[35] In addition to the statue of the god himself, a massive tapestry was placed in the great Temple Hall which "represented the deified Alexander in the garb of Osiris-Pharaoh, ruler of Upper and Lower Egypt," and also the "ruler of the two worlds with the symbols of earthly power and the instruments of eternity."[36] A broadly similar understanding of the unity of civic, political and religious life also characterized the Roman Empire during its pagan period, so that when the Roman Emperor Diocletian later visited Alexandria, he set up a commemorative column in the quadrangle of the Serapeum, "Pompey's Pillar." Roman Imperial rule was celebrated and enshrined in this central place of worship.

Because religious worship played such a central social role, the Serapeum was also more than just a shrine to the god; said to have been the most magnificent of all of the buildings in Alexandria, it was also a center for the study, consolidation and dissemination of Hellenistic culture. Around the temple, therefore, were lecture and study rooms and, as we have seen, a daughter library of the great central library of Alexandria. It was a place of study and learning as well as worship. In the story of the city, the Serapeum was to be the final stronghold of pagan resistance to Christianity—the symbolic

---

[33] Marlowe, *The Golden Age of Alexandria*, 59.
[34] On the cult of Serapis see Arthur D. Nock, *Conversion: The Old and the New in Religion from Alexander the Great to Augustine of Hippo* (Baltimore: The John Hopkins University Press, 1998), 37–41.
[35] Clement gives an account of the origin of Serapis, whom he calls "the arch-daemon himself" (*Protrepticus* 4.48.1-6). Origen, also, refers to the cult as an invention of the Ptolemies (*Contra Celsum* 5:37-38).
[36] Parsons, *The Alexandrian Library*, 351.

close of the pagan period, of this civic and religious unity, gathered about the god of the city, paying homage to the world of the gods, came with the sacking of the shrine by order of the Christian Emperor Theodosius at the close of the fourth century.[37]

---

[37] We must touch briefly on the question of the fate of the great library of Alexandria (or rather libraries, for we remember that there were *two* libraries: the great library attached to the museum and the smaller library at the site of the Serapeum). For a meticulous examination of the evidence, comparing and weighing every ancient source, see Edward Parsons, *The Alexandrian Library*, 273-432. With regard to the daughter library, the Serapeiana, housed in the buildings around the temple of Serapis, one tradition has it that this smaller library was destroyed by a Christian mob when the cult of Serapis was overthrown in AD 391. One can see how this tradition arose, although it seems to be false. The occasion was certainly one marred by violence and by a sense of fanaticism fostered by the reigning bishop, Theophilus. Nonetheless, as Parsons notes, Theophilus' purpose was "not to destroy a *building*, but to destroy a *worship*. When the idol of the false god was smashed and all the instruments of his worship destroyed, the triumph of Christianity over paganism was complete" (359). It was the statue and the sanctuary that were to be destroyed. There was no attempt to destroy the building itself and in fact the temple was converted into a church. John McGuckin notes that the episcopate moved into the Serapeum complex for its own headquarters, "giving the lie to accounts that made of the area a 'wilderness'" ("Origen as Literary Critic in the Alexandrian Tradition," in *Seeing the Glory: Studies in Patristic Theology* [Yonkers, NY: St Vladimir's Seminary Press, 2017], 87, n.16). Moreover, the library was almost certainly not in the temple itself but was housed in one of the buildings in the temple complex. In addition, Theodosius, no obscurantist, whose edict was being implemented by this act, had never requested the destruction of books.

With regard to the main library, one tradition in our sources is that the burning of the great library was essentially an accident: in 47 BC when Caesar was in Alexandria, the local population rose against him and he set fire to the Egyptian fleet in the harbor, in the ensuing engagement of which the conflagration spread to the wharves and the buildings around, including the library. In support, we later find Cleopatra persuading Antony to bring the library of Pergamum to Alexandria, a point that perhaps would confirm that the library needed replacing—or at least supplementing. The clearest source we have claiming this is Plutarch, writing around one hundred and fifty years after the event. The main difficulty in accepting this account is the significant number of sources who would be closer to that event and do not mention the burning of the library or the loss of any books—Strabo, Cicero, Athenaeus, Appian, Florus, Lucan, and Suetonius, all of whom would have been closer to the event than Plutarch. But even without Caesar's action, there are several times during its history under Roman rule when there was considerable violence in the city, or when the city was besieged and taken, and these are each occasions when it is possible that damage was done to the library. Thus, for example, we have the Jewish revolt in the city during Trajan's reign, the massacre of civilians together with some looting and destruction by Caracalla, the besieging and taking of the city by Gallienus, the conquering of the city by Queen Zenobia and the subsequent re-taking of Alexandria by Aurelian, and finally the sacking of the city by Diocletian.

As far as we can tell, then, the main library, very probably suffering various depredations and attacks at intervals during the Roman period, nonetheless survived in some form until the end of the Christian era in Alexandria, as did the

A UNIVERSAL NURSE

An Egyptian papyrus fragment speaks of the city as "a universal nurse," with "every race of men" settling in her.[38] The new Alexandrian church was to teach that God had made possible a new society in Christ, a new society that was at the same time a fulfillment of the heritage brought to her by the nations. In what, then, did this heritage of the nations consist, nursed in Alexandria? In her articulation of the foundations of this new society the Church necessarily distinguished this divinely-accomplished communion of the Church from any existing political form of life. The collusion of gods and civic structures in Hellenism was to be distinguished from this new Catholic culture. This does not mean that representatives of the Christian position saw political unity as irrelevant to the progression of the Gospel, however. Indeed Origen, echoing the work of Philo, in due course presents the gathering of the nations under Roman rule as an act of providence:

> God was preparing the nations for his teaching, that they might be under one Roman emperor, so that the unfriendly attitude of the nations to one another, caused by the existence of a large number of kingdoms, might not make it more difficult for Jesus' apostles to do what he commanded them when he said "Go and teach all nations." It is quite clear that Jesus was born during the reign of Augustus, the one who had reduced to uniformity, so to speak, the many kingdoms on earth so that he had a single empire.[39]

Roman rule (and so Ptolemaic rule, likewise) could be seen by the Church, then, as an act of God's providence. The Church's mission

---

daughter library. What happened then? Newman gives us one view: "After lasting nearly a thousand years, this noblest of dynastic monuments was deliberately burned, as all the world knows, by the Saracens on their becoming masters of Alexandria." (*Historical Sketches,* Volume III [London: Longmans, Green and Co. Ltd, 1885], 93). The basis for this judgement that they were burned by order of Omar who captured Alexandria in AD 641 is an account found in the work of an Egyptian Muslim scholar of the twelfth century, Ibn al Kifti. Parsons concurs with Newman's view, though agrees that what we know is patchy: our key sources are a long way from the event and the evidence hotly disputed. A plausible alternative is that the library holdings were in the main taken to safety to libraries in Rome and Constantinople, taking advantage of a negotiated treaty which allowed Byzantine Alexandria eleven months to continue under Christian rule, and during which time massive amounts of possessions were shipped abroad.

[38] This description is from a third century AD papyrus fragment known as the "Potter's Prophecy," foretelling the fall and destruction of Alexandria. For details see Edwyn Bevan, *A History of Egypt under the Ptolemaic Dynasty* (London: Methuen and Co. Ltd., 1927), 240-41.

[39] *Contra Celsum,* II, 30.

was able to benefit from the natural flow of people, trade and language that was powerfully set in motion by Alexander the Great and then consolidated by the *pax Romana* of the Augustan period around the time of Christ—Rome was famous for the construction of roads, but even more important for travel and trade were her ports. This flow of peoples, religions and ideas enabled many oriental currents and traditions, for example, to find their way to Egypt, and it is clear that the Alexandrian and Indian civilizations were in touch with one another. Thus Eusebius, as he introduces the catechetical school, tells us of Pantaenus's evangelizing work in India.[40] And, travelling in the other direction, we know that the story of the Buddha reached Clement in Alexandria.[41] Still, whatever the advantages flowing from political unification, Origen does not confuse the *pax Romana*, or any form of social organization, with the coming of God's kingdom: at heart, the work of overcoming all fragmentation entails the making of new creatures, and this is a work that belongs supremely to Christ and to his Spirit.[42]

During its Ptolemaic period, the city benefitted from a virtuous circle of intellectual and cultural fame, economic prosperity, and population growth. It is estimated that by the end of the third century BC Alexandria had attracted as many as 80,000 Greek males to settle in Alexandria. We have vivid descriptions of the exuberance and self-confidence of magnificent civic celebrations from the whole of the Ptolemaic period, while the glory and extravagance of Cleopatra's

---

[40] See his *Ecclesiastical History* V.10.2-3 [hereafter H.E.]. Greek art made its way eastward and for a long while the royal dynasty in Bactria, *en route* to India, produced gold coins modelled on those of Alexander and his successors. In 327 BC, Alexander had invaded India and the following year explored the Indus, sailing out onto the Indian Ocean, Alexander's admiral, Nearchus, undertaking the exploration of the area. Elements of the account of Thomas going to India may perhaps be legendary, but the concept itself is not problematic. From the Roman era, significant numbers of coins bearing Nero's and Domitian's heads have been found in Southern India. Trade interests, of course, are the explanation for the extensive Mediterranean finds in India, and these interests were facilitated by the significant improvements in navigation—Pliny describes four phases in the development of navigation between the Red Sea and India, beginning with Alexander the Great (*Natural History* VI.26). For details of the evidence of the Roman presence in India see Mortimer Wheeler, *Rome Beyond the Imperial Frontiers* (New York: Philosophical Library, Inc., 1955).
[41] *Stromateis*, 1.15.71.6. On the Buddhist missions westwards under the Buddhist emperor Asoka see Nock, *Conversion*, 45-47.
[42] Cf. *Contra Celsum*, VIII, 72. For a discussion of Origen and Augustine on this question of the relationship of the *pax Romana* to the peace and civilization of God see Ratzinger, *The Unity of the Nations* (Washington D.C.: Catholic University of America Press, 2015), 33-116.

reign, the last of the Ptolemies, is wonderfully captured in Athenaeus's account of her famous meeting with Antony.[43] The Greek historian Diodorus Siculus estimated the population of Alexandria at the end of the Ptolemaic period as around 300,000 — and he may have been counting here the Greek and possibly Jewish population only; counting the Egyptians and slaves as well we are possibly looking at a city population of around half a million or more.[44]

Ptolemaic Alexandria was highly cosmopolitan and was designed in five main districts, named after the first five letters of the Greek alphabet, with the city organization and allocation of populations reflecting its social, ethnic and cultural make-up.[45] The rich cultural and ethnic makeup of the city, which was undoubtedly a key source of its enormous creativity and wealth, did not always equate to creative interpenetration, or even peaceful coexistence; in fact, it made for an often explosive character, reflected in frequent riots, uprisings and disturbances[46] — from many of which the Christian community was later to suffer. It is generally accepted that there was little integration of the races that made up the city, despite considerable efforts that were made. Roger Bagnell sums up the situation as one of "juxtaposition."[47]

---

[43] Athenaeus, *The Diepnosophists* IV.148. In the format of discussions at a banquet his work contains a potpourri of information about the life and habits of Alexandrians.

[44] Diodorus Siculus, *History* 17.52.6. Diodorus was writing just before the time of the transition of Alexandria from Greek to Roman rule in the first century before Christ. Population estimates of ancient Alexandria are just that, estimates; there is too much that we do not know. For example, when Diodorus offered his estimate he used the Greek term *eleutheroi* (free ones) as the category he was counting, and it is not entirely clear who was included in this. But we know that, whatever the exact figures, it was a massive city, second only to Rome itself. For a discussion of the population of Alexandria in Roman times see Diana Delia, "The Population of Roman Alexandria," *Transactions of the American Philological Association* 118 (1988) 275–92, and for a review of evidence of the likely population at the time of the Arab conquest of Alexandria, see Alfred J. Butler, *The Arab Conquest of Egypt and the Last Thirty Years of the Roman Dominion*, 2nd ed. (Oxford: Oxford University Press, 1978), 368–400. After the Muslim conquest in AD 641 there was a rapid decline in Alexandria's influence and wealth, and in her population, especially after a new capital, Fustat, was established by the Arabs on the Nile. When Napoleon invaded Egypt in 1798, just over a thousand years later, he found Alexandria as a city with a population of only around 5,000.

[45] See Haas, *Alexandria in Late Antiquity*, 47–48.

[46] See Edward J. Watts, *Riots in Alexandria: Tradition and Group Dynamics in Late Antique Pagan and Christian Communities* (Berkeley: University of California Press, 2010).

[47] Roger S. Bagnell, *Egypt in Late Antiquity* (Princeton: Princeton University Press, 1993), 230.

Within this cosmopolitan make up, the Greek community comprised the ruling class and carriers of the original vision of a universalized Hellenistic culture, of Greek *paideia*, as well as the traditions of Greek philosophy. The Brucheion area of the city was the principal district for this community, an area which also contained the Gymnasium, the center of civic life for the Greek community (with the head of the Gymnasium, the "gymnasiarch," functioning as the civic leader for the Greeks in the city).[48]

The Jews were a second, and unique, group, and the Jewish religious heritage in Alexandria was of crucial importance for the school. Alexander the Great had encouraged Jews to settle in the new city in part because he found that they would provide loyal support for him against the Egyptians and so conferred on them particular privileges,[49] giving them a unique position in Alexandria that continued into the Roman era.[50] Under the first of the Ptolemies, therefore, large numbers of Jews settled in the *Delta* district, their own quarter of the city.[51] The district lay directly adjacent to the Royal Palace, a point that is in itself a sign of the value and trust placed in them from the beginning. The district had its own walls and the Jews lived there governed by their own laws and under their own Sanhedrin. Strabo has provide a description of their social position:

> In Alexandria a great part of the city has been allocated to this nation. And an ethnarch of their own has been installed, who governs the people and adjudicates suits and supervises contracts and ordinances, just as if he were the head of a sovereign state.[52]

The Jews had their own ethnarch, their own national leader, in the city. They lived as a city within a city, technically a *politeuma*,[53] an officially recognized body of aliens enjoying the right of residence in a foreign city.

---

[48] The equivalent of our gymnasium today, a venue for physical training, was the palaestra, also located in the Brucheion district of the city. On the overlapping meanings of "gymnasium" and "palaestra" see the discussion in John Lynch, *Aristotle's School* (Berkeley: University of California Press, 1972), 34-35.
[49] See Josephus, *The Jewish War* II.487-89; *The Life Against Apion* II.35.
[50] As H. Stuart Jones puts it, "The Jews were one of the privileged orders in that racial hierarchy that the Romans so strictly maintained in Egypt" ("Claudius and the Jewish Question at Alexandria," *The Journal of Roman Studies* 16, 1926, 29).
[51] So Josephus, *The Jewish War* II.495. According to Philo, the Jews occupied two of the five districts of the city and were scattered about the other districts as well (*In Flaccum* 55).
[52] Strabo is quoted in Josephus, *Antiquities of the Jews* XIV.117.
[53] See Alfred R. C. Leaney, *The Jewish and Christian World 200 BC to AD 200* (Cambridge: Cambridge University Press, 1984), 137.

Alexandria thus became one of the great centers of the Jewish diaspora[54] and it has been estimated that up to a third of the population of the city may have been Jewish during some parts of the Roman era. Philo, living at the time of Christ, claimed that in his day around a million Jews were settled in Egypt, and it is reasonable to suppose that a significant number of these lived in Alexandria.[55] Commercially the Jews were prosperous but they were also divided among themselves as to their attitude to the surrounding populations, and being such a significant group among the whole population can explain why it was easy for unrest between the Jews and their fellow citizens, especially concerning the privileges and rights conferred on the Jewish community, to lead to serious civil disturbances.

The discordant relationships between the Jewish and Greek communities were not inevitable. In fact, in Alexandria "the hope of Jewish philosophers for a fraternal union with the Greek nation was nurtured for many generations,"[56] while an openness of the Greeks towards the Jews and a sense of their unique status *vis-à-vis* the Greek population is reflected in the work of one of the early Greeks to settle in Alexandria, Hecateus of Abdera: in his history of Egypt he actually presented the Jews and Greeks as a single people.[57] The first work in Greek literature to mention the Jews, he presents the Jewish exodus as the result of plagues that covered Egypt so that the Egyptians expelled all foreigners in order to appease their gods. The exiled group, he claims, resettled in both Greece and Judea. This legend, then, saw the Greeks and Jews as originally one people, ejected from Egypt. (Unfortunately, while it united Hellenism and Judaism, this account did nothing to promote a sense of amity with the Egyptian population.)

Despite the clear potential for friendship between Greeks and Jews, the situation of the Jews in Alexandria was complex due in

---

[54] *Diaspora* ("dispersion") is the term commonly used to describe the spread of the Jews outside Judaea. Philo provides us with a list of places to which the Jews were dispersed (*Legatio ad Caium* 281-82) and of course *Acts* provides us with a briefer list as well (2:9-11).

[55] Philo, *In Flaccum* 43. For a careful discussion of the likely Jewish population during the Roman period see Delia, "The Population of Roman Alexandria," 287-88.

[56] Jacob B. Agus, *The Meaning of Jewish History* (London: Abelard-Schuman 1963), I, 119.

[57] The works of Hecateus have not survived. However, we know of his history from the first book of Diodorus Siculus which is based on Hecateus. See *History*, I, 46.8. On the close relationship between the Greeks and Jews we also have the interesting comments in First Maccabees describing the purported kinship between the Spartans and the Jews (1 *Macc.* 12:19-23).

part to an ongoing struggle between two rival traditions in Judaism. On the one hand were Jews drawn to the ongoing Hellenizing of the faith, with many in Alexandria looking to develop philosophical and cultural elements within Judaism that were taken from Greek life and thought. In Alexandria this movement of Hellenization was particularly advanced.[58] The translation in Alexandria of the Scriptures into Greek by a group of Jewish scholars in the third century before Christ, the Septuagint (abbreviated as LXX),[59] was a hugely significant initiative for this movement since it necessarily brought about the deep engagement of the two cultures through the work of translation and subsequent mutual cultural and religious exposure. It made the truths of the inspired word of God for the first time fully accessible to Greek civilization, allowing for Jewish beliefs and convictions to be known and discussed, and from this point onwards the cultural interplay between Greek and Jew would no longer flow in one direction only. The translation began with the Pentateuch, undertaken in Alexandria in the Ptolemaic period, after which the additional books of the Old Testament were also translated—probably within about a century—and from this point on it was the Septuagint translation that was read in the synagogues of the diaspora, wherever Greek was spoken. The Septuagint became symbolic of the identity of Hellenistic Judaism, of those who sought a moderate program of cultural synthesis whilst keeping Jewish distinctiveness,[60] who wanted

---

[58] Nineteenth-century Christian scholarship often proposed an easy contrast, or even an opposition, between the early Christian faith growing out of Judaism and the surrounding Hellenistic environment. But this overly-simple view has gradually been replaced with studies demonstrating decisively how Hellenized even Palestine was at the time of Christ. For example, see Martin Hengel's seminal work, *Judaism and Hellenism: Studies in their Encounter in Palestine during the Early Hellenistic Period* (Philadelphia: Fortress Press, 1974).

[59] The translation was so named because tradition has it that it was undertaken by seventy-two scholars, six translators from each tribe. Septuagint means simply "seventy," and if seventy-two was the original number of translators the number seventy may have been selected to reflect the number of elders who accompanied Moses on Mount Sinai (see *Ex.* 24:1) and the number of the Sanhedrin. We find that same movement between seventy and seventy-two (there are variants in our different manuscripts) in the Gospel when Jesus sends out disciples to preach the Good News, the number representing the count of the nations (see *Lk.* 10:1).

[60] The account of the translation, given to us by Aristeas, sheds much light on this. Aristeas identifies himself as a Greek official at the court of Ptolemy II, Ptolemy Philadelphus. In his account, he writes that he has been sent as part of an embassy from the King, at the request of the royal librarian, Demetrius of Phalerem, to Eleazar the High Priest in Judea to obtain a copy of the Pentateuch and to find translators. The nature of the document and the identity of the author have been much discussed, but it seems likely that it was written by an Alexandrian

to explore the value of the Hellenistic heritage but did not seek its wholesale adoption.⁶¹

The significance of the Septuagint translation for the Church cannot be overestimated. The New Testament writers had used the Septuagint as the main source for their quotations from the Old Testament and the Alexandrian school, in common with all Christians in the first four centuries, benefitted from this translation for their study of the Scriptures.⁶² The Septuagint is also important for preserving a number of books not in the Hebrew canon. Some of these, which manifest the growing fusion of Jewish and Greek education and culture—such as Ecclesiasticus, or the Wisdom of Jesus Son of Sirach, probably written around 180 BC, and the Wisdom of Solomon, whose provenance is almost certainly Alexandria—are found only in the Septuagint.⁶³

Jew around the year 200 BC and that the intended audience of this work is the Alexandrian Jewish community itself. The community is being provided with an explanation of the significance of the translation. While it is often referred to as a letter written to his brother Philocrates, the author himself refers to it simply as a prose account and the reference to Philocrates is simply a dedication. For the questions of authorship and intended readership see Honigman, *The Septuagint and Homeric Scholarship in Alexandria*, 1-3, 27-29. Aristeas's narrative was received without question by both Josephus (the letter is given in a condensed form in Josephus's *Antiquities of the Jews*, XII.2) and Philo, and was accepted as a basically historical account by early Christian writers.

⁶¹ The city of Jerusalem, for example, typically remained the fixed point of reference for all Jews in the diaspora, *the* city of God. Thus, it is interesting to note that in Aristeas's account of the translation of the Septuagint Jerusalem is described as a city built with *symmetria*, that is, with proportion—a reference to the classical principle of building cities that were harmonious and of moderate size, a true *polis*. Alexandria was certainly recognized as an imposing city, one of obvious magnificence, but only Jerusalem has *symmetria*. See *Letter to Aristeas* chapters 83-120 for the description of Jerusalem. Aristotle's prescriptions for the construction of harmonious cities are in his *Politics* 7.4.4, 1326a5-b25. He notes there: "For certainly beauty is usually found in number and magnitude, but there is a due measure of magnitude for a city-state as there also is for all other things." Interestingly, Plato's ideal city in the *Republic* has twelve tribes.

⁶² Origen's famous *Hexalpa*, an arrangement of different versions of the Old Testament, placing the original Hebrew alongside a transliteration of the Hebrew into Greek, and then alongside the Septuagint translation and three other translations into Greek which had been made by Aquila, Symmachus and Theodotion, was probably compiled at least in part in order to establish the original reading of the LXX, which Origen also saw as the privileged text for Christians since it was used and handed down by the Apostles (see the discussion in Heine, *Origen: Scholarship in the Service of the Church*, 73-76). This vast work is unfortunately only extant now in some few fragments and quotations in other works, but its existence shows the seriousness of the engagement of the school with textual questions.

⁶³ The Septuagint divides the Scriptures into narrative, poetical and prophetic books. The additional books found in different manuscripts of the Septuagint are Esdras A and B, Tobit, Judith, some additions to Esther, the Wisdom of Solomon, Ecclesiasticus, Baruch, the Letter of Jeremiah, some additions to Daniel, the Prayer

The most famous representative of this movement of Hellenizing Judaism, a contemporary of Jesus and the apostles, and possible author of the Wisdom of Solomon, was the Jewish exegete and philosopher, Philo (c.15 BC-AD 50). It is natural that Philo's work should have emerged in the cosmopolitan Alexandria since he sought to highlight what he saw as the universal impetus of Judaism. Most of his work consisted of commentaries on the Pentateuch—these were the works of Moses, the unique and great prophet of God, and he wanted to show that Moses's writings were meant not only for the Jews of his day, but for all people.[64] He composed his commentaries to draw out the spiritual significance of Moses's teachings, seeking to show that the Mosaic law, when properly understood, is the most perfect form of universal education—*God's* education, and therefore the summit of all true *paideia*.

For the Scriptures to reveal their deepest meanings, he believed that they must be read allegorically[65] and in concert with a broadly Platonist philosophy, and his exegesis sought to draw out from the text perennially valid meanings that would help readers to understand the relationship of the soul to God, as well as the structure of the soul itself. He also wanted to show that a symbolic account is provided in the Scriptures of the harmony of human nature with the cosmos, for he held the Torah to be the most perfect copy of universal natural law: creation and Revelation flow from a single Source, and mirror one another.[66] This spiritual interpretation of the Scriptures, focusing on the meaning of the text for the individual

---

of Manasseh, and 1 and 2 Maccabees. (In some manuscripts are also found *3 and 4 Maccabees*, the *Psalms of Solomon*, *Odes* and Psalm 151.) The Hebrew canon of Sacred Scripture in fact itself reflects the Hellenic cultural influence on Judaism, especially evident in books such as Proverbs which was probably an Alexandrian compilation made by the religious leaders among the Jews there. This influence, then, is especially evident in the Wisdom literature of the Old Testament, whose dominant theme is the gaining of true wisdom through formation.

[64] As one might expect, he mainly used the Septuagint for his work and believed the translation to be divinely inspired (*De Vita Mosis* II.40).

[65] While Philo is the primary allegorizing figure that the Alexandrian Christians followed in their interpretations of the Scriptures, they were also cognizant of other Alexandrian Jews who had built up a tradition of allegorical interpretation of the Scriptures, as well as of Greek allegorizers who were antecedents to Philo, especially Stoics who offered an allegorical exegesis of Homer, discussing the literal, ethical and metaphysical meanings of passages from Homer (see R. Lamberton, *Homer the Theologian: Neoplatonist Allegorical Reading and the Growth of the Epic Tradition* [Berkeley: University of California Press, 1989]).

[66] "Whoever will carefully examine the nature of the particular enactments will find that they seek to attain to the harmony of the universe and are in agreement with the principles of eternal nature" (*De Vita Mosis* 2.52).

person's journey to God, allowed him to present the Scriptures as containing universally relevant content.

At the same time, while Alexandria was home to this movement of a Hellenizing Judaism, a parallel movement of concerned reaction to this increasing influence of Hellenistic culture grew up, especially among Palestinian Jews, and this reaction proved decisive for the fate of the Jews in Alexandria and for the direction of Judaism in general. It was judged that some had gone too far in the direction of Hellenization: thus, for example, the Jewish philosopher Aristobulus in the second century before Christ tried to show the compatibility of Jewish and Greek thought by equating Zeus with the Jewish God.[67] The two Books of the Maccabees are concerned with dramatic aspects of this extended debate and struggle about Jewish identity, a struggle which was complicated at that time by the violent and antagonistic rule of Antiochus.

A considerable diversity, then, existed among the Jews in Alexandria, in terms of their cultural and religious sensibilities and convictions. Philo's writings give us something of a window onto this range of views and positions among Alexandrian Jews, from proselytes to those who advocated total cultural assimilation and apostasy,[68] and from those who held to a literal interpretation of the Law, to those who read the Scriptures from an allegorical viewpoint like Philo himself—caring, he argued, for both the letter and the spirit of the text as one cares for both the body and the soul.[69] His writings also depict groups of Jews who rejected the Scriptures as mere myth.[70] It is likely that both apocalyptic and gnostic-tending groups were also represented among the Alexandrian Jews.[71]

The social and political situation of this very diverse community of Jews in Alexandria depended, naturally enough, upon their wider relationship to Judaism—and especially to the Palestinian Jews and to the ruling authorities in Jerusalem. Following the Maccabean rebellion there was a resurgence of Jewish nationalism and this increasingly impacted the Jewish population in Alexandria. The division between the Hellenizing Jews on the one hand and those more religiously

---

[67] Unfortunately, extracts from his work now only survive in Christian writings. This particular example can be found in Eusebius, *Praeparatio evangelica*, XIII.12.6-7. But Aristobulus's views were not isolated ones.
[68] *Mosis*, I.31; *De Virtutibus*, 182.
[69] *De Migratione Abrahami*, 89-93.
[70] *De Confusione Linguarum*, 2-14.
[71] For a discussion, see Birger A. Pearson, "Friedlander Revisited: Alexandrian Judaism and Gnostic Origins," *Studia Philonica* 2 (1973), 23-29.

conservative on the other was probably also reflected in a social division, with the former typically being more well-to-do. The Jewish historian, Jacob Agus, comments on the two groups: "while the former took advantage of every opportunity to earn the status of Alexandrian citizens, the latter devoted themselves to the raising of the 'iron walls' ever higher."[72] Quarrels between Jews and Greeks became more frequent in the city, with the "special position" of the Jews in Alexandria frequently being challenged or curtailed, these quarrels reflecting, as we have seen, the inner divisions, and at times the bitter enmity, of the groups within Judaism itself.

As we shall see, the internal divisions in Judaism led to its collapse in Alexandria, and this Hellenized Jewish heritage was at this point taken up by the catechetical school and vigorously developed within Christianity just as it was gradually to fade in Judaism itself. Thus, before the close of the first century after Christ the influence of the Septuagint had declined in importance in Jewish circles, partly from a concern that the Septuagint differed from the Hebrew text that was in use in Palestine and partly from a distrust of the work since it had become the translation used by Christians; thus it was within Christianity that this translation found its home. Philo's work suffered a similar eclipsing within Judaism: while he carried significant weight with many of the Alexandrian Jews of his day,[73] Philo's work, like the Septuagint, has ultimately had little lasting influence within Judaism.[74] But his was a message and an approach to the Scriptures which fitted the Church's commitment to a universal mission, and the grandeur of the Philonic synthesis of Jewish monotheism and Greek philosophy, including his allegorical reading of the Scriptures, found a welcome and home in the Christian community in Alexandria.[75] We will return to Philo and his importance many times, but it is safe to say that the work of the school simply cannot be understood without him. Immensely valued by the Church in Alexandria, with both

---

[72] Agus, *The Meaning of Jewish History*, I, 126.
[73] His influence perhaps rested on his social status as well as on his works. He was from a prominent family and Josephus identifies his brother, Alexander, as the richest man of his time in Alexandria (*Antiquities of the Jews* XX.100).
[74] On this point see Marcel Simon, *Verus Israel: a study of the relations between Jews and Christians in the Roman Empire AD 135-425* (Oxford: Oxford University Press, 1996), 33-64.
[75] In *Philo in Early Christian Literature* David Runia sums up this point starkly: "the survival of Philo's writings was entirely dependent on the intervention of the Christian authors. Pagans were not greatly interested in his thought; Jews either ignored him or condemned him to silence" (Von Gorcum, Assen: Fortress Press, 1993), 17.

Clement and Origen making extensive use of his work, and in the fourth century Didymus the Blind still drawing on his commentaries, through this adoption in Alexandria he was to become, as David Runia puts it, "a Church Father, *honoris causa*,"[76] having a decisive impact on both Eastern and Western traditions of the Church.[77]

From the Jewish heritage we can turn to the Egyptian. The native Egyptians made up the lowest and least privileged portion of the city's population, comprised the main workforce for the city, and lived in the Rhakotis district, the name of the old fishing-village over which the city was built and from which the natives had come. From the beginning, Alexander had in fact taken the Egyptian heritage seriously and he sought legitimacy by visiting the oracle of Amon-Ra who acknowledged him as the son of the god and thus a divinity and the divinely-appointed ruler of Egypt.[78] From the outset, then, the Ptolemies worked to secure the support and acknowledgment of the Egyptian population: Ptolemy Soter based his administration on Pharaonic patterns and practices, and wisely adopted a twofold approach, with Greeks being subject to their own laws and Egyptians to the existing laws of the country, leaving members of the Egyptian aristocracy with their privileges. We do not know exactly when Alexandria became the official capital and the center of Egyptian government, taking over that honor from Memphis, but we do know that in 305 BC Ptolemy declared himself King of Egypt from this new capital and that the glory and prestige of the city ensured that it remained so under both Ptolemaic and Roman rule. To emphasize their connection with the Egyptian nation the Ptolemies fully assumed the ritual

---

[76] *Philo in Early Christian Literature*, 3. According to Eusebius and Jerome, Philo met St. Peter in Rome and the two men formed a friendship which led to Philo's being favorably disposed towards the Christians in Alexandria, where the Church had been founded by Peter's disciple, Mark. (See Eusebius H. E. II.17.1; Jerome, *De viris illustribus* 11.) Marie Verdoner discusses Eusebius's treatment of Philo as a "semi-Christian" in her *Narrated Reality: The Historia Ecclesiastica of Eusebius of Caesarea* (Frankfurt am Main: Peter Lang, 2011), 64–65, 146. Jerome goes so far as to place Philo among the *ecclesiastical* authors, while the Syrian bishop of Halwan around AD 600 mistakenly describes him as a director of the Alexandrian catechetical school (see Runia, 5–6)!

[77] More broadly, Gregory Sterling plausibly argues that Philo provides us with "the single most important body of material from Second Temple Judaism for our understanding of the development of Christianity in the first and second centuries," noting: "I am convinced that the Philonic corpus helps us to understand the dynamics of early Christianity more adequately than any other corpus." "'Philo Has Not Been Used Half Enough': The Significance of Philo of Alexandria for the Study of the New Testament," *Perspectives in Religious Studies* 30 (2003), 252.

[78] The deification of kings and emperors in the Hellenistic and Roman worlds probably takes its origin from this Egyptian practice.

style of Pharaohs for themselves: the Egyptian belief was that the Pharaoh was king *because* he was a god and therefore could act as an intermediary between the people and the gods. Ptolemy, therefore, fully adopted the role of the Pharaoh as the protector of national and local religion, confirming the priests in their privileges and ensuring the building and repair of local temples, while Ptolemy Philadelphus declared his parents to be gods, having temples built in their honor.[79]

Despite these efforts of the Ptolemies, however, the history of Alexandria concerning the relationship between Greeks and Egyptians generally remained one of underlying discontent, breaking out regularly into revolts and resistance on the part of the Egyptians. After an initial enthusiasm for Ptolemaic rule a nationalistic spirit revived among the Egyptian population fairly quickly, with signs of this even under Ptolemy Philadelphus,[80] and the gap between the governing city of Alexandria and the governed country of Egypt tended to widen under the dynasty. Nationalist unrest grew especially under Ptolemy IV, and while Ptolemy Euergetes (170-164 BC) attempted to develop more favorable relationships with the Egyptian population, by doing so he fell foul of Greek sentiment, and in the end failed to undertake the more difficult economic reforms which would have ameliorated the daily lot of the Egyptian population and so diminish the persistent acrimony and strife that bubbled under the surface. Egyptian nationalistic spirit was especially strong in Southern Egypt, centered upon Thebes, an ancient capital of Egypt,[81] and in an effort to curb revolt Thebes was largely destroyed by the Ptolemies in 85 BC. The Ptolemaic relationship to the Egyptian population remained, then, at best half-hearted, and it is interesting to note that even though Egyptian influence in *Alexandria* itself grew a little under the Ptolemies it was only Cleopatra, the last of the Ptolemaic rulers, who took the trouble to learn Egyptian.

Mistakes were made by the Ptolemies, then, who from the beginning had relied too much upon Greeks to rule the city and ensure

---

[79] See Bevan, A History of Egypt under the Ptolemaic Dynasty, 128ff.
[80] See the comments of J. G. M., "Review of E. Bevan, A History of Egypt under the Ptolemaic Dynasty," The Journal of Hellenic Studies 48, 1 (1928), 107.
[81] "The inhabitants of Thebaid were at times virtually a separate state" (Leaney, The Jewish and Christian World 200 BC to AD 200, 132). Thebes was the capital of Egypt during three different periods of Egypt's long history, from 2135 BC-1985 BC, during the XI dynasty; from c.1700 BC-c.1353 BC during the XIII dynasty, and then the XVI to XVIII dynasties, and from c.1332 BC-1279 BC during the XVIII and XIX dynasties. At other times, nationalist Egyptian hopes fastened on a revival of the glory of the ancient city Neni-nesu—or Heracleopolis, as the Greeks called it (for its history and importance see Hermann Kees, Ancient Egypt, 212-30).

the security of the dynasty, with few Egyptians able to rise to high positions in the administration. And while the growing wealth of the city provided lucrative opportunities for Greeks who wanted to settle, and for a cosmopolitan population that was gratefully loyal to the regime, the group always at risk of neglect, subject to economic inequalities, and deeply conscious of its inferior status, was the indigenous Egyptian population, flowing in and around the city from the surrounding rural areas seeking work.[82] The welcome given, in due course, by both Upper and Lower Egypt to a Christian pastoral oversight from Alexandria, from a community composed of Greeks, Jews, indigenous Egyptians, and others, is especially noteworthy in this regard and indicates the reception in the Christian community given to aspects of inland Nilotic culture.

THE MOVE TO ROMAN RULE AND THE GATHERING OF THE HERITAGE

Cleopatra was the last of the Greek Ptolemies. Her relationship with Caesar and then with Antony, marks the turning point from Ptolemaic to Roman rule. In an effort to save and secure Ptolemaic rule in Egypt Cleopatra attempted to draw first Caesar and then, more successfully, Antony into the Alexandrian world, and his willingness to move in this direction, aligning his fate and fortune to Cleopatra, reveals not only her powers of attraction but also the strength of this city and its power of self-assertion on the world stage. With Cleopatra's encouragement, Antony organized a Triumph in Alexandria, something that no Roman general had dared celebrate anywhere except Rome, and he made public his wish to be buried in Alexandria, not in Rome. The self-confidence of the city lent its support to Antony's ambitions, and Rome was quickly reminded of the influential and ambiguous position of Alexandria within the Roman Empire—henceforth it was decided that no Roman senator was allowed even to visit the city without the Emperor's express permission: Senators with political aspirations could all too easily win support and make challenges for the throne from that position, drawing upon a volatile population conscious of its own importance, and with granaries at their behest that were "the pledge of world power."[83] With the deaths of Antony and Cleopatra, then, Egypt

---

[82] For the Egyptian presence in Alexandria during the Roman period see Mohammed Abd-el-Ghani, "Alexandria and Middle Egypt: Some Aspects of Social and Economic Contracts under Roman Rule," in eds. W.V. Harris and G. Ruffini, *Ancient Alexandria between Egypt and Greece*, Columbia Studies in the Classical Tradition 26 (Leiden: Brill, 2004), 161–78.

[83] Emil Ludwig, *The Nile* (New York: The Viking Press, 1937), 472, who adds that

came under the sway of Rome, and from that time on it was a Roman Prefect who ruled Egypt from Alexandria,[84] Octavius Caesar placing Cornelius Gallus as the first Prefect.[85]

Taking up the story of the heritage of the nations, we can say that under Roman rule—during the period of the development of the catechetical school—the Egyptians suffered even more intensely from an economic point of view. A depressed class, it was they who had to bear the brunt of the poll-tax, the so-called *laographia* introduced in 24 BC.[86] Only those possessing Greek or Roman citizenship were exempted from having to pay the tax—and Egyptians were not allowed to become citizens. Henry Green describes the social impact this new tax had on those who had hitherto been "upwardly mobile Egyptians":

> The Romans actively developed criteria to establish who was a Greek. Those who had claimed exemption on the basis of their social status were compelled thereafter to forfeit their civic privileges and be identified as non-Greek, Egyptian.... The immediate consequences for the socially stigmatized were many: occupational mobility was curtailed, jobs in the civil service were closed, Greek education through the gymnasium was restricted, and the tax burden was increased.

Green argues that this polarization of the population into Romans/Greek and Egyptians lay at the root of a profound "social and psychic dislocation" in the first century AD for the educated groups who had

---

the proscription was the greatest honor that could have been paid to Egypt: "so powerful was the seduction of the country that the highest office-bearers of the Empire had to be forbidden to visit it."

[84] A brief unsuccessful attempt to wrest Alexandria back for the Macedonian lineage was made by Queen Zenobia of Palmyra who captured Alexandria during the reign of the Emperor Aurelian (270–75), but was rapidly defeated.

[85] Although the Alexandrian period under Roman rule lacked the relative political stability that the city enjoyed under most of the Ptolemies, a sign of the importance Rome accorded to the city is that the classical sources we have record the names and dates of all of the Roman prefects who ruled Egypt from Alexandria. But the city suffered from the political confusion accompanying the often rapid succession of Emperors during the early Christian era, which was in turn reflected in the rapid turnover of Prefects in Alexandria (over fifty during the first two hundred years of Roman rule). For these details and a discussion see Joseph G. Milne, *A History of Egypt under Roman Rule* (London, 1898), 186–92.

[86] Egyptians in Alexandria as well as in the villages bore this burden, though Egyptian priests appear to have been given some exemptions in both the Ptolemaic and Roman eras. See Andrew Monson, "Late Ptolemaic Capitulation Taxes and the Poll Tax in Roman Egypt," *Bulletin of the American Society of Papyrologists* 51 (2014), 127–60.

previously enjoyed a higher social status.[87] The taxation burden increased and the responsibility for collecting taxes was now normally delegated to local figures and officials who, because of the difficulty in collecting them, found that this task often meant paying a portion oneself.[88] In addition, wealthy Egyptians were increasingly expected to perform "liturgies": "voluntary" offerings of public work—providing supplies for government agencies or warships, for example, or even contributing to the arts. The heavy demand for liturgies and the constant focus on tax-gathering led to a tendency for figures to "disappear" from the system—a phenomenon that was called *anachoresis*, from which we derive the term anchorite. Given this social situation, it is perhaps not accidental that the development of the anchorite way of life, of individuals and communities of religious withdrawing from mainstream society, developed first in Egypt.

Greek and Jewish relations in Alexandria also worsened during the initial cross-over to Roman rule since the Jews, at the instigation of Antipater, the father of Herod the Great, gave support to the Roman army against the Ptolemies. While Herod was on the throne, enjoying a close relationship with the Roman rulers, he was able to lend his support to the Alexandrian Jews and helped to stabilize their position. But after the Jewish revolt in Judaea and the destruction of Jerusalem in AD 70, Roman policy itself towards the Jews became deeply antagonistic and this was reflected in the Roman treatment of the Jews in Egypt. All Jews were now subjected to a special tax levied on them on the principle that the contribution they used to make to the Jerusalem Temple should now be directed to the Temple of Jupiter.

As a result of ongoing Roman hostility, Jewish nationalistic feeling grew in Alexandria during the next generation, eventually spilling over in AD 115-117 into a massive assault by the Jews of Alexandria on their Greek and Egyptian neighbors. The riots in Alexandria spread to the rest of Egypt and to Cyrenaica and Cyprus, with the resulting eventual suppression of the revolt by Trajan leading to an almost complete elimination of the Jewish diaspora in those countries. A further revolt in AD 132-135 was finally put down and temples of Jupiter and Hadrian built over the site of the Jerusalem Temple.[89]

---

[87] Henry Green, "The Socio-Economic Background of Christianity in Egypt," in eds. B. A. Pearson and J. E. Goehring, *The Roots of Egyptian Christianity* (Minneapolis: Fortress, 1986), 109.

[88] See Leaney, *The Jewish and Christian World 200 BC to AD 200*, 132.

[89] For a summary see Leaney, *The Jewish and Christian World 200 BC to AD 200*, 115-25.

It was the end of an era and from AD 135 the Jewish community in Alexandria passed into virtual oblivion. The Jewish heritage in Alexandria was now to be taken forward largely within the Christian community. Origen argued that Israel should be understood not so much as a distinct people, a nation like the other nations, but as that portion of humanity which God has preserved as his own, in direct relationship with him, not bound and delimited by a sense of national allegiance as absolute.[90] Through Israel, therefore, God had given to all the nations a message that there was, in Ratzinger's words, something "primordial, original, and common to all."[91] A "new Israel," a people he would have as his own possession, would be the foundation for the new unified society that God was bringing into being. The school realized that this mission of unification belonging to Christ and his Church asks for, in Newman's phrase, a "very various application." In his *Essay on the Development of Christian Doctrine*, Newman noted that "if Christianity be an universal religion, suited not simply to one locality or period, but to all times and places, it cannot but vary in its relations and dealings towards the world around it.... Principles require a very various application according as persons and circumstances vary, and must be thrown into new shapes according to the form of society which they are to influence."[92]

Newman is writing of the development of doctrine here, but his point can be applied equally to questions regarding the inculturation of the one Gospel truth. The *Directory for Catechesis* describes this as fostering what it calls "relational dynamics" and "reciprocity"[93]—an immensely energetic work that can take place only on the basis of a deep conviction that one is speaking precisely in a world in which there is truly something "primordial, original, and common to all." As one approaches the "heritage of the nations," one seeks points of coherence and sympathy between a culture and the Gospel through a determination to overcome what George Steiner calls "modal" difficulties—points of fundamental experienced disconnect. Faced with such difficulties one needs to seek a broader and new understanding, to be open to a different resonance.[94] A "reciprocity" needs to be achieved.

---

[90] See *Contra Celsum*, V.45–46.
[91] Joseph Ratzinger, *The Unity of the Nations*, 40. See 37–41.
[92] John Henry Newman, *An Essay on the Development of Christian Doctrine* (Westminster, MD: Christian Classics, Inc., 1968), Part I, Chapter II, Section I, Paragraph 3 (2), 58.
[93] *DC* 397a.
[94] See George Steiner, "On Difficulty," in *On Difficulty and Other Essays* (Oxford: Oxford University Press, 1978), 18–47.

Clearly the notion of reciprocity needs to be carefully considered: one person's reciprocity can be another person's compromise, or even betrayal; and so it is important to understand how both Clement and Origen approached this question of inculturation. They did so from a conviction that Christianity brought to every culture something truly foundational: a *worldview of reciprocity itself*, dogmatically enshrined and to be pervasively lived, as the account of the heart of *who God is* and of *how he relates to his creation*. This principle, they taught, lay at the center of Reality as its metaphysical key, and was exhibited in the triple doctrines of the Trinity, the Incarnation, and the divinization of the person through grace, central teachings from which all the individual doctrines and particular practices of the Church take their source and in which they all find their hermeneutical keys. Christianity, the Alexandrian tradition saw, brought to each and every culture the universal truth of reciprocity as the heart of Being itself.[95]

The details had to be worked out, but the basic insight was there. The ultimate reciprocity is in God himself, as the truth of eternal love, and the Alexandrians often used the concept of *philanthropia* (love of mankind) to express the divine work of loving unification exercised by God in relation to his creation. Employed by Isocrates to express the political attitude of the generous city sharing its blessings with the rest of the world,[96] and a key term in Demosthenes to speak of the ideal attitude of rulers, in the Hellenistic period *philanthropia* was used to describe the beneficent monarch in his care for his subjects. This political term was taken up in Hellenistic Judaism by Philo who applied it to the Torah, and from there it was Clement and Origen who "established its Christian usage."[97] As Clement put it, the divine Logos in the Incarnation is *the* perfect all-loving ruler, who brings forth "a spring of love and peace flooding the whole face of the earth."[98]

The promise of *universal truth* as an expression of God's all-embracing *philanthropia* was central to the teaching of the school in Alexandria. The school was to proclaim a message that was for all peoples, for those who were "far off" and those who were "near."[99] Indeed, Clement

---

[95] Eric Osborn insightfully and convincingly uses this concept to illuminate the shape of the argument in Clement's major writings: *Clement of Alexandria*, 132-52, 255-58.
[96] *Panegyricus*, 29.
[97] John Ferguson, *Clement of Alexandria* (New York: Twayne Publishers, Inc., 1974), 66. In the New Testament we find the term in *Tit.* 3:4.
[98] *Protrepticus* 10.110.3.
[99] Cf. *Eph.* 2:13, 17.

pointed out, the Gospel reaches even to Hades, the land of the dead.[100] In Christ there is one covenant for all and there is now no return possible to the ways of the myriads of precursors of Christ.[101] In Christ, God has become a fellow-citizen (*sumpoliteuetai*),[102] the good Shepherd come to save the flock of mankind.[103] The goodness of God reaches out in every way to all persons and to every kind of need.[104] The whole Christ is here and is not to be divided, and so there is now "neither barbarian nor Jew nor Greek, neither male nor female, but a new man transformed by the Holy Spirit of God."[105]

Such universality, then, sensitive to each culture while teaching a divine reciprocity of love that supersedes and perfects every culture, found unswerving expression in the Christian community of Alexandria and in the approach that the school took to its educational and formational practices. Egyptian temple education was reserved for priests and their sons, with other forms of Egyptian education mainly serving royalty and officials. The Greek *paideia* was accessible largely to the elite, with pedagogues living in the households of the well-to-do. It was only the wealthy among Alexandrian Jews who could avail themselves of an education in the liberal arts and sciences.[106] For the Greeks themselves, the "liberal" arts were so called because they were the disciplines and curricula that provided the basis for participation in a free (*liber*) society as a full citizen of that society. The Greek *polis* was seen as an association of free men, a form of political organization that is *chosen* and not just a political grouping which holds its members together in any kind of order. But full membership of such a *polis* was not available to all.

The catechetical school, on the other hand, *was* open to all.[107] The Alexandrian school shared this vision of a greater society of free persons, but it was greater even than that of the Greek *oecumene*, for it preached a society of persons who knew themselves called to the absolute Good, in which every act and choice was to be a preparation, through a disciplining of the whole person, for participation in the

---

[100] *Stromateis* 6.6.48.3.
[101] *Stromateis* 6.5.41.6; cf. 6.18.166.5.
[102] *Protepticus* 11.117.1.
[103] *Protepticus* 11.116.1.
[104] *Paedagogus* 1.9.83.
[105] *Protepticus* 11.112.3.
[106] See James L. Crenshaw, *Education in Ancient Israel: Across the Deadening Silence* (New York: Doubleday 1998), 12.
[107] In fact, the Church had to defend herself against the perception that she catered exclusively to the ignorant and the poor (*Contra Celsum*, III.44).

life of a new creation, a new heaven and earth, a new Jerusalem. The gift of this renewed world, bestowed in embryo to each Christian in baptism, gave to the Alexandrian teachers a breadth of approach as they considered the nature of the preparation required, for nothing in creation, in the world of matter and of the intellect, was to be left untouched. All was ready for transfiguration. All that was created in the one Logos, all of the *logoi* of the created order, were to be gathered. The word of the Teacher "has been diffused over the whole world, over every nation and village, and town."[108] How could the friends of Christ the Logos not love and respect and seek to purify all of the elements of the creation that was being made new? The community received and taught Jews, Greeks, Egyptians and all who came to it seeking baptism. Both men and women were instructed.[109] Members of all classes became catechumens. With the school, as we will see, the Greek *paideia* would be universalized.

---

[108] *Stromateis* 6.167.3.

[109] This equality of women alongside men in instruction was a remarkable feature of the school, reflecting the new Christian understanding of women. Both men and women are equally under the tutelage of Christ: "For if the God of both is one, the master (*pedagogue*) of both is also one; one church, one temperance, one modesty; their food is common, marriage an equal yoke.... And those whose life is common, have common graces and a common salvation; common to them are love and training" (*Paedagogus* 1.4.10.2-3).

CHAPTER 3

The School in its Christian Setting

IN THIS CHAPTER I WOULD LIKE TO PROVIDE further context for our understanding of the school, not in terms of the "heritage of the nations" which the school received in Alexandria, but in the form of different kinds of *Christian* evidence that can help us grasp the nature and significance of the school. The most important evidence concerning the work of the school, its practices and convictions, lies in the writings of the major figures who either led or were connected with the catechetical school—and these writings are extensive. But we can also learn from other sources, and in this chapter I will consider three in particular.

First is the evidence of *Christian life from writings whose likely provenance is Egypt or Alexandria itself*. The school did not come to be in a Christian vacuum, and these additional sources can assist us in further understanding the shape and emphases of the early Alexandrian Christian tradition in the form that it came to take in the school. In the second place are *histories of the early Church* which feature the school and this early Alexandrian tradition, with the main point of interest being, of course, Eusebius's *Ecclesiastical History*. These place the Alexandrian Church in the wider ecclesial context and draw our attention to connections with other great sees and places of learning and formation, especially Rome, Jerusalem, and Antioch. A critical reading of these records of Christian history can help us to identify core elements in the life and teaching of the school that are continuous with other centers of Christian life as well as to appreciate in what the Alexandrian school's particular contributions might consist. Third is *the tradition associating Mark and his Gospel with the Church in Alexandria*. We can remember that the portrait of John Paul II, focusing our attention on the light that comes from Alexandria, included a characterization of the Gospel of Mark as "catechumenal." Reviewing the evidence concerning this tradition of Mark's association with Egypt and Alexandria and setting forth the complexion and key features of Mark's Gospel, I argue here, will enable us to appreciate how deeply this Gospel is echoed in the character of the Alexandrian school and so can form a constitutive aspect of that "light from Alexandria" which can inspire our catechesis and evangelization today.

EARLY CHRISTIANITY IN ALEXANDRIA AND EGYPT

The interpretation of the evidence concerning early Christianity in Egypt is hotly debated. However, while there is much that remains uncertain, we can be reasonably sure that the Christian mission to Egypt *began in Alexandria during the apostolic period* and from there spread into the surrounding *chora*, or "country."[1] We are fortunate that the literary evidence for this mission and for the Christian presence in Egypt is "massive."[2] From Christian papyri, for example, we can see that many of the documents that were in due course formally recognized as belonging to the New Testament canon were present in Egypt by the second century, and it is significant that the very earliest papyrus fragment of the New Testament that we have — a small section of the Gospel of St John — was discovered in Egypt, dating to the early second century.[3]

In addition to the evidence we have of Christian books making their way early into Egypt from elsewhere, demonstrating how the mission from Alexandria had reached into the countryside by the early second century, we also have numerous Christian writings of probable Egyptian origin. The Letter to the Hebrews may have an Alexandrian provenance, and certainly shares many linguistic and thematic links with Philo.[4] Early apocryphal works that we can trace with reasonable probability to Alexandria are the *Gospel of the Hebrews* and the *Gospel of the Egyptians*, two works that speak to the Christian

---

[1] Thus, as a representative comment: "It is...unthinkable that the Christian mission should have bypassed Alexandria for decades. One or several communities must have existed there as early as the second half of the 1st century" (Helmut Koester, "Egypt," *Introduction to the New Testament, Volume II: History and Literature of Early Christianity*, 2nd ed. [Berlin: de Gruyter, 2000], 237).

[2] Birger A. Pearson, "Egypt," in eds. M. M. Mitchell and F. M. Young, *The Cambridge History of Christianity, Vol.1: Origins to Constantine* (Cambridge: Cambridge University Press, 2006), 331.

[3] Held in the John Rylands University Library in England, this fragment is known as John Ryland Papyrus 52. The text from the Gospel, 18:31-33, 37-38, is written on both sides, showing that it is from a codex, or sewn book, rather than a scroll. This is one of a number of early Christian papyri from Egypt and these fragments are the earliest surviving agreed physical evidence for Christianity and the Gospels. See Larry W. Hurtado, *The Earliest Christian Artefacts: Manuscripts and Christian Origins* (Grand Rapids: William B. Eerdmans, 2006).

[4] For a balanced and cautious analysis see Runia, *Philo in Early Christian Literature*, 74-78, and the discussion by Siguard Grindheim, "Direct Dependence on Philo in the Epistle to the Hebrews," *Novum Testamentum* 65 (2023) 517-43. It appears to have a background in diaspora Judaism, and shares many Alexandrian interests, and certainly found strong *acceptance* in Alexandria, as Bruce persuasively argues: F. F. Bruce, *The Epistle to the Hebrews* (Grand Rapids: William B. Eerdmans, 1964), xxxi-xxxv.

missionary interest in the Jews and Egyptians respectively.⁵ We also have the interesting *Kerygma Petri*, the "Preaching of Peter," which is preserved in a number of fragmentary references for us by Clement in his *Stromateis*.⁶ It is also plausible to assign Alexandrian origins to the *Epistle of Barnabus*,⁷ *Second Clement*, the *Apocalypse of Peter*, the *Sentences of Sextus*, the *Teaching of Silvanus*, and the *Epistula Apostolorum*.⁸

Jewish Christianity was almost certainly the earliest form of Christianity in Alexandria and Egypt,⁹ a fact confirmed by the detailed work of the papyrologist, Colin Roberts. He has shown that numerous papyri evidence the practice of treating sacred names, the *nomina sacra*, with special care in manuscripts—names such as *Iesous, Christos, kyrios* and *theos*. Roberts plausibly argues that this early Christian tradition was influenced by the Jewish reverence for God's name, a reverence that we see from Acts was maintained in the early Church. While Jews wrote the Divine Name as the Tetragrammaton, the distinctively Christian practice arose to especially honor the names of Jesus, Christ, and so on, in this way.¹⁰ It makes perfect sense to think of Jewish Christians as the most significant early Christian group in this region because of the proximity of Egypt to Jerusalem and because of the importance

---

⁵ See Birger Pearson, "Earliest Christianity in Egypt: Some Observations," 149-50. Clement knew both of these works: see *Stromateis* 2.9.45.5 and 3.9.63.1. Origen refers to the *Gospel of the Hebrews* in his *Commentary on John* 2:87-88. The *Gospel of the Egyptians* probably originated from gnostic Egyptian Christians living in Alexandria. See further Roelof van den Broek, *Studies in Gnosticism and Alexandrian Christianity* (Leiden: Brill, 1996), 184-85.
⁶ The *Kerygma Petri* is another reminder of the close connection of Alexandrian Christianity to the first apostles from Jerusalem. See A. M. Ritter, "De Polycarpe à Clément: aux origins d'Alexandrie chrétienne," in ΑΛΕΞΑΝΔΡΙΝΑ: *Hellénisme, judaïsme et chirstianisme à Alexandrie. Mélanges offers au P. Claude Mondésart* (Paris: Éditions du Cerf, 1987), 163-65.
⁷ The *Epistle of Barnabas* is one of the oldest complete Christian writings with an origin in Alexandria, and should be dated between AD 80 and 120 (see W. H. C. Frend, *The Early Church: From the Beginnings to AD 461* [Worcester: Billing and Sons Ltd., 1992], 37). The earliest reference to it in Christian literature is from Clement of Alexandria.
⁸ For the plausibility of these as Alexandrian works see the discussions in Runia, *Philo in Early Christian Literature*, 64-118; Heine, *Origen: Scholarship in the Service of the Church*, 34-46, 93-94, 117, and Birger Pearson, "Earliest Christianity in Egypt: Further Observations," 98-107.
⁹ For a clear account, still accepted in general outline, see F. J. Klijn, "Jewish Christianity in Egypt," in eds. B. A. Pearson and J. E. Goehring, *The Roots of Egyptian Christianity* (Philadelphia: Fortress Press, 1986), 161-75.
¹⁰ For example, see *Acts* 3:6, 4:10, 12; 5:28. See Colin H. Roberts, *Manuscript, Society and Belief in Early Christian Egypt* (Oxford: Oxford University Press, 1979), 26-34; Brent Nongbri, *God's Library: The Archeology of the Earliest Christian Manuscripts* (New Haven: Yale University Press, 2018), 37-38.

of the Jewish diaspora in this region, and especially in Alexandria. It is reasonable, therefore, to suppose that Alexandria would have been one of the first places for Christian missionaries from Jerusalem to visit.[11] Alexandria was easily accessible by sea from Palestine, and we know that Apollos, Paul's co-worker, was from Alexandria.[12]

The general scholarly agreement that the earliest forms of Christianity in Alexandria and Egypt were Jewish has replaced an earlier view made popular in the early 1970s by Walter Bauer in his *Orthodoxy and Heresy in Earliest Christianity*. Bauer had proposed that the comparative obscurity that surrounds the origins of Christianity in Egypt is a result of a later orthodox purge of earlier traces of mutant *Gnostic* versions of Christianity that had taken root in Egypt in the first and early second centuries.[13] By "Gnostic" — from the Greek *gnosis* (knowledge) — Bauer was pointing to the different systems of belief that focused on the importance of knowledge, especially esoteric forms of hidden knowledge, as the key to salvation. As Birger Pearson has pointed out, however, the development of this argument

---

[11] Acts 18:24; 19:1. See also 1 Cor. 1:12, 3:4-6, 22, 4:6, 16:12. See also Colin Roberts, *Manuscript, Society and Belief in Early Christian Egypt*, 49-73 and Birger Pearson, "Earliest Christianity in Egypt: Some Observations," in eds. B. A. Pearson and J. E. Goehring, *The Roots of Egyptian Christianity*, 135-37. See also the discussion in Heine, *Origen: Scholarship in the Service of the Church*, 26-31. Benjamin Schliesser offers the argument that it may have been the preponderance of the Jewish presence in Alexandria that meant that Paul, the apostle to the Gentiles, considered it outside of his missionary work: "Why Did Paul Skip Alexandria? Paul's Missionary Strategy and the Rise of Christianity in Alexandria," *New Testament Studies* 67, 2 (April 2021) 260-83. The large Jewish presence did not, of course, mean an easy relationship for the Christians: we can remember that it was the synagogue of the *Alexandrians* in Jerusalem that so violently opposed Stephen (see Acts 6:9).

[12] The reference to Apollos in *Acts* reinforces for us the close links that existed between the Jewish communities in Alexandria and Palestine: "Now a Jew named Apollos, a native of Alexandria, came to Ephesus. He was an eloquent man, well versed in the scriptures. He had been instructed in the way of the Lord; and being fervent in spirit, he spoke and taught accurately the things concerning Jesus, though he knew only the baptism of John." (Acts 18:24-25). Although it cannot be proven, Pearson plausibly suggests that Apollos may have been a pupil of Philo ("Earliest Christianity in Egypt: Further Observations," in eds. J. E. Goehring and J. A. Timbie, *The World of Early Egyptian Christianity: Language Literature and Social* Context [Washington D. C.: CUA Press, 2007], 101). In addition, it is worth noting a variant reading of Acts 18:25 which says of Apollos that he "had received information in his homeland about the word of the Lord"—see Josep Rius-Camps and Jenny Reid-Heimerdinger, *The Message of the Codex Bezae: A Comparison with the Alexandrian Tradition: Volume 4: Acts 18:24-28:31* (London: T&T Clark, 2009), 16. This reading, if historically accurate, would further strengthen the early date by which the faith had reached Alexandria.

[13] *Orthodoxy and Heresy in Earliest Christianity* (Philadelphia: Fortress Press, 1971), 44-53.

led him to over-enthusiastic "discoveries" of heretical Gnostic traces in some of the earliest Egyptian and Alexandrian Christian literature which do not really yield this kind of reading.[14]

It is undeniable, however, that, even if not the earliest form of Christianity, Gnostic literature in Christian as well as non-Christian forms was widespread in Egypt during the period we are investigating and Gnostic groups often found a hospitable environment in Alexandria. Among the most important figures, Carpocrates taught in Alexandria in the early part of the second century, as did his son Epiphanes, while Basilides and his son Isidore also led a prominent Gnostic group there, probably between AD 120 and 140, a group that was subsequently led by Valentinus, another native of Alexandria. Gnostic groups would also have had their own schools,[15] not only in Alexandria and Egypt but further afield as well.[16] Since the findings of the Gnostic library at Nag Hammadi in 1945, a location in southern Egypt just below Luxor, we now have large quantities of firsthand evidence of what these Gnostic beliefs were. The *Gospel of Truth*, for example, may represent Valentinus's beliefs and the *Gospel of Thomas* discovered there is also from the same period. It is clear from this widespread evidence that the form of Gnosticism taught by both Basilides and Valentinus was in some sense Christian. However, it is also clear that the origins of Gnosticism as a whole do not in fact lie in an early perversion of Christianity but must be traced further back and further afield: Gnosticism appears in some forms of Judaism and also in Iranian dualism and in oriental mystery religions found in Egypt and Asia. Gnosticism also seems to have drawn from some forms of Greek philosophy. The collection of beliefs and practices we can describe as Gnostic appeared, then, not first as a Christian heresy but, having arisen from pre-Christian Jewish, Greek and oriental sources,

---

[14] Birger Pearson, "The Problem of 'Jewish Gnostic' Literature," in *The Emergence of the Christian Religion* (Harrisburg: Trinity Press International, 1997), 122–46.

[15] For Gnostic schools in Alexandria, led by Basilades and Valentimus, see the brief discussion in Heine, *Origen: Scholarship in the Service of the Church*, 51–54.

[16] For example, we know that there was a Christian school in the ancient Christian kingdom of Edessa from the second half of the second century and Han Drijvers makes a strong argument that it was led in its early years by Bardesanes, a convert from the Valentinians, and was only gradually brought into the central Christian Tradition under the influence of Ephrem, the Syriac Church Father, who moved to Edessa in AD 363. The evidence for this "School of the Persians" is unfortunately still frustratingly scanty, and we are not necessarily looking at a settled institution here, but at least a place where teachers and pupils gathered regularly. See Han J. W. Drijvers, "The School of Edessa: Greek Learning and Local Culture," in eds. J. W. Drijvers and A. A. MacDonald, *Centers of Learning: Learning and Location in Pre-Modern Europe and the Near East* (Leiden: Brill, 1995), 49–59.

united themselves to Christianity at a later stage.[17] Distinguishing the teachings of the school from these Gnostic beliefs mixed with Christianity, and countering the teaching of Gnosticism in general, were therefore particular preoccupations for the catechetical school.

In the history of the Church in Alexandria and Egypt we have plentiful evidence, not only of the defense of orthodox Christianity in the face of Gnostic variants, but also of a positive *missionary outreach* to Egypt. It is worth noting that it was not obvious that this missionary movement would be effective, for Alexandria, because of the unique features concerning its founding, was always seen as somewhat set apart from the rest of Egypt—for the Romans it was always *Alexandria ad Aegyptum*, Alexandria against, next to, or toward, Egypt. It is a point to remember as we begin to consider the achievement of the school and of Alexandrian Christianity in general since the Alexandrian mission needed to overcome a cultural and social, as well as religious, "distance" of the city from the country. The Alexandrian Christians spoke into an Egyptian context in which, as we have seen, there was deep disaffection with the existing social and political conditions. The city of Alexandria, while in the first place a Greek city, founded to spread Hellenistic culture, was certainly not intended to be an island of Greek culture that would leave the surrounding *chora* unaffected by its founding, its glory and scholarship; yet in the end it was only *Christianity* that finally won the Egyptian population to an intense loyalty, a loyalty even more remarkable given that the pivotal story in the Judeo-Christian narrative, the story that defines it, is one of escape from an Egypt that enslaves. The embedding of the Christian faith in Egypt is perhaps one of the most remarkable of all of the Alexandrian Christian achievements.[18]

Notwithstanding the foundational narrative of the time of slavery and the exodus from Egypt, the Christian mission to the Egyptian population was, of course, able to draw upon a long history of interaction between Egypt and the Chosen People: Abraham had lived in Egypt for a while; Joseph had been Pharaoh's chief minister;

---

[17] A later and popular form of Gnosticism found its way to Egypt from Mesopotamia in the third century AD in Manichaeism, a sect founded by the prophet Mani (d. 276).

[18] The inroads Christianity made into rural areas of Egypt, even by the third century, was in marked contrast to the general picture we have of the expansion of the faith which was largely confined to urban populations (see A. H. M. Jones, "The Social Background of the Struggle between Paganism and Christianity," in ed. Arnaldo Momigliano, *The Conflict Between Paganism and Christianity in the Fourth Century* [Oxford: The Clarendon Press, 1963], 18–19).

Moses had been raised as an Egyptian prince and trained in Egyptian wisdom; and Isaiah looked forward to the fulfillment of God's promises when the Egyptians would honor him and the Lord would say, "Blessed be Egypt my people."[19] This interaction between Egyptian culture and the culture of the Gospel[20] increasingly became expressed in a new language, Coptic—a translation of Egyptian into Greek, using the Greek alphabet with the addition of several letters from demotic Egyptian script, which was developed during the third century by Egyptian Christians for the purpose of translating the Scriptures into Egyptian. "One has only to open a Coptic book to see what an extraordinary number of Greek words were introduced into the language used by the Egyptian Christians."[21]

Alongside the development of this new language, and during the period under study, the Egyptian desert became home to the new forms of Christian community life that we know as monastic. *Christian monasticism* in Egypt, in both its eremitical and cenobitic forms, was closely associated with Alexandria—this is the case both with regard to the physical proximity of many of the communities,[22] as well as their traditions of formation and spirituality. The patterns of Catholic community life which were first established here enabled the Church in due time to hand on her faith and culture in the face of both the Arab invasions in the East and the waves of barbarians in the West.[23] The character of the earliest forms of monastic community and ascetical practice in Egypt may also have been more compatible with ordinary family living than is often presumed, so any view of a simple polarity between desert and city should be avoided.[24] The term *monachos*, "monk," probably first

---

[19] Is. 19:25.
[20] For detailed treatments see David Frankfurter, *Religion in Roman Egypt: Assimilation and Resistance* (Princeton, NJ: Princeton University Press, 1988); *Christianizing Egypt: Syncretism and Local Worlds in Late Antiquity* (Princeton: Princeton University Press, 2018).
[21] Henri Marrou, *A History of Education in Antiquity* (London: Sheed and Ward, 1956) [original French text published in 1948, as *Histoire de l'Education dans l'Antiquité* (Paris: Editions du Seuil), 318].
[22] As Columba Stewart notes, "Alexandria had famous monasteries in its exurbs (the Pempton and Enaton, located five and nine miles west of the city) and offered easy access by canal to Nitria for those interested in a day's outing to see the monks" ("Rethinking the History of Monasticism East and West: a Modest *tour d'horizon*," in eds. S. Bhattacharji, R. Williams and D. Mattos, *Prayer and Thought in Monastic Tradition: Essays in Honour of Benedicta Ward, SLG* [London: Bloomsbury, 2014], 8).
[23] For an overview, see De Lacy O'Leary, "The Egyptian Contribution to Christianity," in ed. S. R. K. Glanville, *The Legacy of Egypt* (Oxford: The Clarendon Press, 1942), 317-26.
[24] For a discussion of this more domestic character in early Syrian monasticism, possibly influenced by Jewish ascetical groups, also see Sidney H. Griffith,

signified solitaries who lived as members of small households, a form of solitary life in the midst of family life, with community forms of monasticism growing from this, so that the earliest monastic communities, like early Christian churches, were located in the private homes of individual ascetics.[25] Both the eremitical and cenobitic forms of monasticism under their respective founders, Anthony and Pachomius, are later developments, growing out of this.

It is significant for our understanding of the work of evangelization undertaken by the school that this desert monastic movement never developed in independence from the mission to Alexandria itself, and that the two worlds, of the desert and the city, did not become antagonistic. This was a major achievement given the wider tensions between the city and the *chora* that we have noted, as well as the different domestic and monastic modes of Christian community life. In fact, the opposite was achieved: "We know of a significant list of the intellectual and social elite of the empire for whom the Egyptian metropolis was the portal to the wilderness and the life of contemplative perfection."[26] In this regard, Layton highlights the importance of the alliance between the bishop, Athanasius, and Didymus the Blind, then leader of the school, who worked together to help prevent the development of a radical asceticism that would stand in opposition to appropriate practices of asceticism expected in ordinary Christian life.[27] We can also note the symbolically important event of Anthony's visit to Didymus, the founder of the eremitical life thereby providing his seal of approval on Didymus as a model of the catechetical, ascetic scholar.[28]

"Asceticism in the Church of Syria: The Hermeneutics of Early Syrian Monasticism," in eds. V. L. Wimbush and R. Valantasis, *Asceticism* (New York: Oxford University Press, 1995), 220-45.

[25] See E. A. Judge, "The Earliest Form of Monarchos for 'Monk' and the Origins of Monasticism," in *Jahrbuch für Antike und Christentum* 20 (1977), 72-89; James E. Goehring, *Ascetics, Society, and the Desert: Studies in Early Egyptian Monasticism* (Harrisburg, PA: Trinity Press International, 1999), 13-35, 53-72; Darlene L. Brooks Hedstrom, "Archeology in Early Christian Egypt," in eds. D. K. Pettegrew, W. R. Caraher and T. W. Davis, *The Oxford Handbook of Early Christian Archeology* (Oxford: Oxford University Press, 2019), 674-77; Birger Pearson, "Earliest Christianity in Egypt: Further Observations," 107-10.

[26] Richard Layton, *Didymus the Blind and His Circle in Late-Antique Alexandria: Virtue and Narrative in Biblical Scholarship* (Urbana, IL: University of Illinois Press, 2004), 19.

[27] "The model of Christian behaviour that [Athanasius] encouraged his congregations to follow has been aptly described as an 'asceticism of everyday life'" (David M. Gwynn, *Athanasius of Alexandria: Bishop, Theologian, Ascetic, Father* [Oxford: Oxford University Press, 2012], 146).

[28] See Layton, *Didymus the Blind and His Circle in Late-Antique Alexandria*, 18-26. The visit of Anthony also helps us to resist any simple opposition between the school's learning on the one hand and a view of uncultured, unlettered monks.

In this connection we should note the presence in Eusebius's *Ecclesiastical History*[29] of a community connected with Alexandria to which Philo had drawn attention in his own writings,[30] the Community of the Therapeutae. The community of the Therapeutae described by Philo was recorded in Eusebius as evidence of an early Christian desert community close to Alexandria, although Eusebius recognizes that this may not be the case since Philo's account does not explicitly mention any Christian beliefs in connection with the Therapeutae.[31] A question worth asking, however, is what purposes this account of the Therapeutae might be performing in Eusebius, and here Sabriana Inowlocki offers a persuasive analysis, through a close comparison with Philo's original text, that Eusebius may be providing an early signal for the catechetical school and its ascetical holiness.[32] Her argument supports that of Robert Grant, who had proposed that we think of Eusebius's understanding of this community as an implicit "portrait," showing that "ideally the Church of Alexandria was a school and, of course, the school was a church." The description of the life of the community shows that it united allegorical exegesis, ascetical practices and an adherence to Church order, the diaconate and episcopate. The descriptions run parallel to how Eusebius describes Origen, thus showing a coherence between Origen's life and practices and this model ecclesial community.[33] If correct, this point further consolidates the view we have been offering here, of a symbiotic relationship between the spiritualty and formation offered by the school and that developed in Egyptian monasticism.

In summary, then, from the evidence of Christian life and writings in Alexandria and Egypt during the period under consideration we can reach certain initial indications regarding the nature and orientation of the school: that it emerged in the midst of a Christian culture that had a controverted identity, with strong Jewish Christian and Gnostic currents and teachings present, and needed to learn how to

---

[29] H. E. II.16-17.
[30] For Philo, the monastic communities of both the Essenes and the Therapeutae were seen as exemplifying the best in the Jewish religious tradition (see his *Vita Contemplativa* and his *Quod omnis probus liber*, 75ff).
[31] The identity of the group remains uncertain, and much discussed. It may have been a Jewish group, but again perhaps even Buddhist since the Buddhist Emperor Asoka had sent missionaries to Egypt. See the discussion in Antoine Guillaumont, *Aux origines du monachisme chrétien: Pour une phénoménologie du monachisme* (Bégrolles-en-Mauges: Abbaye de Bellefontaine, 1979).
[32] "Eusebius of Caesarea's 'Interpretatio Christiana' of Philo's *De via contemplativa*," *Harvard Theological Review* 97, 3 (July 2004) 305-28.
[33] See *Eusebius as Church Historian* (Oxford: Clarendon Press, 1980), 72-76.

shape formation and to articulate the apostolic tradition in relation to these; that it took a deep interest, and almost certainly played a leading role, in strong missionary outreach, not only to the varied populations of Alexandria, but also to the neighboring *chora*; and that in due course it developed ascetical and formational practices that overlap with those of the extensive monastic movement.

THE VALUE OF CHRISTIAN HISTORIES

From the evidence of Christian writings and life in Alexandria and Egypt, we turn to what is clearly the *most significant external source* for our knowledge of the Church in Alexandria and its catechetical school: Eusebius's *Ecclesiastical History*. Exaggerating a little, van den Broek writes, "For our knowledge of the Christian school at Alexandria, as for so many other aspects of early Christian history, we are almost completely dependent on Eusebius's *Ecclesiastical History*."[34] Often called the "father" of ecclesiastical history,[35] Eusebius was a near contemporary of Origen, the most important of the leaders of the school. Eusebius was born approximately AD 260, just a few years after the death of Origen. Because of Eusebius's undoubted importance for our knowledge of the school we are fortunate that, through his own teacher, Pamphilus, he had connections with two of the heads of the school, Origen and Pierius[36] and he notes that Dionysius, Bishop of Alexandria, was alive during his time and that Dionysius was himself previously a leader of the catechetical school and a pupil of Origen.[37] He has excellent reason, then, for his assertion that the Alexandrian school "has lasted on to our time, and we have heard that it is managed by men powerful in their learning and zeal for

---

[34] Roelof van den Broek, "The Christian 'School' of Alexandria in the Second and Third Centuries," in eds. J. W. Drijvers and A. A. MacDonald, *Centers of Learning: Learning and Location in Pre-Modern Europe and the Near East* (Leiden: Brill, 1995), 39. The importance of Eusebius is clear. Nonetheless, van den Broek's judgement here must be received with the obvious comment that we also have the literary sources of leaders of the school themselves, especially Clement, Origen, and Didymus, as well as the liturgical, archeological and other sources concerning Egyptian Christianity and the Church in Alexandria.

[35] Eusebius's *Ecclesiastical History* is the only Christian history of the earliest period. Other Christian historians, such as Socrates and Sozomen, continue the account of the Church from the period of Nicaea onwards. Socrates of Constantinople wrote an *Ecclesiastical History* for the period AD 305–439. Sozomen wrote two volumes of history, the first, which has unfortunately been lost, covering the same period as Eusebius, the second taking up the narrative from AD 323 and running up to 425.

[36] Cf. Annewies van den Hoek, "How Alexandrian was Clement of Alexandria? Reflections on Clement and his Alexandrian Background," *Heythrop Journal* 31 (1990), 179.

[37] H. E. VI.19.3

divine things."[38] Even though he did not have direct contact with the school at the time of his writing, Eusebius is nonetheless relatively close to the events he is recounting and is a source of knowledge of the Church in Alexandria and its school upon which we should be inclined to depend.[39]

His *Ecclesiastical History* is a mature work, written in AD 314/315, shortly after Galerius's Edict of Toleration in AD 311 and Constantine's Edict of Milan in AD 313, and edited around ten years later.[40] Eusebius is writing his history, therefore, at a watershed moment in the life of the Church and sets out to capture an account of her origins, struggles and divinely-guided growth during the first three hundred years. His work culminates in a heartfelt offering of praise to God who secured the peace of the Church through Constantine:

> Thanks be to God, the Almighty and King of the universe, for all things; and abundant thanks be also to the Saviour and Redeemer of our souls, Jesus Christ, through whom we pray continually that peace from troubles without and troubles in the heart may be preserved for us steadfast and undisturbed.[41]

In his dramatic retelling of this tumultuous period of Church history, the Alexandrian Christians play a heroic and not inconsequential role; and at the heart of that lived endeavor of faith Eusebius points us to the catechetical school as a key source of witness, formation and intellectual accomplishment.

There are some characteristics of Eusebius's work that we should note so as to understand how to treat his account of the school. In the first place, we should recognize the remarkable attention and importance Eusebius gave to the compilation of documentary evidence for his *History*. Robert Markus makes the point that, in comparison to

---

[38] H. E. V.10.1.
[39] Together with Eusebius we should note the work of Rufinus of Aquileia, who translated Eusebius into Latin and added further books to his history. Rufinus was himself closely associated with the school, spending eight years studying under Didymus the Blind, to whom he devotes a chapter in his *Ecclesiastical History* which he wrote only shortly after Didymus's death.
[40] It is likely that there was a first edition, completed around the end of the third century and possibly lodged in Alexandria's historical archives before the beginning of the Arian controversy. At this point Eusebius and the Alexandrians' views were in concert, only diverging after Athanasius become the committed opponent of Arius. On this edition see Timothy D. Barnes, "The Edition of Eusebius' Ecclesiastical History," *Greek, Roman and Byzantine Studies* 21 (1980), 191-201; and Tito Orlandi, "The Coptic Ecclesiastical History: A Survey," in eds. J. E. Goehring and J. A. Timbie, *The World of Early Egyptian Christianity: Language Literature and Social Context* (Washington, D. C.: Catholic University of America Press, 2007), 3-24.
[41] H. E. V.10.1.

classical historiography, histories of the Church tended to emphasize this careful attention to establishing our understanding of the past through written evidence,[42] and that this became the case is due entirely to Eusebius and to the immense influence his *Ecclesiastical History* had on subsequent writings. In general, the Church historians Socrates, Sozomen and Evagrius follow his lead in this respect. By comparison with classical histories, Eusebius avoids invented speeches and tries to supplement oral tradition with documentary sources, often presenting them at length in his narrative.[43] To his contemporaries, Markus comments, his work would have ranked "more like an archivist's collection of material than a historical narrative."[44] Eusebius, then, writes his *Ecclesiastical History* with an attention to the accuracy of what he compiled, consciously working from evidence and from sources. For this reason, also, *there is a certain confidence we can vest in his account of the catechetical school.*[45]

This does not mean that Eusebius considered himself in any sense a "neutral" recorder of events. He wants to tell the story well and faithfully, but he also has a clear purpose in his selection of material: to highlight the truth and glory of Christ in his Church. Because the figure of Origen is so pivotal for our appreciation of the school, it is also worth noting that he wants his readers *to share his own*

---

[42] Robert A. Markus, "Church History and Early Church Historians," in ed. Derek Baker, *The Materials, Sources and Methods of Ecclesiastical History* (New York: Barnes and Noble Books, 1975), 1-17.

[43] For a discussion of Eusebius's oral and written sources and their relationship see Grant, *Eusebius as Church Historian*, 61-72.

[44] Markus, "Church History and Early Church Historians," 3. This does not mean that classical historians were indifferent to the question of truth, of course. Thus we have Polybius writing at the beginning of his own voluminous work: "For as a living creature is rendered wholly useless if deprived of its eyes, so if you take truth from history, what is left but an idle, unprofitable tale?" (*Histories* I.14). And Polybius divides historians into three types: those who write for pay, to please political masters, those who compose for rhetorical effect, and those who write to communicate truth (*Histories* XVI.14).

[45] Grant offers a further interesting point concerning Eusebius's relationship to the Alexandrian catechetical school: he comments that while Eusebius's immediate debt for his writing of the *History* is Origen's library and school in *Caesarea*, Eusebius tells us almost nothing about that school but focuses instead on the Alexandrian school. The point might be explained in part by the fact that Eusebius drew extensively on two ecclesiastical libraries for his sources: the library at Caesarea created by Eusebius's teacher Pamphilus and, it seems with a catalog Eusebius himself put in place (see *H. E.* VI.32.3; 36.2), and the library at Jerusalem, founded by Alexander, a pupil of Pantaenus, Clement and Origen (see *H. E.* VI.14.9). These two libraries, then, were either Alexandrian in origin (the Caesarean library) or founded by one who had studied in Alexandria (the Jerusalem library). See *Eusebius as Church Historian*, 41-43, 66, 72-73, 83.

intense admiration for Origen. For Eusebius, Origen "constitutes the ideal Christian."[46] (He devotes most of the sixth book of his history to a presentation of Origen.) Eusebius's mentor was Pamphilus who himself greatly esteemed Origen and who consolidated the academy and library established by Origen in Caesarea. Living in Caesarea where Origen had so recently spent the final twenty years of his life after moving on from his leadership of the school in Alexandria, Eusebius was a personal beneficiary of this work, able to use for his own research the extensive library collected by Origen.

If there is reason to give a certain presumption of trust to Eusebius's presentation of the school and his account of Christian life in Alexandria, then, it is nonetheless important to *read his account of the school critically.* For example, some scholars have argued that the accounts he has provided of both the succession of bishops in Alexandria and of the succession of teachers in the school[47] are artificially constructed in order to provide an enhanced legitimacy to certain figures in the later history of Alexandria and the school. In fact, this argument runs, before Origen began his more theological academy with the episcopal support of Demetrius there really was no "institution" to which we could rightly attach the label of "catechetical school." Eusebius's account is actually a reading back into the second century of *Origen's academy.* Before that time there were, certainly, private teachers of the faith, but these were individual figures who had no or few significant ecclesial connections.[48]

Again, it is also the case that Eusebius's fathering of a new style of writing, of strictly *ecclesiastical* history, involved a deliberate focus — as he himself tells us — upon a narrow range of themes. As Markus explains, Eusebius and his successors were not writing *Christian history* (i.e., history seen from a Christian perspective) as opposed to pagan history (i.e., history written from a pagan point of view) but rather writing *ecclesiastical history,* a history of the Christian Church (as opposed to matters that we would tend to classify as secular history). This difference between "Christian" and "ecclesiastical" entails a certain narrowness of the latter in terms of the selection of material and

---

[46] Verdoner, *Narrated Reality,* 113. This special focus on the person of Origen is one of the ways in which Eusebius's history shares in the Roman historiography from around the second century AD onwards to concern itself with character studies, depictions of holy men, philosophers, emperors and so on.

[47] On his interest in both episcopal and school lines of "succession" see Grant, *Eusebius as Church Historian,* 46-47, 51-52.

[48] Cf. Roelof van den Broek, "The Christian 'School' of Alexandria in the Second and Third Centuries," 41-43.

concentration upon particular themes. Eusebius makes this focus clear in the preface to his *History*, where he provides his "manifesto" for the entire work,[49] explaining that he will be following certain themes throughout his work: the bishops of the most illustrious sees;[50] the heralds of the Word of God; heretics; the fate of the Jews; and pagan attacks on the Word of God, and the sufferings of those who were faithful witnesses to the Word. We might sum up his approach to the selection of material by saying that the substance of his history is the Church herself in some of her aspects and in her relationship to the surrounding culture—which is largely understood as an antagonistic one.

It is helpful to pause to consider both the advantages and the limitations of Eusebius's scope and foci from the perspective of our desire to gain an appreciation of the contribution of the Alexandrian school for our own times. One of the points Markus notes about these foci of Eusebius, which presume a duality between the Church and the secular environment, is that it became less easily applicable after the Theodosian Edict in AD 380 at which point there was a dissolving of sharp boundaries between the Church and the secular world.[51] In this new situation, attempts to follow Eusebius's model of writing history tended to encourage an intensity of focus on internal Church affairs and on clerical aspects of Church life. In our own age, however, where a separation of Church and state is clear in most countries—and where there is often antagonism between the Church and secular society—it can be argued that Eusebius's assumption of such a duality is once again serviceable, and even helpful.

Even so, what is missing from Eusebius's account is any sustained vision or understanding of *the Church as the crown of culture* and as the begetter of a new culture and new humanity, the old transformed through its relocation within a framework of Christian dogmatic truth and transfiguring life. And that broader vision of the relationship of faith to culture is crucial to the approach of the Alexandrian school. Eusebius certainly saw himself writing the history of a "new people," but this was largely conceived along the lines of a nation, a particular group within society, picking up the history of the Jewish people as a group set apart from other peoples.[52] But the *Catholic* nature of the

---

[49] See the discussion in Verdoner, *Narrated Reality*, 77–80.
[50] Eusebius is especially interested in the Sees of Alexandria, Antioch, Jerusalem, Caesarea and Rome (see the discussion in Grant, *Eusebius as Church Historian*, 45–59).
[51] On this point see also the comments of F. Edward Cranz, "Kingdom and Polity in Eusebius of Caesarea," *Harvard Theological Review* 45 (1952), 47–66.
[52] See, for example, H. E. I.4.2; X.4.19. "The Christians were a nation in his view. Thus he was writing national history" (Arnaldo Momigliano, "Pagan and

Church, her assumption of the cultural heritage of the nations, was not articulated or presented in any thematic way by him.[53] For that articulation of catholicity, which is crucial to our understanding of the achievement and continuing relevance of the school, we need to draw especially on the writings of the leading Alexandrians themselves since it was they who, together with figures such as Julius Africanus and Hippolytus of Rome, laid out a Christian philosophy of history, a sweeping and comprehensive presentation of the divine plan that exhibited God's providential rule over times and peoples coming to a climax in Christ's appearing.[54] Alexandrian catechesis taught that all history, all cultures and all time belonged to God. The biblical story, which told the sacred history of God's people, and the secular histories of the world, the Alexandrians taught, belonged to one single overarching story, and the chapters telling of each people led to Christ in whom all fragmentation is overcome. The school saw its role as that of explaining the biblical story so as to reveal this larger account that would be recognized by all the peoples whose traditions would be purified by the Church and united in Christ.

Robert Markus's discussion of Augustine's understanding of the difference between "sacred" and "secular" history is helpful here for appreciating this Alexandrian approach. It is not that one sphere is the action of God and the other not, but rather that "history" is in each case to be seen as the *record* of the past: "The difference between 'sacred' and 'secular' history is... to be defined by distinguishing two different kinds of narrative: the one prophetically inspired, the other not."[55] Sacred history offers us the interpretative key for the reading of all culture and history, local, national and transnational. It was the work of the Alexandrian school to address each of the histories in their own context, uniting in one Body the peoples with their recorded heritage, demonstrating how all was to be seen as a preparation for Christ, the divine Logos indwelling all things who was now made visible, through whom all histories can now be read.

Christian Historiography in the Fourth Century A.D." in ed. A. Momigliano, *The Conflict Between Paganism and Christianity in the Fourth Century* [Oxford: The Clarendon Press, 1963], 90).

[53] While it might be argued that a universal perspective is present in Eusebius in the notion of Christ as the Logos, this is not developed thematically in his history so as to allow his readers to focus with any clarity on the cultural impact of the Church.

[54] See Arnaldo Momigliano, "Pagan and Christian Historiography in the Fourth Century A.D.," 82-84.

[55] Robert A. Markus, *Saeculum: History and Society in the Theology of St Augustine* (Cambridge: Cambridge University Press, 1970), 14-15, and see 231-32.

To stay with this point a little longer, we might contrast Eusebius's approach to the writing of ecclesiastical history with that of Philip of Side who wrote and taught at the turn of the fourth century and who studied under Rhodon, the figure he identifies as the last leader of the Alexandrian catechetical school,[56] and who went on to become head of a branch catechetical school in Side in around AD 405. Philip wrote a Christian history, only fragments of which remain today. It was clearly a massive work with historical, geographical and scientific information alongside its prominent religious themes (the Church historian Socrates records that it consisted of thirty-six books, each book being in several volumes).[57] From Socrates's description of it as *Christian* history, in distinction to his own ecclesiastical history, the closest model would seem to be the ancient "chronicle," with Philip writing a narrative of world history from a Christian perspective.[58] From Socrates's comments we can gather that it was an unwieldly, sprawling work, perhaps indigestible in its scope and organization, though recognized as a work of great erudition. We might surmise that, with his close connection to the catechetical school, Philip's conception of *Christian history* in terms of its scope and breadth *better represents the interests of the Alexandrian tradition*. A comparison of these two histories reinforces for us the importance of staying as close as possible to the writings of the leaders of the Alexandrian school, to writings upon which they drew and also the works of those immediately impacted by them, in order to supplement and, where necessary, amend the picture of the school presented by Eusebius.

HISTORY AND RECEPTION OF MARK'S ASSOCIATION WITH ALEXANDRIA

The question of St Mark's possible association with Alexandria is an inescapable element in our telling of the story of the school and the nature of the early Christian catechumenate. The pursuit of links between the school and the apostolic mission, and also between the school and what is generally now taken to be the earliest of the Gospels accepted into the scriptural canon offers suggestive veins for us to mine. While we might be disappointed, then, in realizing

---

[56] Eusebius refers to him in *H. E.* V.13, noting that he wrote several books, including works against Marcion and Apelles.
[57] Socrates, *Ecclesiastical History* VII. 27.
[58] For a discussion of the character of Philip's work see E. Honigmann, "Philippus of Side and his 'Christian History' (written about 434–39)," in *Patristic Studies* in *Studi e testi*, 173 (1953), 82–91. Christians writing with a more universal perspective in mind would have been able to look to a figure such as Diodorus Siculus who wrote his massive universal history in forty volumes, fifteen of which survive, and which is much quoted in patristic literature.

the ambiguity and the incompleteness of the historical evidence we currently have concerning the relationship of Mark to Alexandria, the tentative conclusions we can reach in this regard should not lead to any hesitation about the value of reflecting upon this evidence since it can reveal much of interest for our understanding of the Alexandrian pastoral and catechetical tradition. The provocative but finally inconclusive nature of the evidence is summed up by Birger Pearson: "The tradition of the association of St Mark with earliest Christianity in Egypt is traceable to the second century and may originate even earlier. The historicity of this tradition, though unproveable, should not be ruled out."[59] Alongside an evaluation of the historical evidence of Mark's association with Alexandria, therefore, we also need to understand the significance of the *reception* of this association within the Church's tradition—both of the Gospel and of the figure of Mark—and what this, also, might reveal to us about the ancient catechumenate and the Church's work of evangelization in these early centuries. We recall that John Paul II, in *Catechesi tradendae*, wrote

> Before being written down, the Gospels were the expression of an oral teaching passed on to the Christian communities, and they display with varying degrees of clarity a catechetical structure. St. Matthew's account has indeed been called the catechist's Gospel, and St. Mark's the catechumen's Gospel.[60]

John Paul's brief statement here concerning the reception of Mark's Gospel in the Church clearly ties its ecclesial reception in part to its perceived catechetical character, paired to the Gospel of Matthew. He also indicates here the importance of an appreciation for the vital place of the oral tradition which preceded the written texts. Viewing the Gospels through this catechetical lens, then, he proposes that the Church's tradition has judged the structure of the Gospel of Mark to be particularly valuable for serving catechumens, those being discipled in preparation for baptism into the Church. John Paul, in the paragraph following the one we have quoted above, then refers his readers to the early catechetical tradition of the Church, specifically identifying works that originate from Alexandria.

---

[59] "Earliest Christianity in Egypt: Some Observations," in eds. B. A. Pearson and J. E. Goehring, *The Roots of Egyptian Christianity*, 144, and for a discussion of what he calls "the Mark Legend," concluding on this note of uncertainty, see 137-45. For an assessment of the evidence in favor of the essential historicity of the "Mark legend" see Leslie W. Barnard, "St. Mark and Alexandria," *Harvard Theological Review* 57, 2 (April 1964), 145-50.

[60] *CT* 11.

The purpose of this section of the chapter, then, is to review the evidence concerning the association of Mark and his Gospel with Alexandria, and its reception, so as to establish the basis on which we might find it reasonable to seek a reciprocal illumination between the Gospel's proposed catechumenal character and works flowing from the Alexandrian catechetical tradition. The question of the Gospel's *catechumenal character* itself and its possible links to the Alexandrian school tradition we will defer until the end of part two, once we have had the opportunity to examine the character of the school and its work in some detail.

We can begin with some striking points about the reception of the person of Mark and his Gospel within the Tradition. The first is to note how the Gospel has risen to an unusual place of prominence since the late eighteenth century's dominating interest in the recovery of the historical origins of the Gospel texts. As Lightfoot notes, "Among students of the New Testament, the Gospel according to St Mark has aroused more interest in the last century than at any other time, so far as we can judge, since it was first put forth."[61] From the patristic period onwards there has been almost no interest shown in Mark's Gospel—or, we might say, any such interest seems to have been eclipsed by the other canonical Gospels, and especially by that of Matthew. Augustine's judgment that Mark was essentially a summary of Matthew[62] both confirmed this initial neglect in the Church and contributed to this continuing lack of interest. Even the inclusion of Mark in the canon functioned as "merely a label and did not contribute to its being read or written on."[63] The Gospel remained a "stepchild" in the canon.[64]

We can place this point alongside a second: that we can find considerable interest in the early centuries in the *person* of Mark himself as founder of the Church in Alexandria. Black neatly sums up the evidence from the patristic age: the fathers "seem to discuss Mark more yet use his Gospel less."[65] It is a point noted also by John A. T. Robinson who compares the lack of interest in the Gospel itself with the significant interest in its author, and especially the

---

[61] Robert H. Lightfoot, *The Gospel Message of St. Mark* (Oxford: Oxford University Press, 1950), 1.
[62] See *De consensu evangelistarum* 1.2.3-4; 3.6; 4.10.11.
[63] Brenda Dean Schildgen, *Power and Prejudice: The Reception of the Gospel of Mark* (Detroit: Wayne State University Press, 1999), 20.
[64] Schildgen, *Power and Prejudice*, 41.
[65] C. Clifton Black, *Mark: Images of an Apostolic Interpreter* (Minneapolis: Fortress Press, 2001), 12.

author's relationship to the tradition that led to its composition: "It is a curious phenomenon that for the Gospel that was least read or esteemed in the early church there is more tradition relating to its date of composition than any other."[66]

The reevaluation of the importance of Mark's Gospel in the light of nineteenth- and twentieth-century enquiries into the relationship between the Gospels, and the generally accepted repositioning of Mark as one of Matthew's sources, has clearly been an occasion for intense reviews of the content of the Gospel; at the same time, it is worth not losing sight of this more ancient interest in the figure of Mark himself, an interest that was preserved and transmitted not only through the familiar figures of Papias, Clement, Eusebius, and Jerome, but also in liturgical and spiritual traditions centered on Alexandria. Thomas Oden, focusing on the reception of Mark in and through these wider traditions, has summed them up as "the African memory of Mark."[67] In this wider memory we can place the naming of the Alexandrian liturgy after the evangelist, a liturgy that is a "tap root," as Gregory Dix says,[68] of all liturgical history and rites, and the liturgy that would have been celebrated in the Alexandrian school, and by Athanasius, Anthony, and Cyril. It is interesting to note that there are no apparent dependencies on the text of the Gospel of Mark in this liturgy and that the naming of the liturgy relies therefore wholly upon the tradition of Mark's own association with the city.

This wider liturgical and spiritual tradition has also given us the story of Mark's martyrdom in Alexandria. The fourth-century *Roman Martyrology* records for 25 April, "At Alexandria the anniversary of Blessed Mark the Evangelist," uniting the memory of his death to that of his successor: "... at Alexandria of St. Anianus, Bishop, the disciple of Blessed Mark and his successor in the episcopate, who fell asleep in the Lord."[69] Mark's martyrdom is also recorded in the Coptic Synaxarion, one of the Oriental martyrologies, in other African

---

[66] *Redating the New Testament* (Philadelphia: Westminster Press, 1976), 107.
[67] Thomas C. Oden, *The African Memory of Mark: Reassessing Early Church Tradition*.
[68] Dom Gregory Dix, *The Shape of the Liturgy* (London: A. & C. Black, 1945), 613. The fortunes of the Alexandrian liturgy followed the wider fortunes of Alexandria itself, and in due course the increasing political and religious prominence of Constantinople and of the Byzantine rite in the East led to its near extinction. The anaphora of St Mark is still celebrated by the Coptic Church. For the text of the Liturgy of St Mark, see ed. Geoffrey J. Cumming, Rome: Pontificum Institutum Studiorem Orientalium, 1990. For summary comments on its provenance and character see also Josef Jungmann, *The Early Liturgy: to the time of Gregory the Great* (London: Darton, Longman and Todd, 1960), 224-25.
[69] *Roman Martyrology* (Baltimore: John Murphy and Co. 1898), 117-18.

Synaxaries,[70] and in *Martyrium Marci*, which gives us an early Egyptian account of his death in Alexandria.[71] The authenticity of this tradition of his martyrdom finds some confirmation in archeological evidence: the locations of the sites of the main Churches in ancient Alexandria, noted by Athanasius and Epiphanius, "correspond closely with literary recollections found in the accounts of Mark's martyrdom."[72] Indeed it appears likely that the main Christian churches in Alexandria were named after events in Mark's life and accounts of his martyrdom.[73] A broad tradition, then, remembers Mark as the founder of the Church in Alexandria and as its first martyr. It is a tradition that would certainly cohere with what we have seen to be a scholarly consensus that the early decades of Christianity in Egypt were of Jewish origin.[74]

From this broad liturgical and spiritual tradition about Mark let us turn to our major written sources, beginning with Jerome.[75] A key source for the identification of Mark as the founder of the Church in Alexandria, he writes in *De viris illustribus*:

---

[70] For an overview of the Coptic Synaxarion and other African Synaxaries, with details of modern editions, see Oden, *The African Memory of Mark*, 61-64.

[71] *Martyrium Marci* can be dated anywhere between the second and fourth century. The topography of Alexandria in this work, especially of the Jewish quarter where it is most likely that early Christians settled, is consistent with what is known from other sources. For a discussion of its provenance and value see Pearson, "Earliest Christianity in Egypt: Some Observations," 140-45. It forms part of the *Patrologia Graeca* (PG 115, cols 167-70); an English translation of the text can be found in E. A. Wallis Budge, *The Contendings of the Apostles* II (London: Henry Frowde, 1901), 309-18.

[72] Oden, *The African Memory of Mark*, 161, and see 162-65; also see Birger A. Pearson, "Ancient Alexandria in the 'Acts of Mark,'" in *Gnosticism and Christianity in Roman and Coptic Egypt* (London: T&T Clark International 2004), 100-13.

[73] The main difficulty regarding the historicity of his martyrdom is the silence about it in some of the key sources in which one would expect it to be mentioned, especially Eusebius, Clement and Origen. But of course one always has to be cautious about arguments from silence: surprisingly, for example, we have no surviving record of Origen mentioning Clement, his immediate predecessor, on whose work he built. For a balanced discussion of the historical value of this tradition see Stephen J. Davies, *The Early Coptic Papacy: The Egyptian Church and its Leadership in Late Antiquity: The Popes of Egypt Volume 1* (New York, The American University in Cairo Press, 2004), 1-14. According to tradition, then, St Mark's relics were placed in the Church of St Mark in Alexandria. They were eventually stolen and taken to Venice in AD 828 — and partially restored by Paul VI in 1968 to the Cathedral of St Mark in Cairo.

[74] For an outline account see F. J. Klijn, "Jewish Christianity in Egypt," in eds. B. A. Pearson and J. E. Goehring, *The Roots of Egyptian Christianity*, 161-75.

[75] The weight of Jerome's attestation to Mark's founding of the Church in Alexandria was especially significant. Other ancient authorities supporting Mark's pivotal role in the Alexandrian Church include Epiphanius, the bishop of Salamis (c. 310-403) (*Adversus Hæresus* li, 6) and the fourth century *Apostolic Constitutions* (VII, xlvi).

So, taking the gospel which he himself composed, he went to Egypt and first preaching Christ at Alexandria he formed a church so admirable in doctrine and continence of living that he constrained all followers of Christ to his example. Philo, most learned of the Jews, seeing the first church at Alexandria still Jewish in a degree, wrote a book on their manner of life as something creditable to his nation telling how, as Luke says, the believers had all things in common at Jerusalem, so he recorded all that he saw was done at Alexandria, under the learned Mark. He died in the eighth year of Nero and was buried at Alexandria, Anianus succeeding him.[76]

There is much of interest contained in this account: that Mark founded the Church in Alexandria after having written his Gospel and that he died in the eighth year of Nero's reign, which would fix his death at AD 62; that his successor was Anianus;[77] and finally, Jerome calls the Jewish Alexandrian Philo as a witness to this account and to the holiness of the Church under Mark. The reference to the community of believers, attested by Philo is, as we have seen, a matter of much debate, and remains unresolved. Thus, while Jerome remains an important witness to the placing of Mark in Alexandria, strongly associating him with the origin and early years of the Church there, there is also reason to see that his account may need to be adjusted.

As a second source, we can turn to Eusebius who treats of Mark in Books II and VI of his *Ecclesiastical History*.[78] Eusebius begins by giving us an account of the writing of the Gospel of Mark, placing Mark in Rome with St Peter: the latter had been preaching and his hearers were not satisfied with an unwritten account of his proclamation. They asked Peter to leave them a written account. Peter calls Mark to assist him in this; this is the origin, Eusebius says, of what we now call the Gospel according to Mark. Eusebius also adds that Peter subsequently confirmed Mark's Gospel account and "ratified the scripture for study in the churches."[79] In other words, the Gospel has the authority of Peter behind it. At this point, Eusebius calls two earlier witnesses to support and verify this account:

---

[76] Jerome, *De viris illustribus*, 8.3–5. See also his reference to Mark as the evangelizer of Alexandria in *Epistle* 146.1.6. Jerome is the only major patristic figure to have written extensively on Mark's Gospel, composing ten sermons on it.

[77] See also Eusebius: "In the eighth year of the reign of Nero Annianus was the first after Mark the Evangelist to receive charge of the diocese of Alexandria" (H. E. II.24).

[78] H. E. II.15–17; VI.14.5–7.

[79] H. E. II.15.

> They say that this Mark was the first to be sent to preach in Egypt the Gospel which he had also put into writing and was the first to establish churches in Alexandria itself.[80]

The "they say" at the opening of this statement refers to Clement and Papias. Eusebius claims that he received from them both the information about Mark's writing of the Gospel and also of his being sent by Peter to Egypt and his founding of the Church in Alexandria. Identifying his sources, he mentions Clement of Alexandria's *Hypoteposes*, or *Outlines*, a work that is now unfortunately lost. Clement, who would have been writing around AD 200, provides us with this account of the origin of the Gospel, Eusebius tells us, in the sixth book of that work. Eusebius then adds: "and the bishop of Hierapolis, named Papias, confirms him."[81] Papias lived a generation earlier than Clement, around AD 60-130, and had personal conversations with "John the Elder" (here he might be referring to either the apostle John or else a younger contemporary of the initial eyewitnesses). Eusebius takes time to underline the credibility of Papias's supporting judgment, explaining Papias's careful searching after the testimony of those closest to the original apostles:

> Papias himself, according to the preface of his treatises, makes plain that he had in no way been a hearer and eye-witness of the sacred Apostles, but teaches that he had received the articles of the faith from those who had known them, for he speaks as follows . . . if ever anyone came who had followed the presbyters, I inquired into the words of the presbyters, what Andrew or Peter or Philip or Thomas or James or John or Matthew, or any other of the Lord's disciples, had said, and what Aristion and the presbyter John, the Lord's disciples, were saying.[82]

About the writing of Mark's Gospel, Papias confirms that he received from the most authoritative source that Mark was indeed the interpreter of Peter, writing what he had received directly from him:

> Mark became Peter's interpreter and wrote accurately all that he remembered, not, indeed, in order, of the things said or done by the Lord. For he had not heard the Lord, nor had he followed him, but later on, as I said, followed Peter, who used to give teaching as necessity demanded but not making, as it were, an arrangement of the Lord's oracles, so that Mark did nothing wrong in thus writing

---

[80] H. E. II.16.1.
[81] H. E. VI.15.2.
[82] H. E. III.39.2,4.

down single points as he remembered them. For to one thing he gave attention, to leave out nothing of what he had heard and to make no false statements in them.[83]

This statement of Eusebius, quoting Papias's *Expositions of the Oracles of the Lord*, describing Mark as the amanuensis of Peter, was crucial in establishing the Gospel in the canon. It was a conviction about the origin of the Gospel affirmed and repeated over and over in the early tradition.[84] And here we alight on the most important element for an assessment of the historicity of Mark's association with Alexandria, and that is the attestation by ancient sources of his close relationship with Peter. On this point several pieces of evidence converge to support such a claim and these in turn make a strong case for us to affirm the plausibility of Mark's connection with Alexandria.

In the first place we can consider the plausibility of Eusebius's account, affirmed by Clement and Papias, of *the Roman origins of Mark's Gospel*. Martin Hengel offers a useful discussion of this tradition and draws attention to the support that can be given purely by linguistic considerations, and especially the extent and nature of Latinisms in the Gospel.[85] It is universally recognized, in addition, that a major recurring theme in the Gospel text is that of persecution and threat, an emphasis that would cohere with a background of a Roman Church facing Neronian persecution.[86] Leslie Barnard, meanwhile, draws our attention to the work of Colin Roberts, the papyrologist we have already noted, and his argument that the introduction of the codex into Egypt is almost certainly a Christian initiative and one very possibly to have been brought from Rome: Mark's bringing his Gospel from Rome would stand out as a candidate for this.[87]

Secondly, we have sources from both the early Roman Christian tradition and from Asia Minor pointing to a *close relationship between Peter and Mark*. Biblical scholars therefore generally accept some kind of link between the Gospel of Mark and a Petrine "tradition" even

---

[83] H. E. III.39.15
[84] Cf. the discussion and judgement in Schildgen, *Power and Prejudice*, 35.
[85] Martin Hengel, *Studies in the Gospel of Mark* (London: SCM Press, 1985), 47-53. See also Bas E. F. van Iersel, *Mark: A Reader-Response Commentary* (Sheffield: Sheffield Academic Press, 1998), 31-57.
[86] Black argues broadly for a probable Roman origin for the Gospel based on what we know of the character and emphases of the Gospel text on the one hand and of Rome and the first-century Christian community there on the other, in *Mark*, 325-28.
[87] Leslie W. Barnard, "St. Mark and Alexandria," *Harvard Theological Review* 57, 2 (April 1964), 145-50. See Colin H. Roberts, "The Greek Papyri," 251-52.

if not all commit to the precise account Eusebius provides for us regarding the origin of the Gospel. Referring to Clement, then, Eusebius tells us that Mark had followed Peter "for a long time,"[88] and he informs us that Clement in turn based his account of the origin of the Mark's Gospel on what he has received as a "tradition of the primitive elders."[89] For the relationship between Peter and Mark we can also note 1 Pet 5:13: Peter concludes his letter (AD 43/44) by sending his greetings and adds, "and so does my son Mark." The question of what Peter means here by "my son" is much discussed: it may signify a spiritual fatherhood, in the way that Paul speaks in his Letter to Philemon of Onesimus as his son who he "begot" in prison. It may also indicate a blood relationship as well. In the Coptic tradition, Mark and Peter are believed to have been related by marriage.[90] It is worth noting that the references to Mark in the Pauline "tradition," in Philemon, Colossians and 2 Timothy, also seem to confirm Mark's association with Roman Christianity.[91]

Thirdly, paralleling the connections between a Roman Peter and Alexandrian Mark are the evident *connections between the Christian communities in Rome and Alexandria*. We have already noted the link of Peter with Alexandria in the early second-century work, *Kerygma Petrou, The Teaching of Peter*, fragments of which have been preserved in Clement's *Stromateis*.[92] In patristic lectionaries, Mark's Gospel was prominent in the Easter rites of both Alexandria and Rome.[93] The connection is also confirmed by the precedence accorded to Alexandria in the early Church. An "ancient custom" according authority to that see was confirmed by the Council of Nicaea which explicitly compared its conferral to that given to Rome.[94] Henry Chadwick points out that the Church's vigorous defense of the precedence of Rome, Alexandria, and Antioch (in that order) was not based on a recognition of their secular prominence but because they were considered

---

[88] H. E. VI.14.6
[89] H. E. VI.14.5
[90] For a discussion of the Coptic tradition on this, see S. F. Girgis, *A Chronology of St. Mark* (Cairo: St. John the Beloved Publishing House, 2002), 27, and Oden, *The African Memory of Mark*, 183-98.
[91] See Black, *Mark*, 50-60.
[92] See *Stromateis* 1.29.182; 6.5.39-41, 43; 6.6.48; 6.15.128. Origen also knows of the work, though he treats it with some caution: see *De Principiis*, I, Prol. 8. See J. K. Elliott, *The Apocryphal New Testament: A Collection of Apocryphal Christian Literature in an English Translation* (Oxford: Clarendon Press, 1993), 20-24.
[93] See Schildgen, *Power and Prejudice*, 50-52.
[94] Nicaea, Canon 6. See ed. Norman P. Tanner, SJ, *Decrees of the Ecumenical Councils, Volume One: Nicaea I to Lateran V* (London: Sheed and Ward, 1990), 8-9.

Petrine sees.[95] The founding of the Church at Alexandria by Mark, Peter's unique "disciple and interpreter,"[96] the chosen carrier of his teaching, would fit this picture. If Peter himself had visited the city, the claim would surely have been made that Peter was the founder of the Alexandrian church. A Markan foundation, however, explains the Petrine link, since it would carry the weight of the Roman church: while Alexandria could not *directly* claim to be founded by the one Jesus had chosen to lead his Church, it could do so through Peter's disciple and interpreter, the recorder of Peter's memories of Christ.[97] The patristic tradition of Mark's founding of the Church in Alexandria and the presence of his Gospel at the roots of the Alexandrian scriptural and catechetical tradition are to be understood, then, as primarily an interest in establishing the apostolic—and especially Petrine—connections to the city. Black puts it this way, "in patristic reflection the Second Gospel's Roman origin appears to have been a function of the tradition of Mark's Petrine authority."[98] Eusebius's references to Mark are reminding us of the apostolic roots of the

---

[95] Henry Chadwick, *The Making of a Rift in the Church: From Apostolic Times until the Council of Florence* (Oxford: Oxford University Press, 2003), 21-23. It was a trio still being urged as unique by Pope Nicholas I (858-867). The displacement of Alexandria as the second see in importance after Rome was attempted only when Constantinople was made the capital of the Eastern Roman Empire, with Canon 28 at the Council of Chalcedon (following Canon 3 of Constantinople I) arguing for the precedence of Constantinople—the "new Rome"—over Alexandria. Even then, Rome did not accept this reduction in importance of Alexandria, ratifying the doctrinal decrees of Chalcedon on March 21 453 but explicitly *rejecting* Canon 28 saying that it contradicted the Nicene canons (the sixth canon at Nicaea had spoken to the authority of Alexandria: "Let the ancient customs hold good which are in Egypt and Libya and Pantapolis according to which the bishop of Alexandria has authority over all these places"). (See Tanner, SJ, *Decrees of the Ecumenical Councils, Volume One*, 22-23, 76, and for a discussion Henry Chadwick, "Faith and Order at the Council of Nicaea: A Note on the Background of the Sixth Canon," *Harvard Theological Review* 53, 3, 1960, 171-95.) As we contemplate this close relationship between Alexandria and Rome in general it is good to remind ourselves that during the first three centuries the Roman Church wrote and spoke in Greek, not Latin.
[96] So Irenaeus, describing their relationship, in *Adversus haereses* 3.1.1. And see Tertullian, *Adversus Marcionem:* "Marcus quod edidit Petri affirmetur, cuius interpres Marcus" (4.5).
[97] Barnard points out that in the early Church the figure of Mark, taken in isolation, as it were, would have been considered a relatively minor figure: "He could not rival the reputations of the great apostles associated with the Sees of Rome and Antioch, and the Alexandrians might well have let their humble beginnings go unrecorded" ("St. Mark and Alexandria," 146). The Petrine connection was the crucial point to establish.
[98] Black, *Mark,* 225. Black judges that in Eusebius, also, "the figure of Mark retains a derivative status" (158), comparing the secondary interest in Mark to that of Luke, another non-apostle. See his detailed discussion in 78-102.

faith, and of the witnesses in the tradition who attest to this. If we accept such a perspective it can make sense of why there could be, alongside this, a comparative neglect of the Gospel itself, even if, as I hope to show, its catechumenal character nonetheless illumines the early Alexandrian catechetical tradition.

If a reasonable case can be made for Mark's bringing his Gospel to Alexandria, the *exact date* nevertheless remains unclear and we have little agreement among our sources. In his *Chronicle*, Eusebius gives the date of Mark founding the Church in Alexandria as AD 43, the third year of the reign of the Emperor Claudius. But while this is possible, it would seem to conflict with the account in Acts, which locates Mark elsewhere during the decade AD 40-50. Nothing in Acts, however, would prevent us from placing an early involvement by Mark with the Church in Alexandria somewhere between AD 50 and 60.[99] As we have seen, Jerome places Mark's death in AD 62.[100] Irenaeus writes of Mark carrying forward Peter's teaching after the latter's "exodus," which is usually taken to mean his martyrdom.[101] Jerome himself seems to have assumed that Peter's martyrdom took place in AD 67, and it seems most likely, following Irenaeus, that Mark's bringing of the Gospel to Alexandria took place following this, even though an earlier date in the 60s is not impossible.[102]

The value of pursuing this question has, I hope, been clear: if we find it credible—as I do—to accept an association between Mark and his Gospel with Alexandria, and also believe John Paul's catechumenal characterization of the Gospel to be worthy of further investigation, this points not only to the importance of Mark's Gospel for studies of the ancient catechumenate but indicates that our enquiry into this dimension of the text should most fruitfully be carried out in tandem with a study of Alexandrian catechesis. Conversely, of course, if we find the historical evidence for the association of Mark with Alexandria unconvincing, while we may still seek to discern the helpfulness of a catechumenal reading of Mark, we will be less inclined to think the Alexandrian connection important.

---

[99] This dating is affirmed by the Coptic encyclopedia: http://coptic.net/EncyclopediaCoptica/.
[100] For a discussion of Jerome's evidence see Black, *Mark*, 165-70.
[101] *Adversus haereses* 3.1.1.
[102] See Hengel, *Studies in the Gospel of Mark*, 28-30, arguing for a date of AD 69.

CHAPTER 4

The Character of the School

THERE IS MUCH THAT REQUIRES EDUCATED guesswork concerning the nature of the Alexandrian school: contours are often blurred, gaps in our knowledge frustrating, and judgments have to rely on a certain amount of intuition. Notwithstanding, there is also a generous amount of light, sufficient, this chapter will be arguing, to discern an *ecclesial institution, catechumenal in character, that places its work of formation within an overarching commitment to the evangelization of culture*. An outline account of the school, its identity and mission, leaders and writings, will be presented in this chapter. We will see that the leaders of the school have left us a significant corpus offering an inspiring pathway of human formation placed under the supervening work of grace. The spirituality and commitments expected of teachers and pedagogues within this pathway of formation are a point of special interest for the school, and we can see the entire craft of catechesis in the process of development. Different elements within this craft come into view more or less prominently during the whole history of the school, depending upon a range of factors—the concrete situation of the Church to enshrine, carry and institutionalize the craft, broader political and social currents, and levels of hierarchical support and involvement. A fuller discussion of certain key elements of the craft—the transformation of the Greek *paideia*, the foundational place of philosophy, the centrality and character of the *kerygma*, the discipline of pedagogy, and expectations regarding an ongoing mystagogical teacher formation—will be treated in Part II.

As we begin to outline the school it is helpful to consider some preliminary, interrelated questions: Was the school an "institution," or something more intangible, a loose-knit grouping that held to a common body of thought and way of life? How far should we be thinking about a school with a stable identity across generations of teachers? Indeed, should we be thinking of a succession of teachers in a *single* school, or is it more realistic to think in terms of a number of different Christian catechetical "schools"? We also need to ask questions about its ecclesial nature: how closely associated was the school with the bishops and presbyters of Alexandria? Should we think of the leaders of the school more as "private" Christian teachers, or as closely connected with the Church in Alexandria?

To illustrate the challenge of identifying the nature of the school we can begin with Eusebius's use of the term "school," *didaskaleion*. This is the term he uses when introducing both Pantaenus[1] and Origen.[2] In both cases they are described as head of the *didaskaleion* and an institution appears to be implied here. But then in Book VI, Eusebius uses the same word to mean simply the teaching that Origen gave—in other words, at that point he means something closer to "school of thought."[3] The elasticity that we find in Eusebius in the use of the term in fact reflects the breadth of its use in the ancient world, including at one end an administrative and identifiable institution with property, a library and a stable place for teaching, and at the other something more like a teacher with his pupils united in holding to a certain body of thought and way of life. Despite Eusebius's use of this single term, some scholars believe that we should think of just such a spectrum, from the more informal to the more consolidated and institutional: perhaps before Origen, figures such as Pantaenus and Clement should be understood as relatively "private" and independent teachers of the faith, with groups of pupils gathered around them, whereas under Bishop Demetrius and the appointment of Origen and his successors we have something more institutionally formal. Together, we might still speak of a continuity of approach that we could term the "Alexandrian tradition."[4]

A POINT OF COMPARISON: PHILOSOPHICAL SCHOOLS

To assist us in reaching some conclusions about these questions it is helpful to understand the character of philosophical schools which we find in Alexandria. These constitute one of the most important points of comparative reference with the catechetical school since the boundary between philosophy and religion was a very porous one in the ancient world and the Alexandrian school consciously expressed itself as belonging to this tradition of school. Eusebius tell us that Origen practiced the "philosophic life"[5] and that Heraclas—whom

---

[1] H. E. V.10.1; V.10.4.
[2] H. E. VI.3.3; VI.15.1.
[3] H. E. VI.21.4. Eusebius is describing Origen explaining to the mother of the Emperor the excellence of the divine teaching (*didaskaleion*).
[4] See the discussion in Robert Wilken, "Alexandria: A School for Training in Virtue," in ed. P. Henry, *Schools of Thought in the Christian Tradition* (Philadelphia: Fortress, 1984), 15-18, and the comments in Bernard Pouderon, *D'Athènes à Alexandrie: études sur Athénagore et les origines de la philosophie chrétienne* (Louvain: Editions Peeters, 1997), 36.
[5] H. E. VI.3.9-13.

Origen selected from among his pupils to assist him with catechetical instruction—offered a "noteworthy example of a philosophic life"[6] and wore the "philosophic garb,"[7] that is, the mantle worn by Greek philosophers (in Latin, the *pallium*).[8] When Origen later founded a school in Caesarea it was depicted in a similar way by Gregory Thaumaturgus, as a Christian philosophical school in which the relationship of master and disciples mirrored that of other philosophical schools in terms of its commitments and ascetical practices.[9] Amongst other things, we can point especially to the development of a prominent Logos theology in early Christianity—especially in the Johannine tradition—as encouraging this view of Christianity as a philosophical school, a school teaching spiritual truths and practicing a spiritual way while being at the same time fully committed to rational exploration. Thus we find Justin Martyr, for example, writing of how other philosophies had a partial understanding of the Logos, whereas in Christianity the Logos had revealed himself fully, becoming incarnate.[10]

The philosophical schools in Alexandria in the period we are considering largely saw themselves as standing in continuity with the four main schools that had been founded in ancient Athens: Plato's *Academy*, Aristotle's *Lyceum*, Epicurus's *Garden*, and Zeno's *Stoa*. Plato's was the first of the four[11] (and the longest-lasting, until the sixth century AD). After the death of Socrates, Plato gathered

---

[6] H. E. VI.3.2.
[7] H. E. VI.19.14.
[8] Other Christians identified themselves in the same way, wearing the philosopher's mantle, including Justin Martyr and Tertullian.
[9] See "The Oration and Panegyric Addressed to Origen," in eds. A. Donaldson and J. Donaldson, *Ante-Nicene Fathers* VI (Grand Rapids: William B. Eerdmans, 1971), 23–38, VI–VII.
[10] *Apology* II.8.1; II.13.3. Whatever the other philosophies contain that is of the truth, Justin argues, is the property of Christians since Christianity has the fullness of the Logos. Eusebius, in his *Praeparatio evangelica*, is delighted to be able to cite the neo-Platonist, Amelius, quoting the opening verses of John's Gospel as a philosophical text in the Logos tradition (see XI.19) and in his *Ecclesiastical History* (IV.26.7) he quotes Melito's description of Christianity as a philosophy. Tertullian and Hippolytus were also significant figures for the development of a Logos theology. The most refined forms of Logos theology in the third century, however, were undoubtedly those found in the works of Clement and Origen: see the discussion in John McGuckin, "The Christology of the Apostolic Fathers," in *Seeing the Glory: Studies in Patristic Theology* (Yonkers, NY: St. Vladimir's Seminary Press, 2017), 41–47.
[11] While the first of these four major schools, the Academy was not in fact the first school of "higher learning" in Athens—that of Isocrates predated it and various other sophists as well as followers of Socrates founded places for higher learning in Athens—but it was undoubtedly the most important.

a group of disciples, both younger figures as well as more mature thinkers, and taught them in his garden and in the gymnasium. In due course, Plato nominated Speusippus as his successor and passed on to him his possessions and garden in trust for the Academy, who in turn bequeathed these to his successor, Zenocrates. The Academy thus became a stable school, with a series of heads, with possessions and a living tradition of teaching. Aristotle spent many years in the Academy, and after Plato's death made the decision, in 335 BC, to found his own school. Zeno's school followed a generation later in 308 BC, and Epicurus's Garden in 306 BC.

The questions we have raised with regard to how far the catechetical school was an identifiable institution with a physical property, possessions, library, and teaching spaces can also be asked about these major philosophical schools and their successors. For example, Eusebius records Origen as receiving pupils into his own home,[12] and in philosophical schools teaching from a private residence was not an uncommon practice: Porphyry tells us that Plotinus taught in a private home, of Gemina.[13] So a philosophical school in the ancient world did not necessarily have the benefit of a physical plant—at least, not all of the time—although this should not be thought irrelevant: the four main schools derived their names "from their sites" as Diogenes Laertius notes.[14] Plato's Academy itself may have lacked a stable physical basis after the collapse of Athens in 88 BC, not recovering as a formal institution until almost the end of the fourth century AD.[15] Nonetheless, even after the fall of Athens to the Roman general Sulla, as a "school" the Academy continued to exist, thanks to the leadership of Antiochus, giving his lectures in the gymnasium, where Cicero heard him.[16] The collapse of an institution, in other words, did not necessarily mean the end of a "school," for most fundamentally the term "school" signified those pupils about a particular teacher, learning from that teacher and developing a pattern of thinking under

---

[12] H. E. VI.15.
[13] *Vita Plotini*, 9. For a discussion of Porphyry's account of Plotinus's teaching see H. Gregory Snyder, *Teachers and Texts in the Ancient World: Philosophers, Jews and Christians* (London: Routledge, 2000), 111-18.
[14] *Lives of Eminent Philosophers*, I, 17. For example, the appellation of "peripatetic" to the Aristotelian school was given because the gymnasium in the Lyceum had a *peripatos*, a place for walking. For a discussion about the importance of place, see Lynch, *Aristotle's School*, 73-75.
[15] See the discussion in Lynch, *Aristotle's School*, 177-89.
[16] See Cicero, *De Finibus* V.1ff. For the vicissitudes that faced the Academy see John Dillon, *The Middle Platonists: 80 B.C. to A.D. 220* (Ithaca, NY: Cornell University Press, 1977), 52ff, 60-61.

the influence of that teacher. Essentially we can say that *there is a school as long as there are teachers, students, and a tradition of thought and practice*. We use the term in this sense today, of course, when we speak of "schools of thought." More formal institutional arrangements were also possible, of course, and philosophical schools could also have property, libraries, and things that were maintained, cared for, and handed on as part of the school. And in this more formal sense both Plato's Academy and Aristotle's Lyceum were definitely real institutions during certain periods. But it is remains true that this more institutional aspect was not always present, nor strictly necessary for something to be classified as a school.

To be described as a philosophical "school" at this time certainly meant, then, that there was an identifiable tradition of thought that was communicated and handed on, a *body of beliefs that was distinctive*. Schools would be distinguished from one another by the teachings that they held and transmitted. [17] The usual term for a philosophical school was *diatriba*, from which we get "diatribe." That word now carries with it a sense of denunciatory and even abusive speech, but it originally simply signified philosophical discourse and lectures.[18] The various traditions of thought would themselves develop over time, and schools also varied as to the importance they placed on holding certain philosophical beliefs and positions in common; in addition, and sometimes just as important, was the methodology of the school and its academic "culture": thus in the early Academy it does not seem to have been the maintenance of a particular curriculum that characterized the school so much as the *manner* of engagement with certain ideas and the common addressing of key problems and questions. One did not have to subscribe strictly to "Platonist positions" to attend — or even to thrive — at the Academy.[19]

---

[17] Lynch's careful review of the evidence in the Imperial period in Athens (the other main center for philosophy, apart from Alexandria) concludes: "In the Imperial centuries, 'Academic,' 'Peripatetic,' 'Stoic,' and 'Epicurean' were no longer the names for the various institutional means by which philosophy was taught at Athens; they had become instead the names which distinguished the *divisions within the subject matter of philosophical studies*. Long before a similar institution was founded by the Neo-Platonists in the fifth century A.D., the self-perpetuating philosophical communities established at Athens by Plato, Aristotle, Zeno, and Epicurus had died out" (*Aristotle's School*, 197).

[18] For a discussion of Greek vocabulary related to philosophical schools, as institutions and as traditions of teachings, see J. Glucker, *Antiochus and the Late Academy* (Gottingham: Vandenhoeck and Ruprecht, 1978), 159–225.

[19] Cherniss, in his study of the early Academy, argues that Plato's own role in the Academy was essentially that of "an individual thinker whose insight and skill in the formulation of a problem enables him to offer general advice and

To be described as a philosophical "school" also meant that there were *recognizable teachers* who led the school, who stood in this tradition and represented it. Battles between rival teachers were common, arguing for the authenticity of their way of understanding the founder's teaching and which developments of the tradition were legitimate or illegitimate. An important crossroads in the Academy was reached in 87 BC, for instance, when Antiochus, living in Alexandria, challenged Philo of Larissa regarding what constituted the authentic Platonic tradition. Writing against Philo in his work *Sosus*, he challenged the whole tradition of Academic skepticism, and held that Plato had clearly taught certain positive views.[20] It was from this successful leadership bid of Antiochus and his successors that the tradition of what became known as "Middle Platonism" developed.

A further key element in all schools was a *shared way of life*, including a *set of practices* that, in addition to beliefs, set a school apart from the others and marked one out as a member of a distinct school. We are indebted especially to the French philosopher, Pierre Hadot, for highlighting this aspect of ancient philosophical schools.[21] He has shown that it is incorrect to think of ancient philosophical schools as concerned only with articulating and defending certain theoretical frameworks for understanding the world. There was a close and mutually synergistic relationship between belief and life. The choice of philosophical school originates in "the choice of a certain way of life and existential option which demands from the individual a total change of lifestyle, a conversion of one's entire being, and ultimately a certain desire to be and to live in a certain way."[22]

All schools had certain criteria and sets of expectations for what counted as *membership in a school*, although they varied in terms of how open they were to those of different views and persuasions—from the Pythagorean brotherhood, monastic in its commitment to detachment from the world, with possessions held in common, and made up of an exclusive group with a secret and elaborate procedure

---

methodological criticism to other individual thinkers who respect his wisdom" (H. Cherniss, *The Riddle of the Early Academy* [Berkeley: University of California Press, 1945], 65).

[20] For a detailed discussion of the nature of the disagreement see J. Glucker, *Antiochus and the Late Academy*, 13–97 and for the possible origins of Arcesilaus's and Carneades's skepticism see 32–64.

[21] See especially Hadot's *Plotinus, or The Simplicity of Vision* (Chicago: The University of Chicago Press, 1993); *Philosophy as a Way of Life: Spiritual Exercises from Socrates to Foucault* (Oxford: Blackwell Publishing, 1995); and *What is Ancient Philosophy?* (Cambridge, MA: The Belknap Press of Harvard University Press, 2002).

[22] Hadot, *What is Ancient Philosophy?* 3.

for joining,²³ to the more open membership commitments of Plato's Academy and Aristotle's school, in which members were divided fairly formally into two groups: the older members as the teachers at the school and the younger members as the students.²⁴ Whatever the differences regarding membership and organizational structures, the philosophical way of life was not to be thought of as one which could be undertaken alone; it flourished in dialogue and in relationship with others. Belonging to a philosophical school meant belonging to a community in which there were forms of mutual support, accountability, and accompaniment. "The living voice and the intimacy of a common life will help you more than the written word. You must go to the scene of action," wrote Seneca. And it is the quality of the *relationships* in the school that would change one's life: "It was not the classroom of Epicurus, but living together under the same roof, that made great men of Metrodorus, Hermarchus, and Polyaenus."²⁵

The schools also had their *central texts and writings* for joint study and their handbooks of core teachings.²⁶ The purpose of such handbooks was in part to make possible a faithfulness to the past, enabling the studying of the teaching of the founders and their tradition. But it would be wrong to think of this study as something petrified, as a system of thought to be mastered independently of life. What was given in the past was to be received as a series of truth claims, as claims about what constitutes the human good and about how the beautiful engages us. The past was to *live* in the members of the school. Texts were studied not merely because they are "in the canon"; the understanding of reality provided was for the sake of

---

[23] For a summary of our knowledge of Pythagorean communities see Thomas Africa, *Science and the State in Greece and Rome* (Chichester: John Wiley and Sons, 1968), 29-32. There is evidence that those wishing to join the brotherhood had to keep silence for five years and even after this to treat Pythagorean teaching with a certain reserve (see W. K. C. Guthrie, *A History of Greek Philosophy* [Cambridge: Cambridge University Press, 1969], III, 151).
[24] See Lynch, *Aristotle's School*, 75-80.
[25] *Epistulae Morales* 6.6. As we will see, the catechetical school would allow no opposition between the spoken and written word, but Seneca's emphasis is still worth noting.
[26] Core teachings were collected in such handbooks with selections of important passages on definite subjects extracted and highlighted for commentary. Thus, for Middle Platonism, the *Didaskalikos* by Alcinous and Apuleius's *De Platone* are important examples. For a detailed discussion of the content of the *Didaskalikos*, see R. E. Witt, *Albinus and the History of Middle Platonism* (Cambridge: Cambridge University Press, 1937), illustrating the eclectic blend of the teachings found there, drawn from the Old Academy and from Aristotelianism and Stoicism.

a present moral and spiritual work in the school.[27] Philosophical schools, then, while certainly "schools of thought" in which pupils gathered themselves around teachers, were also "schools of life,"[28] and the seriousness of the philosophical quest was to be measured by the ascetical and community practices that were put in place in the different schools. In summary, what we find is that all philosophical schools advanced certain spiritual and ascetical practices which were adopted by its members, practices that were shared in common and constituted a way of life that expressed the core beliefs of the school. In many respects, such beliefs and practices were what we might today regard as "religious," being focused on a transformation of the self in the light of what was understood to be the human good, the *telos*, the final end and goal of human life, making clear also the virtues that were needed in order to reach that goal.

In relation to these philosophical schools, the catechetical school certainly saw itself as distinctive, but there were also clear points of overlap, for the school had the confidence to borrow and adapt freely from the practices of the Greek philosophical schools (excepting the Epicurean since, as Clement explained, it denied the providence of God and deified pleasure).[29] Like any good philosophical school, Origen argued, Christianity healed the diseases of the soul, teaching its adherents the way to live well,[30] and in his *Commentary on the Song of Songs* he introduced his readers to the practice of an examination of conscience.[31] Hadot traces the way that Clement adopted a range of spiritual exercises from the philosophical schools and transformed them into Christian ascetical practices—for example, that of cultivating

---

[27] It is in the light of this point that we can understand Lynch's comment that, *contra* Strabo (XIII.1.54), the decline of the Aristotelian school cannot be attributed *simply* to the loss of Aristotle's library, however much that might have been a blow to the school: the lack of energy and interest of the members of the school community itself must have been fundamental (see 146-49).

[28] To couch the point in the language of *John* 14:6, we can say that philosophical schools considered themselves to be not only teaching *truth*, but also maintaining a particular *way* that led to *life*. The tradition of teaching was in service to the way that members of the school followed. So also the catechetical school taught a *way* to be pursued. Christians from the outset described themselves as "followers of the Way" and it was only later that they identified themselves as "Christians" (see *Acts* 9:2; 18:26; 19:9, 23; 22:4; 214:14, 22). This Christian Way, the Alexandrian school argued, was distinctive, for Christ, as God's Logos incarnate, introduced them to *God's* way, his way of acting and being in human form. The way that baptism and faith opened was a privileged participation in the way of the Lord and not simply a path of human wisdom.

[29] For Clement's rejection of Epicurus see *Protrepticus* 5.66.5; *Stromateis* 1.50.6.

[30] *Contra Celsum* III.54.

[31] See his discussion of verse 1:8 in the *Commentary on the Song of Songs*.

peace of mind through various means, and "practicing dying" in the face of pleasure, pain, fear and desire.[32] Many philosophical practices were also taken up into the Egyptian monastic tradition, Christianized versions of Stoic and Platonic exercises. Ascetical practices proposed in Plotinus's *Enneads*,[33] for example, parallel in many respects those found in the desert spirituality that sprang up around Alexandria and flourished under the protection of the leaders of the Egyptian church. Many exercises, moreover, entered into Christian spirituality in general through the Christian philosophical traditions that the school embraced, central to which was an understanding of sharing in the mysteries of Christ and thereby enjoying the new life of his Spirit and learning to see one's brothers and sisters "as Christ" in his Body.[34]

A PATTERN OF ECCLESIAL CONTINUITY AND SUCCESSION

There are two related questions to examine concerning the institutional character of the school. The first is the much-debated issue of the school's origin and the *continuity of succession of leaders in the school*. To what extent do we find in the school a single living tradition, with a line of teacher-leaders handing on the patterns of life and thought of the school, in a tradition of master to disciple, somewhat in the style of philosophical schools? The second question concerns the ecclesial nature of the school: To what extent did the school understand itself as an official *ecclesial institution*, working in close collaboration with and under the authority of the bishops of Alexandria? As we will see, the two questions are closely related to each other.

There is no doubt that the two questions preoccupied the school itself. We have already seen that the overriding interest in the person of Mark in the early Church lay in his connections to Peter and thus the establishing of an apostolic foundation for his Gospel and for the Alexandrian tradition. We should expect this interest in establishing links to the apostles and their successors to be a similar concern for the school also, and indeed this is what we find. The necessity for establishing such an apostolic foundation for the school's teaching

---

[32] The phrase "practicing dying" is from Plato's *Phaedrus* (81a). Clement connects it to Christ's admonition to be prepared to lose one's life and he offers readers a series of ascetical practices in *Stromateis* 2.20.103.1-126.4. For examples of such exercises in philosophical schools see Hadot, *Philosophy as a Way of Life*, 93-101.
[33] For a treatment of Plotinus highlighting the place of such exercises see Stephen R. L. Clark, *Plotinus: Myth, Metaphor, and Philosophical Practice* (Chicago: The University of Chicago Press, 2016), especially 14-20 and 139-45.
[34] For a discussion see Hadot, *What is Ancient Philosophy?*, 241-47.

and practices was no doubt exacerbated by the presence of Gnostic schools in Alexandria and the crucial need to distinguish the school from these and identify it as an authentic point of succession from those apostolic foundations. Gnosticism in all its forms relied upon the notion of secret, unwritten traditions being handed down by the fully initiated, and knowledge of which guaranteed not only a privileged status in the various Gnostic schools but also a secure pathway to salvation. Secrecy was key: initiation into the sect involved the communication of secret rites and sayings. To counter these claims of a secret tradition the catechetical school needed as far as possible to identify a public chain of succession, reaching back to apostolic times. The presence of Gnostic schools may, then, have intensified the need for this evidence to be collected and corroborated. But gathering the evidence for succession from the apostles was understood as necessary in any case, to protect the historical character of the Christian faith and the authenticity of its present teaching. The Founder of the new faith had formed his chosen disciples, who in turn had handed on their authority and testimony to those whom they selected and formed. Current teachers in the Church were the heirs of this formational pathway.

And so we find names, and even lists, associated with the catechetical school in Alexandria, almost certainly of those in a leadership capacity. Some of these names are well confirmed from multiple sources, such as Pantaenus, Clement, Origen, Heraclas, Pierius, and Didymus. Many other names appear in our sources, some who are less well known, others whose links to the school are more debated. But we are able, with a reasonable amount of security, to identify a set of figures who were prominent in the school from the late second century until the beginning of the fifth, even if their precise dating is obscure or role in the school disputed. As might be expected, the nature of the school in its earliest period is the most difficult to discern clearly.

A review of the sources for this evidence is interesting for the light it sheds, not only on this point, but also on the second question we are asking: whether we should consider the school an "ecclesial" one, associated formally with the Church and her structures. In what follows, then, we will be tracing answers to questions of succession and of ecclesial association together.

We begin with our primary source, Eusebius. He first introduces his readers to the school during the time when it was led by Pantaenus: this would be AD 177, the year Commodus began to share the Roman throne with his father, Marcus Aurelius. Alongside this introduction of the figure of Pantaenus he notes that "from ancient custom a school of sacred learning" existed among the Alexandrian faithful.[35] No further names are attached, but Eusebius continues by quoting from Pantaenus's successor, Clement, seeking in the first place to link Clement to Pantaenus. In Clement's *Stromateis*, Eusebius recounts, Clement wrote of many "blessed and truly notable men" whom he had been privileged to meet during his life and mentions one in particular whom he "hunted out from his concealment in Egypt" and thus "found rest."[36] Eusebius surmises this figure — quite reasonably — to be Pantaenus since in another of Clement's works, *Hypotyposeis*, Clement describes him as his teacher.[37] In his description of these "notable men" he had met during his own lifetime, Clement writes of their faithfulness in handing down "the true tradition of the blessed teaching directly from Peter and James and John and Paul, the holy apostles, son receiving it from father ... and by the blessing of God they came down to us to deposit those ancestral and apostolic seeds."[38]

There is a clear double claim here by Clement, of antiquity and authenticity, the two claims grounded in the assertion that through Pantaenus the school and its teaching reached back to the apostles. A further confirming source we have concerning Pantaenus's links to the apostles is from the ninth century compilation of Photius, Patriarch of Constantinople, whose *Bibliotheca* is composed of reviews of around two hundred books he had read. In this work Photius quotes from a (lost) text by Pamphilus and Eusebius, *Apology for Origen*, which affirms that Pantaenus had personally heard some of the apostles and had also been taught by those whom the apostles had taught.[39]

Eusebius and Clement are clearly concerned, then, to demonstrate that the school's teaching can be relied upon as faithful to the Church's tradition because it is rooted in apostolic authority. For

---

[35] H. E. V.10.1.
[36] See *Stromateis* 1.11.2.
[37] Eusebius knew this work, which appears to have been a commentary on the Scriptures, but it has unfortunately been lost. Eusebius has the following to say about the work: "And in the *Hypotyposeis*, to speak briefly, he [Clement] has given concise explanations of all the Canonical Scriptures, not passing over even the disputed writings, I mean the Epistle of Jude and the remaining Catholic Epistles, and the Epistle of Barnabus, and the Apocalypse known as Peter's" (H. E. VI.14.1). That Pantaenus was Clement's teacher, or at least close associate, is confirmed by another of Clement's works: in his *Eclogae Propheticae, Selections from the Prophets*, he names Pantaenus warmly as "our Pantaenus": "ὁ Πάνταινος δὲ ἡμῶν ἔλεγεν (our Pantaenus used to say) ..." (56.2) (https://catholiclibrary.org/library/view?docId=Fathers-OR/Clement_of_Alexandria__Eclogae_propheticae.gr.html).
[38] H. E. V.11.5. See *Stromateis* 1.11.3.
[39] Photius, *Bibliotheca*, Codex 118, ed. R. Henry (Paris, 1969), II, 91.

Origen, also, who was Clement's successor, the claim that he faithfully teaches and hands on the apostolic tradition was crucial. Origen has rightfully gained a reputation as a speculative thinker, but that his intention and concern were always to be a faithful expounder of the apostolic tradition has been increasingly recognized in Origenist studies. For example, John Behr has shown how carefully Origen, in his preface to *De Principiis*, distinguishes between the apostles' preaching itself ("basic elements of the Gospel preaching") and ecclesiastical preaching ("corollaries of this apostolic preaching").[40] We can thus see how the two questions, of the succession of teachers and of the ecclesial character of the school, are inseparable. The school sought to establish the legitimacy and authority of its teaching precisely for the sake of the *ecclesial responsibilities* it had. A catechetical school would necessarily be focused upon establishing a reliable tradition for its teaching since "catechesis" literally means "echo down," indicating a dynamic of receiving and passing on.[41] If the school had a pastoral mission to discharge then establishing the authenticity of the Gospel it proclaimed was vital.

Eusebius, then, provides us with a series of names, even if we cannot always confirm the details of succession from one to another. In fact, grasping the exact relationship even of the central figures of Pantaenus, Clement and Origen to each other is not without complexity. Eusebius certainly seems to imply that Clement was taught by Pantaenus, becoming head of the school on Pantaenus's death, and that he was succeeded by Origen in 202,[42] but the exact relationship between Clement and Origen is not easy to establish for Eusebius

---

[40] John Behr, Introduction, *Origen: On First Principles, Vol 1* (Oxford: Oxford University Press, 2017), xxxix-xlii. Heine thus rightly notes the irony that Origen's consistent attempt to defend and articulate apostolic and ecclesiastical doctrines, distinguishing his speculation from these doctrines, nonetheless led to his being thought "a borderline heretic for centuries" (*Origen: Scholarship in the Service of the Church*, 144).

[41] We find an early example of this assertion of transmission in the *First Letter to the Corinthians* in which Paul writes of handing on "what I in turn had received" (15:3). In John's Gospel, similarly, the coming gift of the Holy Spirit is explained by Jesus to his disciples as a guarantee of authentic remembrance: the Spirit will "teach you everything and remind you of all that I have said to you" (14:26). In John chapter 16 Jesus also describes the Holy Spirit as the one who will "guide you into all the truth" (16:13), and this guiding is to be understood as into the fullness of *what has already been given in Christ*, anchored in the remembrance of what he has taught the disciples but which they have not yet clearly understood (cf. the comments in James D. G. Dunn, *Jesus and the Spirit: A Study of the Religious and Charismatic Experience of Jesus and the First Christians as Reflected in the New Testament* [Grand Rapids: William B. Eerdmans, 1997], 351-52).

[42] H. E. VI.3.8.

nowhere writes explicitly of Clement having been Origen's teacher. Origen was eighteen at the time that Clement appears to have left Alexandria, during the persecution of Christians by the Emperor Severus, the persecution in which Origen's father was martyred, and so he could have been Clement's student only for a short period during his teen years. And yet that there is *something* like a succession involved is indicated by the fact that Alexander, in writing to Origen, describes Pantaenus, Clement and Origen each as his teachers.[43] And that Origen carried out his work with knowledge of Clement's ministry is undeniable, following him in many of his theological emphases and pedagogical priorities. Jerome, for example, writes of Origen composing his *Stromata* (now lost) in imitation of Clement's work of the same name.[44]

The leaders of the school from Origen onwards are mentioned either by Eusebius or by Philip of Side, who provides us with a list of these leaders. As we have already noted, Philip studied under Rhodon, whom he identifies as the last head of the school, after Rhodon had moved the school to Side, and Philip provides us with the following list (in this order): Athenagoras, Clement, Pantaenus, Origen, Heraclas, Dionysius, Pierius, Theognostus, Serapion, Peter (bishop and martyr), Macarius Politicus, Didymus the Blind, and finally Rhodon.[45] The reliability of the list and its ordering is debated—though defended in many of its details by Bernard Pouderon, who argues that some of the apparent errors in the chronology of Philip's list are actually the result of the work of those who conducted the abridgment of his work.[46] For example, the reverse ordering of Pantaenus and Clement in Philip's list seems puzzling since Clement so clearly thinks of Pantaenus as the teacher who attracted and preceded him. At the same time, as they appear to have taught during the same period it may simply be that Clement's renown is being reflected in this reversal. Several in the list—Serapion, Macarius, and Didymus—were also contemporaries and should probably be placed side by side rather

---

[43] *H. E.* VI.14.9.
[44] *Epistle* 70.4. We also know from Clement's text *On the Rich Man's Salvation* that he had by then completed a major work, *An Exposition on First Principles and Theology.* It is plausible that, just as Origen had followed Clement in composing a *Stromateis*, so Origen's *De Principiis* is modelled on Clement's work.
[45] Philip's work is only available to us now in an abridged form in a fourteenth-century manuscript, *Codex Baroccianus graecus* 142, held in the Bodleian Library in Oxford. For the text of our list, see Bernard Pouderon, *D'Athènes à Alexandrie*, 2.
[46] Pouderon's main interest is in the place of Athenagoras, but he discusses at some length the value of the list overall: see 40-70.

than necessarily as successive figures. Philip's list also misses Achillas whom Eusebius places after Pierius.⁴⁷ The presence of Athenagoras (c. 133-190) in the list of teachers and leaders by Philip, who places him as the first of the leaders of the school, is controversial, of course. We know that Athenagoras's work as a teacher and writer took place mainly in Athens, and it is fairly certain that it was while he was there, in AD 176 or 177, that he wrote his apologetic *Embassy for the Christians* to Marcus Aurelius and his son Commodus. Nonetheless, it is also possible that he spent a period in Alexandria, teaching as a Christian philosopher, even though there is no evidence other than Philip's list of his being a leader of the catechetical school.⁴⁸

Willem Oliver has recently attempted an "integrated list," drawing on Eusebius, Philip, and evidence from Athanasius and Jerome, as well as a list preserved in the Coptic Orthodox Church which includes early figures from Mark until Pantaenus.⁴⁹ While we cannot reach final conclusions about the veracity of many of the details, a further important point emerges as we study these lists. A certain amount of the complexity we face arises from the fact that there are two overlapping lines of succession being traced in authorities like Eusebius. One line traces teacher-leaders, the other episcopal figures. At certain points the lists coincide, only to separate out again. We saw that when Eusebius was seeking to establish through Clement the primitive nature of the school, tracing its origins back into the apostolic period, he highlighted the prominent role of the *teacher* as the one who holds in trust the "ancestral and apostolic seeds" and hands them down. It is striking that Eusebius uses the phrase "distinguished members of the apostolic succession"⁵⁰ to refer to this handing on of the faith by teachers. The claim here is clearly to a *succession of teachers* providing a chain of personal transmission of the faith which can be traced back to the apostles.⁵¹ In terms of the structure of Eusebius's *Ecclesiastical History*, however, the more significant lines of succession, dominating Books II to VII, are the political and the ecclesiastical. Thus, we are presented with the succession of the Roman Emperors

---

⁴⁷ *H. E.* VII.32.30.
⁴⁸ For a defense of his having had a role in the school, however, see Leslie W. Barnard, *Athenagoras: A Study in Second Century Christian Apologetic* (Paris: Beauchesne, 1972), 13–18, 174.
⁴⁹ Willem H. Oliver, "The Heads of the Catechetical School in Alexandria," *Verbum et Ecclesia* 36, 1 (2015), Art. #1386, 14 pages. http://dx.doi.org/10.4102/ve.v36i1/1386, and including the work of the Coptic historian El Masri.
⁵⁰ *H. E.* V.11.2.
⁵¹ See also Sozomen, *H. E.* I.1, where he speaks of Clement as a "successor of the apostles."

alongside the monarchical succession of bishops in four sees of the pre-Nicene Church: Rome, Alexandria, Antioch and Jerusalem. In fact, Eusebius constantly presents the Alexandrian school in relation to this succession of bishops in Alexandria: the first mention of the catechetical school, for example, is dated in relation to Julian, bishop of Alexandria,[52] and thereafter the life and progress of the school is continually related to this succession of bishops, the details of which probably came from Julius Africanus.

It is clear that the relationship between teachers and bishops was, from Bishop Demetrius's time onward (189–231), a closely interrelated one, the bishops of Alexandria not only appointing to the school but also originating from it: thus Demetrius appointed Origen to teach while Heraclas, a pupil of Origen, subsequently became head of the school when Origen went to Caesarea, and then succeeded Demetrius as bishop.[53] After Heraclas, Dionysius and Theognostus likewise served as heads of the school before entering the episcopate, as did Peter the Martyr. Athanasius was almost certainly a student in the school[54] and, according to Rufinus, Didymus was said to have taught in the school with the approval of Athanasius "and the other wise men in the church of God."[55] Some level of episcopal oversight of the school appears to have been in place from the early third century until the school's moving at the beginning of the fifth century.[56]

Let us therefore look first at this period from Origen onwards, when it is generally accepted that the school had a definite relationship to episcopal authority, and from that point then seek to go further back to examine whether the nature of the school in the period before Origen can be determined. We can begin by examining what might have taken place at the turning, or demarcation, point of Demetrius's relationship

---

[52] H. E. V.19.
[53] H. E. VI.26.1.
[54] Gwynn, *Athanasius of Alexandria*, 20–25.
[55] Rufinus, H. E. XI.7. Richard Layton cautions that while both Pierius and Didymus were clearly prominent teachers at the school there is no direct evidence that they functioned as its directors (*Didymus the Blind and His Circle in Late-Antique Alexandria*, 15–18). The distinction, though, is perhaps a moot one: leadership and charismatic teaching authority were closely connected.
[56] What precisely happened to the relationship of the school and its leadership to the episcopacy during the heady times of the mid to late fourth century, during the many periods of Athanasian exile and the time of Lucius after Athanasius's death is worthy of more study. Frances Young sensibly proposes that for Didymus there must have been at least a stepping back from his role in the school during the period of Arian ascendency (cf. *From Nicaea to Chalcedon*, 85) if in the general turbulence of the city during this period the school managed to survive in some form without a break.

to Origen as the then head of the school, since the conclusions reached about the nature of the earlier period of the school have often been closely related to the interpretation of this significant interaction between the head of the school and ecclesiastical authority.[57]

It is Demetrius who is normally credited with beginning to consolidate the authority of the bishop in Alexandria and his status in relation to other Egyptian sees. He may have seen the appointment of Origen as head of the school in 202, while the latter was still in his teens, as an element in this consolidation. The relationship began well but concluded badly, with Origen leaving in 231, taking his library with him, to found his own school in Caesarea. Whatever happened, from his episcopacy onwards the school never quite regained the missionary breadth, catechetical vision, and philosophical and theological weight, that it had achieved under Clement and Origen. Nonetheless, even if the school lacked its earlier brilliance one could argue that it benefitted from a certain stability, and there were certainly leaders who loyally took up the work of Clement and Origen again: after a period of episcopal anti-Origenist sentiment under Demetrius and Heraclas, there was a softening of this position under Dionysius, with the subsequent leaders of the school, Theognostus and Pierius, being steadfastly faithful to the earlier legacy of Clement and Origen, both standing firmly in the pedagogical and exegetical tradition that they had established. Indeed, Pierius was known as "Origen the Younger," and had among his students Pamphilus who was in turn friend and mentor to Eusebius. It was Pamphilus who, after his time at the Alexandrian school, went to Caesarea where he revived Origen's academy there and built up his library, including a collection of Origen's own works, afterwards composing with Eusebius the first of five books in the *Apology for Origen*. In the period following Origen, then, it seems almost certain that the school continued its catechetical work, now very much as a part of the ecclesial fabric of the city, until the school finally closed in 405 under the leadership of Rhodon who transferred the school to Sidon. The difficulty leading to the school's eventual closure in Alexandria was probably episcopal in nature, the then bishop, Theophilus (385-412), a "declared enemy of Greek culture,"[58] standing against themes that had played such

---

[57] Among the discussions see C. Wilfred Griggs, *Early Egyptian Christianity from its Origins to 451 CE* (Leiden: Brill, 1990), 61-67, and Stephen J. Davis, *The Early Coptic Papacy: The Egyptian Church and its Leadership in Late Antiquity: The Popes of Egypt* (New York: The American University in Cairo Press, 2004), 22-28.

[58] Roelof van den Broek, "The Christian 'School' of Alexandria in the Second and Third Centuries," 47.

a central part in the school and had been revived under the most recent Origenist leadership of the school.

What led to the falling out between Origen and Demetrius? Among the reasons suggested, one should be removed as unimportant, if not actually false: Eusebius mentions Origen's supposed self-castration as an accusation Demetrius brought against him after Origen had been appointed to the presbyterate by Theoctistus and Alexander, the bishops of Caesarea and Jerusalem. Eusebius defends Origen's act as one of youthfulness and immaturity, though witnessing to his desire to fulfil the Lord's teaching and to avoid gossip, since he taught women as well as men and therefore wanted to circumvent any question of scandal. Eusebius adds that he tried to keep his deed from the awareness of most of his pupils, but unsuccessfully.[59]

Notwithstanding the Eusebian account, we have good reason to be cautious about its accuracy: "that this 'least of all literalists' should have been so caricatured as a literalist ought to have alerted scholars much earlier to the 'smoke-blowing' this tale represented."[60] Even if such an event took place, though—and Eusebius does not question the truth of this account—Eusebius does not see in this action the springs of the evident animus Demetrius had towards Origen. He points out that when Demetrius had first learned of this deed he had, while "marveling" at Origen's "rash act," nonetheless "approved the zeal and sincerity of his faith, bade him be of good cheer, and urged him to attach himself now all the more to the work of instruction."[61]

Eusebius sees Demetrius's opposition rather as resulting from personal jealousy. This is not implausible. Origen had developed an international reputation and was a sought-after scholar of high repute. As his life became busier, he appointed Heraclas to look after the foundational instruction in the school in order to be able to meet the demands being made on him to devote more energies to writing and scholarship. The school was expanding its work, increasingly providing a Christian center of formation that would be a vital support for the universal mission of the Church—and reflective of the reputation of the city in which the great museum and library stood.

Beyond this personal consideration, the challenge for Demetrius might also have been exacerbated by the insecurities of his own

---

[59] H. E. VI.8.1-2.
[60] John A. McGuckin, "Origen of Alexandria on the Mystery of the Pre-Existent Church," in *Seeing the Glory*, 113, n.3; see also ed. McGuckin, *The Westminster Handbook to Origen* (Louisville, KY: Westminster John Knox Press, 2004), 6-7.
[61] H. E. VI.8.3.

situation as he was seeking this episcopal consolidation. And there are two elements which need to be taken into consideration here. The first is the high status of the teacher in the early Christian Church. In the early Church instruction in the faith seems to have been especially given over to specific individuals whom the Church recognized as having the charism to teach (*didaskaloi*). From the beginning of the Church this teaching charism was placed alongside the foundational teaching authority of the apostles.[62] Both the *Didache*[63] and the *Shepherd of Hermas*, a late second-century visionary writing of Roman origin, bear witness to the importance of this role of teacher.[64] Within the Church, then, alongside the apostolic succession of those in orders there was, if not a succession of teachers, then at least a ministry of teaching of the faith, of teachers as bearers and defenders of tradition reaching back to the apostles in a way analogous to the role of the bishop.[65] Roelof van den Broek goes so far as to argue that there was effectively a "double line" of succession during the early period of the school, of teachers as well as bishops, both tracing their legitimate authority back to the apostles, and that this could be seen as, in turn, continuing "the roles of the rabbis and elders of the Jewish community."[66] Henri Marrou proposes a related narrative, that as we see the catechumenal system developing in the Church as a whole we also see a corresponding movement of responsibility from the *didaskaloi* to the presbyterate, with the bishop gradually being recognized as "having the last word." He sees full clarity on this question only being achieved by the "golden age" of the catechumenate in the fourth century.[67]

---

[62] Thus see *Acts* 2:42 referencing the apostles' teaching and *Acts* 13:1 noting the presence of teachers at Antioch. See also *1 Cor.* 12:28; *Eph.* 4:11.

[63] See 13.2; 15.2. In 15.1 bishops and deacons are mentioned as serving in the ministry of prophet and teacher, and the category of prophet and teacher is then repeated, implying that this is also something separate from those who teach as an intrinsic part of episcopal or diaconal life.

[64] See *Visions* 3.5.1 where teachers are listed alongside bishops, priests, and deacons; *Similitudes* 9.15.4; 16.5; 25.2 where apostles and teachers are paired. Popular in the early Church, *The Shepherd of Hermes* is quoted by Origen six times in *De Principiis* (for details see Heine, *Origen: Scholarship in the Service of the Church*, 46–47).

[65] Chadwick judges that in the early period of the Church, "the authority of the expert," and of his "reputation, learning and skill in teaching" were sufficient to create his clientele: H. Chadwick and J. E. L. Oulton, *Alexandrian Christianity* (Philadelphia: Westminster Press, 1954), 137.

[66] "The Christian 'School' of Alexandria in the Second and Third Centuries," 43. Of course we should note that in second century Alexandria little of this Jewish tradition remained after the devastation of the Jewish community following the uprising of 115-17, as Van den Hoek has reminded us ("The 'Catechetical' School of Early Christian Alexandria and Its Philonic Heritage," 86).

[67] *A History of Education in Antiquity*, 315.

If the first point is the relationship between those in orders and those who had a ministry of teacher, the second point is the unusual relationship of the episcopacy in Alexandria to the presbyterate. Possibly as late as the fourth century it appears that in Alexandria the presbyters named one of themselves as bishop, performing the consecration. Jerome calls on the authority of Alexandria to support an argument for the prominent role of the Christian presbyterate, writing: "even at Alexandria from the time of Mark the Evangelist until the episcopates of Heraclas and Dionysius the presbyters always named as bishop one of their own number chosen by themselves and set in a more exalted position, just as an army elects a general."[68] Strong ecclesial organization, it is argued, only began to appear with Demetrius, sometimes known as the "second founder" of the Alexandrian Church because of his work in clarifying and developing the monarchical episcopal system we see outlined by Ignatius of Antioch. It is sometimes proposed that it was under his reign that the episcopal line of succession in Alexandria that we find in Eusebius was clarified.[69]

A picture thus emerges of an Alexandrian tradition giving considerable prestige to Christian teachers, whether ordained or not, together with an ecclesial arrangement that may have left the bishop as more of a collaborator with his presbyters than one who had clear authority over them. If this is a reliable account then it is apparent why Origen might have appeared as a particular threat to Demetrius, especially as the more speculative aspects of his theology were being developed and his reputation grew. Rowan Williams argues that the difficulties of knowing how to resolve questions of disagreement between these two lines of succession was part of the narrative that needs to be understood in the Arian controversy also, with Arius standing in a school or "academic" tradition and looking to be recognized as an eminent and charismatic teacher.[70] Origen, likewise, he sees as standing in the school tradition within this model of dual succession and parallel hierarchies in which the academics operated within a looser model, acting more like philosophical study groups. In the case of Origen,

---

[68] *Epistle* 146.1. For a discussion see Heine, *Origen: Scholarship in the Service of the Church*, 31-34; Rowan Williams, *Arius: Heresy and Tradition*, Rev. Ed. (Grand Rapids: William B. Eerdmans, 2001), 42.

[69] See, for example, Birger Pearson, "Earliest Christianity in Egypt: Further Observations," 105-6; Gwynn, *Athanasius of Alexandria*, 20-25. Robert Grant suggests that Eusebius's episcopal list may have been based upon the, now lost, *Chronographies* of Julius Africanus, a work of uncertain merit (*Eusebius as Historian*, 51-52).

[70] See Williams, *Arius*, 29-91.

Williams sees the school tradition of the authority of the charismatic intellectual and spiritual leader in due course being to some extent resolved through being absorbed on the one hand into the *episcopal* tradition in figures such as Basil the Great and Gregory of Nyssa, while at the same time also taking on new life in the *monastic* tradition, as we see in Athanasius's depiction of Antony as the inheritor of the tradition of the sage living the philosophical life.[71]

This broader ecclesiological picture might affect how we look at the school in a number of ways. In the first place, it helps explain why some scholars regard with skepticism any notion of the school in the period before Origen—or even before Origen's successor, Heraclas—as a ecclesial institution.[72] The argument would be that the Church herself in Alexandria was insufficiently organized under a single bishop with clear authority to sponsor such a school; it "lacked any notion of itself as a single *institutional* unit."[73] The catechetical school before Origen cannot easily be thought of in institutional terms because the Church herself lacked a clearly unified institutional presence, upon which the school would have needed to depend.

But the evidence we have been reviewing can be interpreted in another way, a way which allows us to appreciate the meaning of "ecclesial institution" precisely in the light of this developing ecclesiastical landscape. And, indeed, within Alexandrian scholarship another view of the catechetical school before Origen has gained ground, one that is more sympathetic to the concept of an ecclesial catechetical and scholarly school. André Méhat,[74] in his work on Clement's *Stromateis*, has argued that it is a faulty historical understanding of what it would have been to operate as "private" or "unofficial" Christian teachers that has led to a reluctance to consider the existence of an ecclesial school in Alexandria prior to Origen. Such terms are not applicable in a context in which Christian religious gatherings were illegal. And while we have already indicated that the Alexandrian school shared features in common with philosophical schools of this period, this fact should not lead us to conclude that the catechetical

---

[71] On the integration of the sage and the spiritual ascetic see Williams, *Arius*, 88-89. Also Hadot, *Philosophy as a Way of Life*, 129-30, and the judgement of Stewart, "Rethinking the History of Monasticism East and West," 4.

[72] For example, see Roelof van den Broek, "The Christian 'School' of Alexandria in the Second and Third Centuries," 41-43; Heine, *Origen: Scholarship in the Service of the Church*, 48-64.

[73] *Arius*, 90.

[74] *Étude sur les 'Stromates' de Clément d'Alexandrie* (Patristica Sorbonensia 7, Paris: du Seuil, 1966), 63-66.

school was in some sense "private," in the sense of isolated from the Church. Van den Hoek, also, points to the recent scholarship which is now more inclined to view other Christian schools, like Justin's in Rome, as closely linked to a Christian community.[75]

Van den Hoek[76] also makes the interesting point that the ecclesial nature of the Alexandrian school is in fact signaled precisely by the fact that neither Clement nor Origen *use* the term "school" (*didaskalion*) to describe the context of their own work, arguing that this term was too closely linked to heretical institutions in this period. Their concern is rather to emphasize that they are teaching and working within the unbroken Tradition of the true Church. They are not to be thought of as one "school" among others. Clement therefore identifies himself and his instruction as taking place simply in the "Church," a point which distinguishes his work from heretical sects which see themselves as "schools."[77] It is also worth noting that when Rufinus translates Eusebius he calls the catechetical school the *schola ecclesiastica*, evidence that he thought of the school's primary relationship as being to the Church.[78]

There is one other point of interest: both Clement and Pantaenus are called *presbuteroi*. It is a term which at this time had a number of related meanings, but from the context in which they are described in this way it almost certainly means that they were priests.[79] Jerome, in fact, records that Clement was ordained a presbyter either when he took over the school or else a short while later.[80] And an example from Clement's writings can illustrate how he saw his own role. At the conclusion of the *Paedagogus*, he writes of how "Christ the Pedagogue" has offered his training to the catechumen in and through Clement's guidance, and he now hands the reader over to "Christ the Teacher," that is, to Christ in his teaching, rather than training, role. The catechumen, in other words, is now in a position to receive and benefit from Christ's teaching. In this final passage, with which

---

[75] "The 'Catechetical' School of Early Christian Alexandria and Its Philonic Heritage," 76-77.
[76] See the broad discussion in "The 'Catechetical' School of Early Christian Alexandria and Its Philonic Heritage," 59-87.
[77] See *Stromateis* 7.15.92.7.
[78] Rufinus, H. E. 11.7.
[79] See Eusebius, quoting from a letter from Alexander, Bishop of Jerusalem and a former pupil of Clement's (H. E. VI.11.6). Also see Clement's language in *Protrepticus* 11.113.1; *Stromateis* 3.12.90.1; 6.13.107.2; 7.1.3.3; and *Paedagogus* 3.11.63.1. Van den Hock discusses the possible meanings of *presbuteroi* in "The 'Catechetical' School of Early Christian Alexandria and Its Philonic Heritage," 77-79.
[80] Jerome, *De Viris Illustribus*, 38.6.

Clement concludes his work, he refers to himself as one who has been "appointed" in the Church to assist in this task.[81] The Greek verb is *kathistemi*, "to appoint," a verb used elsewhere to refer to ecclesiastical appointments.[82] It seems clear, then, that Clement saw himself as working in the context of ecclesial authority. He has received from the Church his commission to instruct in the faith.

To conclude this discussion, it seems clear that the leaders of the school, before Origen as well as after, and whether ordained as presbyters or acting as teachers, were not working in isolation from the Church but, on the contrary, saw themselves as working in an *ecclesial* environment. The teaching they gave was consciously transmitted as continuous with the faith that had been handed down by the apostles. The school and its teachers existed *within* the Church and within the overarching authority of Revelation and the *regula fidei*, the rule of faith. Its leaders saw themselves not only as serving the Deposit of Faith but also the sacramental deposit of grace (thus Clement, for example, condemns heretical celebrations of the Eucharist that are "contrary to the rules of the Church").[83] The apostolic Tradition is guarded by the school *for* the Church. It is also clear that, at least from Clement onwards, the teachers at the school prepared catechumens to be received into the Church. They knew themselves commissioned by the Church and they taught as her representatives as they instructed converts to the faith. The picture of a stable ecclesial institution, led by those who identified themselves as faithful to, and in continuity with, the apostolic teaching tradition, as teachers and, in some cases, priests, is therefore a plausible one. Individual Christian charismatic teachers, wandering from place to place, certainly existed in this period (Origen speaks of them in his *Contra Celsum*),[84] but Clement and Pantaenus do not fit the description of such figures.

If this picture is broadly correct, then we must describe the notion of a parallel tradition of Christian teachers and episcopal figures very carefully. The Church—both in her episcopal figures and in the leaders of the catechetical school—saw in heretical sects teachers who claimed

---

[81] See the final prayer and conclusion, *Paedagogus* 3.101ff.
[82] For the use of this verb see, for example, *H. E.* IV.14.3, in which Eusebius quotes Irenaeus's account of the appointment (*katastatheis*) of Polycarp as bishop by the apostles. We can also note *Paedagogus* 1.6.37 which indicates his possible status of presbyter: "Whether we are the shepherds who rule the churches in imitation of the Good shepherd, or the sheep..."
[83] *Stromateis* 1.19.96.1.
[84] *Contra Celsum* III.9 refers to Christian teachers wandering from village to village to spread the word.

an *alternative* tradition and succession. In the face of this, Pantaenus, Clement, Origen, and their successors, understood themselves and the school in which they worked as inseparable from the hierarchy of the Church.[85] This is what distinguished its work from that of the heretical teachers. Authentic teachers in the Church have their own expertise and place of service, and this is precisely one that supports and serves the broad communion of the whole Church.[86] Teachers, alongside deacons, priests, and bishops are *ecclesial* figures. As we will see, this helps us to understand a key feature of the school: that it regarded one of its main purposes to be the *formation of other teachers*, faithful to the apostolic tradition. The school was in part an ancient Christian teacher academy. The catechumenate was the *beginning* of a journey that was aimed at *gnosis*, the wisdom needed by those called to be teachers of the faith.

THE LIFE AND WORK OF THE SCHOOL

An overview of the corpus of writings of three central figures, Clement, Origen, and Didymus the Blind, reveals much about the character of the school and the nature of its work.[87] We begin with Clement of Alexandria (c.150-215), whose writings, as Simon Wood puts it, are "largely the literary account of the instruction and investigation conducted at the catechetical school."[88] A Greek Christian, he is known principally for three works, *Protrepticus* or *The Exhortation to the Greeks*; *Paedagogus*, or *The Instructor*; and *Stromateis*, or *Miscellanies*. There are also some shorter extant writings: *The Rich Man's Salvation*, a short treatise on Mark's account of Jesus's meeting with the rich young man, and a baptismal address, *To the Newly Baptized*. We also have his careful examination of a Gnostic writing, *Excerpts from Theodotus*, his *Eclogae Propheticae*, and some small fragments from

---

[85] Stuart Thomson, for example, argues that Clement's works express a symbiotic relationship between teachers like himself, guaranteeing the transmission of the apostolic Tradition through intellectual and scholarly means, and office-holders in the church, under whose liturgical authority he sits ("Apostolic Authority: Reading and Writing Legitimacy in Clement of Alexandria," *Studia Patristica* LXVI, ed. Markus Vinzent [Leuven: Peeters, 2013], 19-32).

[86] See, for example, the comments by Clement at the close of the *Paedagogus*, in which he lists presbyters, bishops, deacons and widows and then reminds his readers of the need for teachers who help Christians listen to the Teacher (3.12.97.2-3).

[87] Of leaders before Clement, Pantaenus has left no extant writing and the presence of Athenagoras (c. 133-190) in Philip de Side's list of teachers and leaders, who places him as the first of the leaders of the school, is sufficiently controversial for us to omit him from our discussion here.

[88] Simon P. Wood, "Introduction," *Clement of Alexandria: Christ the Educator* (Washington D.C.: Catholic University of America Press, 1954), viii.

his commentary on the Scriptures, the *Hypotyposes*. We must also at this point briefly discuss the fascinating recent discovery of a *Letter to Theodore*—also known as the Mar Saba letter, since it was found by Morton Smith in the Palestinian monastery of Mar Saba—that is claimed to be from Clement of Alexandria.[89] If authentic it would be significant for our study since the *Letter* provides additional confirmation that Mark arrived from Rome to Alexandria—although it says nothing of his founding of the Church there—and so would provide us with our earliest written evidence of Mark's apostolic activity in Alexandria. But the arguments for rejecting its authenticity are strong ones, the text evidencing, as Osborn puts it, the "presence of Clement's language and absence of Clement's ideas,"[90] a successful imitation of Clement's style, but demonstrating a misunderstanding of Clement's ideas on secrecy and tradition. The *Letter*, he argues, is a successful forgery, a view supported by Francis Watson who patiently shows that the *Letter* does not answer the questions with which Theodore was ostensibly concerned but focuses instead on validating the existence and content of a secret Gospel of Mark—a topic that parallels the academic concerns and convictions of the *Letter's* discoverer, Morton Smith.[91] Ironically, the closely imitative nature of Clement's style in the *Letter* has itself been the main reason for doubting its authenticity for some: it contains "too high a ratio of Clementine to non-Clementine traits to be authentic" and should be regarded "as a deliberate imitation of Clement's style."[92]

Clement is a polished and deeply attractive writer, his weighty expositions continually interrupted with a teasing "sense of the

---

[89] The Greek text of the *Letter* together with a critical commentary is presented in Morton Smith, *Clement of Alexandria and a Secret Gospel of Mark* (Cambridge, MA: Harvard University Press, 1973), 446-52. Morton Smith, "Clement of Alexandria and Secret Mark: The Score at the End of the First Decade," *Harvard Theological Review* 75, 4 (October 1982), 449-61, presents the initial range of views as to its authenticity. Griggs offers a useful overview in *Early Egyptian Christianity from its Origins to 451 CE*, 19-21. Stephen Patterson asserts, but overstates: "Today... there is almost unanimous agreement among Clementine scholars that the letter is authentic" ("The Secret Gospel of Mark: An Introduction," in ed. R.J Miller, *The Complete Gospels: Annotated Scholars Version* [San Francisco: Harper, 1994], 408).
[90] Osborn, *Clement of Alexandria*, 195, n.42.
[91] Francis Watson argues that the *Letter* is a forgery by Morton Smith himself in "Beyond Suspicion: On the Authorship of the Mar Saba Letter and the Secret Gospel of Mark," *Journal of Theological Studies*, New Series 61, 1 (April 2010) 128-70.
[92] A. H. Criddle, "On the Mar Saba Letter Attributed to Clement of Alexandria," *Journal of Early Christian Studies* 3, 2 (Summer 1995), 216. Tuccinardi also notes what he calls the "hyper-Clementine" quality of the *Letter*, though he remains neutral as to questions of its authenticity: "A Stylometric analysis of the Mar Saba Letter Attributed to Clement of Alexandria," *Vigiliae Christianae* 74, 3 (2020), 265-88.

humorous."[93] Philip Carrington captures well the breadth and beauty that Clement brings to his writing as the "last exponent of the old literary tradition":

> He loved the songs and myths; he was versed in the philosophers; he had read the poets; he knew something of the Eleusinian mysteries; and he felt the beauty of all these things, even as he condemned their immoralities. He is the last exponent of the old literary tradition with its grace and charm, and its wide and level appreciation of intellectual truth wherever it may be found.[94]

Not without reason, then, Jerome called him the most learned of all the fathers.[95] The Scriptures dominate his work,[96] and from the Alexandrian Jew, Philo, he learned how to unite his exegesis of the Scriptures to philosophical themes.[97] His style is thus a rich one, biblical and Christian, classical and philosophical, and he was concerned to exhibit and weave these sources constantly into his expositions. His sources are not mere decoration, but encourage his audiences to a generous breadth of learning themselves—a searching of the sources, especially biblical and philosophical, is needed for the attaining of truth, the "desirable object of a hunt, secured by hard work."[98] Not content with being an edited handbook of offerings for his readers, Clement is summoning them to an immersion in the sources themselves for the sake of their own growth and sustained learning.

Perhaps in part because of this encyclopedic approach to sources his writing can appear to lack orderliness and system. But this would be to misunderstand Clement: "He did not mean to construct a 'system of theology,' and therefore it is no wonder if his critics cannot find one."[99] His deliberate lack of a determining systematic approach flows from features of his work which are crucial to appreciate: the need to engage with the catechetical needs of the Christian community in Alexandria, with their particular questions and difficulties; the driving soteriological concern and kerygmatic emphasis that characterizes all his writings; and the desire to introduce his readers not to a system—he

---

[93] H. Ritter, "The Christian Schools of Alexandria," *The Dublin Review*, III, 6 (July–October 1864), 305.
[94] Philip Carrington, *The Early Christian Church: Volume II* (Cambridge: Cambridge University Press, 1957), 273.
[95] *Epistle* 70.4.
[96] The Scriptures are cited 5,121 times, according to Osborn (*Clement of Alexandria*, 4). See also Wood, "Introduction," xi.
[97] See Runia, *Philo in Early Christian Literature*, 338–39.
[98] *Stromateis* 1.21.1.
[99] H. Ritter, "The Christian Schools of Alexandria," 304.

was battling precisely *against* the elaborate systems of Gnosticism that were present in Alexandria — but to *Christ*, the living Lord, Pedagogue and Teacher, and to the need to be remade in his image. His work was intended to "hinder and resist the natural craving of the human spirit for a clear, transparent and definite system,"[100] for only in this way would the reader constantly be prompted to seek, beyond all systems, the *Person* of Christ, the Word and Son of the Father.

The relationship between Clement's three major writings has garnered much attention and, as we will see, the works are best conceived as a trilogy which indicate progressive stages in the journey of Christian conversion and growth, from paganism to a fully mature Christian discipleship. They trace the gradual nature of initiation into the Christian life, through the movements of conversion and initial belief, discipline, and finally Christian wisdom (possibly corresponding to the three degrees of the Neo-Platonic mysteries of purification, initiation and vision). He presents the works from a divine perspective, describing these movements as the divine Word undertaking to exhort, to train, and to teach, the opening of the *Paedagogus* setting out the relationship between these three: "Eagerly desiring, then, to perfect us by a gradation conducive to salvation, suited for efficacious discipline, a beautiful arrangement is observed by the all-benignant Word, who first exhorts, then trains, and finally teaches."[101]

Since we will be unpacking this Clementine understanding of God's work of formation carefully in the second part of this book we can be content here with a brief sketch of the content of this trilogy. The first work, *Protrepticus*, is an exhortation, a work of ardent appeal, the text alternating between a soaring beauty and biting satire. Its aim is conversion. Revealing the essential bankruptcy of pagan religion, it seeks to convince the reader of the truth of the Christian message. At the same time, it is at pains to show that there are "seeds of the Word" present in all religions and religious practices and that the Christian journey can take its starting point from these "seeds." *Paedagogus* follows this treatment of the training and formation of the person who has been attracted to Christ and now wishes to place himself under the Word's testing and tutorship. Christ as the supreme Pedagogue, or Formator, has summoned the pupil to be his and now wishes to train him in his ways. *Paedagogus* functions as a guide for the new convert to the Christian faith, placing him securely under

---

[100] The words are those of Josef Pieper ("The Philosophical Act," in *Leisure the Basis of Culture* [London: Faber and Faber, 1952], 160), but they apply well to Clement.
[101] *Paedagogus*, 1.1.3.3. See also *Stromateis* 6.1.1.3.

Christ the Pedagogue, centering on the formation of the person who is now called to take on the discipline of Christ.

The final work in Clement's trilogy is his *Stromateis*, literally a "patchwork." There is intense discussion as to its purpose. The passage we quoted from the opening of the *Paedagogus* clearly sets out the movement of the Word—from exhortation, to training, and finally to teaching—and the second volume in this sequence, *Paedagogus*, concludes the promise of this third step: Christ the Pedagogue tells those whom he has trained that "it is time for Me to lay aside teaching you as Pedagogue, and for you to hearken to the Teacher."[102] The puzzle is that *Stromateis* appears in many ways such a strange work if it is intended for teachers. In no ways does it resemble an orderly handbook, prepared for the learning of teaching skills. A strong case, though, can be made for the view that this work is indeed the promised assistance for those who need to be formed by Christ the Teacher in order to become teachers themselves, even if it appears in this patchwork form, and especially if we take seriously the focus of the first book of the *Stromateis* which concerns the place of written materials in teaching.[103] And the disparate range of topics treated is understandable if the goal of learning is the formation of a formator who can learn how to use the different disciplines, and especially philosophy, with discrimination.[104] The apparently haphazard arrangement of the whole is explicitly addressed by Clement in this first book:

> Why on earth have we judged it right for our notebooks to be organized like this? Because there is a considerable danger in betraying the ineffable word, which truly belongs to the real philosophy, to those who have an immeasurable desire to contradict everything without any justification and throw away words and phrases in complete disorder, deceiving themselves and deceiving those who cling to them.[105]

Christ the Teacher requires a "lover of the chase"[106] in the prospective teacher and catechist. There is a necessary seeking for the sake of the finding. And the "ineffable word" of truth must be protected from the lazy adherent who would communicate to others in

---

[102] *Paedagogus* 3.12.97.3–98.1.
[103] In addition to Osborn's "Teaching and Writing in the First Chapter of the *Stromateis* of Clement of Alexandria," see the discussion in his *Clement of Alexandria*, 5–15.
[104] *Stromateis* 6.10.83.1.
[105] *Stromateis* 1.2.20.1.
[106] *Stromateis* 1.2.20.1.

"complete disorder" because he had not been willing to place himself under the challenging discipline of the Teacher of the mysteries. "My present outline of memoranda" therefore "contains the truth in a kind of sporadic and dispersed fashion, so as to avoid the attention of those who pick up ideas like jackdaws."[107]

Without being systematic in character, then, the *Stromateis* examines a range of questions and points of character necessary for the development of true Christian wisdom and learning how to teach the faith. And the wisdom being offered in the *Stromateis* reinforces the emphases in the *Paedagogus*: his work is aimed especially against Gnostic parodies of wisdom which would tempt new converts into a spiritual elitism derived from a false notion of spiritual illumination, into a way of life reliant upon an intellectualism characterized by a separation between the intellectual and the broader human dimensions of the Christian way. True Christian *gnosis*, Clement argues, consists in following and sharing in the life of the Word who was made flesh and shared in our humanity. The things of the flesh are not unspiritual or to be despised on account of their fleshliness. The stages of conversion and of catechetical development are stages of growing enlightenment on the path to true wisdom, but it is not scholarship or learning in itself that is the goal of this call to Christian perfection but teaching and witness grounded in holiness and the worship of God. It is Clement who is credited with placing the concept of imitation (*mimesis*) at the heart of the Christian approach to formation, with the teacher playing a key role as the mediator of the spiritual life and of Tradition, a figure to be emulated by the student as one who was him or herself an imitator of the divine and saving Logos.[108]

The other pedagogical and theological giant teaching at the school was Origen (c.185-251). His name is Egyptian, literally "Child of Horus" – Horus being the child of the Egyptian goddess Isis by Osiris – and Origen was probably a child of a mixed-class marriage. Epiphanius, a fourth-century antagonist, claims simply that he was Egyptian, and appears to have no reason for trying to mislead on this point,[109] but his Egyptian name is not necessarily a reliable pointer to his ethnicity, for ancients, as well as moderns, named their children with a certain

---

[107] *Stromateis* 1.12.56.3.
[108] See *Stromateis* 7.3.13.1-4. On Clement's importance in the history of spirituality for prioritizing this theme see Henri Crouzel, "L'imitation et la 'suite' de Dieu et du Christ dans le premiers siècles chrétiens, ainsi que leurs sources gréco-romaines et hébraïques," *Jahrbuch für Antike und Christentum* 21 (1978), 32-33.
[109] *Panarion* 64.2.

freedom. Eusebius records Porphyry's description of him as a Greek who benefitted from a Greek education.[110] McGuckin's view that his name "suggests that he was the child of a mixed marriage between one of the *honestiores* and a woman from the class of *humiliores*"[111] is probably a good compromise, and one that would account for the fact that under the persecution by Severus, which was aimed at *citizens*, Origen remained free to attend executions of his pupils without himself suffering this fate since with his mixed-class status he would not have held citizenship.[112]

Whatever his background, his parents were able to ensure that he received a good education. Eusebius tells us of Origen's background studies in secular subjects and philosophy and his subsequent teaching of these:

> He used to introduce also to the study of philosophy as many as he saw were naturally gifted, imparting geometry and arithmetic and the other preliminary subjects, and then leading them on to the systems which are found among philosophers, giving a detailed account of their treatises, commenting upon and examining into each, so that the man was proclaimed as a great philosopher even among the Greeks themselves.[113]

Origen clearly introduced many of his pupils to a range of philosophical positions and schools, studying key texts with them, comparing and examining each, and aiming to provide his pupils with a strong philosophical background. That breadth of approach was characteristic of Middle Platonism at the time, and it seems that he shared with Clement the basic philosophical positions of that eclectic school. He also evidently exhibited a teacher's love for pupils of all degrees of aptitude, for Eusebius goes on to say,

> And many persons also of a more ignorant character he urged to take up the ordinary elementary studies, declaring that they would derive no small advantage from these when they came to examine and study the divine Scriptures. For this reason, he

---

[110] H. E. VI.19.7.
[111] *Westminster Handbook to Origen*, 3.
[112] For further discussion see Ronald E. Heine, *Origen: An Introduction to His Life and Thought* (Eugene, OR: Cascade Books, 2019), 19-21. Origen's father, Leonides, on the other hand, was beheaded while Origen was still young. Eusebius records that Origen's desire to join his father in prison and eventual martyrdom was so strong that the only way his mother prevented this was to hide his clothes. Even so, he wrote his father a letter on martyrdom, steadying him in the face of the persecution and urging him "not to change thy mind on our account" (H. E. VI.2.5-6).
[113] H. E. VI.18.3.

deemed especially necessary even for himself a training in secular and philosophic studies.[114]

Origen, like Clement, urged the serious study of all that we know today as the "liberal arts," and especially philosophy, as a necessary foundation for a true appreciation of the Scriptures and Christian doctrine.

The main body of his works are commentaries on the Scriptures. Origen's are the most extensive early commentaries on the Scriptures that we have and they were written on a massive scale, with his treatment of topics meticulous and exhaustive. His commentary on John, for example, runs to thirty-two books with the first volume dealing only with two words, "beginning" and "word," from the first verse of the Gospel. Later, after his ordination and move to Caesarea, he added collections of more popular homilies on the Scriptures. This huge corpus of homiletic work, which he would have preached following the liturgical cycle, confirms for us his consistent ecclesial focus; as Heine puts it, his scholarship "was always in the context and service of the Church," and he wrote "to solve problems in the Church."[115]

In these commentaries and homilies, the development of an allegorical exegesis was his main preoccupation. Eusebius writes of how Origen, even at a young age, was seeking in the Scriptures for meanings beyond the literal level: "he was not satisfied with reading the sacred words in a simple and literal manner, but sought something further, and busied himself, even at that age, with deeper speculations, troubling his father by his questions as to what could be the inner meaning of the inspired Scripture."[116]

His interest in the spiritual meaning of the Scriptures did not lead to any neglect into the investigation of the literal meaning: on the contrary, he was keenly alive to the grammatical, textual and literary dimensions of the sacred Scriptures, and he composed a remarkable comparative text of the Old Testament, the *Hexalpa*, in which the original Hebrew text was placed alongside a transliteration of the Hebrew into Greek, and then alongside again the Septuagint translation and three other translations into Greek which had been made by Aquila, Symmachus, and Theodotion. We have already seen

---

[114] H. E. VI.18.3-4.
[115] *Origen: Scholarship in Service of the Church*, viii. Origen was the writer of homilies and preached regularly. It is worth recalling, also, the homiletic *form* of many early Christian writings even if they did not originate as actual homilies. Jean Daniélou reminds us of the liturgical setting of much exhortation and instruction in his threefold analysis of catechesis in the early Church of kerygma, catechesis, and homily (*La Catéchèse aux Premiers Siècles*, Paris, 1968, 13-14).
[116] H. E. VI.2.9.

how scholars in the Alexandrian library painstakingly established the methodology for the text of Homer, which was so important since his works were used in all Greek education as the foundational work, the common "textbook." Origen was consciously following in this tradition of the Alexandrian literary scholars in establishing a hermeneutic for the reading of the Scripture which would allow for a consistent interpretation of the sacred Scriptures that was faithful to the Church's Tradition. Origen's wide-ranging scriptural work was also a timely and necessary one in order to respond to alternative readings and commentaries emerging from Gnostic groups:

> The idea of biblical commentary first appeared among the gnostic sages, who relied on the principle of the individual inspiration (or "illumined gnosis") of the commentator to guarantee the spiritual acumen and veracity of the comment. Origen wishes to wrest back the genre from them, by writing his own; and also to subject the idea of individual "enthusiasm"... to the more measured consensus of church tradition and literary interpretative common sense.[117]

This art of authentic scriptural interpretation, of finding the "inner" or "spiritual" meanings of the Scriptures in line with the rule of faith, came to characterize not only the catechetical school but the whole of the Alexandrian theological tradition. It is to Origen, above all, that we can credit the fact that educated pagans' disdain for the biblical text as a series of parochial stories attached to crude, anthropomorphic depictions of divinity, began to be overcome, as he painstakingly united this classical textual analysis to mystical and spiritual interpretations of the biblical text so that the Bible could take its place as the foundational text for the life of the Church and the spirituality of ordinary Christians.[118]

Alongside his work on the Scriptures, Origen also composed philosophically-informed works of theology and apologetics, notably *De Principiis*, "On First Principles," a systematic work presenting the faith which he composed in Alexandria, and his great defense of the Christian faith to a Platonist critic, *Contra Celsum*, which was written towards the end of his life, in Caesarea. Above all, he kept in sight the need to present, over and again, the central mysteries of

---

[117] McGuckin, "Origen of Alexandria on the Mystery of the Pre-Existent Church," 114, n.4.

[118] Francis Young draws attention to the importance of his work in enabling the Scriptures to become a source for *mimesis* for converts to Christianity as they found models for emulation and patterns for living in the texts (*Biblical Exegesis and the Formation of Christian Culture* [Cambridge: Cambridge University Press, 1997], 76–89).

the faith, so that the single plan of God and his love could be kept in view. McGuckin captures this key point in his description of the character of Origen's writings: we find the "grand passion to tell the epic tale... the kerygma of the divine salvation of the cosmos." In this telling, "Origen never lost sight of the one single thread that holds it all together: the restless and unswerving love of a God who is determined to bring back the cosmos to the unity of the circle of love that was its original conception and reality."[119] With this strong pastoral focus, he therefore attended to the pressing matters of practical Christian living in works which unite a warm affectivity towards the person of Christ with philosophical discussions and exegetical explorations. He wrote a powerful and influential treatise *On Prayer*,[120] "the first clear and thoroughgoing exposition, within the Christian tradition, of prayer as the contemplation of God."[121] And this style, uniting the pastoral and spiritual with the theological and philosophical, is very much to the fore in his *Exhortation to Martyrdom*—a pertinent topic for Christians of his times: Eusebius records persecutions in Alexandria under the Emperors Severus,[122] Maximin,[123] Decius,[124] and Diocletian.[125] Witness was indeed often costly for the Christians in Alexandria, and Origen also composed a *Panegyric*, unfortunately now lost, on his martyred disciples.[126] It was also a topic particularly close to his heart given the martyrdom of his own father.[127]

---

[119] McGuckin, *The Westminster Handbook to Origen*, ix.
[120] Origen's work on prayer was particularly influential through Evagrius's taking of Origen's spirituality and ascetical works into the monastic colony in Nitria and subsequently influencing Western monasticism through his disciple, John Cassian.
[121] Joseph W. Trigg, *Origen, The Bible and Philosophy in the Third-century Church* (Atlanta: John Knox Press, 1983), 157.
[122] "Now when Severus also was stirring up persecution against the churches, in every place splendid martyrdoms of the champions of piety were accomplished, but with especial frequency at Alexandria" (H. E. VI.1.1).
[123] H. E. VI.28.
[124] H. E. VI.41.
[125] H. E. VIII.9,10,13. Christian Cannuyer rightly judges that "Egyptian Christianity bore the full brunt of Rome's escalating efforts to control and suppress the growing cult" (*Coptic Egypt: The Christians of the Nile* [New York: Harry M. Abrams, 2001], 26).
[126] McGuckin points to the moderation in his treatment of this theme with the accent lying in the need to remain courageous witnesses to truth and to Christ in the face of tyrannical acts, but being careful to avoid "every hint of fanaticism or populism from the Church's tradition of martyrdom" ("Martyr Devotion in the Alexandrian School: Origen to Athanasius," in *Seeing the Glory*, 73). Cf. Origen, *Exhortation to Martyrdom*, 50.
[127] See H. E. VI.28; on Origen's own torture under Decius see H. E. VI.39. As to why he was not martyred together with some of his students whom he accompanied to their death, we have already noted that Origen was probably not "eligible" for arrest if he was not a Roman citizen since the persecutions of the Emperor

A figure who stands in this Origenist tradition of exegesis,[128] and was the final significant leader of the catechetical school whose works have to some extent been preserved, is Didymus the Blind (c. 313–398).[129] Didymus is important to us as a teacher of Jerome, of Rufinus of Aquileia, of Palladius, and of Gregory of Nazianzus, who carried the work of the school, and especially the allegorical exegetical tradition of Clement and Origen, to the next generation of Christian teachers and scholars.[130] The admiration Didymus enjoyed as a teacher is reflected in Rufinus's moving comments: he tells us that Didymus lost his eyesight as a young child, even before beginning his early schooling, but through prayer for the "illumination of the heart" and great diligence came to have the spiritual eyes that the angels themselves have, by which God is seen.[131] As well as being a memorable and inspiring teacher, Didymus was probably the author of a significant work on the Trinity, and we have extracts preserved of other theological and apologetic works.[132] We now also have a number of Scriptural commentaries available for our study thanks to the discovery of almost two thousand pages of text in 1941, the *Toura papyri*, at the site of the ancient cloister of Dair al-Qusair.[133] Five works of his have been recovered: commentaries on Genesis, the Psalms and Zechariah, together with two records of his oral teaching—on the Psalms and Ecclesiastes—giving us precious further insights into Alexandrian teaching methods, especially as they relate to the Scriptures.

Didymus's writings reveal him as a strongly catechetical figure, following Clement and Origen in reading divine history through an educational lens. Thus, for example, Job's conversations with his

---

Septimus Severus were only directed against citizens (see McGuckin, "Origen of Alexandria on the Mystery of the Pre-Existent Church," 117).

[128] Didymus's general Origenist commitments are noted by Jerome in his *Epistle* 73.
[129] The best overall introduction to his work and life is still Richard Layton's *Didymus the Blind and His Circle in Late-Antique Alexandria*. Didymus's position vis-à-vis the school is debated, but those who strike a cautionary note with regard to his significance in the school tend to do so mainly from a position of greater skepticism regarding the institutional character of the school overall.
[130] So, for example, Jerome went on to translate many of Origen's homilies into Latin, while Rufinus translated Origen's *Commentary on Romans* and part of his *Commentary on the Song of Songs*, as well as *De Principiis*.
[131] Rufinus, H. E. XI.7.
[132] For a discussion of his corpus and of questions of attribution of particular works to Didymus, see Young, *From Nicaea to Chalcedon*, 83–91 and, more recently, Grant D. Bayliss, *The Vision of Didymus the Blind: A Fourth-Century Virtue Origenism* (Oxford: Oxford University Press, 2015), 46–55.
[133] For unsettling comments on the discovery of these precious works, and the miracle of their partial survival, see Brent Nongbri, *God's Library: The Archeology of the Earliest Christian Manuscripts*, 98–100.

friends are understood as the suffering sage's attempts to educate them in the ways of God's providence: "Underlying the entirety of Didymus' hero is... the model of a teaching Job, who both patiently endures suffering and impatiently engages in impassioned debate with his friends."[134] The works reveal an intense interest in the guidance on spiritual and moral progress that the Scriptures provide, a focus that Bayliss characterizes as his "virtue Origenism" as he traces

> a constant struggle against demons, passions, and sophistry which can only be achieved by grace and a journey which is marked out by little steps, by movement from virtuous action to virtuous action, by deepening insight into the truth which lies inside the truth and an occasional hint at endless progress into the mystery of God.[135]

As with other leaders of the school we see, again, a significant use of Philo in his work as he unites the traditional use of typology to a more allegorical exegesis in this service of identifying pathways of spiritual development: "In Didymus we see most clearly how completely and unreservedly Philo had been absorbed into the Alexandrian Christian tradition."[136] A fuller discussion of the place of Philo must wait until part two, but suffice it to say now that we cannot embrace the Alexandrian school without at the same time broadly welcoming Philo's allegorical methodology, even though we shall also see the Christocentric and kerygmatic direction in which this methodology is taken by the school's exegetes.

From this brief survey of key writings of Clement, Origen and Didymus, and some of the light they throw onto the life and work of the school, we can now draw some initial conclusions about the nature and character of the Alexandrian catechetical school.

It will help to return to Eusebius's initial description of the central purpose of the school: to teach the core Christian doctrines and the Christian way of life to those wishing to be received into the Church. In Book VI of his history he tells us that Origen was eighteen when he became head of this catechetical school: he was the one, Eusebius tells us, who was "set apart for catechetical instruction,"[137] "instruction" here being a translation of the Greek *catechesis*, the New Testament term for foundational formation in the faith.[138] This general

---

[134] Layton, *Didymus the Blind and His Circle in Late-Antique Alexandria*, 79.
[135] Bayliss, *The Vision of Didymus the Blind*, 4.
[136] Runia, *Philo in Early Christian Literature*, 204.
[137] H. E. VI.3.1-3.
[138] Cf. *Rom.* 2:18; *1 Cor.* 14:19; *Gal.* 6:6. See also J. N. D. Kelly, *Early Christian Creeds*, 3rd ed. (London: Longman Group Ltd, 1972), 40-52.

use of the term continues in the Alexandrian school, but Clement and Origen begin to use it more specifically also, pioneering its use to signify especially the instruction and training that is given to candidates for baptism,[139] and it is worth noting that Clement is the earliest Christian writer to record Christ's own baptism as the model for Christian baptism in general.[140]

Origen's central task, then, as the head of the school, was to provide catechetical formation, in particular for those preparing for baptism. Later in Book VI, Eusebius notes that Origen "continued to fulfil" in Alexandria "his customary work of instruction with all zeal."[141] Eusebius also tells us that Origen enlisted the help of Heraclas, one of his pupils, to assist him in this work—"he gave him a share in the task of instruction, assigning to him the preliminary studies of those who were just learning their elements."[142] Again, the Greek term translated here as "instruction" is *catechesis*. According to Eusebius, then, the heart of the formation offered by the school is foundational instruction, including preparation for baptism.

We should note, however, that when Eusebius first introduces the school his description is a broad one: it is, he tells us, a "school of sacred learning," one that cares for "the life of the faithful in Alexandria."[143] There is an implication here of a general responsibility for the ongoing education and formation of Christians. If we accept this description at face value, understanding this care to take many forms, with the provision of catechesis being offered within the broad framework of what the Church today would describe as the evangelization of culture, then apparently disparate descriptions and emphases concerning the school and its activities in different phases of its existence can be reconciled. Catechesis in Alexandria, in other words, was undertaken as a "moment" within the broader reality of evangelization,[144] and the initiation of converts into the Christian

---

[139] Cf. the discussion in André Méhat, *Étude sur les 'Stromates' de Clément d'Alexandrie*, 62-70.
[140] *Paedagogus* 1.6.25.2. See Thomas Finn, *Early Christian Baptism and the Catechumenate: Italy, North Africa, and Egypt* (Collegeville: The Liturgical Press, 1992), 185.
[141] H. E. VI.14.11.
[142] H. E. V.15.1.
[143] H. E. V.10.1.
[144] The language of "moments" is that of the recent papal Magisterium on catechesis. In *CT*, John Paul expresses it this way: "The Apostolic Exhortation *Evangelii nuntiandi* of December 8, 1975, on evangelization in the modern world, rightly stressed that evangelization—which has the aim of bringing the Good News to the whole of humanity, so that all may live by it—is a rich, complex and dynamic reality, made up of elements, or one could say moments, that are essential and

faith was inseparable from a wide range of activities surrounding this work. The work overall was one of Christian formation understood in a holistic and inclusive way. The cultures to which the school was bringing the Gospel could not be addressed in a piecemeal fashion: rather, a worldview with an adequate philosophy, theology and pedagogy was needed, one that would *attract* the new convert, *form* the convert in thought and discipline, and provide for an *ongoing conversion* in the faith towards what the school called a true *gnosis*, an *initiation into the mystery of Christ* that would *express itself in charity and teaching*. With respect to this gaining of a fuller understanding of the faith the school maintained that it is baptism and faith that carry one towards salvation, but that providing a deeper spiritual and intellectual engagement, a Christian *gnosis*, was necessary for the establishing of an authentic Christian culture and for the formation of Christian teachers.

For the Alexandrian school, then, catechesis was placed within this broader framework of outreach and the assembling of a rich Christian culture. The elements that made up such a holistic vision of formation are treated in part two of the book: all that was involved in the initial turning to God—a missionary outreach to pagans and Jews, the witness offered by teachers and the Christian community, a formation in the classical *paideia*, and an *apologia* for the faith in response to social, political and philosophical objections (chapters five and six); a proclamation of the kerygma inviting an entry into the mystery of Christ and the adult catechumenate with instruction for baptism (chapters seven and eight); finally, the formation of teachers, mentoring them in close relationships and friendships to assist them in aiming at a Christian perfection of love and knowledge (chapter nine). The school's library and *scriptorium* would enable a particular emphasis on the study of the Scriptures since these were the crown of Christian culture, while the scholarship of its leaders would be of special service to those being formed as teachers.[145] Thus with a competence in areas of secular learning and philosophy, as well as in higher theological studies, Alexandria's catechetical school provided

---

different from each other, and that must all be kept in view simultaneously. Catechesis is one of these moments—a very remarkable one—in the whole process of evangelization" (18).

[145] Such a broad understanding of the needs of formation is continuous, as we would expect, with the earliest practices of the Church. Rétif rightly identifies three overlapping categories of *kerygma*, the basic proclamation, *catechesis* or *didache*, the teaching of converts, and *didascalia*, a more advanced instruction (A. Rétif, "Qu'est-ce que le Kérygme?," *Nouvelle Revue Théologique* LXXI (1949), 910–22).

a way forward for those who found themselves, in the words of Henry Chadwick, faced with the apparent choice between "clever, eloquently defended heresy on the one side and a dim, obscurantist orthodoxy on the other."[146]

It appears that individual leaders and teachers at the school combined different elements within this broad work of the formation of Christian culture. For example, Eusebius tells us that Pantaenus, in addition to his missionary work, was "especially eminent" with regard to his learning, including of Stoic philosophy and a deep knowledge of the Scriptures.[147] Pantaenus was clearly an "evangelist" in the broad sense of the term that we are using here, conducting initial missionary work and also teaching both philosophy and the Sacred Scriptures. Clement united in himself herald of the Gospel, catechist, and scholar. He was "famous for his study of the Holy Scriptures"[148] and also had a thorough-going knowledge of Platonic, Peritpatetic and Stoic philosophies, placing this learning at the service not only of advanced studies in the faith but also of enquirers and those seeking baptism. As we know from the *Stromateis*, Clement also taught selected students at a more advanced level, especially those whom he wanted to form as teachers in the faith. Origen writes and works from such a unified approach as well—as Robert Wilken put it, "he did not make the modern distinction between preaching and teaching,"[149] his written works including homilies, scriptural commentaries, and philosophical treatises.[150] Heraclas undertook foundational teaching and also "wore the philosophic garb."

The school, then, clearly made use of the intellectual and personal capacities of its leaders to support both an initial and an extended formation of those who were attracted to the Christian faith,[151] and it appears to have been a complex reality in which there were many types of leader, teacher, and learner. It seems likely that, in respect of this diversification of focus and interest, the school was following a model found in both the Academy and the Lyceum, with both

---

[146] *The Early Church*, New York: Dorset Press, 1986, 95.
[147] H. E. V.10.1.
[148] H. E. V.11.1.
[149] "Alexandria: A School for Training in Virtue," 18.
[150] As Henri Crouzel writes, in his review of scholarship on Origen in the seventies and eighties, there is much more interest now in understanding his work holistically, "a theology in research, not a complete system." He cites Ulrich Berner that, following Henri de Lubac, one needs to consider Origen "at his work" ("Current Theology: The Literature on Origen 1970-1988," *Theological Studies* 49 (1988), 499-500).
[151] See, for example, H. E. VI.15.1, VI.19.11, VI.19.13.

"younger" members and more mature figures, both those setting out on the catechumenal path and those who could participate in more advanced study and in teaching. Thus, in the Lyceum it appears that there were both younger learners (*neaniskoi*) and more mature figures who were probably concerned with teaching and research (*presbuteroi*).[152] The boundaries between the two groups do not seem to have been rigid and evidence suggests an attempt at personal attention to individual learners, with a variety of curricula offered to accommodate the range of learners.

What, then, might we reasonably suppose to be the curricula of the school that was available for learners beyond the central formation for those being prepared for baptism? Again, with all of the cautions that any depiction of the school must be taken as indicative of particular times and periods, we can begin from Clement's reference in the *Stromateis*[153] to the general curriculum of studies which he saw as leading to philosophy and thence to the study of divine Revelation. He offers there a defense of this kind of liberal education, its value lying in helping one gain critical thinking skills, the ability to distinguish between truth and falsehood, and in learning both how to argue and to communicate truth.[154] Eusebius's account of the school under Origen supports this general picture. Origen's own background lay in secular studies and the humanities and he made his living from early on by teaching these.[155] In order to facilitate and support the work of the school in both the catechumenal and scholarly dimensions, Eusebius tells us, Origen made the decision to divide it into two parts, placing foundational teaching under Heraclas while he dedicated himself to further studies in exegesis and theology.[156] This was perhaps a move encouraged by Hippolytus who, Jerome tells us, supplied Origen with secretaries and resources to undertake his portion of the work.[157] The ability to study and understand Christian doctrine was the prize to be won; all other studies were preparatory to this and oriented towards it. The pursuit of secular and philosophical learning were ancillary areas not to be neglected since they made it possible to

---

[152] See Diogenes Laertius V, 53, 70-71, and the extended discussion in Lynch, *Aristotle's School*, 75-92.
[153] *Stromateis* 6.10.80.1-4.
[154] *Stromateis* 6.10.81.1-6.11.91.1.
[155] H. E. VI.2.15.
[156] H. E. VI.3.1; 15. Origen had reached the point where he decided that his teaching of literature was no longer compatible with the time he needed for divine studies, leading to his disposing of all of the volumes of literature he had "so fondly cherished" (H. E. VIII.9).
[157] *De Viris Illustribus* 61.

enter into the Christian mysteries. Such preliminary studies in general education, followed by philosophy, were considered important, then, to raise one to the level at which the Scriptures could be read with real profit. In his later work, *Contra Celsum*, Origen confirmed his commitment to this pattern of learning: "after the young have been trained in general education and philosophical thought, I would try to lead them higher":[158] in other words, they were now considered ready for the Christian mysteries.

Such a picture of breadth and complexity, of a personal investment by teachers,[159] combined with a scholarship that sought to be faithful to the tradition so that it could creatively engage a range of popular and intellectual cultures, helps make sense of the tension and eventual break between Origen and Demetrius. John McGuckin plausibly argues that Origen's desire to further develop the school in a direction that reached far beyond the usual dimensions of a catechetical program focused on the preparation of converts for baptism into the Church was probably largely responsible for the increased tension between bishop Demetrius and himself. Origen's vision for the school—and here he was in continuity with Pantaenus and Clement—flowed from his keen awareness of what was needed by a Church committed to a universal mission: not only the living witness of teachers within a passionately faithful Christian community, but also the support of a well-articulated philosophy, a reliable biblical text, commentaries that were faithful to tradition and assisted readers into the deeper spiritual meanings of the text, and a high level of theological scholarship so as to reach the intelligentsia of the ancient world. The catechetical school of Alexandria would seek to mirror the universal reach and aspirations of ancient Alexandria itself. McGuckin sees in the extensive library that Origen began to build up in Alexandria, and then transferred and extended in Caesarea, an attempt to imitate the great museum and library at Alexandria.[160] Origen saw that it was essential to place catechesis within the broader task of the development of Christian culture for the sake of the conversion of the cultures around him. Bishop Demetrius may not have shared this vision for the school, although McGuckin points out that it was

---

[158] *Contra Celsum* III.58.
[159] Eusebius provides us with a vivid picture of Origen's daily life of teaching involving a deep commitment of care to his pupils: "those who were coming to him ... did not give him time to breathe (for one batch of pupils after another kept frequenting from morn to night his lecture-room)" (H. E. VI.15.1).
[160] According to Isidore of Seville, Origen's library in Caesarea amounted to thirty thousand volumes in Pamphilus's day (*Etymologia* 6.6).

in fact one that "would later be emulated by all the Alexandrian bishops from the late third century to the sixth."[161]

We have returned to the significance of libraries, that emblematic Alexandrian theme, to the shelf of books in the portrait of John Paul. It appears that there was almost certainly in Alexandria a Christian library of some kind, together with a *scriptorium* for preserving and copying texts, and it is plausible to place this at the school, precisely because of the catechetical school's commitment to scholarship and to commentary on the biblical text in particular.[162] Christian scholars at the school would not have had access to the main museum and library in Alexandria, which was reserved for the scholars in residence there, serving their needs. Using the public library would also have been problematic since it was located at the Serapeum — and later, by the Romans at the Caesarion. As shrines to pagan gods these would have been inimical to Christian leaders and thinkers. Building a collection accessible to Christians would have been necessary. David Runia notes that it was almost certainly the Alexandrian school during the leadership of Pantaenus that rescued the works of Philo from oblivion by placing them in its library,[163] and Clement must have had access to a well-developed library: "The multitude of sources that reached him — whether in the form of extracts or complete works — proves how richly endowed his immediate environment was."[164] It is reasonable, then, to suppose that this was one assembled by the school itself. We also know that, in addition, Origen collected his own personal library, which eventually moved with him to Caesarea.[165]

To close, it is helpful to look to the account given by Gregory Thaumaturgus of how Origen taught his brother and himself in Caesarea. Although this account is from a slightly later period, it fits well

---

[161] "Origen as Literary Critic in the Alexandrian Tradition," 89–91.
[162] Zuntz points to the evidence that Alexandria had a biblical text during the second half of the second century superior to others (G. Zuntz, *The Text of the Epistles: A Disquisition upon the Corpus Paulinum* [London, 1953], 273). On Christian community libraries in the early centuries see also Hengel, *Studies in the Gospel of Mark*, 77–78. "Christian communities, which usually came into being in the larger cities by splitting off from the synagogue communities, would as a rule from the beginning have a 'book chest' with the most important writings of the Old Testament, which were then gradually supplemented by their own Christian writings."
[163] *Philo in Early Christian Literature*, 135.
[164] Annewies Van den Hoek, "How Alexandrian was Clement of Alexandria? Reflections on Clement and his Alexandrian Background," 190.
[165] Books and any real estate were often considered at this time to belong to the head of a school, but we have no reason to think that Origen took with him more than his own private collection, disaggregated as necessary from that of the school.

with what we know of the Alexandrian school.[166] The areas of study through which Origen led Gregory and his brother Athenodorus can be classified in this way: work began with an initial period of moral purification, a training in life; a study of dialectics followed, the most useful part of logic; after this came a study of physics, including the science of the earth (geometry) and of the heavens (astronomy); and this was then complemented by a study of the good life, of ethics. Finally, they undertook together a study of theology, the crown of all subjects. While we cannot pin down with accuracy from this single account exactly where Origen—and indeed Clement—stood with regard to the exact ordering of topics,[167] Gregory's tribute to Origen does confirm for us the broad range of studies offered in the ongoing formation of teachers, as well as the all-important integration of topics around the teaching of the faith.

Indeed, the question of the ordering of studies, while important, should probably not be overemphasized. As Wilken has pointed out, we must not misunderstand what Gregory describes as interested in expressing a rigid curriculum of studies, a set of textbook exercises.[168] What his account reveals is above all the focus on the *individuals* being taught: the whole thrust of Gregory's address is to help us to realize how important to him was the personal, soul-to-soul leading by Origen. We shall return to this point in chapter nine.

---

[166] "The Oration and Panegyric Addressed to Origen." See also the discussion in Pierre Nautin, *Origène: Sa vie et son œuvre* (Paris: Éditions Beauchesne, 1977), 180-97, although he seems unduly skeptical as to whether this represents the range of Origen's teaching in Alexandria.

[167] Schools of philosophy tended to classify subjects according to the three broad areas of physics, ethics and logic but varied in their preferences regarding the order in which they should be taught. Thus, for example, Stoics and the Old Academy typically ordered studies as physics, ethics and logic (see Dillon, *The Middle Platonists*, 63-65), whereas we find Aristotle ordering studies as ethics, physics, logic (*Topics* I.14, 105b19ff). Origen's ordering might owe something to Philo, who generally argued for logic, ethics and physics, although he was not consistent in his preferences.

[168] Cf. Robert Wilken, "Alexandria: A School for Training in Virtue," 19.

PART II

The Alexandrian Catechetical Tradition

CHAPTER 5

Serving the Paideia of the Lord Jesus

THE ALEXANDRIAN CATECHETICAL SCHOOL laid the foundations for a magnificent vision of Christian education and formation through its appropriation of the Greek and Jewish understanding of *paideia*.

As we have seen, classical Greek education in the form of what was called the *paideia* was the foundation of education in Alexander's empire. Inherited from Plato and Isocrates, the liberal arts in the early Christian period were generally agreed to consist of seven subjects: the three literary branches of grammar, rhetoric and dialectic, followed by the four mathematical branches of arithmetic, music, geometry and astronomy, classified in the Middle Ages as the *trivium* and the *quadrivium*. This approach to general education was probably already established by the fourth century BC and was taken over wholesale into the Roman educational world.[1] These studies were generally undertaken as preparatory to philosophy which was regarded as the "crown" of education.[2] This educational heritage was present throughout the whole of the period of ancient Alexandria that we are considering. Greece was eventually to become a province of the Roman Empire and Alexandria governed by prefects accountable to Rome, but the *paideia* was only thereby spread further abroad, through the reaches of the Roman Empire. The words of Horace are often quoted in this regard: "Greece, the captive, made her savage victor captive, and brought the arts into rustic Latium."[3] Classical Rome took over the Greek conception of the *paideia* wholesale; the Greek *paideia* was the prototype which was transferred into the Latin-speaking world of the Romans.

GREEK PAIDEIA

Derived from the Greek for child, "pais," *paideia* denoted the Greek understanding of education. But the meaning of the term is broader than that which we would typically use to describe education. In his classic work on the subject, Werner Jaeger wrote of how challenging

---

[1] See Marrou, *A History of Education in Antiquity*, 244-45.
[2] See, for example, Plutarch, *Moralia* 7c-d.
[3] Horace, *Epistles*, Book II.1, lines 156-57. Marrou writes of the Roman adoption of the Greek *paideia*: "It was not even a case of imitating; it was on the whole a pure and simple transfer" (*A History of Education in Antiquity*, 265).

paideia is to translate: "It is impossible to avoid bringing in modern expressions like *civilization, culture, tradition, literature,* or *education*. But none of them really covers what the Greeks meant by *paideia*. Each of them is confined to one aspect of it: they cannot take in the same field as the Greek concept unless we employ them all together."[4] The Greek understanding of *paideia* was rooted in the centrality of the liberal arts, and the concept included not only the range of subjects to be taught, but also an understanding of the aims of this education—which was ultimately the development of the whole of a culture—and also the educational processes, the inculturation of a person into this cultural heritage which was to be transmitted from generation to generation. It is crucial to appreciate the breadth of this concept, for in time *paideia* came to be translated by *doctrina* and one is in danger of misunderstanding what the Church means by "handing on Christian doctrine" if one thinks of this simply as the art of teaching a range of topics clearly and well. The transmission of doctrine, of *paideia*, is best understood as *the handing on of Christian culture*, which includes the learning of all of the practices involved in Christian living and the expression of Christian life and belief in and through what one makes and how one acts.[5]

To think about what exactly the Church took over in its own vision for education and culture it is helpful to distinguish between "old" and "new" *paideia*. Originally, as the etymology suggests, it indicated an education for children until adolescence. Old Athenian education, or *paideia*, consisted in voluntary formal classroom education for those who could afford it, and was limited to the elementary stage; once completed, one was expected to gain further education through life in the city.[6] It consisted of both physical and intellectual education and the elements together were intended to develop the basic virtues of the good citizen.[7] For each area of education there were private, specialist teachers, paid by the Athenian families who used their services, and the education and training would normally have taken place in either a gymnasium or *palaestra*. At some point—the evidence is not clear as to exactly when, though certainly by the fifth century BC—a compulsory military training for young men aged eighteen to twenty (*epheboi*) was added.

---

[4] *Paideia: The Ideals of Greek Culture*, I, 5.
[5] See the careful discussion of the use of Latin terms to capture aspects of the riches of the Greek in Marrou, *Saint Augustin et la fin de la culture antique*, 549-60.
[6] See Plato, *Laches* 178a-180a; *Protagoras* 326c-d.
[7] For details of Old Athenian education see Marrou, *A History of Education in Antiquity*, 36-45, and Lynch, *Aristotle's School*, 32-37.

The "new" *paideia* appeared with the developments in education in the latter half of the fifth century offered by the sophists.[8] Led in the early stages by itinerant foreign teachers, the sophists offered intellectual education in different disciplines beyond that which was available at the elementary stage, a broader curriculum of studies that completed the general education that the young should study, the *encyclia*, consisting of grammar, rhetoric, dialectic, geometry, arithmetic, music and astronomy. As with the existing teachers, they offered their lessons in gymnasia or *palaestrae* or in private homes. There was no overall "school of thought" that these new teachers represented; what was distinctive about this development was the advanced instruction that they offered. We know that this development, although it clearly seems to represent an advance on what was available within the older form of education, was also controversial. Socrates seems to have clashed with the sophists concerning fundamental ideas about how to practice *paideia* and was by no means the only figure to do so.[9] The points around which Socrates challenged the sophists are instructive, since they indicate themes that are important for understanding the school's conception of formation. From Plato's writings and from those of Xenophon[10] we can see that Socrates agreed with the sophists in believing that education beyond the elementary stage was indeed important, and also that it should be strongly intellectual in character, providing a genuine education in virtue through true knowledge.[11] Where they seem to have disagreed was in how such an education might be acquired.

For Socrates, two closely-related things were vitally important: first, the integration of teaching with the teacher. As Jaeger put it, "The whole of Socratic literature, with one voice, denies that Socrates's doctrine can be detached from his individual self."[12] The person of the teacher is crucial to the other's ability to achieve knowledge. A beautiful description of how Plato saw the potential for insight emerging out of extended dialogue between pupil and teacher is given in his *Seventh Letter*: "after long-continued intercourse between teacher and pupil, in

---

[8] For a discussion of the significance of this new movement in education see Jaeger, *Paideia: The Ideals of Greek Culture*, I, 286-331.
[9] On the general character of the sophists see Guthrie, *A History of Greek Philosophy*, III, 27-54 and for the discussion about the Socratic response, 325-77.
[10] The Platonic view of Socrates is also evidenced in the *Memorabilia* of Xenophon. For a defense of the validity of using their joint account see Guthrie, *A History of Greek Philosophy*, III, 9-10.
[11] See, for example, the discussion in Plato, *Kleitophon* 407a-409a and *Laches* 178a-180c.
[12] Jaeger, *Paideia: The Ideals of Greek Culture*, II, 36-37.

joint pursuit of the subject, suddenly, like light flashing forth when a fire is kindled, it is born in the soul and straightway nourishes itself."[13]

The second point complements this: Socrates seems to have believed that ongoing education is best furthered in a community setting, in dialogue with others, in and through an apprenticeship in what one might call the "school of life." What was needed, then, for this kind of education to be successful, was to purify and spiritualize these associations. Consistent with these points, Socrates remained in Athens, unlike the sophists who moved from city to city. Providing a persistent personal presence to those whom he taught was a key conviction and feature of his life, as he sought out young people in public places to engage them in discussion.[14] This basic stability of life allowed for the growth of friendships among those who were taught. It is significant that, in around 388/387 BC, Plato followed the example of Socrates in committing himself to teaching in Athens and gave expression to this virtue of stability by founding a permanent school, the Academy, that would survive him, both physically and spiritually.

The figure of Plato dominates the most fruitful period for the development of the *paideia* in ancient Greece regarding the emergence of an ideal of culture and education. This new ideal took shape in the fourth century, in the wake of the fall of Athens in 404 BC.[15] The conception of education up to this point had been focused on what was needed to equip the democratic city-state with free persons formed to actively participate in developing that community ethically, artistically, culturally, and politically. The great epics of Homer, the forms of tragedy and comedy that had been laid down in the fifth century, the philosophies of nature, the understanding and practice of the democratic system of self-government by free persons, the founding of the Delian league, and the achieving of all of this even in the face of the might of the Persian empire, came to a point of necessary re-evaluation through the crisis of the Athenian defeat in the Peloponnesian War. Through the work of Plato in particular the concept of the *paideia* now went through a process of spiritualization. "Its journey towards a new paideia started with its realization that a newer and higher ideal of state and society was necessary, but it ended with the search for a new God."[16] The focus and intent of *paideia* moved from a form of education that

---

[13] *Seventh Letter* 341c.
[14] See, for example, Socrates speaking with the group of young men at the Lyceum, Plato, *Euthydemus* 271a.
[15] On the significance of this crisis see Jaeger, *Paideia: The Ideals of Greek Culture*, II, 3-12.
[16] Jaeger, *Paideia: The Ideals of Greek Culture*, II, 8.

enabled a mature participation in a free society, the Greek *polis*, to one that enabled a person to participate in Truth, the ultimate spiritual Reality. The Platonic *paideia* aimed at *participation in the Absolute*. This spiritualizing of the concept meant a new openness to other cultures and also to Jewish and Christian monotheism. Plato's revisioning of *paideia* allowed for the transferring of this education from the Greek city-state onto the universal world stage where, in its new cultural form, it was taken up in Alexander's Hellenistic empire. It would find a point of flourishing in Alexandria. The school was to see itself as bringing this search to completion under the gift of the Christian Revelation.

JEWISH PAIDEIA

The Christian completing of the *paideia* took into account not only this classical heritage of the Greeks and its Platonic revisioning, but also the understanding of *paideia* that was introduced through the interaction between Greek and Jewish culture, and especially of Alexandrian Judaism's adjusting of the concept.

A few words first about Jewish education. The teacher was a crucial figure in Judaism, reflecting the conviction that God has revealed himself to his people both as Teacher and Redeemer, and that this divine Revelation is now to be handed on within human structures and institutions. "Torah" simply means instruction, and it is this instruction from God that is to be taught and learned, and is to form the basis for personal and social life.[17] Those responsible for the transmission of this Revelation were thus accorded a position of great respect. We see from the Old Testament that in the first place this meant the parents, for the family was recognized as the center of education and formation, a point made clear in the account of the *Shema* given in the *Book of Deuteronomy*:

> Hear, O Israel: The Lord our God is one Lord; and you shall love the Lord your God with all your heart, and with all your soul, and with all your might. And these words which I command you this day shall be upon your heart; and you shall teach them diligently to your children, and shall talk of them when you sit in your house, and when you walk by the way, and when you lie down, and when you rise.[18]

---

[17] "The survival of the Jews and Judaism is in a large measure due to the continuous emphasis, throughout Jewish history, upon the transmission of ideas and practices from old to young and from one generation to another" (J. B. Miller, "The Role of Education in Jewish History," in ed. L. Finklestein, *The Jews: Their History, Culture and Religion* [New York: Harper and Row, 1960], II, 1234).

[18] *Deut.* 6:4-7.

The *Shema*, lying at the heart of the Law, is directed towards parents and their responsibility for handing on the commandments to their children, and throughout the Wisdom literature also it is assumed that education is primarily the duty of the father and mother.[19] The education given in the family was then complemented in the period of the Second Temple with that given in the synagogue.[20] Prayers were offered in the synagogue, but its main purpose was as a place for instruction in the Law. The family was supported, then, from exilic times onwards, by synagogue-based education, led by the "rabbi" (the Hebrew term for "teacher").[21] Here the Law was expounded and interpreted as the synagogues became the main centers for education. Elementary Jewish schools also began to appear during the first century AD. In fact, during the reign of Nero, the high priest Joshua ordered that schools, known as "Houses of the Book," be established in every Jewish community.[22] The curriculum was strictly religious: the Law, both written and oral, with the main teaching methodology being learning by repetition, although there was often also discussion of the interpretation of the Law. Once the translation of the Septuagint appeared "it would seem only likely that the Pentateuch would have played a very similar role in Jewish education to that of Homer in Greek."[23] In other words, we can assume that Jewish education in Alexandria was based on the Septuagint, just as Greek education was grounded solidly on Homer.

A further important development should be noted. The rabbis who taught in the synagogues often gathered students around them; communities were formed under these teachers. Here we begin to see the crossover with the philosophical schools, for these rabbinic relationships with their pupils were gradually influenced by the philosophical notion of the teacher with his followers, so that there was

---

[19] For example, see *Prov.* 1:8; 6:20, and so on.

[20] The earliest evidence we have from inscriptions for the existence of buildings designated as synagogues in fact appears in Egypt in the third century B.C. The synagogues were places of meeting, instruction, and worship.

[21] Rabbi is therefore the equivalent term to the Greek *didaskalos*, "teacher." From the period of the Babylonian captivity onwards, in the Jewish Diaspora, *rabbi* was regularly translated by *didaskalos*. In the New Testament, what is provided in the synagogues is always described as *didaskein*, "teaching": see, among many instances, Matt. 13:54; Mk. 1:21; Lk. 4:15; 6:6; Jn. 6:59; Acts 14:1. For an overview of Jewish educational structures during the Old Testament period, see Eugene Kevane, *Jesus the Divine Teacher* (Bloomington: AuthorHouse, 2005), 82–95.

[22] Often these elementary schools were themselves placed in the synagogues, though sometimes in other meeting places with the same legal privileges as the synagogues. Also see Marrou, *A History of Education in Antiquity*, 316–17 on rabbinical schools.

[23] Sebastian Brock, "The Phenomenon of the Septuagint," 16.

an interlinking of the Greek concept of the *paideia* with the Jewish tradition of education. This, in fact, is the origin of the word "disciple" (in Greek, *mathetes*), which is drawn from the Greek philosophical tradition.[24] The Greek term can also refer to an apprentice,[25] and it gradually evolved to indicate an adherent of a great teacher or master.[26] We should note that there was a less well developed tradition of the teacher-disciple or master-disciple relationship in the Old Testament, so this practice was taken largely from Greek culture.[27] The teacher-disciple relationship found its apex, of course, in Jesus and his circle of the Twelve. Thus, as we have already seen, it was natural for leaders of the catechetical school in Alexandria to wear the philosopher's robe and for the school to mirror certain features and traditions of the philosophical schools of the time. They were acting as Jesus himself had when he gathered his disciples to him.

What happened to the concept of *paideia* within Alexandrian Judaism? In the first place, the Jewish form of *paideia* came to be seen as *instruction in Jewish wisdom*, as is clear from the Septuagint where the term *paideia* occurs more than a hundred times, and especially in the Wisdom literature.[28] We know that Jesus saw himself in this tradition, identifying himself with the figure of Wisdom and therefore as the One who is able to lead a person into true understanding through discipleship.[29] Closely linked to the notion of wisdom was

---

[24] For a generally reliable account of this dependence of the rabbi-disciple relationship on Greek models, see the entry by K. H. Rengstorf in ed. G. Kittel, *Theological Dictionary of the New Testament* (Grand Rapids: William B. Eerdmans, 1967), IV. 415–60. Note also the corrections by Michael J. Wilkins, *Discipleship in the Ancient World and Matthew's Gospel*, 2nd ed. (Eugene: Wipf & Stock Publishers, 2015), 13–22, showing that apparent negativity towards the term in many of Plato's writings that Rengstorf takes to mean a general antipathy to the concept and practice of discipleship is better understood as aimed against certain Sophist practices and epistemological positions.

[25] Note that the "disciple" here is one who learns to practice a skill: thus, in Plato's *Meno* (90e), the man learning to play a flute is a "disciple" (*mathetes*) as is the trainee doctor in *The Republic* (X.599c).

[26] See Wilkins, *Discipleship in the Ancient World and Matthew's Gospel*, 41–42.

[27] Wilkins again offers useful corrections to the view that the concept of discipleship is entirely lacking from the Old Testament, drawing attention to the use of *talmîdh* and *limmûdh* that "indicates some kind of learning and training and personal relationship in ancient Israel from a master to a pupil/disciple" (*Discipleship in the Ancient World and Matthew's Gospel*, 52, and see 89–91). But the Hellenistic influence on the development of Jewish educational practices remains the most important point to note.

[28] Thus, Duane Garrett describes the book of Proverbs as in a particular way "the textbook of Israelite paideia" (*Proverbs, Ecclesiastes, Song of Solomon* [Nashville: Broadman, 1993], 57).

[29] Matt. 12:42. See also Matt. 11:28–29 which echoes the call of Wisdom in *Ecclus.* 51:23–27.

the concept of mystery which was also widespread in Jewish literature in the Ptolemaic period, and would have been familiar to the Jewish community in Alexandria. In the Septuagint, "mystery," *musterion*, is found especially in the wisdom and apocalyptic literature—Judith, Tobit, the Wisdom of Solomon, Ecclesiasticus (Sirach), and Daniel.[30]

How does this distinctive Jewish contribution to education mesh with the Greek understanding of *paideia*? We can find one answer in Philo's detailed discussion of the integration of classical *paideia* with the Scriptures.[31] In his work *De congressu quaerendae eruditionis gratia*, Philo developed an allegorical interpretation of Abraham's relationship with Hagar and Sarai as recounted in Genesis 16:1–6 to explore the relationship of the arts and sciences to philosophy and this to divine Wisdom. The allegorical discussion is rich and complex and it is interesting that the main images he uses for these educational relationships are those of marriage and the generation of new life.[32] Philo argues that this story must be more than one simply of jealousy between two women; he understands it to be about Abraham speaking of the role of the liberal arts as the appropriate training of the mind for philosophy, which in turn is the handmaid to revealed theology. Allegorically, then, Sarai is presented as the figure of wisdom, who is not yet capable of bearing a child for Abraham and so has recourse to Hagar who represents the preliminary studies which must first be taken for there to be a fruitful union. "For we are not capable as yet of receiving the impregnation of virtue unless we have first mated with her handmaiden, and the handmaiden of wisdom is the culture gained by the primary learning of the school course ... He then who gains wisdom by instruction will not reject Hagar, for the acquisition of these preliminary subjects is quite necessary."[33] The passage, says Philo, asks the pupil who wishes to learn to go first to the handmaid to learn from her, before turning to the true wife, which is divine wisdom. But in doing so, the pupil must not forget

---

[30] So, for example, see *Jud.* 2:2; *Tob.* 12:7–11; *Wis.* 2:22; 6:22; 14:1ff; *Ecclus.* 22:22; 27:16–21; *Dan.* 2:18–47.

[31] For an analysis of Philo's views on the liberal arts and sciences see Alan Mendelson, *Secular Education in Philo of Alexandria* (Cincinnati: Hebrew Union College Press, 1982), and Jason M. Zurawski, "Mosaic Torah as Encyclical Padeia: Reading Paul's Allegory of Hagar and Sarah in Light of Philo of Alexandria," in eds. K. M. Hogan, M. Goff and E. Wasserman, *Pedagogy in Ancient Judaism and Early Christianity* (Atlanta: SBL Press, 2017), 283–307.

[32] We can find the Platonist background to the notion of education and its transmission as generation in the *Symposium* 206e–207a.

[33] Philo, *De congressu quaerendae eruditionis gratia* III.9; V.24. Hagar is an Egyptian, and Philo sees Egypt as the symbol for the senses and for the lower forms of learning which are concerned with sense knowledge.

his true wife: the handmaiden is necessary but must give way to the sovereign lady, the true wife, divine Revelation.[34] Thus Alexandrian Judaism in its Hellenizing aspects, represented here by Philo, looked to an integration of the Scriptures with the Greek *paideia*.

There is a further important aspect to this when we look at how the relationship between education and correction was developed in Jewish educational thought. The work of human education was placed in the overarching context of God's education of his people, of his redemptive activity as a response to human disobedience and sin. From this perspective, one does not view education simply as a process in which one encourages a natural blossoming of innate qualities in a pupil; rather, educational activity must be accompanied by a necessary *conversion* in the pupil. Becoming educated is a matter of gaining the wisdom that comes from God and this requires training and effort. The discipline that is involved in this educative process is analogous to the authentic love of a parent. Thus, in the book of Proverbs the reader is counseled, "My son, do not despise the Lord's discipline (*paideia*) or be weary of his reproof, for the Lord reproves him whom he loves, as a father the son in whom he delights."[35]

In this understanding of how education is linked to correction we can see an interesting development as Judaism and Hellenism come into dialogue. The Septuagint translation of "discipline" in the verses we have just quoted from Proverbs is a derivative of *paideia* — the reader is asked not to despise the "*paideia* of the Lord." Just as in Greek culture there was a curriculum and sequence of studies leading one ultimately to wisdom, so the Lord has *his paideia*, a pathway of training and formation for the sake of heavenly wisdom. In the Septuagint, the Hebrew verb *yāsar*, meaning both to "instruct" and also to "chastise," "discipline," or "correct," is often translated by the verb *paideuó* while the related *mûsār YHWH*,[36] meaning the chastising guidance, the educational and disciplinary dealings of the Lord in history, is often translated by the Greek *paideia*. What we can see, then, is that in the Septuagint the two concepts of teaching and instruction on the one hand and discipline and correction on the other are brought together to provide an overall vision of *instruction through discipline*.[37]

---

[34] See *De congressu* XIV.73-80.
[35] *Prov.* 3:11-12. It is a Platonic view as well: Plato proposes in the *Gorgias* that it is a good to be punished by God for our remediation (525b). Accepting this truth allows one to take part in the great spiritual contest of life (526d-e).
[36] See *Deut.* 11.2.
[37] In the New Testament we thus find the two meanings of *paideia* present, as instruction and as discipline. So, for example, *paideia* appears as instruction in

In Philo's work that we have just discussed, *De congressu quaerendae eruditionis gratia*, he comments on this same passage in Proverbs that speaks of the discipline of the Lord, and his interpretation sheds further light on how this notion of a disciplining *paideia* was understood in Alexandrian Judaism. He notes there that although the connection between correction and punishment and education might seem a negative and limited perspective, this *paideia* is what turns "our acknowledgement of God into kinship with Him."[38] It is the *paideia* of discipline which makes one a son of his father, which brings one into a filial relationship with God. God's disciplining is not to be thought of as evil, for God is not a doer of evil; on the contrary, "God is good and the cause of what is good, the benefactor, the savior, the nourisher, the enricher, the bountiful giver."[39] What the Jewish educational tradition means by this discipline must not be understood crudely or in a simplistic fashion. The discipline of God's *paideia*, while including the dimension of corporeal discipline, should be understood as the rebuking of vice by virtue and of foolishness by wisdom. God educates us in the midst of life, correcting our crookedness so that we can receive sonship.

---

this passage from *Acts*: "Moses was instructed (*epaideuthe*) in all the wisdom of the Egyptians" (*Acts* 7:22) and as punishment in Pilate's announcement of his decision to whip Jesus: "I will therefore chastise (*paideusas*) him ... and release him" (*Lk.* 23:16). Pilate is treating Jesus as a child who needs to be punished. We can say that, within God's design, Jesus is being disciplined as our Representative. For examples of the scriptural use, see W. F. Arndt and F. W. Gincrinch, *A Greek-English Lexicon of the New Testament and other Early Christian Literature*. 4th rev. ed. (Cambridge: Cambridge University Press, 1952), 608. For the Septuagint translations of Proverbs and the use of *paideuō* and *paideia* see also Karina Martin Hogan, "Would Philo have recognized Qumran *Musar* as Paideia?," in eds. K. M. Hogan, et al., *Pedagogy in Ancient Judaism and Early Christianity*, 81–100. The Septuagint translation has sometimes been seen as a *change* in Jewish religious thinking during the Hellenistic period, from the Hebrew idea of a God who corrects his people to one who educates them towards virtue. But this view is too simple: the Septuagint use of *paideia* and its cognates still includes the notion of bodily correction, a sense that is absent from the classical Greek use. What we in fact see in the Septuagint is a uniting of the notion of *paideia* as formation with the traditional biblical understanding of God's correcting guidance, thus establishing a use of the term that includes both formation *and* correction, so that the classical view of *paideia* now takes on nuances of chastisement. See the discussion by Patrick Pouchelle who, after having mapped the correspondence between *yasar* and *paideuō*, examines the possible reasons Jewish translators would have chosen this Greek term to translate the Hebrew *yasar*: "Kyropaideia versus Paideia Kyriou: The Semantic Transformation of Paideia and Cognates in the Translated Books of the Septuagint," in eds., K. M. Hogan, et al., *Pedagogy in Ancient Judaism and Early Christianity*, 101–34.

[38] *De congressu* XXXI.177.
[39] *De congressu* XXX.171. In Proverbs the disciplining is clearly for the sake of the good of the one being corrected. See 13:24; 19:18; 23:13; 29:17.

The Deuteronomic school had already presented God's educational work in relation to his people, providing a broad interpretative framework for how to understand the history of the people: it saw this history as a recurring cycle of sinful action followed by punishment by God, out of which arises a sense of the need for national repentance and the learning of God's ways anew. This was the pattern of God's ongoing education of his people, teaching them his ways. Disasters, both natural and political, were interpreted as a means of this training and chastisement by God: "I will come against the wayward people to chastise them."[40] And into this cycle of sin, punishment and repentance, the prophets were those who spoke God's words of instruction and guidance. In their teaching, the prophets referred the people to the Law that had been given for their instruction. It is here, in the Law, that God provides his commandments, his statutes and his ordinances for the restoration of human conduct and renewal of life that will allow the people to live in covenant with him.

In essence, the biblical wisdom literature took this broad understanding and approach of God's educational ways and saw this pattern as descriptive also of God's relationship with each *individual*. The wisdom books thus *universalize* the encounter of God with his people, teaching the path to true wisdom for every person, a path that involves not only intellectual application and effort but more fundamentally a reformation of one's life through being placed under God's disciplinary guidance.[41] It is interesting that the Septuagint translation of the wisdom literature also brings out the intensely *personal* nature of this formation. For example, with respect to the father's appeal to his son in Proverbs 19:20, the Hebrew text's more generic advice, "Listen to advice and accept instruction, that you may gain wisdom for the future," has been translated so as to stress the concrete relationship of the father to his son and the personal nature of the father's *paideia* as a summary of the wisdom God has taught him and that he now wishes to hand on to his son: "Listen, son, to the *paideia* of your father, that you may become wise toward your end."

It was upon this joint Greco-Roman and Jewish heritage, then, that the Alexandrian school developed her own distinctive philosophy

---

[40] Hos. 10:10.
[41] While making this general point, we should not think of any artificial divide between Deuteronomy and the Wisdom literature: Deuteronomy is itself associated with the theme of wisdom and shows many points of contact both with the Wisdom literature of the Bible and other Near Eastern wisdom texts. For a helpful discussion see John J. Collins, "Wisdom and Torah," in eds., K. M. Hogan, *et al.*, *Pedagogy in Ancient Judaism and Early Christianity*, 59–79.

of education and curriculum, drawing not only upon the Greco-Roman *paideia*, but also integrating these ways in which Judaism had developed its own understanding of wisdom, discipline and formation. Through the work of Hellenizing Jews like Philo and through the availability of the Septuagint, the Jewish understanding of the disciplining work of the Lord in the history of his people, the *"paideia* of the Lord," was united to the Greco-Roman understanding of *paideia* so that the Greek liberal studies were now united to the truth of the wise and correcting guidance of God. Clement and Origen, then, laid the Christian framework for universalizing the story of God's engagement with the Chosen People. In part this was achieved, following Philo, through an allegorizing of the sacred Scriptures, showing how the particularities of the historical Hebrew story of salvation are also signs of God's universal pedagogy, and in part through uniting the Scriptures to dogmatic frameworks interpreted as pedagogical truths, accessible through the universal avenues of reason and philosophy.[42]

THE CHURCH: THE SETTING OF THE LORD'S *PAIDEIA*

"The Church is the school" and Christians must run to "the good mother as little ones."[43] In the Alexandrian transposition of these Greek and Judaic themes around the concept of *paideia* the community of the Church was seen as the setting for the learning, teaching and practice of Christian doctrine, of *paideia*, the place where Christian culture is received and transmitted, while the key of familial relationality takes on a new prominence. The concept of *paideia* was related to God's one covenantal plan, brought to completion in Christ and now understood in terms of the Father raising up sons and daughters in his only Son through his work of formation and discipline.

We can see this theme already emerging in the Pauline Scriptures: in the Letter to the Ephesians the notion of *paideia* appears in the guidance given to parents to bring up their children in the *paideia kyriou*, the discipline and instruction of the Lord,[44] a clear echo of the Jewish commitment to the centrality of the family in education, now taken into the Christian understanding of the home as a privileged place of formation of children. In the Alexandrian Christian development of

---

[42] Cf. Bertrand de Margerie's comment: "In some sense biblical language only achieves its full universality when it becomes dogmatic language" (*The Christian Trinity in History*, tr. Edmund J. Fortman [Still River, MA: St. Bede's Publications, 1982], 96).
[43] *Paedagogus* 3.12.98.1, 3.12.99.1
[44] See *Eph.* 6:4.

paideia this familial language takes on a central importance. In the following chapters we will see how the Alexandrian school understood the aim of the divine *paideia* precisely as the ongoing formation of adopted sons and daughters of God; the Church, within God's plan, as the mother who nurtures and educates; and the teacher-guide as Christ himself, described as a pedagogue, or household tutor, raising sons and daughters in the household of the Father. Overarching all and contextualizing all is the relationship of the divine Son to his Father, into whose relationship all are called to baptism and Christ-like maturity.

The Church, then, was seen as the living community in which this new perspective was learned and this formation took place. The newness of the Christian *paideia* flowed not so much from its adjustment of the Greek *paideia* in this or that aspect, but rather from its placing *all* natural religion and secular learning in the context of the great truths of Revelation concerning the economy of salvation and of God's action in history and in the life of the person. And these truths were taught, practiced, and celebrated in the Church.

We noted earlier that one of the reasons Socrates criticized the sophists of his day was that he held that education going further than the elementary level is best achieved in a community setting, in dialogue with others, in and through an apprenticeship in what one might call the "school of life." This point the Church took up in earnest, focusing on the Church, the Christian community, as the school in which such education would be achieved. Having this overarching educational setting, Christians did not originally seek to found their own preparatory classical schools of learning, setting themselves apart from pagans studying this same heritage.[45] The Church called herself, in Greek, the *ekklesia*, which was the term originally given to the assembly of the citizens of the Greek small city-state. The Socratic theme of education in the city was now transferred to the Church, the new *ekklesia*, which also embraced schools like the Alexandrian catechetical school, and also — centrally — the family, since the household was the main locus for raising children in the "*paideia* of the Lord." It would in time also embrace types of intentional Christian community such as monasticism.

---

[45] In the early centuries, there was no attempt at developing a parallel school system apart from the time following June 362, when the Emperor Julian forbade Christians from teaching the pagan classics. Evidence for Christians and pagans in Greco-Roman Egypt sharing the same schools, as evidenced by Egyptian school exercises which included both Christian and non-Christian symbols and writing, can be found in Raffaella Cribiore, *Writing, Teaching and Students* (Atlanta: Scholars Press, 1996).

The Alexandrians were not alone in holding this understanding of the Church as the setting for a Christian *paideia*. In his discussion of *paideia* in early Christianity, Jaeger traces how Clement of Rome developed this theme in his *Letter to the Corinthians*, written at the end of the first century, commenting that Clement "conceives of paideia as precisely that which he offers to the Corinthians in his whole letter."[46] In his *Letter*, Clement shows how the organization of the Church needs to reflect the organic conception of society found in Greek political thought in which all of the elements of society work together for the good of all. This will provide an order in the Church in which each element breathes in harmony with the others. The Church herself, he teaches, is to be thought of as the educational setting for every Christian since she has the capacity to hand on to the Christian the *"paideia* of Christ."[47] Clement, then, wants to present an understanding of the Church as the place in which the work of Christ the great educator and savior is received. In his final prayer of thanksgiving at the close of the *Letter* he gives thanks to God for sending Christ "through whom Thou hast educated and sanctified and honored us."[48]

If the Church was seen as the setting within which *paideia* was received and handed on, let us look now at how the content of this classical *paideia* was seen by the Alexandrians to be fulfilled in and through the Church, her teachings, liturgy and practices. We can understand this fulfillment in terms of two, apparently opposite, images: of the Christian faith as the *crowning* of the *paideia*, and also as providing its *foundation*.

In the first place, then, the school saw its catechetical work as the *crowning* of the *paideia*. A monarchical image is perhaps a helpful one since the New Testament and early Church understanding of monarchy was that the power to rule is one given by God, the act of crowning symbolizing the monarch's right to govern. The crowning comes from above. Similarly, in the Christian *paideia*, holistic in the widest sense, uniting core educational principles and methods to the truths of the faith, Divine Revelation now crowns both practical and intellectual formation. With the light that comes from Revelation the mind is provided with secure principles for the framing of all knowledge—the arts and sciences, philosophy and myth.

The Alexandrian conviction that the arts and sciences are a propaedeutic first of all for philosophy, and thence for the highest of all

---

[46] *Early Christianity and Greek Paideia*, 25.
[47] *I Clement* 21.8.
[48] *I Clement* 62.3.

studies, theology, was an affirmation of their belief in the unity of knowledge, a concrete expression of their epistemological commitment to the unity of Truth, that all being coheres in the one Logos.[49] The inclusion of all disciplines in the ladder of learning reaching up to the divine summit was also an affirmation of the *value* of education, of the good of the knowledge to be gained from the different disciplines. There was an explicit ontology affirmed through this commitment to the *paideia* of the goodness of the creation which was studied in and through these disciplines and its capacity to prepare one for the final vision of the Whole, an affirmation of the Truth as Good, as worth discovering. No aspect of the creation was to be discarded or judged useless on the journey home to God. The fragments and disparate paths, under the protective guidance of revealed truth, could lead to the one final, glorious destination.[50]

At this point we should note the generous view of what could be preliminary and potentially helpful in this ascent to the One. The Alexandrians believed that, as part of these preliminary studies, popular myths could also find their place as tributaries that could be carefully guided to join this great river of truth, Christian Revelation both confirming and correcting as needed. Clement notes that one of the psalms, praising the work of God for his people, says "He hath not done thus to any other nation." Notice, says Clement, this word *thus*. "This shows that he hath done, but not 'thus.'" By using *thus*, Clement continues, the psalmist is noting the "pre-eminence"[51] of the Christian Revelation while also making clear that God has not left any people, nor any individual of any race, without his providential

---

[49] The Alexandrian museum provides a case study of the challenges in maintaining this sense of the unity of knowledge, especially when advances in particular disciplines and the adoption of new paradigms need to be integrated into existing knowledge. The need for a continual return to this task, and the patience required to undertake it, can easily be overlooked in the pursuit of more pragmatic concerns. Commenting on this work undertaken in the Alexandrian museum, Jaeger notes that the sense of coherence was to some extent lost over time. Aristotle, through Demetrius of Phaleron, had bequeathed to the scholars in the museum a heritage of a metaphysical worldview united to close scientific research. Jaeger argues that while Alexandrian science continued to see itself as in a continuum with Aristotle's work, the link between philosophy and science was "definitively broken" in that scholarship: "the infinitely refined technique of Ptolemaic research dispensed with the stable intellectual centre that Aristotle's detailed work had possessed in his great spiritualist view of the universe" (*Aristotle, Fundamentals of the History of his Development*, 2nd ed. [Oxford: Oxford University Press, 1948], 404-5).
[50] For a discussion of the good of knowledge see Stephen R. L. Clark, *From Athens to Jerusalem: The Love of Wisdom and the Love of God* (Brooklyn, NY: Angelico Press, 2019), 35-52.
[51] *Stromateis* 6.8.63.4-5

oversight. "He is the Teacher, who instructs the enlightened Christian by mysteries, and the faithful labourer by cheerful hopes, and the hard of heart with His keen corrective discipline; so that His providence is particular, public, and universal."[52]

God provides his preliminary education in many forms, including myth. Greek philosophy had already, of course, challenged the anthropomorphic and crude nature of the Greek myths underlying popular religion and had sought ways of interpreting such stories in the light of general philosophical principles. Stoicism, for example, had proposed a system of allegorical interpretation of Homer, and Aristotle that the gods of popular religion were to be understood as an expression of the summit of all Being, the unmoved Mover, but in mythological form.[53] Within this understanding, popular religion and myth could be seen as narrative entry points into an appreciation of these principles. Alexandrian Christianity did something different, though: teaching the centrality of the doctrine of the Incarnation, it both elevated myth further, as an avenue to the mysteries of Revelation, and firmly anchored myth in the temporal world: in the words of C. S. Lewis, in Christ myth became *Fact*.[54] And it is this Fact that, if one would follow, would lead into *mystery*: the Logos indwelling all things took flesh and appeared not as a myth from which the essential truth needs to be carefully extracted, but truly in history and in the flesh, for the purpose of leading the nations into the mystery of God. Understanding the pedagogy of this mystagogical movement from the myth-become-Fact they judged to be crucial: Christ's temporal appearing was precisely a stumbling block, a sign of contradiction that, if one was to follow, forced one to discover a deeper truth hidden within the outer appearance. The Scriptures that foretold his coming shared this same character, blocking one—even in the simple narratives in the story of salvation—through inconsistencies, paradoxes and puzzles in an effort to force one through to redeeming insight, as Origen emphasized in *De Principiis*.[55]

The character of mystery hidden in fact, in the literal, in what lies at hand, pervades the whole of creation, and so Alexandrian Christianity would speak of the "dispensation of paganism" that would allow

---

[52] *Stromateis* 7.2.6.1-2.
[53] Aristotle, *Metaphysics* XII.8.1074 a38-b14.
[54] Cf. C. S. Lewis, "Myth Became Fact," in *God in the Dock: Essays on Theology and Ethics* (Cambridge: William B. Eerdmans, 2014), 54-60.
[55] For Origen on how the narratives of the faith make spiritual reality accessible for all who are willing to search out mystery, and also include stumbling blocks to push us more deeply into mystery, see *De Principiis* IV.2.7-4.2.9.

the Church to speak into popular religious culture in order to relate it to its doctrines. In his commentary on the Alexandrian approach, Newman captures the concept of this dispensation beautifully: "the vague and uncertain family of religious truths, originally from God, but sojourning without the sanction of miracle, or a definite home, as pilgrims up and down the world."[56] Whatever was true in paganism and popular worship, as in the studies of the old *paideia*, could find a home-coming in the household of the faith, with Christ as the beneficent Head of that household. All that God had spoken to every race and person, in conscience, ritual and myth, and in the study of creation, could now benefit from the security of the fullness of Revelation, with the channels of the sacraments and the inspired word drawing these seeds of the Word into the broader and greater light of the faith. This reaching out to all cultures was determined by a soteriological concern: "We want to gain them all," as Clement says, reminding his readers of Paul's willingness to become a Jew to save Jews and a Greek to save Greeks.[57] Newman goes on to describe the approach to mission and teaching that characterized the teachers of the Alexandrian school, equipped with this understanding of God's dispensation to the pagans: "Believing God's hand to be in every system, so far forth as it is true... while he strenuously opposes all that is idolatrous, immoral, and profane, in their creed, he will profess to be leading them on to perfection, and to be recovering and purifying, rather than reversing the essential principles of their belief."[58] The Alexandrian approach was an affirmation of the essential harmony between Revelation and creation, with both Revelation and creation expressions of God's goodness, and God's Revelation unveiling the full meaning of creation.

As the crown of both secular studies and philosophy, the summit towards which all learning aspired, the school understood God's Revelation as the *ruler* of all that was beneath. There was to be no misunderstanding that human studies or forms of natural religion were at the same level as the Revelation given in Christ. The truths

---

[56] *Arians of the Fourth Century*, Rowan D. Williams (introduction and notes) (Notre Dame: University of Notre Dame, 2001), 80-81.
[57] *Stromateis* 1.1.15.4.
[58] *Arians of the Fourth Century*, 84. John McGuckin describes it thus: "All that human seeking after the truth discovered laboriously in times past is now here, in Christ, presented to humanity full, complete, and in essence. It is nothing other than the life the world has been seeking after throughout history, now given it as a grace" ("The Christology of the Apostolic Fathers," 42). McGuckin is describing Justin Martyr's *Second Apology*, but the thought applies equally to the Alexandrians.

of the faith govern how other subjects are to be interpreted and understood; they provide the light necessary for the other subjects to operate. Revelation was the ruling guide for all formational endeavors at whatever level. As we will see in the next chapter, this understanding was simply an application of the metaphysical principle that we live in a hierarchical universe in which levels of being receive their existence from that which stands above them, participating in the greater fullness of that which is higher. Philo had already articulated such a view of the higher ruling the lower. Philosophy, for example, as wisdom, knows what is beneath it and sheds light on lower areas of empirical study:

> The eyes see, but the mind through the eyes sees further than the eyes... The mind is the eye's eye... and the purified sense of each of the senses... In the same way, what we call the lower or secondary arts, resembling as they do the bodily faculties, handle the questions which they answer without involved consideration, but knowledge in each case does so with greater accuracy and minute examination. What the mind is to sense, that knowledge is to art.[59]

The different arts and sciences each deal with some aspect of nature, but philosophy can see further because it surveys the whole world, can see more deeply and clearly the subject matter of the individual arts. Philo then goes on to argue that the knowledge that each of the lower subjects generates is itself a "gift from philosophy," for the first principles of those subjects depend upon philosophical arguments and conclusions. The nature of things and the human ability to know and to describe depend upon more general and more foundational principles of cosmology, epistemology and language. These are philosophical matters, and it is only by receiving these that the arts and sciences can perform their tasks.[60]

And now, standing even above philosophy, is the Revelation brought in Christ providing, in his own Person and through the first principles and dogmas of the faith, the intellectual light for all study. Revelation provided the criteria for the discerning testing of all that was studied, the measure of what could ultimately be accepted and confirmed, and the interpretative keys for understanding how God was present in every area of study, every philosophical system, and each myth and ritual. As Jaeger comments, "philosophical speculation was used by [Clement and Origen] to support a positive religion that was not itself the

---

[59] *De congressu* XXV.143-44.
[60] See the discussion and illustrations in *De congressu* XXVI-XXVII.

result of independent human search for the truth, like earlier Greek philosophies, but took as its point of departure a divine revelation."[61]

The formation which Christians gave in the renewed *paideia* was presented not only as the fulfillment and crowning of the Greek *paideia*, and its ruler, but also as the temporal source and *foundation* of all *paideia*. The Alexandrian school presented Christianity as the most ancient of all forms of wisdom. Its tenets and truths were that which was, in the words of the First Letter of John, "from the beginning."[62] The truths which crowned the *paideia* were also a recovery of the *paideia*'s own foundations. As we shall see, this theme of Christianity as the fountain of all wisdom was, paradoxically, placed alongside a constant affirmation in the school of the theme of newness and of youthfulness, which also proclaimed a *new* world and a new childhood that had come into being in Christ. Augustine's well-known cry of discovery of God as the ever-ancient, ever-new is anticipated in the Alexandrian theme of the return of a new childhood for humanity, a new beginning of all things, brought about by the incarnation of the only-begotten Child whose days had no beginning.

The Lord Christ, they recognized and accepted, had come late in time, in the last days.[63] And in the face of the accusation of "newness," Christians appealed to the antiquity of the divine *paideia* that they preached. Such an appeal to antiquity was a common one: the ancients knew the value of arguing for a "return to the sources"; the worth of a tradition was its claim to be based on the thinking of a founder. One argues back to an older tradition to validate and support one's position. This was the case for establishing not only intellectual and religious but also social and political authority. Antiochus claimed to be grounding his restoration of Plato's Academy on the Old Academy, and when Eudorus of Alexandria introduced Neo-Pythagoreanism he emphasized that Plato had been a pupil of Pythagoras. When Philo was making his argument for Judaism to the Alexandrians he, in turn, presented Moses as the teacher of Pythagoras—and indeed of all Greek philosophers and lawgivers.[64]

The presentation of truth in terms of its antiquity was perhaps an especially important theme for the Alexandrian school since in Egypt antiquity was prized with a sense of confidence that no other place could match. The Egyptians claimed to be the source of civilizations'

---

[61] *Early Christianity and Greek Paideia*, 47.
[62] 1 Jn. 1.1.
[63] Cf. Heb. 1:2
[64] See the examples in Dillon, *The Middle Platonists*, 119-20.

radiance—and indeed that claim was recognized by the Greeks. Herodotus tells us the story of the Greek Hecataeus who spoke with Egyptian priests about his long ancestry of sixteen generations. In reply, the priest pointed to his, of three hundred and forty-five.[65] Plato has a similar story to tell —of the Athenian, Solon, who went to Egypt and began to speak of the antiquities of Greece. He was met with the Egyptian reply, "Ah! Solon, Solon, you Greeks are always children!"[66] an incident noted by Clement.[67] The Egyptians may have been the oppressed section of Alexandrian society, but Egyptian culture nonetheless was acknowledged by the Greeks as the more ancient, to which the Greeks were indebted, and especially in religious matters. The "wisest of the Greeks"—Solon, Thales, Plato, Pythagoras—came to Egypt to discuss religious matters with the priests, Plutarch was later to affirm,[68] as Clement also argues (indeed, even identifying Homer as an Egyptian).[69] Such a secure claim to antiquity in Egypt may have been grounded in nature, in the sheer fact of the Nile and its annual cycle which dominates all else; alongside this, Frankfurter draws attention to the persistence and continuity of the "literate temple culture" that provided the structure for religious organization and practice,[70] and out of which its wisdom literature grew.[71]

---

[65] Herodotus, *The Histories* 2.143.
[66] Plato, *Timaeus* 22b.
[67] *Stromateis* 1.15.69.3.
[68] See Plutarch, *Isis and Osiris* 354d-f. One of the results of this sense of cultural deference towards Egyptian antiquity was the *interpenetration* that this encouraged of Greek and Egyptian culture during both the Ptolemaic and Roman periods. In the area of religion, for example, we see a certain synthesis appearing. Between the second and fourth centuries AD, a series of Hermetic works were published in Alexandria which flowed out of a union between traditional Egyptian religion and Greek philosophy, especially Platonism. Termed "Hermetic" because they are mainly dialogues either between the Greek god Hermes and the Egyptian god Thoth, who is seen as Hermes's son, or between Hermes and Asclepius, the Greek god of healing associated with Serapis, the Hermetic books did not seek to make a wide appeal on the popular level. The contents were aimed at a set of intellectual devotees, though also with a concern to foster ethical living.
[69] *Stromateis* 1.15.66.1.
[70] "Egypt's temples not only represented the religious infrastructure but also had stood as the axes of Egyptian religion for millennia, distinguishing Egyptian culture from other ancient Mediterranean religions in which priesthoods were neither so ancient nor so institutionalized or socially distinct" (David Frankfurter, *Religion in Roman Egypt*, 14).
[71] It is likely that Egyptian education used hymns, instructions, and proverbs as foundational texts. The wisdom literature in these education materials has much in common with the wisdom writings of the Scriptures (for examples, see John J. Collins, "Wisdom and Torah," in eds. K. M. Hogan, *et al.*, *Pedagogy in Ancient Judaism and Early Christianity*, 60-61; William O. E. Oesterley, "Egypt and Israel," in ed. S. R. K. Glanville, *The Legacy of Egypt*, 245-48).

The Alexandrians enthusiastically engaged with this challenge to demonstrate the ancient credentials of the Christian faith. The truths of Christianity, they argued, while they are made *manifest* to the world in their fullness with the Revelation in Christ, in fact stand at the root of all philosophy and religion. The "race" of Christians was undeniably new, appearing only recently, but the teaching to which they held was not. Christian teaching is the culminating point of the faith of the ancient patriarchs. The Christians tied their claim to antiquity to the source of their faith in the Hebrew religion, joining Hellenizing Jews in the claim that Greek culture and philosophy was in fact derived from an older Hebrew culture. The Greeks have taken the notion of Law from the Jews. Against the claims of the Greeks, then, Clement argues at great length that not only philosophy but all important discoveries go back to the "barbarians," the non-Greeks; Moses was the greatest culture-bearer of the past.[72] Clement is delighted to find support for such a view in the Platonist philosopher Numenius, quoting his rhetorical question, "What is Plato but Moses speaking Greek?"[73] Salvatore Lilla convincingly argues that Clement here is countering a work by Celsus, a pagan Platonist, the *Alethes Logos*, the *True Account*, written sometime between AD 177-180 and which may have had its provenance in Alexandria.[74] Famously, Origen was also later to write a detailed response to this same work. Celsus appears to have been arguing that Greek culture was the pinnacle towards which history had been driving, its most exalted point, to which Clement articulates a detailed response showing Greek dependence on the more ancient barbarians, and thus clearing the way for his own presentation of the Christian Revelation as the high point of culture and truth.

THE KERYGMA OF GOD'S UNIVERSAL EDUCATION

That argument might provide a response to Greek claims. But what about those of the Egyptians? Or of other cultures claiming antiquity? To this, the Alexandrians, in concert with other Christians in the early Church, appealed to Christ as the Logos, the original Wisdom of God who was made manifest in the world for the sake of its salvation. We find such a treatment also in Eusebius's *Ecclesiastical History* which begins with the praise of the Logos who was with

---

[72] *Stromateis* 1.15.66.1–16.80.5.
[73] *Stromateis*, 1.22.150.4.
[74] Salvatore R. C. Lilla, *Clement of Alexandria: A Study in Christian Platonism and Gnosticism* (Oxford: Oxford University Press, 1971), 31–41.

God from the beginning and is before all creation. It is of the Logos that the patriarchs and the prophets speak, with Moses, "the most ancient of all prophets," witnessing to his work in the ordering of creation.[75] Christianity is the religion which holds and teaches the perennial, foundational principles of truth, grounded as it is in the creative work of the divine Logos which permeates all things.

> But even if we are clearly new, and this really fresh name of Christians is recently known among all nations, nevertheless our life and method of conduct, in accordance with the precepts of religion, has not been recently invented by us, but from the first creation of man, so to speak, has been upheld by the natural concepts of the men of old who were the friends of God, as we will here demonstrate.[76]

The *paideia* prepares for the reception of divine final Revelation in Christ. But that human *paideia* itself flows from a deeper and divine source. At this point it is crucial to recognize that this theme of a universal divine *paideia* is the preferred form in which the school presents the essential *kerygma*, or proclamation, of the Good News. Both Clement and Origen wanted to help Christians understand how through Christ, the Wisdom and Logos of God, not only one's studies but the whole of creation can be recognized as a place of redemptive *paideia*.[77] The Church preaches the Good News of a *cosmic salvific paideia* for those with eyes to see, hidden in both the "book" of nature and the book of the Scriptures, and able to be welcomed and responded to in the concrete events of history and one's personal life. God's *paideia*, made manifest in its fullness in Christ, and made present and executed in his Church, is one of education into his merciful and saving plan and that plan is accessible everywhere in traces of wisdom and little sparks which can blaze up helpfully,[78] since all things are created in and through the Logos who indwells all.

---

[75] H. E. I.2.4.
[76] H. E. I.4.4. This claim to Christian antiquity is a major theme in Eusebius's work of apologetics, *Praeparatio evangelica*, in which he claims that Greek philosophy is dependent upon earlier divine Revelation. Philosophy had not only the Greeks for the Gospel, but such philosophy was itself prepared for within divine Revelation. Aaron Johnson argues that this presentation is tied to the way in which Eusebius presents the two peoples of the Greeks and the Hebrews, the former as "latecomers to history" and the latter "the most ancient 'friends of God,' whose way of life embodied piety and wisdom" (*Ethnicity and Argument in Eusebius' Praeparatio Evangelica* [Oxford: Oxford University Press, 2006], viii).
[77] Cf. Jaeger, *Early Christianity and Greek Paideia*, 46–67; John McGuckin, "The Christology of the Apostolic Fathers," 31.
[78] Cf. *Stromateis* 1.17.87.1.

The Church, Origen teaches, is the "cosmos of the cosmos, because Christ has become its cosmos."[79]

The Alexandrians were not alone in this presentation of the heart and center of the divine *paideia* as *kerygma*, and indeed Patrick Pouchelle argues that this articulation was anticipated in the Septuagint since *paideia* unexpectedly appears at times meaning *that which can be heard and announced*. A connection is made in the Septuagint, in other words, between the *paideia* of the Lord and the announcement of God's action.[80] Drawing perhaps on such indications in the Septuagint, we find full, rich, and complementary presentations of this approach in a number of the early Fathers. Eric Osborn has helpfully traced, for example, the parallels between the presentation of the basic *kerygma* in terms of God's *paideia* in Irenaeus's *Demonstration of the Apostolic Kerygma* and Book VI of Clement's *Stromateis*.[81] We know that Clement of Alexandria was familiar with the work of this bishop and early Christian writer, his contemporary. He read him in the Greek edition of his writings and refers to him in his own.[82] They also had a good deal in common: both Clement and Irenaeus were battling Gnosticism, fighting the same great foe in the figure of the Gnostic Valentinius; and both developed, in response, a distinctively Christian understanding of *paideia* that reflected the core doctrines of the faith. The positive role which they assign to both creation and history in God's educational purposes flows from their estimation of the value of both in the Christian faith: they are fundamentally good and so God can use them in his work of maturing his people.[83] The Gnostics, whom both Irenaeus and Clement were opposing, on the contrary, evacuated both history and creation of all educational value. Both Clement and Irenaeus also seek to show how an appropriately-guided literary education and use of philosophy can support, not undermine, the Christian faith, that a proper study of the liberal arts can help to instill virtuous habits and *mores* that

---

[79] Origen, *Commentary on the Gospel of John*, 6, 59, 8-9.
[80] Patrick Pouchelle, "*Kyropaideia* versus *Paideia Kyriou*: The Semantic Transformation of Paideia and Cognates in the Translated Books of the Septuagint," 120, 123.
[81] Osborn, *Clement of Alexandria*, 282-92.
[82] See, for example, *Stromateis* 4.13.91.2. For a discussion of the similarities between Irenaeus and Clement see L. G. Patterson, "The divine became human: Irenaean themes in Clement of Alexandria," *Studia Patristica* 31 (1997), 497-516.
[83] "Because God builds education into his creation and into its history, the mundane, the earthly and the temporal are all construed as holy; they contribute to the perfection of the human race" (D. J. Bingham, "Paideia and Polemic in Second-Century Lyons: Irenaeus on Education" in eds. K. M. Hogan, et al., *Pedagogy in Ancient Judaism and Early Christianity*, 331).

contribute to the formation needed by Christians.[84] For both, the ultimate goal of this education is the development of moral virtue and the love of God for the sake of the adoption of the faithful as children of God restored to his likeness.[85]

It is worth placing Irenaeus's treatment of this theme of divine *paideia* alongside that of Clement and Origen to acquaint ourselves with the rich presentations of the *kerygma* that they provide. In *Adversus haereses*, his major work against Gnostic heresies, Irenaeus presents salvation history as the arena for God's education and formation. In the classical *paideia* the figures of the teacher and the household tutor, or the "pedagogue," work together to form and raise the child in their care on behalf of the father of the house. Irenaeus adjusts this classical model in which the father has only a peripheral role in the education of his children[86] and instead sees salvation history as God the Father himself taking charge of the education of his children, seeking to perfect his children and draw them into unity as one family sharing a common nature and goal through the missions of the Son and Spirit. Human persons are placed in history as in a schoolroom in which the Father gradually educates them through his Word and Spirit.[87] In this process, God assumes the roles of both teacher ("doctor") and tutor ("magister").[88] He teaches his people by the incidents of life and history, both good and bad, and helps them to interpret the meaning of these by giving them the law and the prophets and ultimately the life and teaching of Christ and his apostles. It is a gradual teaching, taking place over the whole period of the Old Covenant, and finding its climax and fulfillment in Christ, with history being a movement towards the time when the Father would adopt the faithful in Christ. The Church's central role is one of providing an understanding of this pedagogy and a formation for the Christian community so that it can interpret the Father's action and cooperate with his grace.

---

[84] The references to physics, cosmology, music, and literature in Irenaeus make it clear that he had received some traditional forms of Greco-Roman education and he proposes that Christians should be familiar with the liberal arts and understand how they can serve the higher ends of Revelation. For example, see *Adversus haereses* 2.32.2.

[85] *Adversus haereses* 5.25.3; 5.28.2; 5.32.1; *Stromateis* 2.22.134.2.

[86] We can recall, though, that Aristotle notes the benefits of a father being a prominent figure in his child's education: fathers know their children and their individual needs and so can mentor them well, while children have a natural sense of filial respect (*Nicomachean Ethics* 1180a29–1180b23).

[87] See *Adversus haereses* 2.25.3; 4.5.5; 4.13.2; 4.15.2; 4.18.6; 4.38.1; 5.1.1.

[88] See *Adversus haereses* 3.20.1; 4.33.4; 4.39.1–2; 5.1.1; 5.2.3; 5.3.1.

Clement's work contains the same strong sense that we find in Irenaeus of God as the universal educator of the human race, this education becoming fully realized for us in the person of Christ. We are all enrolled in God's "universal school."[89] The same familial imagery that is in Irenaeus is also present in Clement, of the Father's plan of goodness being manifested and recapitulated in the Son in whom we return to the Father.

For Clement, the *paideia* of God, his plan of redemptive education, is premised on his universal presence as Wisdom and Goodness. God is the good Father who seeks to lead all people to himself. His unseen presence is everywhere, filling all things. He has no favorites but in his divine dispensation has a purpose for every creature. To further this good he never ceases to work.[90] This good purpose is made fully manifest in Christ. And this manifestation of God's goodness entails the active presence and care of the Father in the Son. Clement loves to use biblical images of vineyards and gardens and presents the Savior as "our spiritual garden ... into whom we are planted, being transferred and transplanted, from our old life, into the good land."[91] As with Irenaeus, the Church is the community in which the purpose and a full understanding of Christ's *paideia* has been made clear so that this good news may be brought to all the nations:

> .... those things which "eye saw not, and ear heard not, nor did it enter the heart of men" (2 Corinthians 11:14) ... the Teacher told the account of them to us; unveiling the holy of holies; and in ascending order, things still holier than these, to those who are truly ... heirs of the Lord's adoption.[92]

Clement refers back to the value of the classical *paideia* in assisting others into this understanding: teachers can help their students to appreciate something of the beauty of Christ's Revelation and the profound coherence of God's work coming to a sublime climax in the Son by comparing it to patterns of numbers, or the order explored in

---

[89] Clement, *The Rich Man's Salvation*, 33.
[90] Clement clarifies that the rest of God on the seventh day cannot be thought of as a cessation of his good work to bring all creatures to himself, "for being good, if He should ever cease from doing good, then would He cease from being God, which it is sacrilege even to say" (*Stromateis* 6.16.141.7). The meaning of the rest on the seventh day is that God's ordering of all of his creation "should be preserved inviolate." Clement knew that the account of creation in the Bible is not a literal account of what happened in time, for "time was born along with the things that exist," but displays God's principles of governance and order.
[91] *Stromateis* 6.1.2.4.
[92] *Stromateis* 6.8.68.1.

astronomy, or how in music there is succession, rhythm and harmony, just as one finds in God's covenants and in his guidance offered to all of the nations. This is the "ecclesiastical symphony" which teachers can play for their catechumens, demonstrating the beauty of God's work.[93]

This kerygmatic account of the *paideia* in Clement is Christocentric, to an even greater extent than we find in Irenaeus: Christ is the recapitulation of all things: all the powers of the Spirit guide us towards the termination point in the Son. He is "the circle of all powers rolled and united into one unity."[94] To live in him is to live in the unity of all things; to disbelieve is to be separated from all things, for outside of him there is nothing. Through the knowledge of all things which is given in the Son the Christian can live securely in the love of God, unshaken by the passions which would disturb him. Not only can this love detach Christians from anger, envy and destructive passions, but even good passions such as courage and cheerfulness are transcended as the faithful who have true wisdom are secure in the promises of God revealed in Christ and so love God and are turned, in Christ, towards him alone.[95] So strong is this kerygmatic focus on the divine *paideia* in Clement's work that he even adds his own phrase to the familiar depiction of the promised Messiah in Isaiah: "Wonderful Counsellor, Mighty God, Everlasting Father, Prince of Peace, *that he might extend his paideia.*"[96] As we will see in chapter eight, Clement also supplies us with a concrete expression of the Father's love for humankind in the metaphor of Christ as the slave-pedagogue, the Tutor of the household who came among his people to serve them through a formation to make them fit to live in the home of the Father.

Origen, as we have seen in other areas, takes up Clement's ideas and develops them "with stronger consistency and in greater detail,"[97] with the understanding of God as the divine educator of the human race central to his theology. His focus, as he develops this theme, is primarily as an exegete: "he moves with his texts and is led along by what they say," and in doing so finds "certain motifs" that occur again and again.[98] Like Irenaeus and Clement, he sees the span of history as, at its core, an educational and purifying process. Even paradise can be thought of as a school in which we can finally learn the answers

---

[93] *Stromateis* 6.11.88.5–11.89.1.
[94] *Stromateis* 4.25.156.2.
[95] *Stromateis* 6.9.73.1–77.2.
[96] This educational addition to *Isaiah* 9:6 can be found in *Paedagogus* 1.5.24.2.
[97] Jaeger, *Early Christianity and Greek Paideia*, 62.
[98] Ibid., 69.

to questions that have baffled us: everything from the properties of certain herbs and why each genus is divided into many species, to why certain angels fell, and fallen angels are allowed to lead us astray. In heaven we will learn about every movement of divine providence and of the care that extends even to the two sparrows that are sold for a penny, and whether we should understand that saying of the Lord literally or spiritually.[99]

Origen's vision, grounded in his exegesis is, again, cosmic in scope. He read Scripture and the universe in a reciprocally illuminating way for he saw the Logos present in both.[100] The way one studies the Scriptures is, "in the final analysis, the rhythm of all thought"[101] because it is the rhythm of the Logos revealed in the text who also dwells in the human mind and heart and in the cosmos in the seeds of the word, the *logoi*. The Church seeks to be attentive to the divine Logos so that she can, obedient to the Spirit, clarify and interpret his movements and illuminate the patterns and intentions of his redemptive *paideia*. The divine story the Church can proclaim is in essence a simple one: the cosmos, created in the Logos, has gone astray, and the history of creation and the story of salvation are one and the same; namely, the magnificent theme of the Logos seeking after the fallen world in order to return it to the Father, to enjoy the life-giving vision of God. Everything in Origen's exegesis and theology is placed at the service of this *kerygma*. As McGucken argues, he "saw all things (especially the Scriptures that demonstrated this teaching in symbolic form) as witnesses to the manner in which the Divine Logos stood at the center of a great cosmic movement of the ascent of creation to the invisible Father."[102] At the center of this all-embracing scheme of salvation, then, Origen places a "mystical Christology of loving communion and *Paideia*."[103]

His work was both comprehensive and integrative as he sought to develop a theology of redemption around this *kerygma* of the divine *paideia*, trying to exhibit on the one hand the unity of Scripture around Christ, and on the other the harmony of this scriptural Christocentricity with an understanding of God's plan, proclaimed in the apostolic Tradition, as one for the whole cosmos. Living in the international culture of Alexandria, a vibrant reminder of the

---

[99] See *De Principiis* II.11.5.
[100] Henri de Lubac, SJ, *History and Spirit: The Understanding of Scripture According to Origen* (San Francisco: Ignatius Press, 2007), 396–406.
[101] Ibid., 396.
[102] McGuckin, "The Christology of the Apostolic Fathers," 44.
[103] McGuckin, "The Christology of the Apostolic Fathers," 45.

aspiration for the unity of the human race, Origen was vividly aware that God's *paideia* for unifying the nations had been made manifest in Christ and was now to be proclaimed and lived. In opposition to all Gnostic schemes, it is no account of the retrieving of divine sparks from a hostile or irremediably lost world, of the *illuminati*, the elect few, who are to be plucked out of a perishing cosmos. There is, in fact, no category of created souls who are beneath the interest and concern of the Logos.[104] God's wise educational work is, on the contrary, patient and inclusive, spanning not just earthly time but taking account of souls' immortal nature. "Like a wise tiller of the land, God is not in a hurry, and what seems difficult or impossible will simply require more time."[105]

Not all of the details of Origen's scheme were accepted by the Church, but its overall approach, linking salvation and pedagogy and uniting this to the purpose of the Incarnation, was to provide a fertile ground for later developments as the Church's Christological and soteriological outline was consolidated. Above all, Origen made the Christian *kerygma*, the core presentation of God's plan, both understandable and attractive: "Origen made his theory of all cosmic life as the yearning of the Logos to re-educate his fallen creation into a story that was not only vastly metaphysical and stunning in all its dimensions, but something that was also tender, loving, and intimately understandable."[106]

AND TODAY

The vision of divine *paideia* which we have seen articulated both as grounding a complete understanding of the educational enterprise and as a presentation of the *kerygma* can clearly offer fruitful avenues for developing the Church's mission of evangelization and catechesis today. The whole of the Greek and Jewish understanding of *paideia* was elevated and crowned with a magnificent vision of the divine Logos taking flesh for the salvation of a cosmos in need of its homecoming to the Father. It was a vision that united education and evangelization in a single whole, capturing within a divine and human synergy the processes of personal conversion and intellectual formation shaped by the work of grace; a right ordering and unification of the fields of knowledge; and principles for guiding the fashioning of Christian

---

[104] See *De Principiis* II.1.8–11.
[105] H. Chadwick, "Philosophical Tradition and the Self," in eds. G. W. Bowerstock, P. Brown and O. Grabar, *Late Antiquity: A Guide to the Postclassical World* (Cambridge, MA: The Belknap Press of Harvard University Press, 1999), 77.
[106] McGuckin, "The Christology of the Apostolic Fathers," 48.

culture within a renewed cosmos following the resurrection of Jesus from the dead. Catechesis found its place, as a sustained formation of the person, within that.[107]

Without seeking to corral unduly some of the possibilities for application today, one can point first to *the importance for educational institutions of the breadth and coherence of vision* that was achieved in the Alexandrian school. In both Eastern and Western traditions of Christianity it was this understanding of education that became the basis for the Christian education that was developed in the monastic and cathedral schools and then in the universities.[108] In today's educational environment, in which very different approaches to educational theory and practice have evolved, a reclaiming of this vision of Christian *paideia* is surely crucial so that the channels of human, moral and spiritual formation can run together in harmony with the truths of Revelation and the practice of Christian virtue. An important strand in the contemporary catechetical *ressourcement*, therefore, must be to focus on how today's Catholic educational institutions can be inspired by this patristic understanding of Christian *paideia*, built on the sources and traditions of the classical *paideia*, so that, in

---

[107] Newman captured the *largesse* of the vision memorably in *The Idea of a University*: "The grace stored in Jerusalem, and the gifts which radiate from Athens, are made over and concentrated in Rome. This is true as a matter of history" (*The Idea of a University* [London: Longmans Green, 1947], 231). For the Western Church, it was especially Augustine who would further this legacy, developed by Irenaeus and the Alexandrians in particular, as the basis for a Christian and classical education. For a detailed discussion of Augustine's understanding of education as the Christian development of the classical *paideia*, see Eugene Kevane, "*De Doctrina Christiana*: A Treatise on Christian Education," *Recherches Augustiniennes* 4 (1966), 97-133, and his "*Translatio imperii*: Augustine's *De Doctrina Christiana* and the Classical *Paideia*," *Studia Patristica* XIV (Berlin: Akademie-Verlag, 1976), 446-60.

[108] It is thus false to argue that the ascendency of Christianity meant the demise and ultimate death of the Greek educational spirit. The classical heritage was, in fact, guarded and crowned by the Alexandrian Christians and it was subsequently preserved in both East and West. Gibbon is a typical representative of this kind of critique: Justinian's decree of AD 529 which resulted in the closure of the philosophical schools in Athens is placed alongside the founding of Monte Cassino in the same year, with the lesson: within Christianity monkish education finally replaced and abrogated the broad liberal tradition of the Greeks (see Edward Gibbon, *The History of the Decline and Fall of the Roman Empire*, ed. J. B. Bury, 7th ed. [London, 1931], 261-67). Gibbon's argument is incorrect, even with regard to the intent of Justinian's decree, which was not to forbid philosophy or reject classical learning, but simply to forbid pagans from teaching philosophy, an action which parallels a similar ban enacted in 362 by Julian the Apostate on Christians teaching. (Julian's decision is appropriately described by Marrou as the "first academic persecution inflicted on the Christians," *A History of Education in Antiquity*, 323.) Lynch discusses Gibbon's and comparable judgements in *Aristotle's School*, 163-77.

suitably adapted and updated forms, the Church's ministry of evangelization and catechesis can crown learning as "a true and proper school of Christian pedagogy."[109]

In the second place, a reclamation of the *Good News of salvation as intrinsically formational* would allow the development of an evangelizing catechesis that is faithful to its Christocentric focus and also unites concrete formational practices to the central proclamation of the faith. The identification of the *kerygma* as the motivating heart of *paideia*, moreover, would prevent any opposition between intentional forms of discipleship and formation and wider concerns for the development and renewal of forms of Catholic culture which are, by definition, seeking to establish patterns of habitual practice and institutional durability. The new *Directory for Catechesis* has asked for the central proclamation of the faith to be considered, not just an introductory step that leads into catechesis, but "the essential dimension of every moment of catechesis."[110] The Alexandrian school went even further and proposed this proclamation to be the essential dimension of every step in the development of Christian culture and education, its living framework and scaffolding. This same *Directory for Catechesis* has already called us also to embrace this broader vision of the *kerygma* underpinning and informing all educational activity, of the whole of God's Revelation as a work of formation in which God himself is the primary educator:

> Revelation is the great educational work of God. In fact, it can also be interpreted through a pedagogical lens. In it we find the distinctive elements that can help lead us to recognize a *divine pedagogy*, one which is capable of profoundly influencing the Church's educational activity. Catechesis also follows in the footsteps of God's pedagogy.[111]

A rich Trinitarian presentation of this pedagogy is provided in the *Directory* as it walks its readers through the living pedagogy of the Father, Son, and Holy Spirit in salvation history and in the Church today.[112] A catechetical approach faithful to the primacy of Revelation will follow "in the footsteps of God's pedagogy," understanding the saving work of the living God to be the heart of all catechetical activity in the Church.

---

[109] Congregation for the Clergy, *General Directory for Catechesis* (hereafter, *GDC*), 1997, 33.
[110] *DC* 57.
[111] *DC* 157.
[112] *DC* 158–63.

Finally, the Alexandrian vision of divine *paideia* can help the urgent recovery of *the formational dimension of the local Church*, so that each community recognizes its call to become a locus for a faithful, holistic catechesis. We saw that the early Fathers saw the Church as the locus for an education-in-life. The 1997 *General Directory for Catechesis* identified the retrieval of this patristic conception of catechesis "as a school of faith, an initiation and apprenticeship in the entire Christian life"[113] as the overriding priority for contemporary catechesis. Clement said that through the coming of the Word who fills all things the whole world has "become an Athens and a Greece."[114] The fullness of Revelation in Christ has made possible an assured pathway of cooperation with God's pedagogical and saving work in each person, and this is made available through the interpretative counsel of the Church, the security and light of her dogmas and teachings, and the graces of her sacramental life so that each member of her faithful can discern God's voice, understand his call, and cooperate with his pedagogy. The 2020 *Directory for Catechesis* therefore called on readers to embrace the reality of the Church as the Mother who begets and carries her children in her womb so that a secure formation can take place "under the guidance of the Spirit and in the living womb of the Christian community."[115]

---

[113] *GDC* 33.
[114] *Protrepticus* 11.112.1.
[115] *DC* 131; Cf. "The Christian is born from the maternal womb of the Church" (21); "the womb of regeneration in faith is the whole community" (64d); catechesis "begets children of God in the womb of the Church" (110); and see also 133; 262a.

CHAPTER 6

Friendship with the Wisdom of God

ONE OF THE POWERFUL CONTRIBUTIONS THE Alexandrian catechetical tradition can make to contemporary catechesis flows from the sustained attention it paid to addressing philosophical questions for the sake of securing an adequate worldview to communicate and fruitfully live the Christian faith. The school of Alexandria was a significant influence in enabling what Ratzinger has called "the decision of the early Church in favour of philosophy."[1] It saw philosophy not as an option, but as a *necessary foundation* for faith. For Clement and Origen, as for Philo before them, philosophy was seen as a vital propaedeutic for Revelation and the union of philosophical thought to Christian Revelation essential for how the faith needed to be understood and presented. Philosophy was never a sideshow for the school, nor a veneer that could be stripped away, nor even merely a useful apologetic tool. Philosophy was needed to provide *pathways* into the mysteries of Revelation as well as *foundations* for those same mysteries. Philosophy could also assist by offering *principles and frameworks* for understanding the mysteries. For this support the school drew, with discrimination and care, especially upon the resources of the Platonic tradition, particularly as this was expressed in the Middle Platonism that was preponderant in Alexandria in the first three centuries of the Christian era.

The school did not merely see the provision of realist philosophical content as crucial. We have already proposed that it understood itself to be standing in the tradition of the philosophical schools in a broader sense, teaching the care of the soul through exercises that stand in the tradition of the philosophical schools, as well as adopting certain styles of interaction between teachers and students, including prioritizing a model of personal discipleship that was characteristic of philosophical schools.[2] In Clement, Origen, and Didymus we can see

---

[1] Joseph Ratzinger, *Introduction to Christianity* (San Francisco: Ignatius Press, 2004), 137. Both Leo XIII in *Aeterni Patris* (7, 12) and John Paul II in in his encyclical on faith and reason, *Fides et Ratio* (38–39), highlighted the contribution of Clement and Origen in this "choice for philosophy," emphasizing their commitment to the importance of philosophy as the "hedge and fence of the vine," and underscoring their interest in the apologetic role of philosophy (cf. *Stromateis* 1.20.100.1).

[2] See Hadot, *Philosophy as a Way of Life*, 126–40. Peter Brown describes the small "study circles" which were typical of the philosophical school tradition of the time

evidence of just such a formation style of small-scale, mimetic teacher-disciple relationships as intrinsic to their approach.³ We can understand, then, why Christianity should have been seen by many as a type of philosophical school and why the leaders of the catechetical school in their turn saw many points of overlap with such schools. And it is perhaps no accident that Catherine, as the patron saint of philosophy, should have been located in Alexandria, represented as the ideal wise woman,⁴ learned in all Greek philosophy and seeing the philosophical craft as preparatory to receiving the true wisdom of Christ.⁵

in *The Body and* Society (London: Faber and Faber, 1988), 104, and the familial style of small discipleship groups in the Platonist tradition is discussed in Carl Séan O'Brien and Sarah Klitenic Wear, "The Figure of the *Diadochos*, from Socrates to the Late Antique Athenian School of Neoplatonism," in eds. J. F. Finamore and S. K. Wear, *Defining Platonism: Essays in Honor of the 75th Birthday of John M. Dillon* (Steubenville: Franciscan University Press, 2017), 253–70.
³ See further Harry O. Maier, "Clement of Alexandria and the Care of the Self," *Journal of American Academy of Religion* 62.3 (1994), 719–45; Heine, *Origen: Scholarship in the Service of the Church*, 48–51.
⁴ Unfortunately, what we know of St. Catherine of Alexandria is possibly largely legendary. The first account of Catherine's life that we have is by Emperor Basil the First in 866, in his *Monologium Basilianum*, published in English as *The Life of St Katherine* (London: Trubner and Co., 1884). It has been argued that her life was based on that of the pagan female philosopher, Hypatia (370–415), whose murder was felt at the time to be a shadow on the reputation of Christian Alexandria: in his *History of the Church*, the Christian historian Socrates said that this event brought opprobrium upon Cyril and upon the whole Alexandrian Church (VII.15). Hypatia has also herself been to some extent the object of legend, a symbol of the best of philosophical paganism, with Charles Kingsley's 1853 novel, *Hypatia*, celebrating—and romanticizing—her life. There is, however, no need to find the source of Catherine's cult in a pagan philosopher, for the school's own work in philosophy was well-known, nor indeed to see Hypatia as a "martyr to philosophy" over and against *Christians* hostile to that craft or to the virtues of philosophical femininity. On the contrary, the catechetical school taught philosophy to women as well as to men, and the figure of a well-known female Christian philosopher should not be viewed as historically problematic in itself; moreover, Hypatia almost certainly came to grief in Alexandria not because she was a woman, nor because she was a philosopher, but more simply as a victim of the crowd violence that sprang up unpredictably in the city, and to which so many—of different persuasions—lost their lives. For a sensible discussion of her death and its likely causes see Maria Dzielska, *Hypatia of Alexandria* (Cambridge, MA: Harvard University Press, 1995).
⁵ Whatever the historical truth of Catherine, the hagiographical account we have draws our attention to the equality of men and women that characterized the early Church, and is so clear in Alexandrian Christianity, both in learning and the pursuit of holiness. Sr. Prudence Allen points out that the figure of Catherine has also assisted the Church in establishing the truth of sexual complementarity, the truth that equality is accompanied by a complementarity of men and women. Middle Platonism tended towards sexual equality but united this to a lack of essential differentiation between men and women because both were sexless rational souls. The Christian belief in the resurrection of the body held onto the importance of the distinction between men and women, whilst affirming their united destiny

In this careful and nuanced act of self-identification, the catechetical school was certainly conscious that by engaging energetically with the philosophical heritage of Hellenism it was also addressing one of the areas of greatest challenge for early Christianity, the conversion of academics: "The strongholds of paganism were the university towns"[6] — and Alexandria, of course, was a uniquely rich academic environment. The philosophical contribution of the Alexandrian school and the strong intellectual formation it provided was crucial for the Church's missionary efforts.

Before unpacking the details of the school's philosophical commitments, it is important to understand that the catechetical school's choice "for" philosophy, and to stand in the tradition of the philosophical schools, was distinctive in the ancient world in an important and costly respect, for its embrace of philosophy was at the same time a choice "against" the pagan gods.[7] This was a fundamental demarcation point for the catechetical school, setting it apart from ancient philosophical schools that were in many ways "religious" in tenor insofar as they were concerned with beliefs related to the ultimate questions of human life. They might be either atheistic or monotheistic in conviction, but all without exception acknowledged the pantheon of the gods, and members of the schools typically participated in popular religious ceremonies. Their highest representatives of mystical philosophy were content to continue their association with pagan worship. Writing to Celsus, his Platonist pagan critic, Origen notes that even Plato, who wrote with such insight and beauty about the nature of the highest good, did not withdraw from pagan worship,[8] while Proclus, who carried forward Neo-Platonism after the end

---

in God (*The Concept of Woman: The Aristotelian Revolution, 750 BC-AD 1250* [Grand Rapids: William B. Eerdmans], 1997, 214-17). Alexandria was not unique in preserving for the Church a figure of the "woman of wisdom": Augustine presents his mother Monica in philosophical terms in his Cassiciacum Dialogues (see *De Ordine* II.1) and in the *Confessions* (IX.10.24), moving from being an earthly mother to a source of heavenly wisdom. The "portrait of Monica in the *Confessions* offers a poignant testimony that reaching God is not a business of a handful of ascetic professionals" (M. Saghy, "Monica, the ascetic," *Studia Patristica* XCI, 2017, 376). For helpful commentary on this philosophical depiction of Monica, see Gillian Clark, *Monica: An Ordinary Saint* (Oxford: Oxford University Press, 2015), 91-115, and Ragnar Holte, "Monica, 'the Philosopher,'" in eds. P. Merino and J. M. Torrecilla, *Charisteria Augustiniana Ioseph Oroz Reta dicta*, 2 (Madrid, 1994), 293-316.
[6] A. H. M. Jones, "The Social Background of the Struggle between Paganism and Christianity," 32.
[7] As Ratzinger also points out: *Introduction to Christianity*, 137, and see also 109 n.7.
[8] *Contra Celsum* VI.3-4, quoting the Seventh Letter and then the examples in *Republic* 327a and *Phaedo* 118a.

of the fourth century, composed hymns to Greek pagan deities and was at ease celebrating Egyptian, Chaldean and Greek pagan festivals.

The Alexandrian Christians, like their Jewish counterparts, however, took up a different position: they rejected the worship of the gods in practice as well as in theory, while at the same time attaching philosophy to belief in God as a necessary handmaid.[9] This choice "for" philosophy, attaching it to Christian Revelation, and "against" the gods, had huge implications for Christians' daily life and commitments. We have seen how closely the political, social, and religious dimensions of life were intertwined in Alexandria, with pagan temple worship a key mark of civic affiliation and an implicit political declaration. The cult of a ruler being treated as a god developed under the Ptolemies after Alexander the Great,[10] and a ruler cult was particularly prominent in Alexandria where, in their elevation of deceased members of the dynasty to the status of divinity, the Ptolemies followed the ancient Egyptian practice of the pharaohs. Ptolemy Philadelphus, for example, who established the museum and the library, erected temples in Alexandria to his second wife, Arsinoe II, ordering that she be worshipped as a goddess.[11] It is easy to see how a refusal to join in the worship of the gods would be perceived as a rejection of the current political rule as well as of social mores and civic loyalties.[12] Such a perception was unfortunate for the Christians of this period since in the main they were, in fact, inclined to encourage obedience

---

[9] So John Paul II, in *Fides et ratio*, notes how Origen, through his development of an early form of Christian "theology," enabled that term to be detached from philosophy, so that it referred instead to Christian doctrine rather than to the highest point of philosophical reflection. In this way his work made possible the distinguishing of philosophy and theology in the Christian Tradition and the use of philosophy as a handmaid to Revelation. Origen, of course, stands in the Philonic tradition in making this move. John Paul writes, "In Aristotelian philosophy... [theology] signified the noblest part and the true summit of philosophical discourse. But in the light of Christian Revelation what had signified a generic doctrine about the gods assumed a wholly new meaning, signifying now the reflection undertaken by the believer in order to express *the true doctrine* about God" (39).
[10] See the discussion in Henk S. Versnel, *Coping with the Gods* (Leiden: Brill, 2011), 439–92.
[11] Pliny provides us with a description of Arsinoe in her temple (*Natural History* XXXIV. XLII.148).
[12] Christians would not compromise by agreeing to worship Christ amid a pantheon of gods. For example, Alexander Severus, who ruled A.D. 222–235, had in his private chapel five statues for veneration: Christ was one, the others being Abraham, Alexander the Great, Orpheus and Apollonius of Tyre (see E. A. Wallis Budge, *The Alexander Book in Ethiopia* [Oxford: Oxford University Press, 1933] for this and for a translation of the *Romance of Alexander*, a second century A.D. Alexandrian work that was successful in spreading the cult of Alexander, particularly during the Middle Ages).

towards the Emperor and other political rulers whom they saw as exercising a legitimate authority that had been given by God.[13] However, like the Jews, it was anathema to them to participate in any kind of pagan worship and—unlike the Jews—they were not easily recognizable as a distinct group that could be offered privileges of exemption: Judaism was an officially "authorized" religion, a *religio licita*, but Christianity did not have this status. For this refusal to engage in pagan worship Christians drew opprobrium as "atheists," as well as excluding themselves from public and political office.

PHILOSOPHICAL TRADITIONS IN ALEXANDRIA

To appreciate the nature and significance of the school's philosophical commitments, we must understand the philosophical heritage present in Alexandria. Aristotle's philosophical legacy was built firmly into the very foundations of Alexandria in the person of Demetrius of Phaleron who oversaw the collection of manuscripts and organization of the library and indeed was central to the founding of the museum under Ptolemy Philadelphus. Before coming to Alexandria, he had studied in Athens at the Lyceum as a disciple of Aristotle's successor, Theophrastes, and one of the early collections of books secured for the Alexandrian library was reportedly Aristotle's own library, bought from Neleus, Theophrastes's successor.[14] This strong connection to Aristotle seems particularly fitting given that Alexander the Great had Aristotle as his personal tutor. Platonism also made its home in Alexandria. After the fall of Athens to the Romans in 88 BC, the center of Platonist philosophy moved to Alexandria, with Antiochus's pupil, Dion, carrying the torch for Platonism there, followed by his pupil Eudorus. In fact, it may have been from Alexandria that Platonism in time subsequently returned to Athens.[15]

Although I have introduced Aristotelianism and Platonism separately, they should not be regarded as insulated traditions of thought; the philosophy that grew up in Alexandria was eclectic,[16] coming

---

[13] For an overview of early Christian beliefs in this matter see Robert M. Grant, *Early Christianity and Society* (London: Collins, 1978), 13-43.
[14] Athenaeus, *The Diepnosophists* I, 3a-b. For a discussion of the complexities surrounding the fate of Aristotle's library, see also Lynch, *Aristotle's School*, 146-49.
[15] We have little idea what was taking place in terms of Platonic thought in Athens from the fall in 88 BC until around AD 50, but in AD 66-67 we find the Egyptian Ammonius in Athens teaching Plutarch; thus it was possibly he who brought back Platonism to Athens from Alexandria (see Dillon, *The Middle Platonists*, 185-86, 232-33).
[16] While the philosophical environment was eclectic, this did not necessarily imply peaceful coexistence. There could be fierce competition between different schools

to be largely represented by what is known as "Middle Platonism" (roughly 80 BC–AD 220), a form of Platonism that was influenced not only by Aristotelianism but also Stoicism and Pythagoreanism. The ethical seriousness of the Aristotelians and Stoics, together with the vitalistic cosmology of Stoicism, and the mystical speculations of the Pythagoreans, including their numerology,[17] all found a place as elements of the streams of thought and practice which fed Middle Platonism.

Middle Platonism was eclectic, then, but there was a core set of beliefs nonetheless, a core drawn from the central convictions of the major traditions. Jaeger is probably correct in seeing this convergence on a common set of beliefs as a reaction to the rise of skepticism, the traditional philosophical schools undertaking "a strange sort of self-defense by joining forces and concluding a *grand alliance* to which Platonists, Stoics, Pythagoreans, and (to a lesser degree) Aristotelians made their contribution."[18] It was the foundation of the *philosophia perennis* which was to coalesce in Neo-Platonism.

In the area of *metaphysics and cosmology* the philosophical convictions of Middle Platonism included a belief in a transcendent, non-material principle of the universe: God, the Monad, the One, from whom all being flows and after whom the material world is patterned. The typical understanding of God that developed within Middle Platonism shared many points in common with God as he was understood within the Christian Revelation: he is the Supreme Being, eternal and unchanging, spiritual (i.e., not material) and simple (i.e., not composed of parts). He is One, all-good and all-knowing, the One who governs all things. It was also understood that the universe is ordered and knowable: it is a coherent, patterned whole, a fitting object of contemplation, especially through mathematics (number has a mystical significance because of this patterning). In the area of *anthropology,* Middle Platonism understood the supreme good of human life to be to become "like God": Pythagoras had

---

for "converts," and fragmentation within schools was also common, as members founded their own schools. Diodorus of Sicily describes the often antagonist spirit: "if someone examined the most famous schools of philosophy, he would find them differing with one another as radically as possible and deliberately assuming contrary positions on central tenets" (*History* 29.6). Some of the mutual opposition probably arose from political differences and allegiances, and Diodorus was perhaps overly impatient of the mutual challenges and counter-challenges, but his comment also indicates the importance of personal identification with a school.
[17] The Pythagoreans in this Middle Platonist tradition saw Plato, of course, primarily as a follower of Pythagoras (see Dillon, *The Middle Platonists,* 341-83).
[18] *Early Christianity and Greek Paideia,* 42.

exhorted his disciples to "follow God," Plato defined the goal of the human person as assimilation to the divine,[19] and Aristotle, also, left his followers with a mystical understanding of the good life.[20] Alongside this conviction of the divine *telos* of the human person came an affirmation of free will and responsibility and of personal immortality. These beliefs made up a consistent body of philosophical doctrine, the Platonic "heritage," that was passed on in Middle Platonism and took final shape in Neo-Platonism, in which the key concepts can be summed up as the *One*, from which all that exists derives its being; *intellect*, or *nous*, which grasps the reality of being; *soul*, which animates nature; and *nature* itself.

Dillon writes touchingly of the many minor philosophical figures in Middle Platonism who contributed to the securing and transmitting of this heritage of the *philosophia perennis* upon which the catechetical school drew:

> Like those humble sea-creatures whose concerted effort slowly builds a coral reef, the philosophers of this period each contributed some detail to the formation of what was to become perhaps the greatest philosophical edifice of all time, that Platonism which, gathering to itself much of Aristotelianism and Stoicism, was to dominate the Late Antique world and the Middle Ages, and continue as a vital force through the Renaissance to the present day.[21]

At this point we must connect with the person of Philo once again, for his works were one of the main avenues through which the Christians in Alexandria received this Greek philosophy in a form already united to biblical Revelation.[22] Philo was steeped in both the Greek literary heritage and in Greek philosophy, especially that of Plato, and his *corpus* includes a small number of works that are mainly philosophical in nature, treating questions about the nature of God, the cosmos and the human person. And while these works

---

[19] *Theatetus* 176B. Socrates advises Theatetus to "make all speed to take flight from this world to the other" and adds "and that means becoming like the divine so far as we can" (See F. M. Cornford, *Plato's Theory of Knowledge* [London: Routledge & Kegan Paul, 1935], 87).

[20] For the argument that Aristotle offered a more unified mystical interpretation than is commonly appreciated see Stephen R. L. Clark, *Aristotle's Man: Speculations on Aristotelian Anthropology* (Oxford: Clarendon Press, 1975), and especially the final chapter on body-mind unity.

[21] Dillon, *The Middle Platonists*, 415.

[22] Henry Chadwick makes the point simply and starkly: "The history of Christian philosophy begins not with a Christian but with a Jew, Philo of Alexandria" ("Philo" in ed. A. H. Armstrong, *The Cambridge History of Later Greek and Early Medieval Philosophy* [Cambridge: Cambridge University Press, 1970], 137).

explicitly focused on philosophical topics are limited in number, at the heart of all of his exegetical writing lies the conviction that the Scriptures contain a divinely inspired philosophy, one that is coherent with the fundamental doctrines of the Platonism of his day. He identified Moses, in fact, as the true father of philosophy to whom the Greek philosophers are indebted[23] and so held that whoever reads the Law of Moses correctly will find the doctrines of Platonism there.[24]

From this initial excursus into the identity of the catechetical school in relation to other Alexandrian philosophical schools and their teachings, we can now turn to the fundamental question: What, for the school, was the place of philosophy in Christian formation? What were the purposes that philosophy served? Essentially there were two: philosophy *opened a pathway into faith*, and it provided necessary *foundations for faith*.

OPENING A PATHWAY INTO FAITH

Clement argues that, just as the Law and the prophets prepared the Jews for the Gospel, so the same is true of philosophy for the Greeks. "For philosophy was to the Greek world what the Law was to the Hebrews, a tutor escorting them to Christ. So philosophy is a preparatory process; it opens the road for the person whom Christ brings to his final goal."[25]

This understanding of God's provision of philosophy follows from the Alexandrian school's conviction that God's *paideia* is in the whole world. There was a dispensation of preparation from God for the Greeks and, through the Hellenistic expansion following Alexander's conquests, for the wider world, that paralleled the preparation of the Law and the prophets for God's chosen people. God in his goodness has supplied many tributaries that flow into the "perennial river" of truth; "the roads to righteousness are many and various and lead to

---

[23] *Legum Allegoriae* I.108 mentions that Heraclitus followed Moses's teaching and *De Aeternitate Mundi* 18-19 that Hesiod and Plato are both indebted to Moses for the correct understanding of creation.

[24] Philo's *Life of Moses* grounds the convictions about the Platonism in Moses's teaching by outlining Moses's education: for this adopted child of Egyptian royalty, "Teachers at once arrived from different parts, some unbidden from the neighbouring countries and provinces of Egypt, others summoned from Greece under promise of a high reward.... Arithmetic, geometry, meter, rhythm and harmony and the whole subject of music...were imparted to him by learned Egyptians" (*De Vita Mosis* I.21, 23). Cf. *Acts* 7:22: "he was instructed in all the wisdom of the Egyptians."

[25] *Stromateis* 1.5.28.1, 3.

the master road and master gate," the "Lord's gate."[26] Quoting from the Wisdom of Solomon, "The spirit of the Lord has filled the world," Clement argues that we should expect to find, through God's good providence, means and ways of reaching him everywhere.[27]

Clement writes of philosophy "opening the road," for he saw the roads that could lead to Christ hampered by many things—attachments, a laziness about seeking truth that might challenge one's views and lifestyle, and a contentment to live with a general skepticism about how much we can know. Skepticism, he saw, tended to towards lethargy when it came to choices about important matters, and he believed that philosophy can play a vital role in "opening" the road by placing the call of Truth before his hearers. In his *Protrepticus*, Clement addressed those who were content to order their lives simply according to tradition and custom: "But, you say, it is not reasonable to overthrow a way of life handed down to us from our forefathers."[28] But a challenge to custom and tradition is only possible if there are rational grounds for other, and better, choices; *metanoia* presupposes that there are objective realities that can be known and are worth choosing i.e., that would be rational to choose.[29]

In the *Stromateis* Clement argues that there must be some self-evident, undemonstrated principles from which true judgments can be drawn.[30] His target is especially the Pyrrhonian suspension of judgment, those who say that nothing is certain.[31] He points to the self-defeating nature of such skepticism: the skeptic, being doubtful as to the validity of any particular epistemological, moral, or religious standpoint, must also withhold judgment as to his own skepticism. Clement has the practical implications of such a skepticism in sight as well, for in withholding commitment from affirming any proposition as true the skeptic also withholds affirmation of any form of behavior which is grounded on the truth of certain propositions. But of course the person suspending judgment cannot remove the need to act in *some* way. He is therefore in the position of having to do something, to act in some way, without having any rational

---

[26] *Stromateis* 1.7.38.6.
[27] *Stromateis* 1.5.29.1, 3, 5 (quoting *Wis.* 1:7).
[28] *Protrepticus* 10.89.1.
[29] I offer a form of this argument in the account of my own conversion, "Climbing the Wrekin," in eds. B. Besong and J. Fuqua, *By Strange Ways: Theologians and Their Paths to the Catholic Church* (San Francisco: Ignatius Press, 2022), 239–62.
[30] See *Stromateis* 8.3.6.7–7.2; 8.5.15.2–16.3
[31] For an account of such skepticism see Sextus Empiricus, *Outlines of Scepticism* (Cambridge: Cambridge University Press, 1994). For Empiricus on the suspension of judgement see I.22:196.

grounds for preferring one course of action as better or worse than any other. How, then, *can* he act in practice? "We live in accordance with everyday observances, without holding opinions," says Sextus Empiricus, living according to a fourfold "guidance by nature, necessitation by feelings, handing down of laws and customs, and teaching of kinds of expertise."[32] Lacking all reason to move away from custom and laws and the traditions of his elders the skeptic is content with conformism, unable to consider *metanoia*. Clement recognized how essential it was, then, that the school provide a response to the deadening inertia of skepticism through the principles of the *philosophia perennis*, making possible its challenge to the power of custom: "Let us then shun custom; let us shun it as some dangerous headland, or some threatening Charybdis, or the Sirens of legend. Custom strangles man; it turns him away from truth; it leads him away from life; it is a snare, an abyss, a pit, a devouring evil."[33] Opposing local custom and tradition is the truth of Christ as the universal Savior: "And how is He Saviour and Lord, if not the Saviour and Lord of All?"[34] Clement's question is predicated on the philosophical foundation of belief in one Truth, for either the meaning of things is held in the divine Truth or their meaning is arbitrated by individual or community desire, opinion, and custom and it is we who give things their meaning, corresponding to our *own* patterning of the world.[35] Only from within a philosophy of universal objective truth—who is Christ, and who alone is to be worshipped—could the Church break free from the power of the gods, from the forces of political and social convention that so easily presented themselves as absolutes.[36]

Philosophy opens the pathway; the Lord who is the Truth is the *goal*, just as the Old Covenant is crowned and fulfilled by the Person of Christ. Clement reminds us of Jesus's image of fledglings being gathered about the mother bird: "Jerusalem, Jerusalem, how often have I wished to gather your children together to me like a bird with her fledglings!"[37] Clement draws our attention to Christ's phrase,

---

[32] *Outlines of Scepticism* I.11.23-24. And see the discussion in Clark, *From Athens to Jerusalem*, 4-6.
[33] *Protrepticus* 12.118.1.
[34] *Stromateis* 7.2.7.6.
[35] Cf. Gerard Boersma, *Heavenly Participation: The Weaving of a Sacramental Tapestry* (Grand Rapids: William B. Eerdmans, 2011), 31-32.
[36] In a striking passage, faith in the voice of God in the Scriptures is presented as having the power to resist the "supernatural power" of the Sirens who put all who passed them into a state of shock (*Stromateis* 2.2.9.7).
[37] Matt. 23:37.

"how often?" and insists it be taken seriously, for "it indicates the varieties of wisdom" and the offering of salvation "in individual ways, qualitatively and quantitatively, universally, in time and in eternity."[38] The one salvation is to be found in Christ, but the paths to him are universally available, gathering points to Christ along which the children are brought. Clement clarifies that he is not saying, of course, *every* path leads to Christ; quite the contrary, for one can either listen to lady philosophy or follow the way of folly. There are paths that lead to Christ and others—often tempting and apparently charming—that lead to ruin and death. Pathways require discernment. What we can know, however, since we believe in the goodness of God, is that he has made paths of wisdom that lead to truth universally available.[39]

The commitment to philosophy made by the Alexandrian school was not a commitment to any particular tradition of thought. "When I speak of philosophy, I do not mean Stoic, Platonic, Epicurean or Aristotelian. I apply the term philosophy to all that is rightly said in each of these schools, all that teaches righteousness combined with a scientific knowledge of religion, the complete eclectic unity."[40] It is Truth one needs to follow, not any particular branch of philosophy. Clement insisted that he was not a member of any the four main schools of Greek philosophy but belonged to the truth and justice contained in them all. It is to the *philosophia perennis* that he is committed.[41]

From the report we have by Gregory Thaumaturgus we find this same attitude in Origen.[42] In studying with Origen, Gregory found an openness to all schools of thought—excepting, as we noted earlier, the Epicurean system. All other schools, Origen taught him, might be studied for truths that could be gleaned from them: "we should read with utmost diligence all that has been written, both by

---

[38] *Stromateis* 1.5.29.4-5.
[39] *Stromateis* 1.5. 29.6-10.
[40] *Stromateis* 1.7.37.6.
[41] See Lilla, *Clement of Alexandria*, 41-51 for a close comparison between the positions held in Middle Platonism and those of Clement.
[42] "The Oration and Panegyric Addressed to Origen" XIII. The collection of Origen's writings in the *Philokalia* includes a letter to Gregory Thaumaturgus in which Origen makes the point that one should draw from Greek philosophy whatever can be turned to a Christian purpose, comparing this practice to the children of Israel, on making their exodus, begging valuable objects from their neighbors and so "spoiling the Eygptians" (13:1-2). On Origen's philosophical allegiances see also Mark Edwards, *Origen against Plato* (Aldershot: Ashgate Publishing, 2002), 3-9.

the philosophers and by the poets of old, rejecting nothing... but hearing what all of them have to convey." This kind of openness to truths taken from different schools is, as we have seen, typical of the Middle Platonism that was found in Alexandria.

This spirit of freedom in the study of philosophy speaks both to Origen's familiarity with the teachings of the schools and to the confidence he had in the ultimately compelling nature of the truth. What Origen asked from his pupils, wrote Gregory, was a spirit of discernment—he wanted his pupils to be familiar with all schools of thought, to understand each, and to be able to weigh and evaluate the merits of each. In the review of philosophical schools, Gregory writes, "he himself went on with us, preparing the way before us, and leading us by the hand, as on a journey."[43] He would interpret and explain terms, unpack arguments, and stretch out a saving hand to rescue those who were being "submerged" in the writings and in danger of drowning. He would conclude the work with his pupils by "selecting and setting before us all that was useful and true in all the various philosophers and putting aside all that was false," especially "in all that concerns piety."[44]

Pathways, then, had to be carefully discerned. But philosophical pathways, though they could be challenging to navigate, and hence needed the support of a good teacher, were seen as absolutely necessary. One could not simply receive the truth in its fullness as a first step. There was a process that must be followed, a gradual unfolding. Everyone was called to receive sovereign wisdom, the wisdom of Christ, but Clement and Origen were convinced that they could only do so when they showed themselves ready for it, and this readiness was manifested by a willingness to take "labor and discipline"[45] to track wisdom down. There is a chase involved that entails a commitment of intelligent and focused energy: "The lover of the chase catches his prey by a process of hunting, searching, tracking, and using the speed of hounds. Similarly, truth is clearly a desirable object of a hunt, secured by hard work."[46]

A final clarification worth making on this question of philosophy as a pathway to Christ is that both Clement and Origen saw philosophical formation as important for *all* Christians. It was not understood as necessary only for pagans who were without Revelation.

---

[43] "The Oration and Panegyric Addressed to Origen" XIV.
[44] Ibid.
[45] *Stromateis* 1.4.26.1-2.
[46] *Stromateis* 1.2.21.1.

How does this position cohere, then, with Clement's teaching that within God's dispensation there was a way of the Law for the Jews and of philosophy for the Greeks, with both able to bring a person to Christ? That would seem to suggest that for a convert—such as Clement—the pathway to Christ would be philosophy, whereas for one raised a Christian and already possessing the Scriptures—such as Origen—the pathway of the Law was sufficient. In fact, neither Clement nor Origen thought in such either/or terms because the Alexandrian school built on what Philo had discovered in his reconciliation of Jewish prophecy and Greek philosophy in which true philosophy is seen as already contained in the Sacred Scriptures. For those who know how to read the Bible spiritually and truly, in other words, the precepts of Revelation discovered there unfold the principles that are *also* found in all sound philosophy. Philosophy and Revelation will be read in concert. There is certainly a difference of emphasis between Clement and Origen on this matter, with Clement stressing the importance of studying philosophy for the sake of understanding how to rightly interpret the Scriptures and Origen unveiling the true philosophical principles at the heart of the Bible by developing his allegorical exegesis. The "philosopher" and the "exegete" have different methodological approaches.[47] But whether the philosophical foundations were to be presented explicitly in and through the study of teachings from the main philosophical schools or received implicitly from the engagement with the Scriptures, both leaders of the school saw the foundational teachings of philosophical wisdom as necessary for the sound formation of the Christian and as intrinsic to the right reading of the Scriptures.

FOUNDATIONS FOR FAITH

What, then, are these foundational teachings of philosophical wisdom that are necessary for sound formation and for the right reading of the Scriptures? What needs to be believed about human persons and about the world if the Christian Gospel is to be embraced and accepted? What philosophical principles are necessary to hold if the journey of conversion into the Christian mystery is to be made, for a participation in the formational work of God's *paideia*?

---

[47] For this difference in emphasis between Clement and Origen cf. *Stromateis* 7.16.95.9 with *Contra Celsum* I.62. But the distinction should not be overplayed: God's wisdom is the measure of all things, not human wisdom, and having that measuring rule allows one to discern philosophical truth from error. Clement agreed with Origen that philosophy "adds" nothing to the Savior's teaching, which is perfect in itself since Christ is the wisdom of God (see *Stromateis* 1.20.100.1-5).

We can begin with a principle enunciated by Origen. In his *Commentary on the Song of Songs* Origen comments on Paul's teaching in Romans 1:20, that the invisible things of God are to be understood by means of what is visible and offers us a clear summary of the principles underlying Christian Revelation:

> So, as we said at the beginning, all the things in the visible category can be related to the invisible, the corporeal to the incorporeal, and the manifest to those that are hidden; so that the creation of the world itself, fashioned in this wise as it is, can be understood through the divine wisdom, which from actual things and copies teaches us things unseen by means of those that are seen, and carries us over from earthly things to heavenly.[48]

This has been described as "the cosmological-theological key to his exegesis,"[49] the key that underlies his theological outlook and his methodology for interpreting the Scriptures. For the Church's evangelizing catechesis to be received, Origen judges that those being formed need to be confident that they inhabit a purposeful universe in which heavenly realities can be known in and through the things around them that are evident, because of the divine wisdom at work in them and in the universe. Origen goes on to say that this relationship of visible to invisible does not only characterize creatures, but that "the Divine Scripture itself is written with wisdom of a rather similar sort."[50]

Wisdom and the Logos

Origen expresses in this passage the fundamental Christian conviction that the world is created in and through a divine "Wisdom," a Wisdom in which human beings share in some fashion. This is another way of speaking about the place of philosophy in the Christian faith since "philosophy" is, of course, literally "friendship with wisdom," *philo-sophy*; strikingly, it is the only academic discipline to be framed in terms of friendship, which speaks, perhaps, to its inescapably personal and fulfilling character. In addition to the centrality in the Greek tradition of this notion of friendship with wisdom, the figure of Wisdom was powerfully expressed in Judaism, as we have seen, and served as one of the main ways of speaking of

---

[48] Origen, *Commentary on the Song of Songs* III.12.
[49] So R. P. Lawson, in his introduction to Origen's *Commentary on the Song of Songs* in the Ancient Christian Writers Series, 26 (New York: The Newman Press, 1956), 9.
[50] *Commentary on the Song of Songs* III.12. In the final chapter we will be able to see how this exegetical principle is unfolded in both typological and sacramental ways.

God's immanence, of his presence in his creation. In the Hellenizing Judaism that we find in Alexandria the figure of Wisdom comes to a particular prominence and is closely associated with the idea of God's *paideia* as an expression of his wise, formative action in history and in the world. We have noted that Jesus himself stands in this tradition and identifies himself as the embodiment of Wisdom, calling the people to find life and rest in him. The "pathway" of philosophy, of developing friendship with wisdom thus has, in the Christian tradition, a natural trajectory leading to friendship with the Person of Christ.

For Origen, the importance of knowing through the divine Wisdom was crucial for guaranteeing not only the intelligibility of the universe and its unity, its coherence, but also to enable a response and movement on the part of the one who was seeking. Only if wisdom is discoverable can it provide the basis for the practical choice of direction for one's life. The first step needed for participation in God's work of *paideia* was a willingness to respond to a call to *metanoia* – that is, to go beyond one's current way of thinking and, with this, to embrace a new way of life. Without such an openness to conversion no progress could be made. Origen told Gregory that there could be "no genuine piety towards the Lord of all in the man who despised this gift of philosophy."[51] An openness to *metanoia* is the first essential movement of the religious person.[52] A life directed by wisdom entails a fundamental choice of a way of life that leads to fullness and completion, not to a diminishing of one's being. To set one's priorities according to this foundational choice one must be able to discern and respond to the voice of Lady Wisdom: "To you, O people, I call, and my cry is to all who live."[53] The call is a universal one, and a foundational principle must therefore be to establish the human capacity to hear, understand, and respond.

Only an acceptance of the principle of a divine Wisdom that orders

---

[51] "The Oration and Panegyric Addressed to Origen" VI.
[52] The Christian call to conversion in Christ cannot, of course, be equated with any other model of conversion in the ancient world, as we will see in the next chapter for, as Martin Hengel rightly argues, Jesus ultimately "confounds every attempt to fit him into the categories suggested by the phenomenology or sociology of religion" (*The Charismatic Leader and His Followers* [Edinburgh: T&T Clark, 1981], 69). Nonetheless, while there are no exact parallels, there are overlapping points of contact between Christian and philosophical understandings of conversion, as one would expect, and most fundamentally the importance of developing a new way of "seeing" as a key aspect of initiation into a new way of life (cf. Nock, *Conversion*, 181–83).
[53] *Prov.* 8.4.

the universe and in which humans share enables the possibility that we can arrive at a true knowledge of objective being. And it is only from this foundation that setting out on the path of conversion can begin. Origen wrote of moving "from actual things," from "those that are seen," "from earthly things" to those things which are heavenly and unseen. A basic belief in the trustworthiness of perception is required, and is certainly characteristic of both Origen and Clement, moving from things that are seen and manifest. They begin from a position of taking the "signs" seriously. So, for example, in the second book of the *Stromateis* Clement refers to the position that one can have faith in what appears evident to sensation—"perception is the starting point of faith"—a position he attributes to Theophrastes, Aristotle's successor in the peripatetic school.[54] This commonsense position did not mean that Clement thought acts of perception unchallengeable, of course; only the voice of God in the divine Scriptures is irrefutable.[55]

Still, why should one take basic human perceptions and judgments to be generally reliable? In the uncompleted eighth book of the *Stromateis* (a book which consists simply in notes he made on further topics he wished to treat, prominent among which are questions of skepticism and epistemology) Clement argues for a foundational epistemological position of the capacity of the human being to reach true knowledge. He proposes here that there must be at least some undemonstrated principles from which true judgments can be drawn, describing this as undemonstrated belief.[56] That the universe can be understood, argued about, have conclusions reached about it, depends upon prior, "undemonstrated" beliefs in its rational patterning and of the mind's ability to grasp these beliefs and work from them. All demonstration needs to begin from a trusted, foundational point or no demonstration can be undertaken, for each principle would need to rest on something prior to it in an infinite regress. If there is to be movement it must begin from a firm starting point. In arguing for this Clement shared the central position of Middle Platonism[57] which drew upon arguments from both Plato[58] and Aristotle.[59]

The metaphysic that explains why the mind can work from these undemonstrated principles and have faith that the universe

---

[54] *Stromateis* 2.2.9.5.
[55] *Stromateis* 2.2.9.6-7.
[56] For his argument against skepticism see *Stromateis* 8.3.6.7-7.2; 8.5.15.2-16.3.
[57] Albinus, *Didaskalikos* 157.9ff, 21-22.
[58] *Republic* 511b 6-7.
[59] *Topics* 100b18-21; *Posterior Analytics* 71b20-23; 72a7-8; 72b20-21; 84a30-33.

is discoverable flowed, for both Clement and Origen, from their understanding that human reason shares in divine Wisdom and is an image of the divine Logos.[60] This was again a position the Alexandrian school would have found in Middle Platonism, especially as it drew on Plato's *Timaeus*.[61] The divine Logos was seen as the governing Agent of God in the world, imaged in the intellect of each person, thus making possible for each person a self-governance under God and a knowledge of the cosmos. Origen argues, consistently with this Middle Platonist tradition, that the regularity and order in the universe points to the Logos working behind and through the phenomena we perceive.[62] The ordered environment in which we live is the result of the *logoi*, or essential ideas of things upon which they are patterned, being held in unity in the one Logos. Through the human intellect's sharing in the Logos it, too, could hold the elements of the cosmos in a unity.

Philo had already performed the important work of uniting this understanding of the Logos to the Genesis account of man's being in the image of God. Drawing from the fact that there are two creation narratives in Genesis, he explained the account of creation in Genesis as consisting of two stages: God first created the intelligible world, the world of ideas that are held in his mind. All of these ideas dwell in the one Logos, held in unity there. These ideas become the models and archetypes by which the physical world is then created: the ideas, the *logoi spermatikoi*, are the creative, generative principles of the world. The term "image" appearing in Genesis 1:26-27 signifies that the human intellect has a kinship with the universal Logos. The human person, made in the image of that which exists in the mind of God, the Logos, is thus able to know the created world and can also penetrate the transcendent world.[63]

Philo taught, then, that the eternal realm of ideas which the creation mirrors are the thoughts of God[64]—a development of Platonism to which Philo is the earliest witness that was crucial to subsequent Christian thinking.[65] In fact, the Logos language in Philo comes very close to Christian descriptions: he calls the Logos the first-begotten

---

[60] See *Stromateis* 1.7.37.2; 5.14.94.4-5.
[61] *Timaeus* 31b-32c. In 34b 3-4 and 36a 6-37a 1 we also see the concept of the rational world-soul stretching to the boundaries of the sensible world as the cause of the order and harmony in the universe. See also Aristotle, *Physics*, 8:2, 252b, 26-27.
[62] *De Principiis* I.7.3.
[63] *Legum Allegoriae* I.31.
[64] *De Specialibus Legibus* I.47-48; *De Cherubim* 49.
[65] H. Chadwick, "Philo," 142.

Son of the uncreated Father[66] and the "second God,"[67] the heavenly food from God, like the manna given in the desert,[68] and the great high priest interceding to God.[69] But in the end Philo draws back from a full incarnational language, and distinguishes the Logos from God: the Logos is God's image, not God himself.[70]

This Logos theology gave the Alexandrian Christians a way of approaching cosmology with Christ the Logos at the center. To create a cosmos, an ordered whole, God made all things in accordance with his own Logos. Following the lead of Philo, they located Plato's eternal Forms, or Ideas, in the mind of God, giving them their theological home there—in the divine Word, the eternal Logos, the overarching Reason who holds all things together. Origen explicitly rejected the notion of *self-subsistent* Platonic forms; rather, God holds all things in his mind,[71] and the final happiness to which we are called is not to a contemplation of the Forms but of the divine hypostases, the divine Persons.[72] Origen systematically developed his theology of the *logoi* of creation, regarding them as created ideas present in Christ that together form the intelligible world, the archetype of the world of the senses and representing the original goodness of things,[73] "the principles according to which the world not only will come into being, but also will be held and sustained . . . in the Logos."[74] The eternal Ideas, the

---

[66] *De Vita Mosis* II.134.
[67] τὸν δεύτερον θεόν. For this see Eusebius *Praeparatio evangelica* VII.13.1.
[68] *Legum Allegoriae* III.175.
[69] *De Migratione Abrahami* 102; *De Somniis* I.215.
[70] *Legum Allegoriae* III.207.
[71] See *De Principiis* II.3.6. For an excellent article placing Origen's thought within currents in antiquity that were developing Platonic thought in this direction see Audrey Rich, "The Platonic Ideas as the Thoughts of God," *Mnemosyne*, Vol. 7, Fasc. 2 (1954) 123-33.
[72] See Peter Widdicombe, *The Fatherhood of God from Origen to Athanasius*, Rev. ed. (Oxford: Clarendon Press 2004), 44-46. For key areas in which Origen distinguished himself from Plato see Edwards, *Origen against Plato*, 159-61.
[73] See *De Principiis* I.2.2.
[74] Panayiotis Tzamalikos, *Origen: Cosmology and Ontology of Time* (Leiden: Brill, 2006), 44. This theology of the *logoi* is relevant to a broader question about Origen's views on creation and his relationship to Platonism. Much Origen scholarship has understood Origen to have taught that God created a separate world of independent rational souls and then a second creation of "earthly" humanity as a result of the fall of this world of rational spirits. But this view is being increasingly challenged: Origen taught, rather, that God has patterned his creation on the archetypal intelligible world held in unity in the one Logos. There was no world of "pre-existent souls" whom God created and whose fall was the occasion of this material universe. For scholars responding to the earlier "double creation" view see Edwards, *Origen Against Plato*, 89-92; Tzamalikos, *Origen: Cosmology and Ontology of Time*, 81-99; John Behr, ed. and tr., Introduction, *Origen: On First*

logoi which are held in unity in the Logos, are the principles of order and unity in creation so that we face, not into a world of fragments and dissociated objects, but a world of beings sharing common natures.

With these fundamental convictions about the order and knowability of the universe in place, the practical choice for wisdom in one's life and the intelligibility of the universe come together in the adoption of a single sapiential worldview, enabling one to follow a pathway of divine wisdom. Origen taught that the path of wisdom in one's daily decisions is the good life, the ultimately fulfilling life, because this is to live according to the way of the cosmos itself: the way of wisdom is life in harmony with what is Real. Origen, said Gregory, "filled our minds with a rational instead of irrational wonder at the sacred economy of the universe, and irreproveable constitution of all things."[75] He taught Gregory to appreciate the order and harmony of the universe and its laws and to live in accordance with them. The good life is in the end the rewarded life, the life that leads to the supreme Good and to true happiness, because there is a coherence between paths of justice and virtue and the ways upon which the universe is patterned. There is an order underlying creation that is set there by Wisdom. The one who "reaches mightily from one end of the earth to the other," and "orders all things well," is the one whom one should take for a bride.[76]

Hierarchy and participation

The Alexandrians, then, developed their Christian worldview premised upon a creation that is intelligible and open to human discovery. Following the *philosophia perennis*, they also held this ordered, unified world to be symbolic and structured in a hierarchy. There are levels of being, with each level receiving its being from that which stands above it and dwelling in that higher level by which it is assumed and transformed. The realities of this world participate in heavenly realities and do so in an analogous way, appropriate to their own way of being. This cosmic order was often described in terms of a "Golden Chain," an image taken from Homer's *Iliad*, in which he

---

Principles, Volume 1 (Oxford: Oxford University Press, 2017), lvi–lxii; Ronald E. Heine, *Origen: An Introduction to His Life and Thought*, 93–116.

[75] "The Oration and Panegyric Addressed to Origen" VIII.

[76] Wis. 8:1-2. In Hellenistic Judaism the notion of divine wisdom penetrating all things in the cosmos and ruling over them was prominent in the Wisdom of Solomon which, as we know, had an Alexandrian provenance, and we find such an understanding expounded in chapters 8–13: the Wisdom through which God created the world is accessible to all and guides them in the paths of righteousness.

writes of such a chain stretching from heaven to earth.⁷⁷ From the lowest elements of the world to the transcendent One all were bound together in a single, stratified unity, a "ladder of being" stretching up to the heavens and embracing the depths of the material world. The key philosophical concept in this framework was that of *participatory reality*, which was the way of explaining how many individual subjects could possess a given attribute, each individual sharing, or "participating" in the attribute, which each receives in part, according to the nature of that being, the attribute itself transcending the individuals who participate in it.

This hierarchy of being was clearly expressed in Origen's hermeneutical principle that was quoted at the beginning of this section, which presented "all the things in the visible category... related to the invisible, the corporeal to the incorporeal, and the manifest to those that are hidden." In general terms, then, the lower level of sensible reality may be said to participate in, and point to, the intelligible world of the spirit, which is why Jesus's disciples, Origen explained in a later work, begin by looking at the things around them and use these as "steps to the contemplation of the nature of intelligible things."⁷⁸ Theologically, this philosophical approach corresponded to, and supported, a sacramental view of reality, that things are signs of that which is higher, which they can truly signify since they share in them. All of creation was thereby seen as sacramental, bearing the glory of the invisible Logos.

This understanding of a hierarchical universe, with the key concept of participation governing its structure, was reflected in the Alexandrian understanding of the human person; philosophical vision was thereby unfolded in the practical guidance given on the spirituality of the Christian life. The human person was seen as the central point of the created order, the intelligible and sensible realms, the visible and the invisible, united in the human person, who belongs to both and is therefore a microcosm of the whole of creation. "By the power of the Holy Spirit He arranged in harmonious order this great world, yes, and the little world (*smikon kosmon*) of man too, body and soul together; and on this many-voiced instrument of the universe He [i.e., the Logos] makes music to God, and sings to the

---

⁷⁷ See Zeus's speech in *The Illiad* VIII.18ff. For a discussion of this understanding of the order of being, with a rich historical perspective, see A. O. Lovejoy, *The Great Chain of Being* (New York: Harvard University Press, 1936).
⁷⁸ *Contra Celsum* VII.46. For an earlier presentation of a process of spiritual ascent through a Trinitarian participation in the Persons see *De Principiis* I.3.6-8.

human instrument."⁷⁹ The human person is a "little world," mirroring in miniature the unity of the cosmos. Imaging the divine Logos in his rationality, man, the "human instrument" of the Logos, is the connecting point in creation between the visible and the invisible, able to share in the knowledge of the *logoi* in all that is created and to represent those levels of the created world in worship and in action. This image of a cosmic order, which was in turn connected to the notion of a scale of value, was thus linked to prescriptions concerning how to achieve a right ordering of the *person* that would place it in harmony with such a divine ordering. Clement employs musical images to express this cosmic harmony and the work of bringing human life to mirror and share in such a harmony, taught by God's Logos, and in the next chapter we will see how he picks up this same musical metaphor to articulate the basic proclamation of the Gospel, the Good News as the new and "pure song" of the Logos who is "the stay of the universe... stretching from the centre to the circumference," bringing "this whole to harmony... in accordance with the fatherly purpose of God"⁸⁰ through his Paschal mystery.

A spirituality of doctrine

Origen noted, we remember, that the divine wisdom's ordering of visible to invisible and earthly to heavenly does not only characterize creatures, but that "the Divine Scripture itself is written with wisdom of a rather similar sort."⁸¹ The rich understanding expressed in the school, of the "little world" of the human person and of the whole cosmos, as a wise arrangement hierarchically structured, explains why the Scriptures were to be read spiritually as well as literally, as we will unpack in a later chapter. The Scriptures not only trace the passage of God's salvific work through time, conveying in linear form the

---

⁷⁹ *Protrepticus* I.5.3. For a discussion of Didymus's interpretation of the creation stories in Genesis revealing the human person as a microcosm of the universe see Layton, *Didymus the Blind and His Circle in Late-Antique Alexandria*, 88–91. Later, this microcosm theme will be especially richly developed by Maximus the Confessor: see Adam Cooper, *The Body in Saint Maximus the Confessor: Holy Flesh, Wholly Deified* (Oxford: Oxford University Press, 2005). In due course Lateran Council IV would declare: "from the beginning of time made at once out of nothing both orders of creatures, the spiritual and the corporeal, that is, the angelic and the earthly, and then the human creature, who as it were shares in both orders, being composed of spirit and body" (*DS* 800). It appears again to inform our contemporary Catholic anthropology in *Gaudium et spes* 14. See J. Ratzinger, "Introductory article and Chapter 1: The Dignity of the Human Person," *Commentary on the Documents of Vatican II*, Vol. 5., ed. H. Vorgrimler (New York: Herder and Herder, 1969), 129.
⁸⁰ *Protrepticus* 1.5.2.
⁸¹ *Commentary on the Song of Songs* III.12.

drama of the gathering of the nations, the plan of his Wisdom, but also present us with the Logos incarnate who recapitulates all things in himself and is, for the whole cosmos, the Center and magnetic point of attraction, now having been lifted up and gathering all to himself through the levels of being. The mirroring of this cosmic restoration is mirrored centrally in the human person, and so in the holy Scriptures we are taught to place ourselves in relation to the incarnate and risen Logos, in whose virtues and powers we can share as the great drama of redemption is enacted in each of us.

A *Christocentric* adaptation of these teachings from Middle Platonism was brought to bear on all areas of the spiritual life. With the understanding that all being is held in the Logos, united in a hierarchy of participation, everything on earth can be a point of attraction to Christ if the soul can be rightly awakened. To enable such an awakening a love and desire for truth has been implanted in us, a yearning for what is true and right. Origen reflects on how people devote themselves to study, expending enormous labor even when the reward is only "small fragments" of discovery. The mind burns "with unspeakable longing" to know the realities of God's creation. Such a longing, he argues, would make no sense if it could not be satisfied,[82] and ultimately only the perfect good and fullness of truth will allow the soul to rest. At this point Origen sketches something like a theology of study as "the pencil of our Lord Jesus Christ" faintly outlines the forms and natures of all things in our hearts as we pursue this quest for knowledge. In knowing the world, I am finding the tracks and traces of the Logos in whom I and all things cohere.[83] Perhaps less obviously to me, an inner transformation is also taking place, if I will allow this, for the Logos himself is gradually purifying the one who bears his image in this process of discovery, working to restore it to the Father who is the final point and object of contemplation. As I seek to uncover the mysteries of creation, I am myself being led on a path of transformation through this dedication to truth, towards a purity of heart and the capacity to

---

[82] For this and what follows see *De Principiis* II.11.4.

[83] Visually, one can see this understanding stunningly presented in a later period, in the depiction of Christ and the apostles in the tympanum of the central narthex portal of Sainte-Madeleine at Vézelay which was completed in AD 1132. The figure of Christ, human and divine, stands at the center of the cosmos, with the four elements of the earth, the peoples of the world and the zodiac and months of the year surrounding him. For a discussion and explanation of its spirituality see Conrad Rudolph, "Macro/Microcosm at Vézelay: the Narthax Portal and Non-elite Participation in Elite Spirituality," *Speculum* 96, 3 (July 2021), 601–61.

see God. The inner quest and the outer realities thus belong together because the one Logos, the Person of Christ, inheres all things and places his beckoning to beatitude in every place for the sake of those who bear his image.[84]

The Alexandrian doctrine of the Logos underlay not only the school's passion concerning the value of study, but also its commitment to mission employing a spirit of dialogue and debate. Mission to all was the mandate of Christ and dialogue with all was possible because one speaks to the other from "within" the Logos (*dia-logue* across, or through logos). In this the Alexandrians were again following the Platonic tradition on the importance of dialectics in philosophical training. They saw the practices of study and communication as more than just a training of the mind; they were also ascetic practices, for truth always requires a humility before it, and individual truth must be transcended for the sake of the Logos who is shared by all.[85] Undertaking dialogue in the school of Christ the Logos one commits oneself to *metanoia*, to a losing of one's life for his sake, a losing that leads to a transcendent *finding* both of oneself and of the other with whom one is in dialogue, in a shared love of the good of Truth.

The themes which we have been treating, of Wisdom, the Logos and participation, were also central to how the Alexandrian tradition explained the doctrines of the Incarnation and Redemption, reinforcing this strong sense of coherence in the accounts the school sought to provide as it united doctrine and spirituality. The two doctrines of the Incarnation and Redemption were held to be inseparable: in the wise plan of God, the divine Logos took human flesh to himself in order to redeem it. Clement and Origen both employ a double analysis of descent and ascent in their accounts,[86] reflecting a double movement that was already present in the Platonic account of how the Forms constitute themselves in bodies and material reality—thus, for example, the Form of Beauty was understood as appearing in the realities of the world it informs, doing so in order to draw the soul upwards towards itself. There is a descent and instantiation *for the sake of the ascent* to the eternal Form. All the appearances of beauty in the world are to awaken the soul to the transcendent Form, to raise the soul to its true home.

---

[84] This path to the contemplation of God is traced in *De Principiis* II.11.5-7.

[85] Cf. Hadot: "the individual transcends himself towards something which lies beyond him" (*What is Ancient Philosophy?*, 63).

[86] For a helpful discussion of how Clement and Origen's teaching on the Logos use these themes of descent and ascent see Williams, *Arius*, 124-48.

Building on this understanding from Platonism, creation, incarnation and redemption flow together in Clement and Origen as free acts of God, not necessary to him, yet his fitting self-expression, acts of his reason as well as his will—not arbitrary, but ordered according to the patterning of the divine. Clement expresses the character of the inner life of the Trinity as one of divine Self-gift, providing the logic of this movement of descent for the sake of drawing all things to himself in the concluding appeal of the *Protrepticus*, in a passage in which Clement's voice gives way to Christ's:

> I desire, yea, I desire to impart to you even this gracious favour, supplying in its fulness the good gift of incorruption. And I freely give you divine reason, the knowledge of God; I give you Myself in perfection. For this is Myself, this is God's desire, this is the concord, this the harmony of the Father: this is the Son, this is Christ, this is the word of God, the arm of the Lord, the might of the universe, the Father's will.[87]

Divine desire, will, and reason all come together here in the Self-gift of Christ as an act of freedom and grace from the Father. Christ acts in complete unity with the Father, in concord (*symphonia*) and harmony (*harmonia*) as he gives himself for the sake of drawing all to the Father.[88]

The doctrines were taught as cosmic in scope: the whole of creation participates in these great acts of God. The Incarnation of the Logos was an affirmation not just of the human person but of the whole of creation since the Logos penetrates into every part of creation; the human person the central point of God's redemptive activity because he sums up in himself the whole of material creation and because he is fallen. Athanasius, also, was later to teach this cosmic scope of the central Christian doctrines, employing these same central philosophical concepts of Logos and participation. Human transgression was the immediate "cause" of the Incarnation, "our sorry case that caused the Word to come down, our transgression that called out His love for us,"[89] but this point of sickness was also to be the point of gathering, of a cosmic healing. It would be a paradoxical

---

[87] *Protrepticus* 12.120.3–4.
[88] We see the musical analogy appearing again here in Clement, and for a discussion see Petroc Willey and Scott Sollom, "The *Catechism of the Catholic Church*: Some Anniversary Considerations," *International Journal for Catechesis and Evangelization* 3, 1 (2022), 49–64. This harmony and concord is expressed by Origen and Clement in terms of the unique Father-Son relationship: a Father cannot be a Father without a Son (see Origen, *De Principiis* I.2.9; Clement, *Stromateis* 5.1.1.3–5).
[89] Athanasius, *De Incarnatione* 1.4.2.

and hidden healing in the lowliness of flesh, for God became flesh in a "mere man" rather in "other and nobler" parts of creation, such as the sun, moon or stars, precisely because he came to teach and to heal rather than dazzle the human person: the manifestation had to be "according as they could bear it."[90] And this work of Redemption would encompass all: through the healing of the person, creation was also to be healed as the divine Logos took his image upon himself to establish harmony with the *logoi* of creation. In and through the Logos taking flesh, then, to use an image from Clement, the creation will be restored and lifted up to God, being drawn upwards and inwards to Christ the Logos, as minute particles of steel are drawn to a magnet through "many steel rings."[91] Here is the movement of ascent, Christ drawing the soul upwards through the levels of participatory being until it is restored to him in a state of holiness. In a final passage in the *Protrepticus* Clement places on the lips of Christ an appeal to his images to allow him to make them into his likeness:

> O ye who of old were images, but do not all resemble your model, I desire to conform you to the archetype, that you may become even as I am. I will anoint you with the ointment of faith, whereby you cast away corruption; and I will display unveiled the figure of righteousness, whereby you ascend to God.

The image is to be restored to its true likeness by Christ the Archetype through an anointing. We are being pointed towards the cleansing of the image in the bath of baptism and the anointing of the gift of faith. "Let us take up His yoke; let us take upon ourselves incorruption; let us love Christ, the noble charioteer of men," Clement then exhorts his readers, and he recalls how Christ "led the foal and its parent under the same yoke"[92] as he entered into Jerusalem. Christ made the journey to his sacrifice on the Cross having "yoked together the team of mankind" so that he might ride in this chariot first into Jerusalem and then into heaven. The descent of the Logos was to enable Christ to "yoke" humanity to him and in this way lead them, through the depths of his descent, back to the Father.

AND TODAY

Philosophically, our culture has moved a long way from the principles of the *philosophia perennis* that were embraced and used in the

---

[90] Athanasius, *De Incarnatione* 1.43.1-2.
[91] *Stromateis* 7.2.9.4.
[92] *Protrepticus* 12.121.1. See Matt 21:1-7.

Alexandrian catechetical school. In *Catechesi tradendae*, John Paul warns of "certain contemporary philosophical schools" which exercise "a strong influence on some theological currents and, through them, on pastoral practice,"[93] requiring the Church to put in place a sound philosophical formation for catechists that will enable them to provide a convincing response to these negative currents. To help us understand the importance of regaining the Christian and Platonic synthesis that was achieved in the school for underpinning and sustaining a realist philosophical approach for the new evangelization today it is helpful to remind ourselves briefly of Alasdair MacIntyre's project to address what he describes as the "disquieting" contemporary situation of metaphysical loss and cultural amnesia, of the partial loss of traditions of understanding and of a consequent living and teaching among "fragments" of such traditions, only half-seen and, even where seen, only half-understood. His characterization of our Western situation is immediately recognizable: "What we possess . . . are the fragments of a conceptual scheme, parts which now lack those contexts from which their significance derived."[94]

In *After Virtue* he traces and explores this notion with reference to ethics and moral living in which we possess "simulacra of morality" and "continue to use many of the key expressions," but have — "largely, if not entirely — lost our comprehension, both theoretical and practical, of morality."[95] In a subsequent work, *Three Rival Theories of Moral Enquiry*, MacIntyre compares three traditions from which we variously draw, comparing and evaluating each for its capacity to provide a satisfactory account of morality and of cultural transmission in order to respond to the crisis of cultural incoherence.[96] The first is the Enlightenment rationalist tradition such as it is expressed in the ninth edition of the *Encyclopedia Britannica*. It offers a conception of the unity of enquiry, and therefore of human knowledge and achievement, rooted in a clear intellectual approach which was enshrined especially in the science of the day: it finds coherence in an approach which begins with data to be scrutinized and examined; constructs conceptual frameworks which can provide

---

[93] CT 60.
[94] *After Virtue*, 2.
[95] Ibid., 2. For a discussion of the application of this concern to the sphere of catechesis, see the opening chapter of Pierre de Cointet, Barbara Morgan and Petroc Willey, *The Catechism of the Catholic Church and the Craft of Catechesis* (San Francisco: Ignatius Press, 2008).
[96] Alasdair MacIntyre, *Three Rival Theories of Moral Enquiry* (London: Duckworth, 1990).

means of unifying this data; involves methods of moving between the data and these conceptual frameworks to test, verify and improve understanding; and, finally, offers a history of continual progress to support the veracity of this approach and methodology. This tradition also offers a way of understanding how we might frame human goods, centered on the values of rationality and autonomy, and proffers scientific achievement as the highest expression of knowledge. This tradition was manifested, MacIntyre suggests, in the concept of the lecture form as the most appropriate means of educational transmission. The lecturer held a position of authority, providing a focal point of academic achievement, summing up and drawing together the whole tradition from the vantage point of its current position, which was necessarily the highest point.[97]

A movement against this tradition arose, a reaction to this Enlightenment understanding of rationality, which was experienced as overly prescriptive in its view of the human person, governed as it was by a universalist and unitary understanding of reason. The view of the person, it was felt, took too little account of the need to unite the cognitive and affective dimensions, and also underplayed man's social identity. The Enlightenment view of the human person had an insufficient understanding of how the person is "embedded" in his nature and in social contexts and traditions that are also intrinsic to his nature. The understanding of individual liberty, paramount in this tradition, was also limited in being considered as liberty from all but economic relationships with others. MacIntyre takes Nietzsche's *Zur Genealogie der Moral, On the Genealogy of Morals,* as the representative work of a "rival version" of enquiry, therefore, a version which also necessitated a new form and model for educational processes and a complete review of the Enlightenment's conception of what might be held to be suitable aims for education. In this work, Nietzsche, as a "genealogist" of morals, sets out to write an account of academic history and the history of moral thought as ideology, seeing it as in reality the history of the will to power, which is the reality underlying social, moral and educational development, disguised as the search for truth. Nietzsche sees Christianity playing a key role in this distortion, as the religious culture that places a "priestly" veneer over the set of heroic values enshrined in classical Homeric culture.[98] The lecture format of the nineteenth century could not be sustained in the face of this challenge. No longer an

---

[97] See ibid., 21–31.
[98] See ibid., 39–42.

authoritative summing up of available knowledge and understanding of a topic, a lecture now, MacIntyre argues, "can only be an episode in a narrative of conflicts."[99]

One of the questions MacIntyre asks is whether the Nietzschean position can give rise to a tradition which can incarnate and demonstrate its viability and vitality, or whether it is incapable of propagation, or is even necessarily self-destructive. It is a question that touches upon a crucial theme running through this work on the Alexandrian school as we seek to uncover principles for current "fruitfulness" in the Church's pastoral ministry. A central question is that of the generative capacity of a principle or a teaching: To what extent, and how, does it contribute to the transmission of greater and fuller life i.e., in Christian terms, an entering into the Mystery of truth? MacIntyre argues that Nietzsche, in attempting to avoid "taking a position," which could then in turn be subject to ideological undermining, disintegrates the sense of self and the possibilities of communication. Nietzsche's work on morals necessarily "represents no more than a temporary stance, a mask worn only for the purposes of certain particular addressings of certain particular audiences." His nightmarish project is ultimately how to "assume the contours of a given mask and then to discard it for another, without ever assenting to the metaphysical fiction of a face which has its own finally true and undiscardable representation."[100] MacIntyre here signals the central difficulties for this rival version of moral enquiry. Nietzsche does have, in fact, a project and he wants to communicate this to others. And yet he undermines this very project by not making room either for himself as an enduring self with intentions which can be pursued over time, or for the possibilities of communication, which also requires stable identities in his audience, who can receive what he is offering. Beliefs and forms of life which disintegrate the person and which undermine the possibilities of communication are self-defeating.[101]

MacIntyre's analysis of the deficiencies of both the "encyclopedist" and the "genealogist" positions draws our attention to the need to provide a metaphysics and anthropology that can do justice both to

---

[99] Ibid., 33.
[100] Ibid., 47.
[101] In the light of this MacIntyre makes what he calls a "modest, albeit metaphysical" claim: "it is ... necessarily presupposed by the act of writing for a particular reader or readers that the ego of writer and that of reader have enough fixity and continuity to enter into those relationships constitutive of the acts of reading-as-one-who-has-been-written-for and of writing-as-one-who-is-to-be-read" (*Three Rival Theories of Moral Enquiry*, 46).

universality and what is shared in common on the one hand and also to the integrity and reality of individual persons and things, allowing individual beings truly to signify that which transcends them without an evaporation of being. MacIntyre himself proposes that we look to a third tradition of philosophical and moral enquiry from which we can draw. He finds this in Thomism, a tradition that sits firmly on the shoulders of the philosophical commitments that were adopted by the Alexandrian school.[102]

MacIntyre's conclusions parallel the teaching of John Paul II in his encyclical on faith and reason. There, after surveying a number of schools of philosophy and thought problematic for the Christian faith, John Paul II identified certain *indispensable philosophical requirements for catechesis*[103] — requirements, in other words, for the communication and reception of Christian Revelation. The three requirements parallel those of the *philosophia perennis* that we found in the school and the use of these in Christian formation is seen as essential. In the first place there is the need for a foundational "sapiential dimension" in one's worldview — that is, the conviction that there is an overarching purpose and meaning in life, a rationality and unity in the patterning of the cosmos. It is this sapiential approach, the *Directory for Catechesis* confirms, that enables an integration of different elements of the faith, acting as a principle of unity.[104] Secondly, he asks for a recovery of the conviction that the mind can arrive at knowledge of "the very being" of the objects it knows — that there is a coherence between anthropology and cosmology, the human mind "made" to know the truth of objective reality. Finally he argues that the word of God requires a philosophy of "genuinely metaphysical range," of depth and value, enabling one to move from "phenomena" to "foundation" — a hierarchy of being and of value.

Perhaps significantly, John Paul does not commit us to a particular philosophical tradition at this point, referring the reader instead to St. Thomas and St. Bonaventure, two points of philosophical synthesis of the *philosophia perennis* that was so essential to the Alexandrian school.[105] The central philosophical themes that we have found in

---

[102] On the Platonic contribution to St Thomas see W. Norris Clarke, SJ, *Explorations in Metaphysics: Being, God, Person* (Indiana: University of Notre Dame Press, 1994), 65–88 and Sebastian Morello, *The World as God's Icon: Creator and Creation in the Platonic Thought of Thomas Aquinas* (Brooklyn, NY: Angelico Press, 2020), 13–36.
[103] FR 80–82.
[104] DC 101.
[105] FR 82 n.99 refers us, on the question of knowledge of the true, to St Thomas's *Summa Theologica* I.16.1 and St Bonaventure's *Collationes in Hexaemeron* 3.8.1.

the Alexandrian school are intrinsic to both these points of synthesis which rightly reflect some development of the philosophical work of Middle Platonism, especially in its understanding of participatory reality. Both Clement and Origen ultimately remained within the framework of Middle Platonism in holding that God could not be called "Infinite." To be knowable to any extent, it was believed, God must have Form, must be circumscribed. Infinity was formlessness, being without boundaries, and therefore strictly unknowable. The next step towards a fuller and more adequate Christian understanding of participatory reality was taken by Origen's contemporary, Plotinus,[106] who made the philosophical move necessary for God to be identified with the Infinite, using the Greek term *apeiron* to express the notion of the One who contains all perfections and all plenitude in which limited Forms participate. Following Plotinus's breakthrough, the work of systematization by Proclus in his *Elements of Theology* and the subsequent Christianization of this by Pseudo-Dionysius, this Neo-Platonic notion of participation was able to find its resting place in Christian theology and cosmology, a place reflected in due course by both Thomas and Bonaventure.[107] Only then would the notion of participation be able to describe the mode of being of all finite beings, with all that is finite, limited, participating in *God* as the Unlimited, their creative Source and Goal.

---

[106] Origen and Plotinus shared much in common and had possibly benefitted from the same teacher in Alexandria, Ammonius Saccas—although the evidence on this is uncertain because there are two figures of this name as well as two Origens, the leader of the school, and a pagan Origen!

[107] Cf. Clarke, *Explorations in Metaphysics*, 76-77. Thomas, for example, fused this notion of participation with the Aristotelian metaphysics of act and potency, taken from the latter's account of how individual substances change; he applied this to the relationship of Creator to creation, such that God, as subsistent *esse*, the pure act of existence, was seen as related to his creation as beings who participate in him as potency in relation to act (see the discussion in Morello, *The World as God's Icon*, 37-66).

CHAPTER 7

The Good News of Christ and the Call to Conversion

IN THIS CHAPTER WE EXAMINE HOW THE school announced the Good News of Christ, making the initial call to conversion and preparing converts to take their first steps toward the baptismal assent of faith.

We noted earlier that Clement composed a trio of works that trace the stages of Christian conversion and discipleship, and we will use these as the framework for the final three chapters. Without neglecting Origen or later leaders of the school, this emphasis on Clement's writings will allow us to focus on the earliest period of the Alexandrian school and see the shape and contours of the catechumenal path at the end of the second century. The stages in this catechumenal way can be thought of by analogy to human life and growth: Clement's *Protrepticus* calls a person to conversion and welcomes him or her as a *new creation* in Christ; his *Paedagogus* describes the discipline that Christ undertakes with the *growing child*, the new Christian, while his *Stromateis* addresses the *Christian in maturity* who is called to holiness and knowledge (*gnosis*), and a capacity to support this new life in others, learning to teach and disciple, to father and mother new converts to the faith.

THE LURE OF GNOSTICISM

As we begin our investigation into the character of the school's catechumenal path and its opening exhortation to conversion, it will be good to preface this with a slightly more extended account of the Gnostic alternative that was a living presence in Alexandria during the second and third centuries. Like the catechetical schools, Christian Gnostic schools offered their own *kerygma* and pathway of initiation, and a review of the main characteristics of the Gnostic message offer a point of reference and comparison to the presentation of the faith that we find in the catechetical school and will help us to identify some of the distinctive features of the school.

The Alexandrian catechetical school was vehemently opposed to Gnosticism in all its forms, but it is nevertheless important to note the overlapping nature of some of orthodox Christianity and Gnosticism's concerns so that we avoid an overly simplistic dichotomy between them.[1] While Gnosticism as a system was rejected, some points of coherence between Christianity and heterodox Gnosticism must be recognized. Gnosticism, that "passionately wild idea, whose urges had long been suppressed"[2] was, like orthodox Christianity, best conceived as a religion of redemption. It spoke out of an awareness of the experience of alienation in human life, with the world, and especially bodily reality, a source of profound pain and distress as well as pleasure. It conjured up a picture of life as a battle in which one must live in holy rebellion, antagonistic to all that would constrain one. The Gnostic spirituality the school faced was fueled, one might say, by a divine discontent, an awareness that to accept life "as it is" meant certain death and loss. A response was needed, centered on a recovery of understanding of one's true nature.

At this point, the commonalities probably end. For the Gnostic *kerygma* was one of a rescue mission that retrieves *from* the world, a redemption of trapped divine sparks that left creation itself untouched and unhelped. In broad terms we can say that the Gnosticism that the school was countering, while there were certainly variations of emphasis,[3] identified evil with the material world. It saw the earth as ruled by demonic forces ("Archons"), who were utterly opposed to the First Life. The tyrannical rule of the demon was *heimarmene* — that is, universal fate — which in its physical aspect corresponded to the laws of nature. Unlike Platonism, Gnosticism did not say, then, that there is a less than perfect order in nature, which shows the world to be deficient in goodness. On the contrary, it viewed the world as bound by a rigid and demonic *order*.[4] The world, for Christian Gnostics, was the domain of Satan, and all temporal realities were understood to be inevitably heading for perdition.

---

[1] These commonalities go some way to explaining why Christianity and Gnosticism were at times equated. See, for example, the comments of Plotinus, *Enneads* II.9.
[2] Ratzinger, *The Unity of the Nations*, 19.
[3] Compared to many other Gnostic groups, Valentinian Gnosticism, for instance, seems to have held beliefs on creation that were in some respects relatively close to the Christian understanding. The creation of the world was not seen as the result of the clash of two eternally dueling principles but came about as a result of a fall within an otherwise perfect system. Creation, in other words, while *de facto* fallen, has not sprung from a source that is eternally alien to the Good.
[4] Hans Jonas put the point well: "The blemish of nature lies not in any deficiency of order but in the all-too-pervading completeness of it." (*The Gnostic Religion: The Message of the Alien God and the Beginnings of Christianity*, 2nd rev. ed. [Boston: Beacon Press, 1963], 253).

What was the Gnostic way of salvation? Facing a world like this, the only hope for humanity lay in learning the truth that sensible reality was valueless and completely opposed to what one must understand as one's True Self which flows from the Lord of Light, an emanation from that original Light. One's bodily nature was a prison, and this imprisonment was understood variously either as justified punishment for some unearthly sin, or else the work of the Dark Force who had captured the human race.[5] Nature opposes us at every moment: it not only reveals nothing of God's glory, it distracts one from true worship: "Come let us make a great upheaval, that he may forget the heavenly voices."[6] Any concern with behavior or with the natural order was thus simply a further consorting with evil and in this lay the danger of forgetfulness of one's true identity, which could only be discovered when one lives as a stranger to the world.[7] Ignoring the world and showing one's disregard for material reality could take many forms, but principally the way to enlightenment in this tradition consisted in either a life of extreme dissipation and self-indulgence, or else an equally extreme asceticism. Both ways were dismissive of the life of normality, cluttered as it was held to be with its superstitious taboos, an over-concern with earthly affairs and a moral scrupulosity, all things opposed to the way of salvation, which lay only through the gaining of a spiritual knowledge (*gnosis*) far transcending such matters. The Church's task, then, was restricted to the invisible empire of souls.

A story of divine redemption accompanied this dark account of the world which we inhabit and throughout which we search for our True Self: God, the First Light, became involved in the world's tangled destiny in order to retrieve the divine sparks imprisoned in the universe. The First Light was not identified with the Judeo-Christian God. Christian Gnostics believed, in fact, that the Creator God of the Old Testament is not the Father of the Lord Jesus Christ, nor the Supreme

---

[5] For the Egyptian rural population, trapped in an apparently unchanging economic order, deprived, socially stigmatized and constantly humiliated, such a cosmology might have reflected their sense of the natural order, and one can imagine that a message of salvation *from* creation would have been appealing and intuitive. For details of the ordinary life of the majority of the Egyptian population, see Henry Green, "The Socio-Economic Background of Christianity in Egypt," 107-13.
[6] Cited in Jonas, *The Gnostic Religion*, 53.
[7] Philo perhaps provides us with a vivid description of those who were tempted to some form of *Jewish* Gnosticism. They are, he writes, "as though they were living alone by themselves in a wilderness, or as though they had become disembodied souls and knew neither city nor village nor household nor any company of human beings at all, overlooking all that the mass of men regard, they explore reality in its naked absoluteness" (*De Migratione Abrahami* 90).

Being of Christian belief. He is rather the "Demiurge" — one of the lowest beings in the complex spiritual hierarchies of the Gnostics, and an obstacle to those seeking salvation. The Demiurge intervenes to *prevent* the possibility of divine knowledge, seeking to deny this to human beings. The Old Testament narrative of the temptation and fall is reversed in Gnostic mythology, a reversal that can be seen, for example, in the Gnostic sect of the Ophites (from the Greek *ophis*, "snake") or the Naasseni (from the Hebrew, *nahash*) which saw the serpent as the one who offers access to *gnosis*, and who is to be identified with the Logos or Sophia.[8] Wisdom comes to the earth through the knowledge of good and evil and it is the serpent who offers this wisdom to the human race. Jesus himself is a reincarnation of the serpent-logos, providing secret knowledge for the elect.[9] In all Christian Gnosticism Christ is the one who seeks to rescue the divine sparks imprisoned in the universe by bringing true spiritual *gnosis*, thereby enabling the elect to enter the higher spheres of reality.

Before leaving this account of the essential features of the Gnostic worldview, we must note one or two other features that are crucial to it, for just as the Gnostic story of salvation parodies that of orthodox Christianity, so the Gnostic pathway of response parodies the catechumenal way of the Church. Foundationally, then, it was the Gnostic understanding of *the relationship between creation and salvation* that determined the gulf between its presentation of religious belief and practice and that of the Church. The Church held to the belief in one God who is both the Good and the Creator. God the Creator, in other words, is not other than God the Redeemer. This position was established as normative by the Church in and through debates and pronouncements countering the schools of Gnosticism which sought to hold a contrary position, driving creation and redemption apart. For orthodox Christians, soteriology and cosmology were not to be opposed nor viewed as irrelevant to each other. In fact, for both Clement and Origen it was their soteriology that governed their understanding of cosmology: knowing what God's plan and intention is for creation allows one to understand the nature of that creation.[10]

---

[8] Clement writes of them in *Stromateis* 7.17.108.1-2 and Origen discusses their mysterious diagram in *Contra Celsum* VI.24-38.
[9] Gnostic sects noted that Jesus alluded to the serpent figure as an image of himself in John 3:14.
[10] Thus for Origen, Paul's account in 1 *Cor.* 15:23-28 of glorification in and with Christ, when God will be "all in all" dominates his thought. Origen refers to this as the "restoration" (*apokatastasis*). See, for example, *De Principiis* III.1.15-19; III.6.1-6. A point of controversy in scholarship about Origen, it is important to

The pathway to salvation in Gnosticism is essentially, as the name suggests, one of gained *gnosis*. As such, a wedge was placed between faith and knowledge, the former being inadequate, the latter the privileged possession of its adherents. While the Alexandrian Christians strongly opposed Gnosticism, they at the same time did propose that Christians possess true and authentic *gnosis* for "God our Savior desires all men to be saved and to come to the knowledge of the truth."[11] Clement and Origen wanted to win for orthodox Christianity an authentic understanding of the nature and place of *gnosis*. Combatting the Gnostic teachers, they taught that Christianity necessarily leads to true *gnosis* since God is the True and being is knowable. Clement sought to explain the nature of this knowledge in the *Stromateis*, not as the possession of some arcane knowledge, but as a right holding to principles of rational thought, a faithfulness to the moral teaching of the Church, and a more adequate understanding of the meaning of the Scriptures.[12] The leaders of the school also held that knowledge never replaces the obedience of faith as *the* pathway to salvation since that which is finally to be known in perfected *gnosis* is nothing other than the great net of revealed mysteries which are held by all in faith. The path to greater *gnosis* is thus a path *within* faith, a deepening understanding of what has been given to all and is held ecclesially, knowledge of the Mystery of Christ. Moreover, as we will see when we consider the central place of mystery for the school, *gnosis* was ultimately understood not as a series of resolutions of "problems," or even the achieving of a "right perspective" upon truth as an object to be studied, so much as the penetration of a mystery through a deeper understanding achieved through participation, one that is inseparable from the path of virtue and prayer and which depends, above all, on the work of grace. The school's approach, therefore, while it prized its intellectual character, should not be characterized as narrowly intellectualist.[13] The knowledge sought was always framed within a call to holiness as part of a wholistic vision for formation.

---

note Heine's discussion of this topic in Origen's thought and his conclusion that more consideration should be given to his evolution of thought in this area: "It seems to me a defensible, but not an unquestionable, conclusion that in Caesarea Origen was in the process of rethinking his view of the ultimate salvation or restoration of all beings" (*Origen: Scholarship in Service of the Church*, 256; and see 242-56).

[11] 1 *Tim.* 2:3-4.

[12] For an unpacking of these different meanings in Clement see Méhat, *Étude sur les 'Stromates' de Clément d'Alexandrie*, 489-522.

[13] See, for example, allegations of intellectual arrogance by Marlowe, *The Golden Age of Alexandria*, 255, and Charles Bigg, *The Christian Platonists of Alexandria* (Oxford: The Clarendon Press, 1913), 18.

Finally, in all Gnostic systems a radical divide was introduced between the elect and others. According to Irenaeus, Valentinian theology, for example, distinguished between three categories of human beings: those with a spiritual nature (*pneumatikoi*), those with a soul-like nature (*psuchikoi*), and those with a material or earthly nature (*choikoi*). Christ assumed a spiritual nature and a soul, but not an earthly nature, for this group could not be redeemed.[14] (Because of its view that material reality was evil there could be, of course, no true doctrine of the Incarnation in Christian Gnosticism.)

We have already noted that it would be wrong to see in the catechetical school a form of Christian Gnosticism that contradicted the Gospel message of the saving power of faith, or that we should think of different "classes" of people in the school, the simple and the elect, with a path of virtue and holiness being proposed for the former group while one of knowledge was mapped out for the "advanced" Christian. On the contrary, there was no exclusivity with regard to persons in the Alexandrian school, which knew that the Church is for all, not just for the intelligent. Christianity offers "short roads to salvation" [15] to all because Christian teaching is accessible to all and the truth can in principle be grasped by everyone. The Gnostic claim that an occult and secret knowledge is the pathway to salvation must be rejected. The school sought to appeal to all and to receive all for baptism. The allegation that Origen had to counter from Celsus, the pagan critic of the Church was, in fact, that the Christian Church in Alexandria,[16] as elsewhere, *avoided* the company of the intelligent and instead sought out the ignorant: "whenever they see adolescent boys and a crowd of slaves and a company of fools they push themselves in and show off."[17] The Christians seek to attract "anyone ignorant, anyone stupid, anyone uneducated, anyone who is a child."[18] Some Christians, Celsus says, do not try to give reasons for the faith but say, "Do not ask questions; just believe."[19]

Interestingly, in addition to the accusation of intellectual disinterest among Christians, one can see in Celsus's comments the common

---

[14] *Adversus Haereses* 1.6.1.
[15] *Protrepticus* 7.77.1.
[16] Celsus probably wrote his attack on Christianity either in Rome or in Alexandria. If the latter, then his remarks would be especially pertinent regarding the Christian church in Alexandria: see the comments in Henry Chadwick's introduction to Origen's *Contra Celsum* (Cambridge: Cambridge University Press, 1965), xxviii-xxix.
[17] *Contra Celsum* IV.50.
[18] *Contra Celsum* III.44.
[19] *Contra Celsum* I.9.

Hellenistic presumption that the good life is in fact only available to those capable of a strong intellectual formation.[20] The Christian interest in the formation of all its members was distinctive and unusual. Origen makes no attempt to deny that Christians seek to attract the ignorant and slaves; the Christian faith is for "anyone interested."[21] Of course, he replies, if a person could abandon the ordinary business of life and devote himself to philosophy this would no doubt be the best path to follow. But most cannot, and to restrict Christianity to intellectuals would be wrongly to suggest that God is only interested in a small portion of humanity.

THE ALEXANDRIAN KERYGMA

From the lure of the Gnostic worldview and pathway to salvation we can now turn to examine that offered by the school. The first work in Clement's trilogy, then, is his *Protrepticus*, his *Exhortation to the Greeks*. The exhortation was addressed specifically to the Greeks since, as we have seen, after AD 135 the Jewish community in Alexandria was virtually nonexistent. The pressing needs regarding evangelization required a particular focus on the Hellenistic heritage. In doing so, the Christian school was handing on the Hellenized *Judaism* that had been developed in Alexandria, a union of Athens with the strict monotheism of Jerusalem. Indeed, there is much to be said for Guy Strousma's argument that it was with "Jewish weapons" that "Christianity conquered the Roman Empire."[22] And now Christianity had worked a further transformation on this union of Judaism and Hellenism with its joyful annunciation of the appearing of Christ, a coming that had transfigured the world.

The title of Clement's work describes a *genre* of writing that was found in the ancient world: *Protrepticus* indicates a form of "hortatory literature that calls the audience to a new and different way of life."[23]

---

[20] As Clarke notes, excepting the Cynics, philosophical schools "drew their pupils for the most part from the well-educated" (*Higher Education in the Ancient World*, 122).
[21] *Contra Celsum* IV.51. Justin says as much a hundred years earlier (*Apology* II.10), as does Augustine, a hundred and fifty years after Origen (*De Catechizandis Rudibus* 12.13.23)
[22] Guy G. Strousma, *The End of Sacrifice: Religious Transformation in Late Antiquity* (Chicago: University of Chicago Press, 2009), 11. Thus, for example, the Greek philosophical tradition of the "care of the self" was broadened in Christianity, taking on a deeper ethical and personal dimension informed by Revelation and a Jewish anthropology of sin and repentance, as well as of the central importance of the body and community. "The great caesura in the self is no longer between body and soul, but between the sinning self and the sound self" (*The End of Sacrifice*, 25).
[23] Stanley K. Stowers, *Letter Writing in Greco-Roman Antiquity* (Westminster: John Knox Press, 1986), 92. On common elements between Clement and Roman rhetoricians see also Laurence Emmett, "Clement of Alexandria's *Protrepticus* and Dio

This type of text would have been recognizable to his hearers: it was used in philosophical schools where it took the form of an "inaugural lecture that tried to gain converts and attract young people to the philosophic life."[24] Plato's dialogue, *Euthydemus*, contains an example of a Socratic speech in the form of an exhortation of this kind and Aristotle wrote a *Protrepticus* that was often imitated. A later, Roman, example is Cicero's exhortation, *Hortensius*, which was in due course to have a profound effect on Augustine's call to Christ.[25] The form of the work, then, is one found in ancient philosophical schools — a point that reinforces for us the school's conviction that Christianity should be seen as the true philosophy, the true wisdom that is calling to the reader, inviting to a new way of life and thinking.[26]

As for the context in which Clement's work was heard, or read, we have no accounts of Christianity being presented in open-air gatherings and so it was probably shared in smaller, more informal settings with those who had expressed an interest in the faith. Recalling the fundamentally religious and ascetical character of the philosophical schools and the inseparability of ethos, practice and belief in such schools, we will resist, however, images of the catechetical school as a kind of refined literary group or drawing room association, an academic gathering for the exploration and discussion of ultimate mysteries. And we have already seen the distinctive way in which the school approached the question of philosophy itself, involving a break with pagan religion.

Clement describes the call to conversion that stands at the beginning of the process of initiation and formation in the school as a *pro-catechemenous*, a preliminary instruction.[27] Leading into the extended period of teaching (*didache*), a basic proclamation of the faith is given, the *kerygma*, which is aimed at the initial conversion of the person. From the account of the Alexandrian catechetical school Eusebius gives us we can see that the school was known for its kerygmatic qualities and emphasis. Eusebius introduces his readers to the school through the figure of Pantaenus who, Eusebius tells us, was made head of the school after a period of missionary activity in India.[28]

Chrysostom's Alexandrian Oration," *Studia Patristica* 36 (2001), 409-14. Mark Edwards points out that Origen's *Exhortation to Martyrdom* bears the title *Protreptikos* in Greek (*Origen Against Plato*, 41, n.66).
[24] Marrou, *A History of Education in Antiquity*, 206-7.
[25] See Augustine, *Confessions* III.4.7.
[26] *Protrepticus* 11.112.1.
[27] *Protrepticus* 10.96.2.
[28] The links between Alexandria and India have already been noted. The Ptolemies also constructed a new port, Myos Hormos, on the Red Sea, and Strabo

In Eusebius's words, "he showed such zeal in his warm disposition for the divine word that he was appointed as a herald for the gospel of Christ to the heathen in the East and was sent as far as India."[29] "Herald" here translates the Greek *keruka*, part of the word family that includes *kerygma*. In the person of Pantaenus, then, the catechetical school of Alexandria had clearly secured a veteran missionary as its head and it is not unreasonable to suppose that the catechesis and further studies undertaken at the school under Pantaenus would always have kept a formation for mission in mind, appreciating the need for some converts to move beyond an initial reception of the Gospel and subsequent period of discipling to embrace a missionary work.

From apostolic times, the Church had drawn a distinction between these two elements in the handing on of the faith—kerygma and teaching—while at the same time holding them in unity. The apostolic Church had also distinguished the two in terms of *ministry* since *kerygma*, like *teaching*, can refer to an activity as well as to the content of that activity—*kerygma* can signify the act of proclaiming as well as the content of the proclamation. We can see St Paul using the term in these two ways in his First Letter to the Corinthians: thus on the one hand he writes, "it pleased God through the folly of what we preach (*kerygma*) to save those who believe,"[30] which seems to refer to the *content* of what Christians teach, while on the other hand he writes that his *kerygma* lay "not in plausible words of wisdom, but in demonstration of the Spirit and power, that your faith might not rest in the wisdom of men but in the power of God," which seems to point to the *way* in which he preached the message.[31] Because the terms for both *kerygma* and *teaching* can, then, refer to an *activity* as well as a *content*, we find that the early Church sometimes distinguished the ministry of the evangelizer, who drew the new convert to the Church, from that of the catechist, who then deepened the understanding of the faith and prepared the convert for baptism—see, for example, the Letter to the Ephesians which mentions both evangelists (*euangelistas*) and teachers (*didaskalous*).[32] In the Alexandrian school, as we have seen, this distinction between *kerygma* and teaching was definitely

---

tells us that by his time there were more than a hundred ships leaving for India every year (*Geography* II.5.12).

[29] In India, Eusebius tells us, Pantaenus discovered that the Apostle Bartholomew had preceded him and had left the Indian converts with the Gospel of St Matthew written in Hebrew (*H. E.* V.10.2-3).

[30] *1 Cor.* 1:21.

[31] *1 Cor.* 2:4-5.

[32] *Eph.* 4:11.

appreciated, though from the evidence we have the main leaders of the school appear to have been at ease ministering in each of what the Church now describes as the "moments" within evangelization.

We can look now, then, at the key content of the Alexandrian *kerygma*, its annunciation of the central Christian message, especially as it appears in Clement. Clement has left us no account of his own conversion, but the clues are all over his work and are perhaps especially to be found in the *Protrepticus*. From the profound sense of newness of life that pervades all his writings, speaking palpably to a radical discovery of joy, Richard Tollinton has judged that Clement's conversion was probably untroubled by stress and pain,[33] but it may not have been that simple—even in this *kerygmatic* phase we find him focusing on the realistic demands for change this call to joy makes on one's life, while one of his final works provides a moving account of John the apostle rescuing a young man who had fallen away from his baptismal commitments, indicating at the very least a profound empathy for those involved in extended struggles to gain and regain the Christian path of life.[34]

But joy is definitely one of the notes sounded most prominently and insistently in this work. I want to look now at four ways in which Clement presents the *kerygma* in the *Protrepticus* and should preface these presentations by noting that in every framework chosen it is always given as *the supremely good news of the love of God*. Clement speaks over and again of God's *philanthropia*, God's love of the human race. He contrasts this with the actions of the pagan gods and spiritual powers, *deamons* who are *misanthropoi*, that is, hostile to man. The tales of the immorality, pettiness, and viciousness of the gods make this antagonism to human welfare clear, he argues, since they mislead those who worship them into a life of perversity and death, while the stark fact of human sacrifice in pagan worship sums up the antagonism.[35] The conversion Clement seeks from his reader-hearer from his initial annunciation of God's love, then, is crucially a release from the power and influence of these "gods." Nothing could be further from the gods of paganism than the character of the true God, Clement cries: "O surpassing love (*philanthropias*) for man!"[36] The Lord God goes beyond all expectations: "He speaks not as a teacher to disciples, nor a master to servants, nor as God to men, but as a 'tender father' admonishing his sons."[37]

---

[33] *Clement of Alexandria: A Study in Christian Liberalism* (London: Williams and Norgate, 1914), 13.
[34] The story is found in *The Rich Man's Salvation*, 37-42.
[35] *Protrepticus* 3.42.1.
[36] *Protrepticus* 9.82.2.
[37] Ibid.

The paideia of love

We can see from this quotation how natural it is for Clement, in his proclamation of the faith, to draw immediately upon the theme of *paideia*. As we saw in chapter five, the content of the *kerygma* might be summed up as the coming of a new, divine *paideia*. God's *philanthropia* is inseparable from the loving education and training of his children. The Good News of the love of God is that he has undertaken to adopt and form humanity as his children. The Good News to be proclaimed is that the Father has sent the Son for man's salvation and will not leave the human person unaltered. God's work of redemption is transformative. It is an enlightenment and expansion of the person and of his capacity to receive divine life, to be educated into the Lord's own ways, for the actualization of the supreme gift of divine kinship. The offer of a new life in Christ and the pathway of formation to be fully united to him, made in his likeness, are thus presented together in Clement's *kerygma*.

In his *procatechemenous* Clement in this way prepares the new convert to expect the blessings of the kingdom to be gained through a discipline that will include trials and even persecutions—as indeed the Lord Christ himself did in his presentation of the Beatitudes. The loving Father acts by admonishment. The *kerygma* includes the frank recognition of the challenges that face one in the world, together with the assurance that the Father uses even the most painful of these to bring his children home; that not only can nothing separate the believer from the love of God, but that all can be put to *use* in the Father's education of the person. Clement's doctrine of God's providential oversight is far from the impersonal providence of the Stoics for whom the goodness of the Whole justified the inclusion of evil within it. Clement taught rather the Christian doctrine of the saving action of God who permits evil only because he knows how to derive good from it, turning evil into the medicine of salvation.[38] Evil is never treated as a good nor ugliness as beauty, but even evils such as the actions of the rebel angels can be directed towards good for the universe, within God's providence, for he will not allow "the evil which springs from that freely chosen rebellion to lie in unprofitable uselessness, still less to become totally baneful."[39] The intelligent and resourceful love of God is the key to understanding the divine *paideia* and Clement exhorts his readers to trust in his work of gathering humankind into one in the image of the union of his own Being. And here Clement offers a musical imagery again:

---

[38] *Stromateis* 7.11.61.5
[39] See *Stromateis* 1.17.86.1–3.

And the union of many into one, bringing a divine harmony out of many scattered sounds, becomes one symphony, following one leader and teacher, the Word, and never ceasing till it reaches the truth itself, with the cry, "Abba Father." This is the true speech which God welcomes from his children.[40]

The Good News of this divine education is presented by Clement in the most comprehensive way: the teacher who fills the universe with his instruction has now come:

> Wherefore it seems to me, that since the Word Himself came to us from heaven, we ought to no longer go to human teaching, to Athens and the rest of Greece, or to Ionia, in our curiosity. If our teacher is He who has filled the universe with holy powers . . . this teacher now instructs us in all things, and the whole world has by this time become an Athens and a Greece through the Word.[41]

Clement urges his readers to place themselves under "the really true wisdom which leaders of philosophy only hinted at."[42] With the coming of Christ, the work of Athens has been fulfilled and divine wisdom is now available everywhere the Gospel is proclaimed, with every moment providing an opportunity for formation in this divine school of learning. John Ferguson puts the point memorably: "We might say, in a pun which Clement could not make but would approve, that the universe is our university."[43] God's educative and transformative *philanthropia*, then, is the heart of Clement's *protocatechesis*. In his introduction to his next work, the *Paedagogus*, Clement will make clear that this same *philanthropia* is in fact the key for understanding God's *entire* work in our lives: "Eagerly desiring, then, to perfect us by a gradation conducive to salvation, suited for efficacious discipline, a beautiful plan (*oikonomia*) is observed by the all-benignant (*panta philanthropos*) Word, who first exhorts, then trains, and finally teaches."[44] The *kerygma* offers the foundational explanation for each moment of the journey of formation.

The kingdom of the Logos

If one central way of articulating the *kerygma* is that of God's *philanthropia* expressed in a new, divine *paideia*, a second prominent articulation is the Good News of the Word's saving plan. The call to

---

[40] *Protrepticus* 9.88.3.
[41] *Protrepticus* 11.111.3–112.1.
[42] *Protrepticus* 11.112.2.
[43] *Clement of Alexandria*, 63.
[44] *Paedagogus* 1.1.3.3.

conversion is a call *to enter the world of the Logos*. The title of Clement's work reveals this message—and here we see Clement's love for word-play—since *Protrepticus* can be rendered as *The Exhortatory Word*, the title of the work functions as a title of Christ. Clement's book is presented to his readers as an exhortation made by the Word himself, the Logos incarnate.[45] Throughout the text Clement in fact refers to Christ under this title as he challenges his readers to undertake the "glorious venture to desert to God's side" in the battle of life, so as to become a lover of the Word,[46] to join in the struggle for truth in an arena in which the "holy Word" is the umpire.[47]

The call to conversion that Clement makes in his *Protrepticus* is a call to enter into *the world of Truth that transcends one* since the Word who has come down to us is the very Truth of God. The Word calls us beyond all particular cultures, customs, social norms, and opinions to measure ourselves against Truth himself. Importantly, therefore, Clement's call to conversion is a call to enter into *a common world* rather than into a realm set apart from others, because it is the world shared by all rational beings who have turned aside from personal opinion to place themselves under the "charioteer" of the universal Logos. One is making the only sane choice: to live in the order of God's economy which is governed by the Word. The act of faith in Christ enables one to enter the kingdom of Truth, the world of intelligibility, since the forms of all things are held within the Logos, the mind of God, and the things themselves are dependent on God as the fullness of being. The notion of the Logos, present in nature and placed deeply in the human mind and heart is, as we have seen, the key to how the Alexandrians understood that all peoples have the possibility of knowledge of God and of a relationship to him.[48] And the notion of the Logos held in common is Clement's pathway for introducing the convert to the Church, the gathering place of all who follow and put their faith in the Word incarnate: "As His will is creation, and is called the universe, so His desire is the salvation of

---

[45] See Ferguson, *Clement of Alexandria*, 44-45.
[46] *Protrepticus* 10.93.2 (the language here is reminiscent of Plato's *Phaedo* 114d).
[47] *Protrepticus* 10.96.3.
[48] The figure of the Logos was understood to have been present in God's Self-revelation in the history of his people as well, for all the divine epiphanies in the Old Testament were seen as manifestations of the Logos who in due course became incarnate. This understanding also underpins a sacramental view of creation as well as explaining why the Scriptures have to be read Christocentrically, aglow with the illuminating presence of the Logos. Cf. the discussion in McGuckin, "The Christology of the Apostolic Fathers," 39-40.

men, and is called the Church."⁴⁹ The Church is the place in which one awakes finally to the common world governed by the divine Logos.

Thus, the notion of Christ the Word, the Reason and Wisdom of God, who has come among us to make an appeal to each of us to enter his kingdom, grounds Clement's explanation of why the act of faith is a rational one to make. As the religion of the saving Logos, Christianity is the rational religion *par excellence*. In fact, those who reject the Christian message are irrational, *alogos*,⁵⁰ while to be baptized into Christ is to enter into the water of reason.⁵¹ "The gates of the Word are the gates of reason, opened by the key of faith."⁵²

Origen shares this approach and in a passage in *Contra Celsum* explains how the rationality of faith underpins the most ordinary human decisions and actions. The assumptions of intelligibility, moral order, and a predictable universe are common to all. Making acts of faith in this world of the Logos, Origen argues, is the natural foundation for human life as a whole. The most ordinary undertakings in life presume a rationally ordered world and make implicit acts of faith in the stability and consistency of the universe, in causation, and in the capacity of the person to reliably predict. Faith exercised in these ways in ordinary life is both necessary and all-pervasive: "all human life depends on faith.... Who goes on a voyage, or marries, or begets children, or casts seeds into the ground, unless he believes that things will turn out for the better, although it is possible that the opposite may happen—as it sometimes does?"⁵³

Origen then builds upon this natural set of assumptions in the intelligibility and goodness of the world's order to speak of the distinctive *Christian* faith in the Logos who took flesh out of love for us. How much *more* rational is faith in this Logos, who suffered "a death supposed to be disgraceful, which he endured for the sake of mankind."⁵⁴ Origen here not only defends faith in a good Creator and rational Ground of being, as a making explicit of the kind of natural faith entailed in everyday life and its decisions, but also argues that Christ's demonstration of love underlies the rationality of Christian practices and the Christian way of life. Those who embrace the Christian faith participate in the greater and fuller *rationality of divine love*, the "divine magnanimity" of God.⁵⁵

---

⁴⁹ *Paedagogus* 1.6.27.
⁵⁰ *Protrepticus* 10.99.1.
⁵¹ *Protrepticus* 10.99.3.
⁵² *Protrepticus* 1.10.3.
⁵³ *Contra Celsum* I.11.
⁵⁴ Ibid.
⁵⁵ Ibid.

Faith, reason and love are thus brought into unity under grace. The only rational response to this love will be a moral purification and an advancing in the work of love oneself. Only this path can lead to a knowledge of the Father in and through the person of the divine Son. The call to conversion is to an *obedience of faith*,[56] a unity of intellect and will, both powers implicated and committed through the act of faith. It is the pure in heart who see God.

The call of divine beauty

In addition to the kerygmatic emphasis on formation in the divine *paideia* and on Christ as the great figure of the incarnate Logos, both Origen and Clement place *the awakening of desire* at the beginning of the Christian path. From the opening of the path that will lead into the catechumenate, and placed at the heart of the catechetical process, must be a *desire* to receive more and more deeply the Revelation which is being transmitted.[57] When a soul has once clearly seen the beauty of the divine Word, Origen wrote, it will be moved thereafter by "heavenly love and longing," with the "blessed fire" of God's love.[58] Alongside the capacity in the catechumen for understanding truth there must also be a desire for what is offered. The exercise of one's intellectual capacities look to the engagement of desire and of the will, and of the perception of the truth being offered as attractive since the whole life of the learner is to be aligned, gladly and fully, with this truth.

To awaken and then sustain this desire, Clement's catechesis seeks to attract the convert through communicating a sense of the lyricism and beauty of the new life available in Christ. "No other writer sets out the wonder of the new age as does Clement."[59] For this newness Clement uses the Greek term, *kainos*, indicating especially a qualitative newness, a superseding of what has gone before.[60] Christ has brought

---

[56] See also Clement on faith as obedience to God's commands in *Stromateis* 2.11.48.4.

[57] The Alexandrians were following Plato in the central importance they gave to the place of desire in education and formation. In the *Meno*, Plato writes of the encounter between Socrates and the young man, Meno, who has received his education at the hands of the Sophists in Athens. The dialogue revolves around the question of how knowledge can be gained, and Socrates insists that there is no way that knowledge can be imparted independently of the learner's desiring to receive it. As every teacher knows, the learner must be motivated to learn and to be active in the learning process. For a discussion see R. S. Brumbaugh, *Plato for the Modern Age* (New York: Crowell-Collier, 1962), 56–63.

[58] *Commentary on the Song of Songs*, Prologue.

[59] Osborn, *Clement of Alexandria*, 34.

[60] The distinction with the temporal term for newness, *veos*, must not be pressed too hard. Christ's coming was in the sequence and order of the economy of

about a new stage in the economy of salvation. The theme of Clement's opening chapter of the *Protrepticus* is Christ the Logos incarnate who in the newness of his coming brings about the harmony of the person and of creation.[61] Musical imagery, as we have seen, provided Clement with some of his favorite analogies for the spiritual life. The Logos is portrayed as "an all-harmonious instrument of God, melodious and holy," sharing with mankind "the wisdom that is above the world."[62] The world has "grown old,"[63] but his coming among us has made the universe a "sea of blessings."[64] He is the one who sings the new Song of his truth to awaken and attract us — indeed, Clement describes him simply *as* the New Song.[65] Clement builds on the imagery of his time, that the heavens resound with beautiful music, and Christianizes this, transforming a "cosmocentric vision of musical harmony into an incarnational one"[66] and placing the *fullness* of harmony in the incarnate Person of the Word.[67] From the very beginning it is to Christ that the believer must learn to listen, for he plays to us the music of heaven, seeking to persuade us to hear the heavenly song in his human form. The true Orpheus, his song has revived those who were dead and has made them share in his own "real and true life" and his transforming power can make "men out of stone and men out of wild beasts."[68] Christians are those whose ears are opened so that they can hear this music and live according to this call of beauty. The one who responds to the Logos will live in harmony with nature, with God's providential plan for his creatures.

If Clement's text is expansive and mellifluous, seeking to communicate the wonder of the coming of Christ, is no surface aestheticism that he promotes. As always in Clement, challenge and appeal are presented together. As a Platonist, he wants to show that physical

---

salvation. Nonethless, *kainos* focuses on the sense of something appearing that is greater, superior, a new order of things. For a discussion see Andreas Kramarz, LC, "A Call for Universal Harmony: The 'New Song' in Scripture, Patristic Commentary, and Liturgy," *Antiphon* 26, 2 (2022), 105-33.

[61] *Protrepticus* 1.5.2-3.
[62] *Protrepticus* 1.5.4.
[63] *Protrepticus* 1.2.2.
[64] *Protrepticus* 10.110.3.
[65] "... because He lately took a name, — the name consecrated of old and worthy of power, the Christ, — I have called Him a New Song" (*Protrepticus* 1.7.1).
[66] Andreas Kramarz, LC, "Christian Reception of the 'New Music' Debate in the Church Fathers and Clement of Alexandria," *Greek and Roman Musical Studies* 6 (2018), 374.
[67] See also the discussion in Calvin Stapert, *A New Song for an Old World: Musical Thought in the Early Church* (Grand Rapids: William B. Eerdmans, 2007), 42-59.
[68] *Protrepticus* 1.4.1.

beauty is always at the service of the higher beauty of the soul and of divine things. Christ, therefore, had a quite ordinary body because he needed to draw people by the beauty of the truth, and not by outward charm; he is the Lord "who to outward seeming is despised, but in very deed is adored."[69] Clement is referencing Isaiah 53:2–3 here and this prophecy of Christ was accepted by the early Fathers as indicating that Christ had no obvious physical beauty to attract. It is the mind and the soul that Christ would beautify. Spend time on those things, Clement will urge believers in the catechumenate, not on embellishing the body: "The man who would be beautiful must adorn that which is the most beautiful thing in man, his mind, which every day he ought to exhibit in greater comeliness."[70]

Origen takes up this point of Christ's lack of outward beauty in a response to Celsus. Surely, Celsus argued, if Christ was divine then his body must have reflected this in its outward appearance, its strength and beauty.[71] Because Origen, like Clement, reads the Gospels as a *pedagogy* he understands Christ's appearance as a pedagogical feature also, and in his response to Celsus refers to another teaching that he has received: that how Christ's outward appearance is perceived depends on the capacity of the viewer. For while Isaiah speaks of his despised form, the psalms refer to his beauty and fairness,[72] and indeed to Peter, James and John he appeared transfigured in glory. The Logos, Origen argues, appears in the form that can be borne by the viewer. Everyone has the capacity to see Jesus as he really is, but it is the pure in heart who are promised the vision of God, and this requires the putting away of sin. Only the true disciple, willing to follow the Lord up the mountain, will be able to see him as he truly is or hear the voice of God.[73] Origen proposes that it was an act of mercy that Jesus did not manifest his brilliance to everyone for even his apostles "were unable to receive his divinity without some periods of relief."[74] Jesus appears as all things to all people,[75] so as to be able to save each by presenting himself to each person according to his or her capacity, seeking to draw each one on to bear more and more. In both Clement and Origen, then, the presentation of the *kerygma*

---

[69] *Protrepticus* 10.110.1.
[70] *Paedagogus* 3.3.20.6.
[71] *Contra Celsum* VI.75.
[72] Ps. 44:4–5.
[73] *Contra Celsum* II.72.
[74] *Contra Celsum* II.65. If Jesus had appeared in his glory to those who condemned him, he would have smitten them with blindness (II.67).
[75] See *Commentary on John* 1.31.217.

as the call of divine beauty contains both the implication that one will be setting out on an ascetical journey, learning how to respond to a deepening of that call, and that the call is an intensely personal one: there is an invitation to an accompanied pedagogy in which the believer will be introduced progressively to the Lord's glory, working with the development and free responses of the person.[76]

A point of particular attraction in this call, highlighted by Clement, is that it is made by the One who promises to reveal our *own* truth to us, and "the greatest of all lessons is to know one's self. For if one knows himself, he will know God."[77] Christ's coming is the call from the Image to overcome all estrangement and alienation by knowing oneself as made in him, and to welcome in oneself the awakening longing to be reshaped into his likeness. God is the supreme artist and the human person made in the Image, in the Logos, is a work of art far greater than any work that could be fashioned by man.[78] It is precisely in and through this recognition of one's true nature that one finds it possible to transcend custom and the limitations of partial and local judgments, and to reject the worship and practices of paganism with their attendant idolatry, a worship of idols and gods that had shrunk one to their size and enmeshed one in their immorality. A recognition that one is made in the image of the Logos lifts one into the world of rationality, able to heed the voice of Truth which is universal and transcendent. In his mercy and condescension the Father has made himself known through his "healthful Logos" who is the Sun of the soul and who alone can rise in the depths of the mind and illumine the soul's eye.[79] The Word has come down and our response must be to *lift* our gaze.[80] We must not worship the elements of the world, but only its Creator, not the sun but the Maker of the sun.[81] Why, Clement asks, do you imagine winds, air, fire, the earth itself, to be gods? Why do you babble in high-flown language about "the divinity of the wandering stars"? This only has the effect of making the worshippers of such things into the real "wanderers," lost in this world.[82] Those who worship idols mock the true God—or rather, he says, "mock and insult themselves."[83] "I long

---

[76] I am grateful for the discussion in John McGuckin, "The Changing Forms of Jesus according to Origen of Alexandria," in *Seeing the Glory*, 103-12.
[77] *Paedagogus* 3.1.1.1.
[78] *Protrepticus* 4.61.4; 10.98.3-4.
[79] *Protrepticus* 6.68.4.
[80] *Protrepticus* 1.2.3.
[81] *Protrepticus* 4.63.5.
[82] *Protrepticus* 6.67.2.
[83] *Protrepticus* 2.39.3-4.

for the Lord of the winds," says Clement, "the Lord of fire, the Creator of the world, He who gives light to the sun. I seek for God Himself, not for the works of God."[84] The incarnation of the Logos, then, is the full and final confirmation of the truth of our nature.

The journey from image to likeness

Finally, it was characteristic to present the initial proclamation using the imagery of a journey—and the catechumenal process itself, with its steps and stages, drew on this idea. It was a deeply biblical image, of course, rooted in Abram's setting out from Ur and separating himself from polytheism, with the attendant costs that such a detachment required. The school drew attention to this key moment in salvation history.[85] Crucially, of course, the theme of the exodus from the slavery in Egypt and the subsequent journey to the promised land framed the way in which the Christian story was presented. The canonical Gospels themselves employed such an exodus theme in a range of ways, with Jesus's journey to Jerusalem characterized as the definitive exodus from the slavery of sin and death.[86]

This initial period of *kerygma* and inquiry, therefore, was often presented as the moment of setting out on the journey, with the *protocatechesis* providing a view of the landscape of the journey and its destination. Origen, for example, in homilies delivered later in Caesarea, would compare the initial response of the believer to the setting out from Egypt, leaving behind its idols, the crossing of the Red Sea as the moment of entrance into the school of the catechumenate, into the period of training and formation on the desert journey, and the crossing of the river Jordan into the Promised Land as baptism into the new Christian life of sacramental grace.[87]

In his *Protrepticus* Clement provides the journey *kerygma* in simple narrative terms, as the story of a young child in an earthly Paradise who was led astray into a false and distorted manhood and is now invited by the Savior to begin a journey to the heavenly Paradise to discover his true self in a new, spiritual childhood. As we think about this journey theme in the Alexandrian catechesis it is helpful to remember that the early Church thought typologically, with earlier

---

[84] *Protrepticus* 6.67.2. Clement is agreeing here with Plato: *Timaeus* 28c.
[85] For the use of this story in the later stages of the school's development cf. Layton, *Didymus the Blind and His Circle in Late-Antique Alexandria*, 144–51.
[86] Thus Jesus, in the account of the Transfiguration in Luke's Gospel, speaks to Moses and Elijah "of his coming departure (*exodus*) which he was to accomplish in Jerusalem" (Lk. 9:31).
[87] See *Homily on Numbers* XXVI.4.1.

stages of salvation history anticipating and finding fulfillment in the earthly life of Christ and the life of heaven—when the *Christus totus*, the "whole Christ," will be finally gathered. Typology, in other words, always looks forward, with the past as the foundation for what is to be made new. There is no "return" to a Golden Age in Christian thinking. The age of true and everlasting gold lies ahead, not behind.

In the beginning, then, God created us so that we were naturally constituted for the acquisition of virtue. The Gnostics, Clement argued, place before us a false dichotomy, asking: was Adam created perfect or imperfect? If imperfect, then how is that the work of a perfect God? If perfect, how is it that Adam fell? But the answer is that Adam was made with an affinity for the good, "adapted to the reception of virtue,"[88] and was created for a *journey* towards maturity. And that journey towards ultimate goodness and truth requires learning the good use of "hands and mouth and heart,"[89] that is, it requires "purpose, action and speech."[90] The training of that child as he makes his journey will dominate the description of formation in the *Paedagogus*, which will climax in the gift of baptism in which the renewed child, released from slavery at last, will learn the "true speech" of the Christian, beginning with the word *Abba*.[91]

In the *Protrepticus*, Clement begins his telling of the story with a reminder of God's goodness and then traces in summary fashion the scriptural account of creation, fall, incarnation, and redemption.

> Now consider briefly, if you will, the beneficence of God from the beginning. The first man played in Paradise with childlike freedom, since he was a child of God. But when he fell a victim to pleasure... and was led astray by lusts, the child, coming to manhood through disobedience and refusing to listen to the Father, was ashamed to meet God... The man who by reason of innocence had been free was discovered to be bound by sins. The Lord purposed once again to loose him from his bonds. Clothing Himself with bonds of flesh (which is a divine mystery) He subdued the serpent and enslaved the tyrant death; and most wonderful of all, the very man who had erred through pleasure, and was bound by corruption, was shown to be free again, through His outstretched hands. O amazing mystery! The Lord has sunk down, but man rose up; and he who was driven from Paradise gains a greater prize, heaven, on becoming obedient.[92]

---

[88] *Stromateis* 6.12.96.1-3.
[89] Clement points us to *Deut.* 30:14.
[90] *Protrepticus* 10.110.1.
[91] *Protrepticus* 9.88.3.
[92] *Protrepticus* 11.111.1-111.3.

Adam is presented here as a child playing in Paradise, setting the scene for Clement's presentation of salvation as a recovery of a true childhood. The mystery of a divine exchange is central to the presentation of the *kerygma*: the Lord became man in order that man might become divine; the bonds of slavery are freed by the Lord who takes those bonds on himself; the Lord sinks down and man rises. The work of the Cross is expressed through the gesture of Christ's "outstretched hands," a beautiful reminder of both the cost and the breadth of the saving work.

The one playing in Paradise is the "child of God"—in other words, he bears the image of his Father. The journey to be made, correcting the misorientation, will involve a shaping of that image into the likeness of the Lord who is the bearer of the Archetype of that image.[93] "Image" and "likeness" in Clement and Origen stand as the beginning and end points of the whole of the human journey. Christ the Archetype inscribes his image upon us and then comes among us, modeling for us the way of growth that enables us to reach our *telos*, the true likeness to God. Thus, for the Alexandrian school, the doctrine of the Image grounds human freedom in its potential for participation in the work of grace that will mold it into the likeness of God. Layton points to the centrality of this doctrine of the image and its renewal into true likeness as the "basis for the mimetic pedagogy" of Didymus's work as well:[94] Christians, as those who share in the Divine Image who took flesh, as images in the Image, receive his work of grace for their restoration into a true likeness and can therefore act as witnesses to this work and models for each another along this pathway of reclamation.

CROSSING THE THRESHOLD

Clement's *Protrepticus* concludes with a call to the reader to come to a decision. Moved by love, he has run on for too long, pouring out what he has himself received from God. The greatest of all things is offered: salvation, God's gift of himself in love. "But with you now remains the final act, namely this, to choose which is the more profitable, judgement or grace."[95] For those who chose in favor of the Christian faith, an extended period of testing followed the *protocatechesis*, including a thorough moral training and instruction, as well as the requirement to disengage from all practices and beliefs

---

[93] *Protrepticus* 1.8.4.
[94] Layton, *Didymus the Blind and His Circle in Late-Antique Alexandria*, 113.
[95] *Protrepticus* 12.123.2.

that were considered unworthy of the new life to be received. An extensive examination of the enquirer's life and motivation, including his or her professions, took place, and the journey towards baptism now began as the school prepared its candidates.

For our knowledge of the rite and requirements accompanying this in Alexandria, at least in the third century, we can lean especially on Hippolytus's *Apostolic Tradition*. Composed in Rome at the close of the second century or beginning of the third, it reflects Roman liturgical practice at that time. It was adopted in Egypt and appears in an adapted form under the later *Canons of Hippolytus*. Jungmann confirms how confident we can be that Hippolytus's work accurately portrays third-century liturgy in Alexandria also, reminding us of the close interchanges between Rome and Alexandria, including Origen's visit to Rome and attendance at one of Hippolytus's homilies.[96] We also have, in *Contra Celsum*, Origen's own explanation to Celsus of how one needs to receive and convert a person through a process of initial testing:

> ... as far as they can, Christians previously examine the souls of those who want to hear them, and test them individually beforehand; when before entering the community the hearers seem to have devoted themselves sufficiently to the desire to live a good life, then they introduce them.[97]

The "examination" to which Origen refers, and which we also find in Hippolytus, was conducted by those in the community who knew the candidate, together with catechists who would be instructing them. It also included a commitment to abandon any profession that was contrary to essential Christian morality.[98] Origen also writes of the readmittance to the catechumenate of those who "have been overcome by licentiousness or some outrageous sin." These the Church admits "some time later as though they had risen from the dead provided that they show a real conversion, though their period of probation is longer than that required of those who are joining the community for the first time."[99] Although by the time of writing this work Origen had been teaching at the school he founded in Caesarea for more

---

[96] See Jungmann, *The Early Liturgy*, 52-58. The second part of the *Apostolic Tradition* describes the reception of converts into the Church—the catechumenate and the regulations for the administration of baptism and confirmation. Jungmann provides a helpful summary account in *The Early Liturgy*, 74-86.
[97] *Contra Celsum* III.51.
[98] See Hippolytus, *The Apostolic Tradition*, 24-28.
[99] *Contra Celsum* III.51.

than a decade, it is reasonable to suppose that his descriptions are an accurate representation of the Alexandrian setting as well. And in confirmation of some kind of rite or moment of formal agreement that was undertaken before entry into the catechumenate proper we also have a passage in his *Exhortation to Martyrdom* that refers to the "promises" made by those who were about to begin instruction in the faith.[100]

In his *Stromateis*, Clement explains what this initial period of testing was seeking to achieve in terms of one's attitude towards the instruction that was to be given. He confirms that mere interest or intellectual curiosity was not sufficient for a person to receive instruction in the faith; before a person is received into the community to receive instruction he or she must have demonstrated a sufficient devotion to right living. Entrance into the community required the stability of a good will and a commitment to develop in virtue.

> It is not right to entrust the Word to hearers to make a test of it on the basis of comparison or to hand it right over for investigation to those who have been brought up to all kinds of sophisticated arguments and who vaunt the power of their intellectual proofs, those whose souls are already determined beforehand instead of being emptied of prejudgments.[101]

It is not that Clement was disallowing the place of reason in the catechetical process or the appropriate testing of arguments. On the contrary, this was necessary. But there was a point at which one was looking for a certain docility to the divine Wisdom which one was introducing to a soul and for a certain humility to be present. God is mystery and his ways higher than man's ways, and the soul who would approach God making "man the measure of all things"[102] instead of being "emptied of prejudgments" was not yet able to progress further. When one came before the Word one was not to "make a test of it," for it would be the *Word* that was testing the soul. One must not think of handling the Word "objectively," as a matter of scientific investigation, an object to be measured and studied. The time for review and analysis needed to give way before the Word's power to transform; otherwise the new life being offered could become a mere acquisition, with God the latest token for the "vaunting" ego to display. The time of testing that the school required was not, then,

---

[100] *Exhortation to Martyrdom* 17.
[101] *Stromateis* 1.1.8.1.
[102] Cf. Plato, *Protagoras* 333d.

for the sake of displaying spiritual prowess or even simply for making good intentions so much as a growth in humility, of the gradual acceptance of the deep *need* for Jesus. The death of the ego had to be faced: the catechumenate would be the beginning of *learning how to move towards dying with the Lord in baptism*. Clement gives us the criterion for moving on:

> Whenever anyone elects out of faith to go to the banquet, he has faith as a reasonable criterion of judgement, and is strong to receive the words of God. From that point, conviction pursues him out of his superfluity. This is the real meaning of the prophet's words, "If you do not have faith, you cannot understand" (Is.7:9).[103]

"Faith" here signifies that the soul has reached the point of a rational assent. The enquirer has established that making an act of faith is reasonable. That conviction arises from a considered self-knowledge that knows its poverty of spirit and is open to receiving the promises of God. The ongoing growth in faith and trust will not now be a blind leap in the dark, but the free movement of the will made in concert with an intellectual judgment. This act of faith opens the person to receive the divine formation and teaching that the Word will now give.

AND TODAY

The *Directory for Catechesis* has asked that there be a restoration of a *kerygmatic* catechesis, explaining that this should be understood as the basic annunciation of the faith and the call to conversion being seen not only as a preliminary moment in the catechumenal process, to be subsequently left behind. Rather that this *kerygmatic* call to conversion be considered "the essential dimension of every moment of catechesis."[104] The proclamation and content of the *kerygma* is not only the "first step" in evangelization but its *character*. The *kerygma*, as the most fundamental expression of the Good News, holds the central truths surrounding the Mystery of Christ. It is therefore the foundation for each and every truth that is handed on, whether an aspect of the creed, a petition of the Lord's prayer, a sacrament, or a requirement of justice and love.

The inseparability of the *kerygma* and catechesis is profoundly and inspiringly present in the Alexandrian school. We have seen that at each stage of Clement's framework—of exhortation, of formation and

---

[103] *Stromateis* 1.1.8.2.
[104] *DC* 57.

of teaching—he focuses on the central truth that it is the one Lord working out of love, his *philanthropia*, to execute his plan, expressive of his desire for our salvation. The content of this initial proclamation, expressive of this central truth, is both imaginative and varied: the recovery of spiritual childhood as the true likeness of the perfect Image; the call of the All-Beautiful One, to be discovered even under the guise of a Face that was despised; the entry into the glorious sanity of the kingdom of the Logos; learning the ways of the Lord's gracious and sanctifying formation in his divine *paideia*. And in each of these presentations of the *kerygma* Clement announces the determination of "the love that never ends"[105] not only to invite but to *complete* his work of humanity's restoration to happiness and truth. The content of the *kerygma* is always the unveiling of the whole of God's plan, including its costly nature and its promise of blessedness.

The current retrieval of the Church's emphasis on a *kerygmatic* catechesis that we find in all recent magisterial teaching on catechesis and evangelization is particularly the result of the work of two twentieth-century Jesuits, Josef Jungmann and Johannes Hofinger.[106] Their work was significant in emphasizing both the scriptural and the liturgical dimensions of such a *kerygmatic* catechesis, as well as in drawing attention to the narrative character of patristic presentations of the faith. A return to a fully *kerygmatic* catechesis is thus at the same time a recovery of the importance of these elements as well—as is reflected in the most recent *Directory*.[107] And of course we find an exciting shaping in the Church of just such a biblical and liturgical catechesis in the Alexandrian school.

The way of beauty, the *via pulchritudinis*, prioritized by the Alexandrian school, is also central to the contemporary understanding of catechesis set within the contours of the new evangelization, reflecting

---

[105] We can note here the overarching *kerygmatic* principle proposed in the *Catechism* (and taken in fact from the sixteenth century *Roman Catechism*) that "The whole concern of doctrine and its teaching must be directed to the love that never ends. Whether something is proposed for belief, for hope or for action, the love of our Lord must always be made accessible, so that anyone can see that all the works of perfect Christian virtue spring from love and have no other objective than to arrive at love" (25).

[106] See Josef A. Jungmann, *Handing on the Faith: A Manual of Catechetics*, 92–97; Johannes Hofinger and Francis Buckley, *The Good News and its Proclamation* (Notre Dame, IN: University of Notre Dame Press, 1968), *passim*.

[107] The breadth of this *kerygmatic* retrieval is seen in the account of the sources of catechesis: the Word of God in Scripture and Tradition, the Magisterium, the liturgy, the testimony of the saints and martyrs, theology, Christian culture, and beauty (*DC* 90–106).

the conviction of Benedict XVI that it represents "the privileged path for evangelization and dialogue."[108] Thus, "catechesis should know how to point out 'the attractiveness and the ideal of a life of wisdom, self fulfillment and enrichment' so as to form believers as 'joyful messengers of challenging proposals, guardians of the goodness and beauty which shine forth in a life of fidelity to the Gospel.'"[109] We should also note that the *Catechism* authors' decision to open its treatment of the Deposit of Faith with a consideration of the place of desire in human life, followed by the quest for wisdom, again finds a well-developed background in the Alexandrian school.

Moreover, Clement's depiction of Christ as the true Orpheus, the divine Logos, drawing all into harmony through the heavenly music he plays, also finds an unexpected presence in contemporary catechesis, in the pedagogy of the *Catechism of the Catholic Church* which uses just such a musical image to provide the entry point into the content of the Deposit of the Faith. A simple illustration intended for the front cover of every edition depicts a pastoral scene of a shepherd, seated under the shade of a tree, playing panpipes. Lying attentively at his feet, gazing at the shepherd, is a lamb. Inside the *Catechism* is a short explanation of this simple image that "suggests certain characteristic aspects of this *Catechism*: Christ, the Good Shepherd who leads and protects his faithful (the lamb) by his authority (the staff), draws them by the melodious symphony of the truth (the panpipes) and makes them lie down in the shade of the 'tree of life,' his redeeming Cross which opens paradise." The faithful are represented by the lamb, lying at the feet of the Shepherd, held there, rapt, attentive, because the Shepherd is playing the "melodious symphony" of heaven. When the faithful listen to Christ "playing" the Deposit of Faith, they are transported into the heights of heaven by its beauty. It is precisely a desire for a participation in the harmony of life in Christ that the *Catechism* depicts to draw the reader into formation under the heavenly Word.

Finally, we should not omit to mention one of the remarkable emphases of the school, the union of mission and outreach with its catechumenal process. We will be able to unfold this in greater detail in chapter nine, and here simply note that the *Directory for Catechesis* calls precisely for a recovery of a "missionary understanding of catechesis,"[110]

---

[108] Pontifical Council for Culture, Introduction, *The Via Pulchritudinis, Privileged Pathway for Evangelization and Dialogue: Concluding Document of the Plenary Assembly*, 2006.
[109] DC 84, citing EG 173; see also DC 106-9.
[110] DC 5.

linking this closely to the need for a *kerygmatic* catechesis and asking that "in the context of the renewed proclamation of the Gospel in the changed situations of contemporary culture, the Church [be] attentive to giving every one of her activities an in-built connection with evangelization and mission."[111] Intrinsic to this development of a "missionary" approach in the Alexandrian school is the character of its extended preparation for baptism: it takes place, as we will see, within a community that practices a pedagogy of ascetical commitment and self-gift for the sake of developing a profound capacity for Christian witness in a life of holiness. It is to this understanding of the catechumenate that we can now turn.

---

[111] *DC* 41.

CHAPTER 8

The Catechumenate: The Pedagogue Forms his Children

WE HAVE NOW ARRIVED AT THE CENTER OF the candidate's formation. The baptismal catechumenate provided the central structure and shape for this process. As Ratzinger has pointed out, "the baptismal formula, which is, properly speaking, a dialogical creed, presupposes a long learning process" which entails that, since this confession of faith is essential for baptism, "the catechumenate itself is a part of baptism."[1] The catechumenate thus has a sacramental character, with the central content of the catechumenate entering "directly into the *forma sacramenti*."[2] Ratzinger notes the "long learning process" in the reception of the baptismal formula: those seeking membership in Christ through baptism in Alexandria were normally given an ascetical formation and an instruction in the basic elements of the faith over a period of three years, presumably taking its inspiration from the period of Christ's own formation of the apostles.[3] "Time is needed for strength in a catechumen," Clement writes, and he refers by analogy to the practice of farmers taking care of their young trees "right to their third year."[4] Three years was also the usual length of formation in the catechumenate that we find in Hippolytus's Rome[5] and in Origen's Caesarea.[6]

Clement's *Paedagogus*, the second work in his trio of writings, is a handbook for this central period of instruction and formation. In the *Stromateis* he describes the purpose of the handbook: the *Paedagogus* exhibits "the training and nurture up from the state of childhood,

---

[1] *Principles of Catholic Theology*, 35.
[2] Ibid., 36.
[3] It is likely that by the time of Clement this notion of a three-year period was just being consolidated. André Turck notes that in Clement's contemporary, Tertullian, it is difficult to identify a standard length ("Aux Origines de Catéchuménat," *Revues des Sciences philosophiques et théologiques* 48, 1, January 1964, 20).
[4] *Stromateis* 18.95.1-96.2. See also Méhat, *Étude sur les 'Stromates' de Clément d'Alexandrie*, 221-22.
[5] Hippolytus, *The Apostolic Tradition*, 17.
[6] From the evidence we have of Origen's homilies, Nautin argues for a reconstruction of Origen's preaching that would entail him covering the whole of the Old Testament during a three-year period, a length that correlates with that of the catechumenate according to Hipploytus (*Origène: Son Vie et Son Oeuvre*, 389-409).

that is, the course of life which from elementary instruction grows by faith" and "prepares beforehand the soul, endued with virtue, for the reception of true knowledge."[7] This period, then, was concerned with gaining virtue and strengthening the spiritual life of the catechumen, building faith through the giving of an "elementary instruction" in preparation for the final stage of the journey beyond baptism—that of an ongoing formation, a mystagogy, led by Christ the Teacher. Clement's focus in this present work is squarely on this training of the person in the disciplines of a Christian life. Other elements that were also central to the catechumenate are not equally represented in the *Paedagogus*, although their presence is implied. Additionally to the training in virtue with which the *Paedagogus* is mainly concerned, then, catechumens would receive expositions of the Scriptures, both from the Old and the New Testaments,[8] probably in the context of liturgies.[9] These liturgies of the Word probably took place early in the morning and it is likely that such liturgies were held in Alexandria on Wednesdays and Fridays, which were also days of fasting. Catechumens would also have been able to attend the Eucharistic liturgy up until the conclusion of the homily.[10] Prayer supported the ascetical practices that were so essential in the catechumenal formation and an intensification of both prayer and these practices would accompany the latter part of the catechumenate, with exorcisms and the formal renunciation of Satan forming the climax to the preparation for baptism.

We have no description of the actual baptismal ceremony in Clement's writings, but from what we know of third-century practice we can say that the baptism itself would have been by full immersion, and immediately after the reception of the sacrament the new converts would be fed milk and honey,[11] pledges of the heavenly Jerusalem. Intense and demanding as this preparation had been, the release

---

[7] *Stromateis* 6.1.1.3; and see the broader context of 6.1.1.1-2.4.2.
[8] It is worth noting that Clement is the first Christian author to refer to the "New Testament" as a composite body of inspired writings to be heard and read (see *Stromateis* 5.13.85.1).
[9] See *Paedagogus* 2.10.96.2. We also have Origen's recommendations in Caesarea (again, we do not have direct evidence of his practice in Alexandria) for scriptural books that he considered especially helpful for teaching matters of conduct in this catechumenal period—Esther, Judith, Tobias and the Wisdom books (see his *Homilies on Numbers*, XXVII.1.3).
[10] Cf. Socrates H. E. V.22, though he is not always reliable in matters of detail. Pierre Nautin presents a plausible reconstruction of the kind of liturgies that were celebrated during Origen's time in Caesarea in *Origène: Son Vie et Son Oeuvre*, 391-94.
[11] *Paedagogus* 1.6.45. For comments on this passage see Harry A. Echle, *Terminology of the Sacrament of Regeneration, according to Clement of Alexandria* (Washington, D.C.: Catholic University of America, 1949), 88-89.

from evil and rebirth in baptism was seen as only the beginning of God's work of salvation in the believer. Just as Paul had denied that he had reached the goal,[12] so the goal of the newly baptized lay ahead of them, Clement tells the new Christians. Baptism is a regeneration,[13] the beginning of the new life of the child and now a growth in the Christian life to maturity must follow.[14] He calls them onward and points them to Christ who, having trained them in essentials, is now ready to lead them into his mysteries.

What is distinctive in the understanding of the catechumenate in the Alexandrian school is the notion of placing the person aspiring to baptism under the tutelage of Christ in the form of "the divine Pedagogue." It is significant that Clement titled his work *Paedagogus*, the Pedagogue, since in the ancient world the pedagogue was the figure in Greek and Roman households—usually a slave—who would be tasked by the father of the household with the supervision and care of the child on behalf of the parents, the custodian or guide to the child in the early years of instruction and formation.[15] The pedagogue complements the work of the teacher and of formal instruction by undertaking the pastoral and moral care and training of the child, supervising and disciplining the child on behalf of the father. The pedagogue attends especially, then, to the formation of character through a personal relationship with the growing child, as well as an integration of the studies learned at school with the virtues and qualities of character expected in the household, helping the child to put into practice that which is given by the teacher.[16] Clement of Alexandria explains his use of the metaphor: "That ... pedagogy is the training of children is clear from the word itself. It remains for us to consider the children whom scripture points to; then to give the Pedagogue charge of them."[17] Regarding the children to

---

[12] See *Phil.* 3:15.
[13] *Paedagogus* 1.12.98.2. The terminology of regeneration is Clement's preferred imagery, as Ferguson notes (*Baptism in the Early Church*, 309-13).
[14] For helpful treatments of the relationship in Clement between the perfection brought about in baptism and the call to grow and develop within that baptismal grace see John Behr, *Asceticism and Anthropology in Irenaeus and Clement* (Oxford: Oxford University Press, 2000), 152-59; Henry Chadwick, *Early Christian Thought and the Classical Tradition*, 2nd ed. (Oxford: Clarendon Press, 1987), 51-54.
[15] For the background to this metaphor of "pedagogue" in the ancient world see N. H. Young, "παιδαγωγός: The Social Setting of a Pauline Metaphor," *Novum Testamentum* 29 (1987), 150-176.
[16] Cf. Marrou, *A History of Education in Antiquity*, 142-49. To a certain extent the position of the pedagogue is in continuity with the older Homeric figure of the tutor.
[17] *Paedagogus* 1.5.12.1.

be trained: "We are the children."[18] Regarding the Pedagogue: "He is called Jesus."[19] "The Word who leads his children to salvation is unquestionably a Pedagogue of little ones."[20] Clement addresses his readers from the first: "O you who are children!"[21] and introduces the Word from the outset by his new title, "Let us call him, then, by the one title: Pedagogue of little ones."[22] This abundance of images about spiritual infancy is remarkable, as Behr comments, in an age in which there was "no real appreciation for the state of infancy."[23] The gaining of a true spiritual childhood is crucial for Clement's understanding of the catechumenate.

Fittingly, the *Paedagogus* concludes with a call to give an "eternal offering of holy thanksgiving" to the Lord "in return for his wise education."[24] A beautiful baptismal hymn to Christ, celebrating the Pedagogue who guides his children, follows. If not by Clement himself, the hymn is perhaps taken from an earlier Alexandrian liturgy and seems to have been designed for antiphonal singing.

> Bridle for wild horses,
> Wing of birds unerring,
> Dead-set helm for ships,
> Shepherd of royal lambs,
>
> Gather your simple children
> To praise holily,
> To hymn guilelessly
> With innocent mouths,
> Christ the Guide of children.
>
> Lord of saints,
> All-subduing Word of the Most High Father,
> Master of Wisdom,
> Strong support of griefs,
> Rejoicing in eternity:
> Jesus, Saviour of the Mortal race,
> Shepherd, Ploughman, Helm, and Bridle,
> Heavenly Wing over the all-holy flock,
> Fisher of men who have been saved,
> Catching pure fish with the sweet bait of life,

---

[18] Ibid.
[19] *Paedagogus* 1.7.53.2.
[20] *Paedagogus* 1.7.53.3.
[21] *Paedagogus* 1.1.1.1.
[22] *Paedagogus* 1.1.1.4.
[23] Behr, *Asceticism and Anthropology in Irenaeus and Clement*, 152.
[24] *Paedagogus* 3.12.101.3.

From a sea of evil and the enemy's waves.
Shepherd of rational sheep,
Guide us, Holy King,
As unspoilt children,
In the footsteps of Christ.

Heavenly Way,
Ever-flowing Word,
Immeasurable Aeon,
Eternal Light,
Fount of Mercy,
Adept in Virtue.
How noble is the life
Of those who sing to God.
Christ Jesus, Heavenly Milk
Of those sweet breasts
Of the graces of the Bride,
Pressed from your wisdom.

Gather your simple children
To praise holily,
To hymn guilelessly
With innocent mouths,
Christ the Guide of children;

Little children,
So tender their gums,
Feeding to the full
With spiritual dew
From the nipple of your Wisdom.

Together let us raise a merry sound
To Christ the King,
Of simple praises, and true hymns,
Rewards of the Doctrine of Life.
Let us sing together,
All you who are Christ-begotten,
A Sober People,
A Chorus of peace,
To the God of Peace.[25]

The *kerygmatic* themes we have met are wonderfully drawn together in this hymn, celebrating Christ's wise formation offered in this divine *paideia*, his role as the Word of the Father, shepherding his "rational

---

[25] This translation is taken from John McGuckin, *At the Lighting of the Lamps: Hymns of the Ancient Church* (Harrisburg: Morehouse Publishing, 1995), 15-17.

sheep" and "royal lambs," the beautiful "graces of the Bride" that attract and nourish, and the heavenly way on which the children can safely follow. We can see the *Paedagogus*, then, as a work collecting the *kerygmatic* themes and unfolding them within a structure of broad formation and moral instruction, describing the discipline that needs to be undertaken to reach the goal of formation—the maturity of a new spiritual child, enlightened by baptism. This formation in the art of living well is presented as both a broad and as a narrow way: broad in the sense that it was to be followed by all; narrow in that it required an ascetical engagement with the work of grace that called for the transformation of all the details of one's life: in the catechumenate Wisdom will lead in the practice of "corporate exercises and discipline."[26]

The *Paedagogus* is divided into three books. The first focuses on Christ as the true Pedagogue—his person, aims, methods and means; his character, faithfulness, graciousness, and goodness. It also explores why Christ's goodness is compatible with an apparent severity at times and a system of punishments. Clement spends considerable time on this question, which perhaps reflects the struggles that many of his catechumens experienced. The second and third books present detailed guidelines for living so that the Pedagogue and his principles might shape the whole of one's life. The topics Clement covers here, interspersed with extended homiletic-style reflections, are intensely practical in character, focusing on the most mundane and familiar aspects of life: how a Christian should walk, sleep, speak, laugh, dress, adorn, eat and drink, and take general care of the body. What is appropriate footwear for a Christian? How should one sit in the company of others to show attentiveness and respect? What should we do if we have a sneezing fit? Wisdom has come to teach us the "art of living"[27] and every detail must be brought under the sway of the new Christian way of life: those who belong to her will not separate themselves from her, even when they sleep.[28] As Clement unfolds these details, the tenor of the remarks, the constant encouragement and gentle probing of societal attitudes offer numerous insights into the habits and proclivities of well-to-do Alexandrian society. A particular kind of writing was needed for a work like this, a work that was to confirm the

---

[26] *Stromateis* 2.20.122.1. See also the *Eclogae Propheticae* 14-16, where we find indications of the catechumenal practices of fasting, prayer and good works. In general, the advice in the second book of the *Paedagogus* follows the path of Clement's admiration for "an austere life" (2.2.20.2).

[27] *Paedagogus* 2.2.25.3.

[28] *Paedagogus* 2.2.25.2.

conversion and deepen it—not *protrepsis* but *paranaesis*,[29] the giving of advice and counsel for those who have entered a new way of life.[30] It is an impressive guidebook: as Osborn observes, while other writers "recognized the need for a regimen which covers all human behaviour, no one in antiquity achieved this aim as completely as Clement."[31]

It is easy to smile at some of the details in Clement's instructions or be bewildered by the attention to detail. But the underlying conviction in the Alexandrian school's understanding of what was involved in this path of formation is that it must include all that pertains to what is properly human: the body, senses, affectivity, consciousness, reason, soul, and all human capacities for the aesthetic, personal, moral and spiritual dimensions of existence. The work of the Logos, drawing one into unity and harmony with oneself, with others, and with the Father, embraces all the dimensions of one's humanity. In the opening section of the work Clement explains that it is therefore helpful to think of the work of the Pedagogue as employing different forms of address for different aspects of life. We can think of the Pedagogue as concerned with our *habits*, our *actions* and our *passions*, and these correspond to three different modes of address he uses—he exhorts, he prescribes, and he persuades. To establish us in good habits, the Pedagogue seeks to rouse us to faith through an exhortatory form of address, to lead us to embrace certain dispositions. To provide a set of structuring principles for our actions, the Pedagogue secures us with commandments, stabilizing our discipleship and placing it within firm boundaries. Finally, to provide us with an ongoing healing of our passions, the Pedagogue employs the art of persuasion to assist us in embracing the life of Christ in its fullness.[32]

THE WORK OF HEALING AND THE *DISCIPLINA ARCANI*

At the beginning of the work, Clement sets out to explain why this disciplined catechumenal formation concerns the *healing* of the catechumen. Before Christ can appear as the teacher in our lives he must first heal us, give us health. Christ's first task is "to improve the soul, not just to instruct it, guide to a life of virtue, not just to instruct

---

[29] For a helpful discussion of the relationship between *paraenesis* and *protrepsis* see Diana M. Swancutt, "Paraenesis in Light of Protrepsis," in eds. J. Starr and T. Engberg-Pedersen, *Early Christian Paraenesis in Context* (New York: Walter de Gruyter, 2004), 113-55.
[30] For examples of Clement's paraentic style see the illustrations in Clarence E. Glad, "The Rhetoric of Moral Exhortation in Clement's *Pedagogue*," in eds. J. Starr and T. Engberg-Pedersen, *Early Christian Paraenesis in Context*, 433-66.
[31] *Clement of Alexandria*, 243.
[32] *Paedagogus* 1.1.1.1-3.

it."[33] Yes, Clement confirms, Christ is the teacher as well, "but in this work we are not considering Him in that light," but as a *practical* educator.[34] And there is also an order within this work of healing itself: Christ seeks first to establish right dispositions and character, then he persuades us to keep the commandments, finally healing our emotions by a gradual strengthening of our souls. And then, at last, he is ready to teach:

> As, then, for those of us who are diseased in body a physician is required, so also those who are diseased in soul require a pedagogue to cure our maladies; and then a teacher, to train and guide the soul in all requisite knowledge when it is made able to admit the revelation of the Word.[35]

Until this healing has taken place we *cannot* learn what Christ wants to teach us. Health must precede knowledge.[36] Concrete, specific changes need to take place in the catechumen for the sake of the engagement with the deeper mysteries of Christ. The Lord himself, in the promptings and graces he provides as the Pedagogue will render a person teachable, to be *able* to receive the teaching given both in the transmission of doctrine and in life itself. He will "bridle" the "wild horses." This, then, is the ordering that brings salvation, the wise arrangement put in place by the all-loving Logos. The themes of healing, of the restoration of harmony, and of the need to establish unity and integrity—morally, intellectually and spiritually—recur frequently in the writings of the school. It is only at the very end of the *Paedagogus* that Clement finally hands his readers over to Christ the Teacher.

It is in the light of this understanding of the order and purpose of the catechumenate that we can best appreciate one important aspect of this formation that was developed in the early Church, the discipline of the *arcanum*—i.e., the reservation of certain teachings and practices for the fully initiated, the practice of keeping certain teachings "secret." Certain mysteries of divine truth, "instead of being exposed to the gaze of the profane and uninstructed, are kept hidden in the bosom of the Church,"[37] to be given to those who are more

---

[33] *Paedagogus* 1.1.1.4.
[34] *Paedagogus* 1.1.1.2.
[35] *Paedagogus* 1.1.3.3.
[36] The bones of humanity are broken and the work of resetting the broken limbs belongs to the divine Pedagogue. "Society had to be reset" (H. Ritter, "The Christian Schools of Alexandria," 302). Clement is not original in this analogy: the Stoic philosopher Epictetus describes the philosopher's lecture room as a hospital (see *The Discourses of Epictetus* [London: Everyman, 1995], 3.23.30).
[37] *Arians of the Fourth Century*, 37. In his insightful analysis Newman attributes to the Alexandrian Church some specific practices for which we only have clear

fully prepared and initiated. For example, only the initiated could partake fully in the Eucharistic liturgy, and certain teachings were only given to believers after baptism. Christians who were baptized were strictly required not to reveal certain secrets of the Christian faith to outsiders, and even to catechumens—in particular certain practices and formulae associated with baptism and the Eucharist. As we have seen, even before an enquirer was accepted into the catechumenate there was a probationary period, a period of testing.[38] The catechumenate as a whole might be considered an extended period of testing in some sense: the believer had left the slavery of Egypt but was in transition to the Promised Land.

This discipline of secrecy and practice of restraint in Christian initiation should certainly not be confused with what Rowan Williams describes as Gnosticism's "spiritual technology"—the provision of arcane knowledge to the fully initiated as a way of successfully navigating one's way to salvation.[39] The school knew that salvation comes from God's grace and through the response of faith, shown by works of love, with an "equality" of salvation in God's plan; as Clement insisted, salvation was not reserved for those few to whom special hidden knowledge was communicated: "faith is salvation reaching the whole of mankind . . . an impartial share of union with the just and loving God, given to all."[40]

While the need for caution about too open an expression of faith in periods of persecution may have contributed to the development of the discipline, the preservation of a profound reverence before God's transcendent mystery, and of Revelation as the unveiling of the mysteries of the faith, was undoubtedly the deepest religious motivation. God is the unmeasurable. The incomprehensible nature of God was a truth prominent in Hellenistic Judaism where the prohibition of images and the fact that the holy Name of God was never pronounced led to a certain "negative theology." That God "dwells in unapproachable light"[41] and is beyond our comprehension is reinforced in the

---

evidence from the fourth and fifth centuries, but his discussion of the rationale for the *disciplina arcani* is helpful in identifying the *pedagogical* concerns at stake. And while he recognized that the discipline was open to possible abuse, he further defended it in his *Apologia* as an entirely appropriate expression of God's economy of salvation (see Note F. The Economy).

[38] This practice in some ways mirrored Pythagorean practice, as Origen reminds Celsus (see *Contra Celsum* I.7).

[39] Rowan Williams, *The Wound of Knowledge* (London: Darton, Longman and Todd, 1979), 26.

[40] *Paedagogus* 1.6.30.2.

[41] *CCC* 52. Cf. 1 *Jn.* 1:5 and *Jas.* 1:17: God is the "Father of lights."

writings of the apostles.[42] As one comes closer to the God who is all light and in whom there is no darkness one's eyes need time to accustom themselves to his brightness for the "blaze of Divine glory to the enlightened is the blinding of unbelievers."[43] The discipline is one of *mercy* towards the believer not yet ready to bear the light of God. In the face of the divine mystery and the distance between the holiness of God and the limitations of the human person—both in understanding and in the orientation of one's life—a pedagogy of gradual enlightenment and purification must be taken seriously, both for the sake of guarding the mystery of God, and for the sake of success on the journey. Jesus made the point memorably and graphically: it is not right to throw pearls before swine.[44] Human nature, Origen pointed out, is "in no way sufficient for the search for God, or for finding him in an unsullied way unless aided by him who is being sought."[45] The human mind cannot reach up to meet God; only God's Revelation of himself in the Logos makes possible a true knowledge of him.[46] And this in turn requires a personal and moral transformation, for all such "true knowledge is saving knowledge; it brings moral perfection to the soul."[47]

Entering the mystery was thus seen as inevitably an *arduous* task, for the school knew that in every convert—as in themselves, for Clement was honest enough to speak of "we," not "you"[48]—there was a deep *reluctance to grow*, a tendency to perversely refuse grace. The call to maturity was resisted and imperfection preferred to the demands of a more satisfying and substantial life. The "discipline and instruction of the Lord"[49] took place within a context of a fallen human nature and fallen creation. And so God's education was patient and gradual, forceful and gentle as necessary, wise and loving. Because of sin, the Lord must often walk "contrary" to his people.[50] The

---

[42] Cf. 1 *Tim.* 6:16, *Rom.* 11:33, and *Eph.* 3:8. See Frances M. Young, "The God of the Greeks and the Nature of Religious Language," in eds. W. R. Schoedel and R. L. Wilken, *Early Christian Literature and the Classical Intellectual Tradition* (Paris: Editions Beauchesne, 1979), 65-66.
[43] *Arians of the Fourth Century*, 48, quoting here from Cyril of Jerusalem.
[44] *Matt.* 7:6.
[45] *Contra Celsum* VII.42.
[46] See the discussion in Peter Widdicombe, *The Fatherhood of God from Origen to Athanasius*, 44-62.
[47] Widdicombe, *The Fatherhood of God from Origen to Athanasius*, 50.
[48] Cf. *Protrepticus* 10.92.5-93.1.
[49] *Eph.* 6:4.
[50] See *Lev.* 26:18, 28. This "contrariness" is the crooked walking of humanity which must make its paths straight. It is the human antagonism towards the good, flowing from sin. Sin introduces a perverted view of the Goodness of Being in

overarching understanding of the life of faith was a divine education in which the Lord gradually raised the eyes of humanity to himself, cleansing the understanding together with a purification of life. This education, though resisted, would overcome the work of sin which distances humanity from its true fulfillment, life with the Lord in a perfect and everlasting happiness. God's disciplining which accompanied the educational process was always given "in just measure,"[51] according to the growing capacities of each person as he or she could bear that which the Lord wished to show them. Clement explains it in this way using the parable of the talents:

> ... the Savior appears in person out of his superabundance. He distributes his goods among his servants, proportionately to the capacity of the recipient—and this ought to be increased by disciplined practice. He returns and demands an account from them. Those who have increased his money and have "been faithful in a small matter," he welcomes and promises "to give wide responsibilities," telling them to "enter their master's joy."[52]

The discipline of the Pedagogue was therefore just, and in itself an education in the virtue of justice; it was wise, and an education in wisdom. The restraint that was followed in instruction and in the teaching of certain practices, the "method of concealment," as Clement calls it,[53] was not as a deceptive process, for truth was given as it could be received, the capacity for reception increasing insofar as the catechumen engaged freely with the disciplines offered, and in no way would the deeper Revelation that the disciple could expect in due course overthrow an earlier teaching but would sit upon foundations well and securely laid. As Newman observed, "the elementary information given to the heathen or catechumen was in no sense undone by the subsequent secret teaching, which was in fact but the filling up of a bare but correct outline."[54]

This practice of gradual initiation into the mystery of Christ was needed, in addition, because only gradually was the human

---

which it is seen and experienced as contrary to one's good. Such a contrariness, as the conception of experienced evil as a repugnance towards the goodness of being is powerfully treated in Charles Williams's novel, *The Descent into Hell*. For a discussion see Dorothy Sayers, "Charles Williams: A Poet's Critic," in *The Poetry of Search and the Poetry of Statement* (London: Victor Gollancz, 1963), 69–90.
[51] Cf. Jer. 10:24; 46:28.
[52] *Stromateis* 1.1.3.1.
[53] *Stromateis* 5.4.19. See 5.4-10 for an extensive discussion of the discipline, with prefigurations identified from Egyptian and Greek religious practices and from the Old Covenant.
[54] *Arians of the Fourth Century*, 53.

formator-learner relationship developing and the whole of the process required the active judgement of the one assisting the divine Pedagogue, who had to come to know the person being instructed, and to enter, by empathy and understanding, into his or her world.

> The person who addresses people who are present uses time as a test and judgement to come to a verdict. He distinguishes the one who is capable of hearing from the rest. He keeps an eye on their words and ways, their character and life, their impulses and attitudes, their looks, their voice, the parting of the ways, the rock, the well-trodden path, the ground that bears fruit, the countryside that is thick with trees, the land which is fertile, excellent, praised, the soil which is capable of multiplying the seed.[55]

The person leading the catechumen is clearly a kind of chaplain, spiritual director and formator whose discernment was needed concerning the developing character of the catechumen as a whole, including his attitudes, ways of speaking and behaving, his choices,[56] and his capacity to receive what is given, noting the fruitfulness of the teaching that was evident in his life. It is interesting to note the reference in Clement's text to Jesus's parable of the Sower which he sees as describing this pedagogy of the Word moving from the hard ground through a series of obstacles to final fruitfulness. Jesus told his disciples that understanding the meaning of this parable was the criterion for understanding all the other parables,[57] presumably because it does indeed depict the process of the reception of the divine mysteries he had come to reveal and of the purification that must take place. Clement draws attention to the same parable in his discussion of the dialogue of the rich young man with Jesus, drawing out the practical implications in this case of the young man's capacity to receive the words of Jesus.[58] As is well known, Clement invites one to see Jesus's invitation to the young man as a process of detachment for the sake of discipleship: he must learn to divest himself from his anxious attachment to things, and also from the riches of his "extravagant boasts"[59] — "I have done all these things" — for the sake of receiving the "hundredfold" from the Lord. He turns away at this point, Clement says, for he "did not truly wish for life, as he said, but aimed solely at a reputation for good intentions." "He could be

---

[55] *Stromateis* 1.1.9.1.
[56] The "parting of the ways" is a reference to the Pythagorean symbol of choice.
[57] Mk. 4:1-20 and see v.13.
[58] *The Rich Man's Salvation* 11.
[59] Ibid., 10.

busy about many things, but the one thing, the work that brings life, he was neither able nor eager nor strong enough to accomplish."[60] Clement's analysis of character, his interest in discerning the spiritual state of the young man, illustrates the kind of role one can see was expected of the formator who was intent on leading the catechumen on the path of deeper discipleship.

Origen, too, discusses the Parable of the Sower[61] from a pedagogical point of view, seeking to understand how God overcomes the hardness of heart which is perhaps symbolized by the path upon which the seed falls without being able to penetrate it, leaving it vulnerable to the birds which seek to snatch it away. Such hardness is not of God's design, he teaches, for God desires all to receive his Word, and there is no category of person unable to receive the education God wishes to provide. There is nothing hidden that will not be brought to light, nothing secret except to be made manifest. A lamp is made to give light and is therefore to be put on a lampstand. God seeks to bring each person to be light and participate in his communication of love to others; he shines on every life, as the sun. God is the great Farmer who wisely sows his seed slowly in the rocky soil, "putting in seeds that will be able to endure, the slower method being better for this ground."[62] Souls are innumerable, and their habits innumerable, Origen comments, "and equally so are their movements, their purposes, their inclinations and their impulses." There is only one who "has full knowledge both of the times and the appropriate aids and the paths and the ways, namely, the God and Father of the universe."[63]

The heat of the sun will harden clay just as it melts wax, and so God must tend to the quality of the soil first to make it capable to receiving his judgments and formation, and this he does by *engaging* the response of the person being formed—desire, will, and intellect—for, as Origen comments, "our perfection is not effected while we rest and do nothing."[64] The reason for holding back certain doctrines, then, arose from the desire of the formators, Newman suggests, "to rouse the moral powers to internal voluntary action," while at the same time reflecting "their dread of loading or formalizing the mind."[65] The delicacy here is that of being able to discern at what points one needs to be able to provide intellectual structure,

---

[60] Ibid.
[61] See *De Principiis* III.1.14-24.
[62] *De Principiis* III.1.14.
[63] Ibid.
[64] *De Principiis* III.1.19.
[65] *Arians of the Fourth Century*, 49.

and when rather to press for a further deepening of understanding and assent that is only possible from a deeper moral commitment.

Engaging with this process required a profound spirituality on the part of the formator, who was not simply working through a syllabus in the catechumenate but rather seeking to attend with sensitivity to the needs of each soul. "The great duty of the Christian teacher was to unfold the sacred truths in due order, and not prematurely to insist on the difficulties, or to apply the promises of the Gospel."[66] The formator must not go ahead of God's work in the soul of the learner, but know how to facilitate and foster that relationship. This was the faithful attitude and approach of the Alexandrians—a patient probing, and then a drawing out of each responding step needed to enter more fully into the mystery of God. As Newman points out, this educational approach is one of charity towards learners, for the Alexandrian teachers saw them as "likely to be perplexed, not converted, by the sudden exhibition of the whole evangelical scheme."[67] The pedagogy they presented, therefore, was one of gradual steps, for the sake of a deep and lasting conversion. A delicate synchronizing action governed the pedagogy: the gradual emergence of light accompanied by a corresponding fostering of the capacity of the person.

STRIVING UNDER GRACE

With the prominent place given to ascetical practice in the Alexandrian catechumenate and the learning of specific disciplines, it is important to note how this is contextualized within a broader theme of *receptivity* that runs throughout the *Paedagogus*. The definition of the Church offered by Clement is instructive in this regard: she is the community of those who practice "submissive endurance."[68] He provides an interesting commentary on this phrase:

> The Church, too, has been given the reassuring name "submissive endurance", either because her enduring continues in unending joy, or because she is formed of the submission of those who believe: of us who are members of Christ. The testimony given by those who have submissively endured until the end, and their gratitude, as well, is a mystical *paideia*; the helpmate of this holy gladness of heart is salvation. The king is Christ, looking down from above on our laughter, and "peering through the door", as Scripture

---

[66] Ibid., 51.
[67] Ibid., 47.
[68] *Paedagogus* 1.5.22.2.

says, on our gratitude and benediction that works in us joy and cheerfulness with submission.[69]

The character of the Church, as the end and goal of creation, offers us penetrating insights into Clement's Christian anthropology. In the first place the character of the Church illuminates the receptivity of created being as one of "submission." It is a "reassuring" characterization, Clement writes—the Church *enjoys* her receptivity. This enjoyment is paralleled by Christ's delight in his children, which shines through Clement's text. Christ peers through the door and sees Christians laughing and blessing the Creator: their submission is a matter for cheerfulness and rejoicing. The name is also "reassuring" for it reminds Christians that their submissive enduring will continue for all eternity in a state of unending joy. The Christian lives in an enduring *place of blessing*, lives before the Father who continually pours out his graces, the God who never ceases working and whose work is nothing but the unending sharing of his life. The task of Christ the Pedagogue in the life of those preparing for baptism and of the newly baptized is to train and form the Christian to *receive* this new life in ever-increasing fullness. The use of the term "endurance," although reassuring, also points to the challenges the baptized will face. An extant baptismal address we have from Clement is titled *Exhortation to Endurance*. In this he counsels: remember the Lord's goodness and care and make up your mind now to be courageous in the face of illness and death. Even in those matters "let Christ be to you continual and unceasing joy."

The receptivity that characterizes the Church and each Christian is part of the Alexandrian account of created reality *receiving* its nature and characteristics from God through his Logos. A created being receives its nature from the Creator and its end must be fitted to the capacity of that nature as its fulfillment and good. The *capax* of created being lies first in its receptivity. All that is—a human life, a tuft of grass, a dream, a thought, an artifact—is contingent, receiving its being from Being itself. Each person draws his or her life from that which transcends it. "Being created" therefore refers to a relationship, to the absolute and enduring dependence of each creature on God who is at each moment that creature's source and end. Towards his creature, God is a goodness that is always active: "for what is the use of good that does not act and do good?"[70] The dependence of the

---

[69] *Paedagogus* 1.5.22.2–3.
[70] *Stromateis* 6.12.104.3.

creature on God is also, for Clement, a mirror of an eternal dependence within God himself, for the Son eternally receives his being from the Father. The unity in God of Father and Son is accompanied by an eternal overflow of the good and of receptivity. The human person, made in the image of the Logos, the Son, is *defined* by the Son's reception of absolute Being from his Father.

This depiction of the essentially receptive nature of the person and the Church is crucial for our appreciation for how Clement transforms the classical understanding of the spiritual life. The *Paedagogus* places what we can call a "pedagogy of ascent," of striving towards the perfection of the divine, within a wider "pedagogy of descent," of the Logos through whom all things and persons were made, reaching down to lift the believer to him by his grace. So, for example, Stoic understandings of the virtues of self-sufficiency (*autarkeia*) and a passion-free life (*apatheia*) are central to Clement's thought—and some have proposed that the second and third books of the *Paedagogus* are to some extent dependent on a treatise by Musonius, who was the Stoic teacher of Epictetus.[71] Clement's appropriation of Stoic thought, however, is always placed within the envelope of Revelation,[72] transposing themes within a Christian framework of receptivity and vulnerability in which the figure of the mature person is the redeemed "child."[73] The second and third books of the *Paedagogus* cannot be viewed in isolation from the first, which provides the controlling principles for appreciating all that follows in the more detailed proposals in the later books. Clement's introduction to Book Two, in fact, leads with a clear statement of his intention of laying before his readers the practical wisdom of the Scriptures in which we find the instructions of the heavenly Pedagogue.[74] As Eric Osborn stresses, Clement is "not merely giving good advice to his readers," but is rather "explaining the kind of response which they must make to the love of God so that their love may resemble in reciprocity the love of the son to the father."[75] The practical advice—often, indeed, paralleled by Stoic thinkers—is given a new context, that of adoption into the dynamic of divine Trinitarian

---

[71] See, for example, Charles P. Parker, "Musonius in Clement," *Harvard Studies in Classical Phliology* 12 (1901), 191–200, whose interest is in salvaging from Clement a reconstruction of a lost treatise from Musonius.
[72] On this, see the judgement and examples offered in John Behr, *Asceticism and Anthropology in Irenaeus and Clement*, 164.
[73] Origen similarly transforms the classical Greek understanding, offering a pedagogy of ascent "Platonist in hue," that is made possible "only through the grace of God in the Logos" (*The Fatherhood of God from Origen to Athanasius*, 120).
[74] *Paedagogus* 2.1.1.1.
[75] *Clement of Alexandria*, 244.

love so that he or she becomes a child in the Son, living from his life. Within this new vision, authentic maturity is understood as learning what is needed for relationships of respect and intimacy that avoid the manipulation and domination of others and instead finds a route of service. Rather than resort to employing slaves to avoid work oneself, Clement counsels, or useful Celts to carry one around town in expensive litters, one should wait on oneself, and remember Jesus's injunction to care for the least of his little ones.[76] Such a childlike vulnerability will be learned from those who are themselves usually characterized as the weak: "if one appear needy or ill-clad or ungainly or weak, do not in your soul take offence at this and turn away. This is a form thrown round us from without . . . that we may be able to take our place in this universal *paideia*: but hidden within dwells the Father and his Son who died for us and rose with us."[77] If we want to learn the ways of God we should surround ourselves with "an army of God-fearing old men, of God-beloved orphans, of widows armed with gentleness, or men adorned with love."[78]

The pedagogy of ascent

Let us look at how the school understood the ascending movement of the human person towards healing and virtue. The school built upon the classical foundation of the Greek *paideia* and then developed it in certain distinctive ways.

In common with the thought of Middle Platonism, the Alexandrians understood the movement towards integrity and unity as the soul's free choice to move from the less to the more spiritual. For Middle Platonism, drawing on themes from both Platonist and Aristotelian thought, as well as from Stoicism, the human *telos* was to be "like God." It was a path to wisdom, culminating in contemplation of the divine.[79] The preferred pedagogy is that which enables a person to strive towards this highest kind of life and this entails training a person to integrate pleasure into this quest: to learn to love the good by feeling pleasure in the good and avoid the bad by learning to feel displeasure in the bad. The lovers of what is truly noble find pleasure in the noble.[80] All forms of education in the

---

[76] See *Paedagogus* 3.4.26.1–30.4.
[77] *The Rich Man's Salvation*, 33.
[78] Ibid., 34.
[79] For a study of Plato's understanding of the path and goals of formation, upon which this pedagogy of ascent is broadly set, see R. C. Lodge, *Plato's Theory of Education* (New York: Harcourt, Brace, 1947).
[80] Cf. Aristotle, *Nicomachean Ethics* 81099a11–16.

paideia should contribute to a person's progress towards the highest possible life. Thus, both Plato and Aristotle distinguished between living and living well. Clement agrees—only the second is worthy of the human person.[81]

Plato and Aristotle are in broad agreement regarding the kind of formation suitable for a human being to enable this living to one's full capacity, though Plato emphasizes the cognitive dimension and Aristotle the formation of habits. For both, however, it is always the *whole person* who acts. Even in periods of self-conflict, confusion, struggle and division, it is always *I* who am thus confounded and at odds with myself. Their educational visions are therefore holistic, consisting in the training and formation of character and virtue alongside intellectual development. Reason and action, words and deeds, belong together. This was a key feature of the Greek *paideia* as a whole. Jaeger defined the Greeks' ideal of human perfection as "that character which united nobility of action with nobility of mind." He draws attention to Phoenix's advice to Achilles who, when faced with a crisis in action, reminds him of this ideal in which he has been molded: "to be both a speaker of words and a doer of deeds" and comments: "The later Greeks were right in believing this verse to be the earliest formulation of the Greek educational ideal."[82]

Both Plato and Aristotle also knew that our passions, the passageway between thought and action, are themselves conceptual, and the Stoics encouraged their categorization for the sake of understanding their better integration. Our emotional and cognitive lives do not live in separate compartments. We fear to venture out at night precisely because we fear what we know, or think we know, might happen to us. When angry, one is in a certain "state of mind," and there are certain "frames of mind in which men are easily stirred to anger"—for example, we are prone to anger with the one whom we *think* is contemptuous of us.[83] The formational quest, therefore, included the need for emotional responses to be appropriate, to be measured against the real, establishing a rationality of the emotions through a kind of spiritual therapy. This understanding of the place and nature of the emotions explains why ancient Greek culture provided an important place for music in education: it is precisely because of the integrating properties of music, its capacity to assist

---

[81] *Stromateis* 6.12.100.2. For Plato and Aristotle on this point, see *Crito* 48B; *Politics* 125b29.
[82] See Jaeger, *Paideia: The Ideals of Greek Culture*, I, 8.
[83] See Aristotle's discussion of anger in *Rhetoric* 1378a20–1380a4.

in the rational structuring of the emotions, to support the ongoing integration of the person in the direction of contemplation.[84] Music therefore played a fundamental role in the *paideia*, assisting in the development of habits of harmony, gracefulness and gentleness.[85] We can understand why it holds such a prominent place in Clement's thought and why he should have opened his appeal to conversion with a depiction of Christ as the true Orpheus—he is signaling the beginning of a pathway of formation. Other subjects in the *paideia* had their part to play in the formation of character as well. Studies undertaken in geometry and the mathematical sciences assisted the mind in its purification from sensible representations.[86] Even the development of rhetorical skills, learning different patterns and examples of formalized speech, was seen as a form of training in virtue as one mastered the disciplines of grammar and speech, bringing them under the control of reason and thus enlisting the power of language in the service of persuasion to the truth. Rhetoric asks for a mastery in the control of speech and therefore prepares for, and contributes to, other forms of self-control.[87]

From the Platonist tradition, the Alexandrians had received an understanding of the human person in tripartite fashion, comprising of reason, energy, and appetite, faculties of thought and contemplation, of will, and of sensation. In order to live a harmonious life, according to what is best in us, three corresponding virtues of wisdom, courage and temperance need to be developed, corresponding to these three "parts" that make up our selves.[88] The virtue of justice corresponds to the ensuing harmony of the three, and Plato outlines the path towards this harmony, using the image of a line, divided into four parts, and corresponding to different degrees of knowledge and understanding.[89] Coming-to-know is a gradual, deepening movement,

---

[84] For details of the role of music in ancient Greek education and within the Christian Tradition see Basil Cole, O.P., *Music and Morals: A Theological Appraisal of the Moral and Psychological Effects of Music* (Alba House, 1993).
[85] See the description in Plato's *Protagoras* (326b) and Aristotle's discussion in the *Politics* (1339a12-1342b34), of the place of rhythms, modes and melodies in education, where he judges that any modes and melodies that have been "approved by philosophers who have had a musical education" (1342a30) may be accepted as contributing towards good character development.
[86] *Republic* 526e.
[87] Thus one's words, as well as one's thoughts and actions, must be pure (*Stromateis* 6.12.97.2). See also Peter Brown, *Power and Persuasion in Late Antiquity: Towards a Christian Empire* (Madison: University of Wisconsin Press, 1992), 48.
[88] See, for example, *Phaedrus* 246aff.
[89] For this image and for Plato's discussion of the path, see *Republic* 510aff.

a clearing away of confusion as one's "eyes" become accustomed to the sight of the real. Formation in habits leads gradually to a focus on the development of rationality. The earliest level of schooling emphasizes practice through imitation of what is worthy of admiration: children will come to resemble that which they imitate because of this habitual practice.[90] Thus is the mind disciplined and trained until finally the student is ready to synthesize his understanding. This path of gradual movement towards a fuller understanding and a life of virtue ultimately enables the person to reach true wisdom in the knowledge of the Good.

Aristotle, in his anthropology and his understanding of formation, writes with conscious reference to Plato, his master. Like Plato, he proposed a clear path towards wisdom on the basis of his conception of the person as threefold: the level of physicality, the life of the body; of instinct and sensibility; and of intelligence. He basically follows this order in his scheme of educational development: it begins with physical care and training; then moves to the education of the senses and emotions; and finally turns to the education of the mind. For Aristotle, therefore, the path of formation needs to draw into harmony the behavioral, the affective and the intellectual dimensions of the person. He uses concepts of "nature," "habit" and "rational principle" to discuss this movement towards unity, the last two of these being the province of education.[91] The cultivation of habit and reason enable the perfection of the potentialities of the human person.[92] A particular emphasis, which Clement echoes, is placed on habit in Aristotle's schema. He strongly believed that only the sheer force of repeated action until it becomes habitual can gradually enable change and development in a person. Understanding and reasoning alone cannot change character; nor can resolution.

The end, or *telos*, of the whole process informs and gives purpose to the whole. Understanding the end, which is participation in the life of God, or the Good, gives direction, purpose, and structure to the development of all levels of the person. In this matter the Alexandrians were again in accord with Middle Platonism with its uniting of Platonist and Aristotelian elements. Man is the only animal with

---

[90] This conviction about the relationship between inspiration and imitation explains Plato's strong views about the importance of selection of appropriate material for children. In Book III of the *Republic* he explains the necessity for careful censorship and challenges the place of honor given to Homer in the educational system of his day.
[91] See *Politics* 1332b10-11.
[92] See *Nicomachean Ethics* 1104b17 and 1105b13.

something of the divine in him, Aristotle taught,[93] the life of *nous*, the mind, and so the cultivation of intelligence constitutes the highest level of human development. The fulfillment of the human person is realized in its capacity for contemplation of the Supreme Being[94] which is the crowning of the stages of formation.[95] In his *telos* the human person finds his own good and this is the good of the whole person.

Finally, as we look towards the transposing of this classical model in the catechetical school, we should note how Philo, as so often, functions as a kind of bridge, uniting his Greek philosophical understanding to the divine models provided in the Scriptures. In his treatise on the life of Abraham he taught that the successful following of the path to the goal of true knowledge of God requires three elements: nature, instruction and practice. One must have a nature open to receiving moral teaching, an instructor to guide one in the path, and one must faithfully follow the practices that the instructor gives.[96] Philo links these three elements with the three patriarchs who, he judges, incarnate the qualities needed. It is interesting to see Philo's returning instinct for the importance of models of scriptural figures to support the teaching he gives. Clement adopts the same mimetic style, holding before his readers the examples of God's personal education of Abraham, Jacob, Moses, Jeremiah and David.[97]

---

[93] *On the Parts of Animals* 656a66.
[94] For a discussion of the nature of *nous* in Aristotle, see Clark, *Aristotle's Man*, 174-90.
[95] *Nicomachean Ethics* 1177b15-26. Thus Aristotle asks, What is the *ergon* of the human person? One of the critiques of this classical approach (e.g., see W. F. R. Hardie, *Aristotle's Ethical Theory* [Oxford: Oxford University Press, 1968], 23), both of Aristotle with this notion of finding the *ergon* of human life, and of Plato's arguments concerning the good life of man in *The Republic*, is that to argue for the proper life of man as corresponding to his *ergon* is to reduce him to being a means to an end. Man becomes a means to achieving ends outside of himself. He is merely a cog in a larger machine. This critique has some validity with respect to Stoicism: the wise learn to see themselves only within the good of the Whole. And it is true that Aristotle does use analogies at times which seem to suggest a tool-like understanding of *ergon*, as in the *Nicomachean Ethics*: "But is it likely that whereas joiners and shoemakers have certain functions (*erga*) or activities, man as such has none, but has been left by nature a functionless being?" (*Nicomachean Ethics* 1097b28f). But other, more organic, images are preferred by him, as when he says that sight is the *ergon* of the eye (*Nicomachean Ethics* 1097b24f), and both Aristotle and Plato are best understood as pointing us to the need to employ an analysis of the human person that focuses upon the proper ends in which we find fulfillment. Thus, "For the *ergon* is the end, and the activity the *ergon*" (*Metaphysics* IX, 1050b22). For further discussion see Stephen R. L. Clark, "The Use of 'Man's Function' in Aristotle," *Ethics* 82 (1972) 269-83, and *Aristotle's Man*, 15-18.
[96] *De Abrahamo* 52-54.
[97] *Paedagogus* 1.7.56.1-61.3.

Turning now to how the Alexandrian school took up and developed this classical and Philonic model, we can note two important areas in which adjustments to this ascending movement were made. In the first place, in the development of the right ordering of the person toward the Good, the stages of formation were not thought of as necessarily following a simple sequential pathway such that one leaves behind more primitive levels as one ascends towards the higher life. Clement's selection of the *child* as the key image for the Christian—after baptism, as well as before, and therefore after one has received illumination—allows him to continue to engage with all dimensions of the person: the arc within which all development takes place is the movement from the immature to the mature *child*. Living well, as one of the "perfect," will always be that of the perfect child. And Clement recognizes how difficult it is to leave the imperfect child behind: the "younger child" lives in us beyond his years and emotional scars return to haunt. Thus we find that Clement's more advanced theological and ethical reflections for his catechumens on spiritual nourishment, for example, are interspersed with lower level recommendations and reprovals about not speaking with your mouth full or always reaching for the sauce,[98] while his challenges to the upwardly-mobile whose homes and possessions, he suggests, always hint at a delicate exclusivity, demonstrate his awareness of an ongoing need to find ways of addressing the not-yet-outgrown adolescent desire for peer admiration and social acceptance.[99] In all these matters, he appeals for simplicity and an avoidance of ostentation, and promises that there is a better way if we follow God.[100]

In the second place, in the path of ascent the highest reaches of the person also embrace the body as intended for redemption. The economy of the sacraments witnesses to the importance of the natural life in God's dispensation. It is often supposed that the Alexandrians, influenced by Platonism, distrusted the physical, and had a tendency to downplay the significance of human activity: the sensible universe was to be ignored, in order that the only Real world, that of the spiritual Ideas, might be attained. It is important, in fact, to be fair to Plato himself on this point, not least so that we may better understand how the Fathers of the Church believed his thought might be profitably employed within a Christian view of the world. Aristotle credits him with a straightforward dualism, and on this point ranges

---

[98] *Paedagogus* 2.1.11.3; 2.1.13.1.
[99] *Paedagogus* 2.3.37.2–3.
[100] *Paedagogus* 2.3.36.2.

him with Empedocles and Anaxagoras.[101] It is not easy to find a clear text in Plato to justify Aristotle's assertion, however, and if this were the case the principle of evil for Plato would be matter, whereas it seems fairly clear that he did not consider matter itself to be evil, or the source of evil. It is a lesser reality than the Ideas, certainly, but the dark region is not the earth—which has a sort of being, however tenuous—but non-being itself.[102] There is no need to suppose, then, that a Platonic outlook must lead to a denigration of the material world. Physical objects are shadows of the Forms and are thus neither wholly real nor wholly good (since reality and goodness are correlative). Plato clearly held to a theory of value which placed matter at the foot of the scale of Being and there is in Platonism—and in Philo who followed him in most respects here—an understanding of the spiritual path as involving a gradual detachment from sensible reality, an ascent to the intelligible world that involved a lessening engagement with the world of matter.[103] Still, we must remember that even at the lowest level of reality, material reality remained a manifestation of the eternal, archetypal world, and as such is worthy of respect. This is why the Fathers, though they needed to adjust the valuation of the body and of matter, were able to "baptize" Plato and use his philosophical thought as a foundation for Christian doctrine.

We can see just such a "baptism" taking place in the *Paedagogus* in which we can follow Clement's concern to correct both Gnostic extremes and Platonic underestimations of matter in favor of a proper Christian valuing of the body and of bodily action: "a middle course is good in all things."[104] The *Paedagogus* is neither romantically unreal about bodily life nor disdainful, and Clement displays a subtlety of thought about the body as also the place of the passions in the Christian life. While much of Clement's intellectual argument countering Gnosticism is found in his *Stromateis*, a careful anti-Gnostic stance also informs the whole of the *Paedagogus*, with its detailed interest in the concrete ethical practices of the new Christian disciple. The formation of the person undertaken by the Pedagogue, as we have seen, involves not only the intellectual, but also the affective and behavioral dimensions, a point which follows from Clement's

---

[101] *Metaphysics* A, 6, 988a 7–17.
[102] Cf. *Republic* 514aff.
[103] For Philo, the soul is enslaved in the body as Israel was enslaved in Egypt and it must seek an exodus from this slavery. Philo is not entirely consistent in his views on this matter, but on the whole his ethic and spirituality, as Henry Chadwick puts it, "inclines towards a world-denying asceticism" ("Philo," 146).
[104] *Paedagogus* 2.1.16.4.

commitment to a unified account of the human person: there may be angels and demons warring over me and there may be recalcitrant and ignorant parts of myself, but I dare not divide myself. What is needed is the right ordering of my *entire* being.

For the Alexandrian Christians the Incarnation changed everything. Because of the Incarnation of the Son of God there were new possibilities for the body: it was to be changed, to undergo transformation and eventually resurrection.[105] Whereas Platonists saw the religious ascent as a movement to pure immateriality, Origen insisted that, like the Lord, Christians would be clothed in glorified bodies in the afterlife, our earthly bodies modeled on his, transformed and refined.[106] Against Celsus, Origen clarified the Christian position on the body: "in our view it is not true that 'the matter which dwells among mortals' is responsible for evils. Each person's mind is responsible for the evil which exists in him, and this is what evil is. Evils are actions which result from it. In our view nothing else is strictly speaking evil."[107] The Christian life is an embodied one, of good actions undertaken in the body. Origen therefore presents baptism as the radical beginning of a new life in the *body*, the point of the "first resurrection." Baptism marks the moment when a new life in the body begins. There is a bodily resurrection to be expected after physical death, but the new life in Christ has begun now. Our bodies are to be raised at the end of time in a state of glory, but the baptized Christian already enjoys the fruits of the resurrection "for he walks in a certain newness of life, but without being yet resurrected with the blessed and perfect resurrection for which we hope."[108]

A particularly high value was placed upon the finite human body that was assumed by the divine Person of the Word, since everything about the human nature which he assumed was put at the service of expressing the character of the divine Person of the Son.[109] And there were implications for all human beings in the Word's assumption of human nature, including a new valuing of every human body. Clement also transforms the Stoic *apatheia* by reading the meaning of this virtue in the light of Christ's teaching and life. God falls into passion

---

[105] See Peter Brown, *The Body and Society* (London: Faber and Faber, 1989), 31.
[106] *Contra Celsum* III.41-42. See also *De Principiis* I.6.4. For a careful discussion of Origen's understanding of the place of the body and its destiny see Benjamin P. Blosser, *Become Like the Angels: Origen's Doctrine of the Soul* (Washington, D.C.: The Catholic University of America Press, 2012), 38-59, 247-53.
[107] *Contra Celsum* IV.66.
[108] *Commentary on John* 10, 35, 232.
[109] Origen writes movingly of the wonder of the Incarnation in *De Principiis* II.6.2.

for our sake,[110] and was afflicted, giving us "the greatest thing he has, his own life."[111] In this divine condescension he means to teach us how to be passionless, which means service of others, forgetting oneself and forgiving the sins that others have committed against us.[112] And this virtue of true Christian *apatheia* can be won only through grace, for we can do nothing without God.[113] Again, Richard Layton, in his analysis of Didymus's teaching techniques, shows how Didymus also takes the classical approach to the passions in this Christocentric direction, carefully explaining how Christ handled each of the passions—in Gethsemane, for example, mastering sorrow, purifying it and placing it at the service of his Father's mission, modeling courage for us as well in the face of fear.[114]

The pedagogy of divine condescension

The Alexandrians, then, followed the broad outline of Middle Platonism in understanding the worthy life as an ascending movement towards the divine. But, as we are beginning to see, they transformed this through placing this within the larger framework of God's active love in creation and his descent—his pursuit of his creatures, fallen, disfigured and scattered, to retrieve them and bring them to share in his glory and life. In the school's understanding of formation, the core doctrines of the faith radically adjusted the way in which the growth to maturity we have just traced was understood, drawing together all that was best in the perennial philosophy of the period and infusing it with the light of the Gospel. A primacy of place was given to the divine initiative manifesting itself in a movement of condescension, drawing the human person through a journey of responding ascent.[115] In the Old Testament Scriptures, Origen saw

---

[110] *Paedagogus* 1.8.74.4.
[111] *Paedagogus* 1.9.85.1.
[112] *Stromateis* 7.14.88.4.
[113] *The Rich Man's Salvation*, 21.1.
[114] *Didymus the Blind and His Circle in Late-Antique Alexandria*, 51–86, discussing in particular his Christocentric treatment of the Book of Job and of the Psalms.
[115] For the synergy in Clement between divine grace and human freewill see Werner Jaeger, *Two Rediscovered Works of Ancient Christian Literature: Gregory of Nyssa and Macarius* (Leiden: Brill, 1954), 103–6, and John Behr, *Asceticism and Anthropology in Irenaeus and Clement*, 167–70. In his *Stromateis* Clement describes the place of human effort and will within this synergy as that of a "cooperating cause" (see 8.9.25.1–33.9), a concept he uses to depict the closest possible dependence of the will upon God. While this suggests a close living from baptismal grace as the pattern for understanding Christian growth into maturity, Behr argues that Clement does not *sustain* this approach in a consistent way, allowing himself to think more in terms of a more "external collaboration" between grace and human freedom (170).

the allegory of this cosmic drama of descent and pursuit especially vividly present in the Song of Songs, a drama enacted at once on both the personal and the ecclesial levels. The bride of the divine Logos, whom he seeks to purify and redeem, is at once each human soul and also the *ekklesia*, the one Body of the Church.[116]

A Trinitarian, kerygmatic approach is taken to frame the work of formation, then, emphasizing our being lifted to share in divine relationality. This is the key to understanding both Origen's and Clement's approach to formation. Clement places it at the center of the first book of the *Paedagogus*: "O the great God! O the perfect child! The Son in the Father and the Father in the Son."[117] For Clement, this is the core principle we need to understand in order to appreciate the nature of God's formative work, for he immediately then speaks of our own incorporation into this divine relationship: "And how shall not the discipline (*paideia*) of this child be perfect, which extends to all, leading as a schoolmaster (*paidagogousa*) us his children, who are his little ones?"[118] Christ provides the perfect *paideia* to lead us into this mutual indwelling of love, into the very "mysteries of love."[119]

The Rich Man's Salvation climaxes on this same truth: "Behold the mysteries of love, and then you will have a vision of the bosom of the Father, whom the only begotten God alone declared. God in his very self is love and for love's sake became visible to us."[120] And divine relationality is the prize to be uncovered in the mystagogical phase of formation as well: as Clement nears the conclusion of the *Stromateis* he returns to this doctrine by offering us an allegorical reading of the distinction in the Law between clean and unclean animals, the clean being those which divide the hoof and chew the cud. The division of the hoof, he proposes, refers to the relation of the Father to the Son in the Godhead, of God to his Logos. It is this life of divine reciprocity, into which each Christian is invited through baptism and faith, that is the great truth that gives "stability" in the Christian life.[121] And in the mystagogia the divine Teacher leads us to learn this greatest of all truths by our chewing the cud—ruminating upon the Scriptures—for when we practice such a divine reading we

---

[116] See, for example, *Commentary on the Song of Songs* I.1; 2:1 (personal meaning); 3:3 (ecclesial meaning).
[117] *Paedagogus* 1.5.24.3.
[118] Ibid.
[119] Ibid.
[120] *The Rich Man's Salvation*, 37. For the central importance of love in Clement see Méhat, *Étude sur les 'Stromates' de Clément d'Alexandrie*, 480-81.
[121] *Stromateis* 7.18.109.1-110.3.

are the clean animals God desires us to be. Clement reads everything, then, in the light of the reciprocal relationship of Father and Son.[122] The way of formation is that of the child who gradually learns how to be fully mature with the fullness of Christ.[123] That full maturity, because it is growth into Christ the *Son*, never loses its filial character.

Origen, too, sees knowledge of the Father and of his love in and through Christ who reveals him as the foundation for understanding the path of formation as well as the goal of salvation.[124] The Fatherhood of God is eternal and the Father's generation of the Son eternal, for Father and Son are correlatives. All of creation finds its origin and destiny within this divine reciprocity. He writes in a powerfully affective way of the love of the Father, drawing on the adoption language of Paul in Galatians 4 and Romans 8. Like Clement, he also draws extensively from John's Gospel on the relationship between the Son and the Father in order to explain how we come to live in the Son. The Christian life consists in moving from a Lord-to-servant relationship to a Father-to-adopted son relationship, a sharing in the eternal relationship of the Father to his only Son, and as this transformation takes place the relationship moves from that of fear to love.[125] It is through Christ himself and his work in us that this change is effected for he is the only one by whom we can come to know the Father.[126] The Christian's new status is expressed when he prays the *Our Father*,[127] pointing him towards his destiny, that of sharing in the Son's "uninterrupted contemplation of the Father."[128]

If the Holy Trinity is the source and goal of the formation offered in the catechumenate, the doctrines of the Incarnation and Paschal mystery are the keys, for Clement, for explaining the nature of the journey which the catechumen is making. Clement's choice to identify Christ with the figure of the Pedagogue becomes a means for a profound reflection on the *kerygma*. The social reality of the pedagogue is important to remember, for the presence of a pedagogue in a household was associated, socially, with a certain level of privilege:

---

[122] See the convincing emphasis that Osborn places on this structural theme in his treatment of Clement's thought: *Clement of Alexandria*, 107–36.
[123] *Paedagogus* 1.5.18.3.
[124] For an exposition of Origen's teaching on our adoption by the Father see Widdicombe, *The Fatherhood of God from Origen to Athanasius*, 93–118.
[125] Origen, *Commentary on John* 1.29.201–2.
[126] *Commentary on John* 20.17.135–39.
[127] Origen, *Prayer* 22.1.
[128] *Commentary on John* 2.2.18. See Widdicombe, *The Fatherhood of God from Origen to Athanasius*, 119–20.

it is the freeborn child who is placed under the tutelage of the slave. Plutarch, in an essay that deals with the care that parents need to take in their educational choices, regrets that his advice will not be able to be followed in the homes of the poor who cannot afford a pedagogue. The choice of this image is a striking example, then, of how Clement wants to accentuate the theme of the divine exchange, for here Christ who is the free and eternal Son of the Father takes on the bondage of slavery in order to train to the likeness of true sons and daughters those who are poor and without resources.[129] In Christ his Son, God the Father sets about forming our characters, helping us to learn what is necessary for growing up well in *his* household.

It is only right to note that the term had gradually come to also signify "educator" in a broader sense. Thus in the *Laws* Plato describes God as the pedagogue of the whole world, meaning by this the teacher and educator of the human race.[130] Jaeger, reasonably enough, suggests that it was the theological dignity that Plato had given to the concept of the pedagogue through his use of it to describe the relation of God to the world that made it possible for Clement to use this term of Christ.[131] However, it seems in keeping with what we have seen of Clement's kerygmatic concerns that he should have wanted to emphasize the pedagogical implications of the Incarnation and of the divine exchange which enables the adoption of the baptized into the reciprocity of divine love by maintaining this concrete reference point of the domestic slave and tutor. In such a depiction, after all, Clement was following the Gospel portrait of Jesus who had prepared his disciples to understand his relationship to them in this way, as the one who came among them as a slave, to serve.[132] How great an error it is not to see who our Pedagogue really is, Clement exclaims: he, the humble God, Lord of the universe, is girded with a towel, and carried a foot basin.[133]

Christ, then, is not being identified for the catechumen simply as a heavenly "model" of perfection to be emulated. Those in formation are being asked to "grow up" into the One who first "came down," who condescended to come among them, who followed the downward stages of the human fall into error and the bitter effects of sin, in order that he might lead them up from their unlikeness.

---

[129] It is noteworthy, in this respect, that the *Directory for Catechesis* describes the pedagogy of the faith as being "inspired by the self-abasement of God" (*DC* 179).
[130] *Laws* X.897b.
[131] *Early Christianity and Greek Paideia*, 133 n.29.
[132] See Mk. 10:45; Phil. 2:7; Jn. 13:2ff.
[133] *Paedagogus* 2.3.38.1.

Thus, through this image of the Pedagogue the great biblical theme of the cosmic fall of the angels and of man, and the unloosing of the order of created being, is introduced. It is made clear that what was needed was not just an ascent according to the patterns of order established in creation, but a restoration, a remaking of what had come apart, through a divine descent, a condescension and a work of grace. Because of the sin that had compromised man's fundamental covenantal relationships, human virtue was now to be understood as "a remnant to be stored and held sacred out of some primordial ruin."[134] The integration of the person was to be achieved in the face of the disfigurement caused by sin. For this restoration the Word came. He would not be good, Clement argued, unless he rendered us service,[135] and so he came precisely to do this, to render the service of salvation. "Such is our Pedagogue, good beyond a doubt."[136]

From this identification of Christ as the Formator working in humility Clement can appeal for a serious attentiveness on the part of catechumens to the area of their own lives that is the proper responsibility of the pedagogue, that of physical, and more especially moral welfare. The association of the role of pedagogue with that of a growing child made it natural that this educational reality should form an image of the way in which the body and the passions need to be governed by rationality. So, for instance, Aristotle, in his treatment of the virtue of temperance, had argued that the appetitive part of us should be ruled by principle, "just as the child ought to live in accordance with the directions of his tutor (*paidagogon*)"[137] and Clement's concentration in this work is precisely on this cultivation of virtue. Clement's choice of metaphor thus allows him to emphasize the ordering of formation: first the healing of the emotions and the development of virtue and then the pursuit of knowledge. Such a healing focuses upon certain central points in the development of character, especially of trust, gentleness, simplicity and guilelessness: "children are those who look upon God alone as their father, who are simple, little ones, uncontaminated."[138] Developing the quality of trust is especially important for Clement: "the Only-begotten sent from the bosom of the Father" is the "Word evoking trust."[139] Clement hammers the

---

[134] The phrase in this case is Chesterton's: G. K. Chesterton, *Orthodoxy* (London: Collins, 1961), 64.
[135] *Paedagogus* 1.3.9.2.
[136] *Paedagogus* 1.9.85.1.
[137] *Nicomachean Ethics* 1119b13–15.
[138] *Paedagogus* 1.5.17.1.
[139] *Paedagogus* 1.3.8.2. So significant is this quality in Clement that it is puzzling

point home: "Evoking trust, indeed, trust in abundance."[140] When Jesus speaks of becoming like little children, Clement notes, he is not in the first place offering a "figure of speech for some kind of rebirth" but is recommending "the simplicity of childhood for our imitation."[141]

The metaphor of Christ as Pedagogue allowed Clement to focus, then, upon this theme of spiritual childhood. The status of a child was something to be embraced. Catechumenal formation was for the sake developing a "godly" childlikeness before the Father.[142] This understanding of the goal of formation stands in stark contrast to the classical view, in which the mature adult was the standard for education. Marrou, in fact, argues that the "barbaric severity" of much education in the classical world was a result of the view that the education of the child was only for the sake of the grown adult, without the child being valued for its own sake: the whole point of such an education was "to teach the child to transcend himself."[143] In the light of this conscious shift from the usual classical view, Clement's discussion of the rationale for conceiving of the goal of Christian formation as a call to mature childlikeness is therefore detailed and careful. Some falsely charge, he writes, that we call ourselves children because "the learning we acquire is puerile or rudimentary."[144] On the contrary, we receive enlightenment and knowledge of God when we are reborn.[145] Rather, then, the formation given by Christ the Pedagogue should be conceived as a movement from "childishness" to "childlikeness"—and at this point Clement provides an extensive account of the differences between a childlike and a childish character.[146] Clement then connects the catechumenal journey to the figure of the Pedagogue himself, with

---

that Behr in one place judges Clement's anthropology to be one characterized by protection against any state of vulnerability or dependency (*Asceticism and Anthropology in Irenaeus and Clement*, 211), even viewing it as "diametrically opposed" (218, n.11) to a spirituality of simple entrustment to God.

[140] In the *Stromateis*, Clement writes that the Christian must learn the childlike quality of *parrhesia* (7.12.71.3), speaking with confidence to God. This is the concept highlighted in the *Catechism* in its description of the life of prayer before the Father: "straightforward simplicity, filial trust, joyous assurance, humble boldness, the certainty of being loved" (CCC 2778). This is, says the *Catechism*, a "characteristically Christian expression," summing up the qualities of the divine education that needs to be received in the new state of being into which Christians are introduced through the gift of the Spirit.

[141] *Paedagogus* 1.5.12.4, referring to Matt. 18:3.
[142] *Paedagogus* 1.5.21.4.
[143] Marrou, *A History of Education in Antiquity*, 219, and see 218–20.
[144] *Paedagogus* 1.6.25.1.
[145] Ibid.
[146] *Paedagogus* 1.5.12.1–1.6.25.1.

the ultimate justification for the notion of spiritual childhood as the Christian standard being a Christocentric one:

> But there is another and even greater support for this argument of ours, which I shall now explain. The Spirit inspired Isaiah to call the Lord a child: "Behold, a child is born to us, and a son given us, and the government is upon his shoulders..." What is this child, this little one, after whose image we also are little ones?... Is not the childhood of this child perfect, embracing as it does all of us children, educating us little ones as his children? This is he who stretches out his hands to us, hands so clearly to be trusted.[147]

The Pedagogue is himself the perfect Child. And Clement then focuses on the end point of the catechumenal journey: it is in baptism that Christians are adopted as sons and "being made sons, we are made perfect."[148] This baptism, in which the catechumen receives perfection as a child, restored to the Father, is modeled on Christ's own baptism when, of course, the voice of the Father was heard, "Thou art my beloved Son, today have I begotten Thee."

Finally, the image of Christ the Pedagogue allowed Clement to place the catechumenal journey of formation within the theme of salvation history, showing how Christ fulfilled the promises made to the Chosen People and universalized these to make them available to all. In the *Paedagogus*, therefore, Clement uses, and develops, Paul's reference in his Letter to the Galatians to the Mosaic Law as the pedagogue within God's economy of redemption, a custodian bringing God's people to Christ.[149] For Paul, the time before Christ was a period of being placed under a pedagogue, a period both of preparation and of constraint. In Paul's thinking, then, the relationship between the Law and Christ is essentially one of moving to a state in which one can claim one's inheritance. The child is the "heir" who will be able to inherit when he is no longer a child under a pedagogue but has been adopted as a son. Law cannot deliver our inheritance. The Law, as pedagogue, does not provide us with fulfillment, but prepares us for it, leads us to our inheritance and makes it possible for us to receive it. The metaphors of educational maturing, of inheritance rights for sons, and of the legal entitlements of adopted children are all brought together in this complex Pauline passage.

---

[147] *Paedagogus* 1.6.24.1-4.
[148] *Paedagogus* 1.6.26.2.
[149] Thus, "the law was our custodian (*paidagogos*)" (*Gal.* 3:24). Paul's argument continues in 4:1-7, where he uses the related analogy of being like a son in a patrician household.

Because Clement is committed to this image of *Christ* as the slave-Pedagogue, raising up the fallen children of his Father, he expands the references to the presence of the Pedagogue under the dispensation of the Old Covenant. From the beginning of the history of salvation, Clement argues, we see the divine Pedagogue at work. "As far as I can see," Clement writes, "Scripture is undoubtedly presenting a picture of the Pedagogue of children, and describing the guidance he imparts."[150] He illustrates his point by citing the passage from Deuteronomy of the eagle teaching its young to fly.[151] The name of the Pedagogue remains hidden during this period, he argues, as we can see from the refusal of the mysterious figure who wrestles with Jacob and will not reveal his name. "For he was saving his new name for his new people, the little ones."[152] Through Moses, again, the Lord showed himself to be the Pedagogue of his children.[153] And in due course, Moses made way for the *perfect Pedagogue* to come in the flesh, to lead his children face to face.[154] The divine Pedagogue who has been accompanying his people, hidden in this role, takes flesh now as the divine servant, bringing the full Revelation of the Father and of his saving love.

At the close of the *Paedagogus*, Christ the Pedagogue speaks directly to the reader: "It is time for me to lay aside leading you as Pedagogue, and for you to hearken to the Teacher."[155] The Church is the school and we must run to that good mother as little ones, to be taught there.[156] A new stage is to be entered upon in the Christian life. Clement's short talk to the newly baptized, *Exhortation to Endurance*, indicates how Clement understands the relationship between the formation received by the Pedagogue and the ongoing growth in knowledge and love in the life of the Christian, for here he turns to the responsibilities of the baptized: to "learn gladly, and teach ungrudgingly." The learning of the baptized is to continue and deepen, but it is now to be associated with handing on the faith. The learner now is to become fruitful in teaching. "Never hide wisdom from others by reason of a grudging spirit." The baptized must now "listen and converse in turn." It is a beautiful depiction of what the Church is now describing as "missionary discipleship."

---

[150] *Paedagogus* 1.7.56.1.
[151] *Deut.* 32:10-12, quoting from the Septuagint.
[152] *Paedagogus* 1.7.57.1-2.
[153] *Paedagogus* 1.7.58.1.
[154] *Paedagogus* 1.7.60.2.
[155] *Paedagogus* 3.12.97.3.
[156] *Paedagogus* 3.12.98.1-99.1.

This call to continue moving is not for a select few. "You are all one in Christ Jesus," Clement had earlier reminded them. "It is not, then, that some are enlightened Gnostics and others are only less perfect Spirituals in the same Word, but all, putting aside their carnal desires, are equal and spiritual before the Lord."[157] There is no division of Christians into the simple faithful and the elect Gnostics. All are being called on. The Christian life is lived at a stretch, going from fullness into fullness, the Pedagogue leading the Christian ever more deeply into the realization of the defining relationship to God the Father and learning how to mirror his generosity in drawing others into the place of blessing: "the new people are called young, having learned the new blessings; and we have the exuberance of life's morning prime in this youth which knows no old age; in which we are always growing to maturity in intelligence, are always young, always mild, always new."[158] It is time for the Teacher to receive his pupils.

AND TODAY

There are many points we may wish to draw from this understanding of the catechumenal process to assist the contemporary renewal of catechesis. The striking identification by Clement of spiritual childhood as the character of baptismal maturity has been reinforced by the declaration of Thérèse of Lisieux as a Doctor of the Church by John Paul II, and concomitantly with this the theme of God as pedagogue being brought to the fore during his pontificate, especially in the *General Directory for Catechesis*.[159] It has since been developed further, in the *Directory for Catechesis*, as a central way of understanding both God's activity in salvation history as a whole and the style of the Church's catechesis.[160] The identification of Christ *as* the divine Pedagogue after the manner of Clement's treatment would assist in gaining a greater focus on catechetical apprenticeship, further strengthening the Christocentricity of catechesis and its kerygmatic nature.

Clement and Origen, as we have seen, emphasized an approach to formation that asked for an intensely individual fostering and support. It is challenging, but worthwhile, to consider how this personal approach might be made a feature in all forms of catechetical ministry. The understanding of a catechumenal pedagogy as deeply personal, attending to the needs of each unique individual, is also

---

[157] *Paedagogus* 1.6.31.1-2.
[158] *Paedagogus* 1.5.20.3.
[159] See GDC 33, 38, 99, 112, 129, 137-47.
[160] DC 157-81.

reflected in a key pastoral principle presented in the *Roman Catechism* — and repeated in the prologue of the *Catechism of the Catholic Church* where the new *Catechism* sets out its pedagogical priorities:

> Whoever teaches must become "all things to all men" (I Cor 9:22), to win everyone to Christ... Above all, teachers must not imagine that a single kind of soul has been entrusted to them, and that consequently it is lawful to teach and form equally all the faithful in true piety with one and the same method! Let them realize that some are in Christ as newborn babes, others as adolescents, and still others as adults in full command of their powers... Those who are called to the ministry of preaching must suit their words to the maturity and understanding of their hearers, as they hand on the teaching of the mysteries of faith and the rules of moral conduct.[161]

Such an affirmation of individual and small-group mentoring suggests that it would be worthwhile to revisit the value of the *disciplina arcani* in the catechumenal process. Certainly, the magisterial teaching on catechesis is leading now with a strong affirmation of a gradual, step by step approach as God "communicates himself to man gradually," preparing his people "by stages" to become capable of welcoming, knowing and loving him "far beyond their own natural capacity."[162]

What is also clear is that the mimetic pedagogy of the Alexandrian school is particularly suited to a *home* environment, just as the identification of Christ as Pedagogue also places the accent on the home as the key *locus* for formation. For Clement, this language of pedagogue and child may in fact have been an opportunity to reflect on his own family situation as he seems to have associated himself with married men.[163] Whether he was married or not, it is also interesting that when commenting on Jesus's promise to be wherever two or three are gathered in his name Clement assumes that this saying refers to husband, wife and child.[164] That assumption perhaps simply reflects the catechetical realities in these early centuries where it was parents who were considered their children's catechists, providing their religious training and then representing them as sponsors at baptism.[165] In his classic account of educational

---

[161] *Roman Catechism*, Preface II; cited in *CCC* 24.
[162] *CCC* 52–53.
[163] See the general tenor of the comments in *Paedagogus* 3.11.
[164] *Stromateis* 3.10.68.1. Though we should note that Origen interprets the promise in a similar way in his *Commentary on Matthew* 14.2, and of course was not himself married.
[165] See Hippolytus, *The Apostolic Tradition*, 33.

practice in the ancient world, Henri Marrou suggests it can be difficult for us today to appreciate the significance of the role of the pedagogue since "we have made the school the decisive factor in education" whereas "for the Greeks the decisive factor was the surroundings in which the child grew up—the family with its surroundings and friends."[166] Marrou was writing in 1948, before the threat to children's catechesis in the family became acute because of the widespread family breakdown in so many Christian cultures and societies. The papal Magisterium has certainly been urging a major shift towards family forms of catechesis, in which attention can be given naturally and appropriately to questions of moral and spiritual development and readiness, and John Paul II recaptured something of this ancient vision of the Church when he described the parish as "the *Church living in the midst of the homes of her sons and daughters*"[167]—the formation in the gathered Christian community of the parish standing in a symbiotic relationship to the pedagogy and formation offered in the home. If this is indeed the vision for the way forward in catechesis it speaks to the need to prioritize the strengthening of Christian marriage and family life.

Another point that has emerged from this review of the school's catechumenal process is the close attention the school gave to grounding practical expressions of faith in core areas of doctrine. The danger of pastoral drift from dogmatic teaching is an ever-present one. Newman, in his *Arians of the Fourth Century*, made the point that in the pre-Nicene Church the integrity of the faith was necessarily held through a determined union of doctrine and discipline, and in his account of early Christian *paideia* Werner Jaeger places that felt need for a strong unification of faith and life within the framework of the evangelization of culture:

> They felt that if Christianity proved unable to take over cultural and intellectual leadership, even its external political victory, of which they felt certain in the long run, would be illusory... it would never achieve its goal without passing through the severest training of hand and mind, just as the ancient Greeks had had to learn the hard way. They had to start from the elements and then build man up systematically. What they needed was the kind of school that would teach them that. In a word, they had to build up a Christian *paideia*.[168]

---

[166] Marrou, *A History of Education in Antiquity*, 221.
[167] *Christifidelis laici* 26. Italics in the original.
[168] *Early Christianity and Greek Paideia*, 72–73.

One point for our contemporary ministry, then, is the need to teach concrete disciplines to accompany doctrine. Disciplines, like doctrines, can develop authentically within the Church, and the coherence between the two is vital. This is not to argue for an inappropriate universalizing of culturally-specific practices—some points in the *Paedagogus* that Clement urges upon his readers are clearly specific to his Alexandrian setting; the point is rather to accentuate the *recovery of concrete disciplines*, especially those that challenge levels of unexamined comfort, explicitly teaching them alongside and organically connected to doctrine, attending to the unity of faith and life within each culture, and grounding every discipline and faith-practice in the central Mystery of Christ. A renewal of this kind has certainly been sought in the catechetical Magisterium since the Second Vatican Council. The *General Catechetical Directory* of 1971 pointed to the urgent need for a renewal that went beyond the dichotomy of either a reemphasis on the place of teaching doctrine on the one hand, or of an attempt to show the relevance of the faith to contemporary life.[169] The 1997 *Directory* subsequently specified the need in terms of the recovery of an "organic" approach in catechesis, which it described as the *"principal characteristic"* of catechesis.[170] Again, the *Catechism* made an organic reading of its contents its *principal* recommendation.[171] The 2020 *Directory for Catechesis*, similarly, places a key accent on this organic approach, identifying the catechumenal process as "an organic and cumulative whole for initiation into Christian faith and life"[172] and asking in numerous places for the unifying of catechetical work with ecclesial pastoral care.[173]

---

[169] *GCD* 9.
[170] *GDC* 67, n.203 (italics in the original). See also nos. 115, 119, 121, 124, 130, 132, 178, 203, 221, 240, 241.
[171] See *CCC* 18.
[172] *DC* 61.
[173] See, for example, *DC* 262, 297, 301, 393, 402, 410, 421, 422.

CHAPTER 9
Christ in his Mystery: Formation for Transmission

IN CLEMENT'S TRIO OF WORKS TRACING THE stages of Christian conversion and discipleship we now come to the *Stromateis* which addresses the Christian in the ongoing call to holiness and knowledge of Christ. This is the period of mystagogy, of a continuing and deepening formation in the faith. The *Paedagogus* had identified Christ as the Pedagogue, responsible for the training of the catechumen in the Christian life. Towards the end of the *Paedagogus* Clement places these words in the mouth of Christ:

> ... it is time for Me to lay aside teaching you as Pedagogue, and for you to hearken to the Teacher.... He will take us and teach us the word of God. The Church is the school and the Bridegroom is the one only Teacher; His noble desire, as of a noble father, is excellent wisdom, the holiness of knowledge.[1]

Christ the Teacher would now be assisting the newly-baptized Christians to grow in the capacity to support his generation of new life in others, learning to teach and disciple, to father and mother them in the faith. Through an ongoing mystagogy the school wanted to prepare *teachers* of the faith, new catechists to serve the Church. This required the provision of a formation that included a deepening understanding of the sacramental and spiritual life and the development of scriptural and exegetical skills for the support of believers. While it is hard to find a formal structure in the Church of the first three centuries for a designated period of postbaptismal formation,[2] the Alexandrian Church stands out for its determination to engage the newly-baptized with a vision of responsibility for growth towards holiness and solicitude for others on the path to baptism.

ENTERING THE MYSTERY

The time of the Teacher with the baptized was dedicated to leading them more deeply into his Mystery. For the development of this period of formation the school looked principally to Jesus himself

---

[1] *Paedagogus* 3.12.97.3–98.1.
[2] Cf. Dujarier, *The Rites of Christian Initiation: Historical and Pastoral Reflections*, 207–20.

and his own pedagogy. Jesus had identified himself with the figure of Wisdom and therefore as the One able to lead a person into a true understanding of the Father and of his plan progressively, through a gradual unfolding of truth and a discipline of encounter, conversion and instruction.[3]

In addition to this definitive reference point of the life of Christ for the development of a mystagogical process, the school presented Christianity as *the authentic mystery cult*. Henri Marrou, in his history of education in antiquity, argued that "In its form, Christianity is a mystery religion,"[4] and Odo Casel's work has highlighted the ways in which the sacramental "form" of the Christian faith received a providential preparation in ancient understandings and cults of mystery, prefiguring the true Christian mysteries.[5] The concept of "mystery" in its Greek, Jewish, and Egyptian faces was indeed central to the world the early Christian Church encountered. Important in the Greco-Roman environment were "mystery religions," cults which involved the initiation of adherents into the mysteries associated with a particular god. "Mystery," *musteria*, was originally the Athenian term for one of these cults, the Eleusinian festival of Demeter and Kore,[6] and from that first reference it was then gradually applied to a whole range of cults that involved a measure of secrecy, initiation and, typically, an interest in the afterlife — Greek mystery cults associated with Orpheus and Bacchus, for example, and the Egyptian cult of Isis.[7]

Typically, then, participants were received into the cult through an initiation that included a form of purification and a crowning or garlanding of the initiate, with the climax of this initiation being the communication of some mystical knowledge as the initiate was

---

[3] Matt. 12:42. Cf. Matt. 11:28-29 which echoes the call of Wisdom in *Ecclus*. 51:23-27. On Jesus as the figure of Wisdom see the helpful treatment in James D. C. Dunn, *Christology in the Making*, 2nd ed. (Grand Rapids: William B. Eerdmans, 1996), 163-212.
[4] *A History of Education in Antiquity*, 315.
[5] See his 1960 classic, *The Mystery of Christian Worship* (The Crossroad Pub. Co., 1999), especially chapter three on the ancient mysteries and Christianity. Christianity fulfils ancient myths of dying and rising gods with the historical fact of the life, death, and resurrection of Christ, re-presented for us in the sacraments.
[6] "Eleusinian" is so called from the fact that the annual procession took place from Athens to Eleusis.
[7] Of the prominent place of the Isis mystery cult Plutarch writes: "As for Isis, and the gods associated with her, all people own them and are familiar with them" (*Isis and Osiris* 377d). For a survey of Greek mystery religions, see Jan N. Bremmer, *Greek Religion*, 2nd ed. (Cambridge: Cambridge University Press, 2021), 97-113. For a helpful discussion of early Christian liturgy in relation to the mystery cults see Jungmann, *The Early Liturgy*, 152-63.

brought into the presence of a holy object associated with the god. So Plutarch writes of three components in initiation into a mystery religion: things said, things done, and things shown, with the highest being those that were shown at the climax of the mystery by the hierophant, the highest official presiding at the initiation.[8] Some kind of ritual enactment took place that made the one being initiated a sharer in the life of the god. Together with these initiation rites there were also recurrent celebrations associated with each cult, ceremonials associated with the gaining of salvation through this mystical association with the god being worshiped.

Many details of these individual mystery cults can be found in Clement's—sometimes hilarious—attack on many practices of the mystery cults in his *Protrepticus*.[9] But alongside these vehement attacks, especially of the more barbaric and licentious forms the cults could take, he also proclaimed Christianity as the *true* mystery cult, looking to the model of Jesus's teaching and self-gift as the pattern of initiation into mystery. Thus—and probably with reference to the Bacchanalian mystery cult—Clement calls for conversion to Christ the giver of the true mysteries:

> O truly sacred mysteries! O pure light! In the blaze of the torches I have a vision of heaven and of God. I become holy by initiation. The Lord reveals the mysteries; He marks the worshipper with His seal, gives light to guide his way, and commends him, when he has believed, to the Father's care, where he is guarded for ages to come. These are the revels of my mysteries! If thou wilt, be thyself also initiated, and thou shalt dance with angels around the unbegotten and imperishable and only true God, the Word of God joining with us in our hymn of praise.[10]

As always with Clement, it is striking to see how consistently he amends and develops the practices he finds around him, to bring the surprising newness of Christianity to speak into existing models of religious devotion. In the passage just quoted, Clement refers to the moment in which, in the typical mystery cult, the initiate "sees" the divine object and so is transformed, becoming like that with which one associates.[11] The better one knows something the more one is assimilated to it and so it is by contemplating the divine that one

---

[8] See *Isis and Osiris* 378b and *Alcibiades* 22.3.
[9] See especially *Protrepticus* Books 2-4.
[10] *Protrepticus* 12.120.1-2.
[11] A principle that Plato enunciated: see *Republic* 500c; also Empedocles, Fragment B109, "like is known only by like."

becomes divine.[12] That understanding of initiation and its climax, however, he then significantly shifts in the *Paedagogus*. As we have already noted, Clement was the first in the Christian tradition explicitly to connect Christian baptism to the baptism of Christ. By thus referring the Christian initiate to Christ's baptism, Clement reinforces his theme of a receptive childlikeness since the climax of Christ's baptism is, of course, the moment in which the divine Son *receives* the confirmation of his identity from the Father, "this is my beloved Son," and the Spirit alighting upon him.[13] Rather than focus on the seeing of the divine object as the climactic moment of initiation, then, Clement reminds his readers of what happens in baptism, modeled on Christ's: "This is what happens with us, whose model the Lord made Himself. When we are baptized, we are enlightened; being enlightened, we become adopted sons; becoming adopted sons, we are made perfect; and becoming perfect, we are made divine."[14] The eyes of the Christian are indeed to be made pure so that by gazing upon what is good[15] they may ultimately see God himself, and that training of the custody of the eyes is the work of the divine Pedagogue. But the high point of Christian *initiation* is to become aware of the confirming gaze and voice of the Father.[16] And Clement returns to this same point of the divine seeing of the person by the Father in the period of mystagogy as well, in which he recalls Jesus's teaching that prayer is being in the "secret chamber" of the heart where one is before the Father, to be seen by him.[17] As so often, Clement's approach finds some anticipation in Philo's description of what is involved in the final vison of blessedness, highlighting the relationship of joy to which the human person is called as a state of "seeing and being seen," a "drawing near to God who has drawn the mind to himself."[18] The discipline of the Christian who seeks perfection, then, is that of placing oneself under the Father's gaze. It is to be known

---

[12] See *Timaeus* 90a.
[13] *Paedagogus* 1.6.25.1–3. It is Christ's humanity which is perfected in Jesus's baptism by John, a perfection and sanctification which the Christian who is initiated also receives.
[14] *Paedagogus* 1.6.26.1.
[15] *Paedagogus* 2.6.49.2.
[16] Cf. the teaching of Jesus as he transformed the three traditional Jewish practices of prayer, fasting, and almsgiving into opportunities to be seen and approved secretly by the Father (*Matt.* 6:1–6, 16–18).
[17] See *Stromateis* 7.7.49.6–8.
[18] *De Somniis* II.226; *De Plantatione* 64. Chadwick points to similar statements made by St Paul, in whom we find this same sense of reciprocity expressed: "... I press on to make it my own, because Christ Jesus has made me his own" (1 *Cor.* 8:3); "... if one loves God, one is known by him" (*Phil.* 4:13). Cf. "Philo," 148.

by God the Father, in union with Christ the Son, and to know the Father in return. And "what is wanting to him who knows God?"[19]

Before we turn to the most extended treatment of Clement's transformation of this theme of pagan mystery to become a true Christian mystagogy, it is also important to note that Greek education, the *paideia*, was often compared to being initiated into a mystery religion: education, too, was seen as setting one apart, placing one amongst the "initiated" — one becomes one of those who know, gaining knowledge from the master,[20] from teachers who are the "high priests of God's mysteries and torch-bearers of wisdom."[21] In the Platonic *paideia*, then, Socrates is presented as the true mystagogue, the master in dialogue with his pupils initiating into wisdom, especially in the *Symposium* where a group of friends gathers to discuss the nature of love. Here Socrates relates how he was led into the mystery of love by Diotima and he rehearses her speech for them, referencing the Eleusinian initiation rites and using the language and images of those rites to propose the true Socratic *paideia*: there is a pathway towards the mystery of love and for a secure following of this one needs a guide, a mystagogue. The path on which the mystagogue leads the person is a series of steps, leading from the beautiful things of the body to those of the soul and from there to the Form of Beauty itself, "the final and highest mystery," the Beauty which "always *is* and neither comes to be nor passes away, neither waxes or wanes."[22] Significantly, a desire for *generation* is placed at the beginning of the pathway: the pathway towards the mystery of love is desired because a person is "pregnant" and wants to give birth to something beautiful. Love desires "reproduction and birth in beauty" because this is the means to immortality — one wants to leave something beautiful behind.[23]

To understand how Clement developed these themes to enunciate a Christian mystagogy, of Christ the Word as the Beautiful one who begets new life in the soul and by stages forms the one being initiated

---

[19] *Paedagogus* 1.6.25.1.
[20] The teaching of rhetoric was also often compared to an initiation process into wisdom, Plato's work in the *Phaedrus* on the nature of rhetoric being hugely influential in this regard. See Christina Schefer, "Rhetoric as Part of an Initiation into the Mysteries: A New Interpretation of the Platonic *Phaedrus*," in ed. A. N. Michelini, *Plato as Author: The Rhetoric of Philosophy* (Leiden: Brill, 2003), 175–96. And the concept transferred to Roman thinking about rhetoric as well: Quintilian refers to the teaching of rhetoric as an art of initiation into the mysteries (*Institutes* 5.13.60; 5.14.27).
[21] So Plutarch, *De Liberis Educandis* 10e.
[22] See *Symposium* 210a–211a.
[23] *Symposium* 206e–207a.

to be a generator of new life in others, we can turn to his short treatise, *The Rich Man's Salvation*, which is an extended reflection on Jesus's call to the rich young man as found in Mark 10:17-31. After quoting the entire passage, he notes that the children of the kingdom must now be instructed in the "secret meaning" of this passage.[24] He will gradually demonstrate that the real meaning of this teaching is "the mysteries of love"[25] and will remind them of the ultimate mystery of love, the divine exchange: Christ made himself vulnerable, coming among us, enduring being measured to the scope of poor human love. In return, Christ then says, "I give you my love." And how great is this? "On behalf of each of us He laid down the life that is equal in value to the whole world."[26]

Now consider, Clement says, what it is to be led into the mystery of this divine education, what it is to receive and to live in this exchange. In this education we learn the measurement of this divine love as we are formed by Christ to see our neighbor as he does. "He demands this sacrifice from us on behalf of one another."[27] This is the measurement of the depth of conversion needed, the extent and meaning of God's education of each person. He refers the reader to Paul's panegyric of love: faith will depart when we see God with our own eyes; hope vanishes when what we have hoped for is given; but love "goes with us into the fullness of God's presence and increases the more when that which is perfect has been bestowed."[28]

To illustrate what it is to be educated in the mysteries of Christ's love, and to emphasize the vital importance of establishing an ongoing mystagogia in the Church, Clement then recounts a story from tradition, "a true account of John the apostle that has been handed down and preserved in memory."[29] While John was travelling to organize and support the life of the local churches he identified a young man of great promise and asked one of the bishops to care for him. The bishop took the young man into his care, "brought him up, made a companion of him, cherished him, and finally enlightened him by baptism."[30] The young man had completed his catechumenal formation. Then, however, the bishop "relaxed his special care and

---

[24] *The Rich Man's Salvation*, 5.
[25] Ibid., 37.
[26] Ibid.
[27] Ibid.
[28] Ibid, 38.
[29] Ibid., 42. It is worth noting that this story was thought worth recording by Eusebius as well, appearing in *H. E.* III.23.19.
[30] *The Rich Man's Salvation*, 42.

guardianship, thinking that he had set over him the perfect guard, the seal of the Lord."[31] But that relaxation was fatal: the work of education in the Lord's *paideia* was only now beginning, not coming to an end. Lacking the ongoing mystagogical care and formation, the young man gradually fell away from God until at last he despaired of his salvation, eventually deliberately choosing the life of a violent robber to confirm himself in his ruin.

Later, the apostle John returned, asking: "Now, bishop, return us the deposit which Christ and I together entrusted to your care in the presence and with the witness of the church over which you preside."[32] The term "deposit," *paratheken*, used in this account, is that which is found in Paul's first Letter to Timothy to describe the treasure of the faith, the Deposit of Faith.[33] As a term taken from banking, the bishop thought he was being accused of stealing money, but John clarified, "It is the youth and soul of our brother that I demand back." When John heard what had happened, he went in search of the young man, eventually finding him through being captured by the robber band. The young man, recognizing John, was smitten with shame and turned to flight. But John appealed:

> Why do you fly from me, child, from your own father? . . . Have pity on me, child, do not fear. You have still hopes of life, I myself will give account to Christ for you. If need be I will willingly undergo your penalty of death, as the Lord did for us. I will give my own life in payment for yours. Stand; believe; Christ has sent me.[34]

Witnessing to the divine exchange through the offering of his own life, John won the young man back. And now, Clement writes, John stayed with him, prayed and fasted for him, and taught him with "siren-like words," casting a "soothing spell over his mind," and did not leave him "until he had set him over the Church"—a position of leadership in the Church is implied here.[35] The mystagogical path continues to the point of yielding for the Church one who will in turn form others.

Clement composed this short treatise on the rich young man after he had completed his trilogy of major works and the story he provides here not only sums up his own passion for the salvation of souls, but illustrates what he means by the phrase we have already encountered,

---

[31] Ibid.
[32] Ibid.
[33] 1 Tim. 6:20.
[34] *The Rich Man's Salvation*, 42.
[35] Ibid.

of "the true tradition of the blessed teaching" which is "handed on directly from Peter and James and John and Paul, the holy apostles, son receiving it from father" so that "by the blessing of God they came down to us to deposit those ancestral and apostolic seeds."[36] Clement stands in the line of the transmission of the deposit which was to be communicated in such a way that the one receiving can in turn *become a formator and teacher of others*. That is what it is to truly "receive the deposit," to enter into the "mysteries of love." The *Protrepticus* marked the beginning of the journey. It advances to the point at which the initiated Christian is able to express the "generative" capacity planted by Christ in his or her soul. The example of the apostle John illustrates what is needed: a formational process that teaches a person how to know the breadth and depth of the love of Christ in order to communicate that to others.

A key element in this process is a person to accompany, train, form, teach, intercede, and fast, as John was for the young man. It is an absolute necessity, Clement says, that each person should appoint "some man of God as trainer and pilot."[37] Only with this kind of accompaniment will one be able to progress into the mystery of the knowledge and love of God. Speaking to the rich in his audience he draws attention to Christ's parable of the unjust steward who learned how to be wise,[38] noting that the Lord does not ask the steward to simply "give" or "help" others, but to "make a friend" with his money—"And a friend is not made from one gift but from complete relief and long companionship."[39]

Origen would say that the image with which we should leave ourselves, as we consider this delicate mystagogical pathway accompanying an individual soul, is that of the divine Bridegroom drawing his bride to himself, in intimacy and love. The entering of the soul into mystery, guided by the catechist-mystagogue, a friend of the Bridegroom, is to be understood in the light of the economy of God's love, following a pathway that is sacramentally structured and deeply personal. Origen's *Commentary on the Song of Songs*, which describes this mystagogical part of the journey, uses personal and ecclesial language interchangeably: the bride sought by the divine Bridegroom is both the Church and the individual soul.[40] From the point of

---

[36] See *H. E.* V.11.5.
[37] *The Rich Man's Salvation*, 41.
[38] *Lk.* 16:1–9.
[39] *The Rich Man's Salvation*, 32.
[40] See *Commentary on the Song of Songs* I.1–3. For a discussion of Origen's "personalism" see J. Christopher King, *Origen on the Song of Songs as the Spirit of Scripture*, 14–23.

initial conversion the path of formation led to the bridal bath of baptism, and thence to the wedding feast, and now the Bridegroom-Logos wishes to share the spiritual understanding of the Scriptures, a teaching which is given only in the bridal chamber.[41] The mystagogical pathway of formation as a teacher is also that of the mystical union of the bride with her Lord. Andrew Louth puts it simply: the Church is following a way "which leads us back to those ultimate unities... that draw together the mind and the heart... unities that are nourished by love, ultimately by the love of God which is the mystery of our faith."[42]

ASSISTING CHRIST THE TEACHER

Just as the divine Pedagogue is assisted by human pedagogues, so also in his role as Teacher, Christ is assisted by human teachers. The *Stromateis* betrays a fascination with the whole process of learning and with the knowledge and skills needed for a broad teaching, not only of matters of faith, but of history, science and philosophy, aimed at the development of Christian culture. The work teems with discussions of genealogies, civilizations, and the rising and falling of cultures. Discussions of the invention of the alphabet, and of boxing gloves, of Critolaus the Phaselis on "word-soldiers," and Metrodorus on the good of the soul, stand alongside the lengthy treatments of faith and knowledge in Book 2, and marriage, concupiscence, and procreation in Book 3.[43] A feature of the Alexandrian church, in fact, which "distinguished it from other Christian churches in the 2nd century was the prominent role accorded to its teachers."[44]

We concluded earlier that the school was a deeply *ecclesial* entity: one learns and teaches as a member of the Church, of the whole Christian Body. The ongoing journey towards Christian perfection unfolded in Clement's *Stromateis* is no "flight of the alone to the Alone."[45] We also find in these pages how profoundly *Christocentric*

---

[41] *Commentary on the Song of Songs* I.5.
[42] Louth, *Discerning the Mystery*, 72.
[43] Cf. *Stromateis* 1.16.75.1; 1.16.76.3; 2.7.33.1; 2.21.131.1.
[44] Runia, *Philo in Early Christian Literature*, 123. Roelof van den Broek also argues for this particularly strong tradition regarding teachers in the early Egyptian church ("The Christian 'School' of Alexandria in the Second and Third Centuries," 39–47).
[45] The phrase is from Plotinus (*Enneads* VI.9.11.51) and is often taken to characterize Neo-Platonism, indicating a preference for an individualistic over a communal spirituality. But in fact this is unfair to Plotinus himself as Daniel Tolan makes amply clear: "The Flight of the All-One to the All-One: The φυγὴ μόνου πρὸς μόνον as the Basis of Plotinian Altruism," *Harvard Theological Review* 114, 4 (October 2021), 469–90.

was the understanding of the teacher in the Alexandrian church. The teacher is one who has learned how to stay close to Christ. He or she is Clement's true Gnostic, which means the one who knows Christ personally and from this participation in his life is able to assist others into a similar participation. Clement's teacher is someone committed to the life of holiness, and is also called to be something of a spiritual director, one who can help others learn how to surrender into the mystery of Christ.

A preoccupation for Clement, as he considered the formation of teachers, was the respective place of oral and written transmission.[46] Jesus, like Socrates, had left no teaching in written form. For both, their oral teaching was carried forward by their disciples. Yet in both cases, while handing down the teaching and formation that they had received in this personal form, their disciples had also left written accounts. Plato's preferred written form was the dialogue, maintaining in this fictional format a primacy of oral discussion and debate; the Christian Gospels declared the good news in narrative format, with the oral formation of the apostles as the golden thread of the narrative. In some sense, then, an oral and a written transmission belonged together, and teasing out the relationship between the two was a primary focus in both the Platonic tradition and in the Christian Church.

The oral word

We can begin our discussion with Socrates—and therefore with his disciple, Plato, for whom the written and oral word belonged together, but with the written word in a secondary place. In the *Phaedrus* this relationship of written to oral teaching is considered at length. In Plato's discussion of each, the value of each of the two media is judged in relation to their capacity to be agents of formation, the purpose of speech, whether written or oral, being to direct the soul to its true end. Jaeger argues that the dramatic form of the dialogue was so important for Plato precisely because of this concern for formation:

> With Plato the primary impulse was originally the formative one. He did not write in order to set out the contents of his doctrine. His desire was to show the philosopher in the dramatic instant of seeking and finding, and to make the doubt and conflict visible; and that not in a mere intellectual operation, but in the fight against pseudo-science, political power, society, and his own heart;

---

[46] See Osborn, "Teaching and Writing in the First Chapter of the *Stromateis* of Clement of Alexandria," 335–43.

for the spirit of Plato's philosophy necessarily collided with all these forces.[47]

Hadot concurs, emphasizing the primacy of formation in Plato's conception of philosophy:

> He did not aim to construct a theoretical system of reality, and then "inform" his readers of it by writing a series of dialogues which methodically set forth this system. Instead, his work consisted in "forming" people—that is to say, in transforming individuals by making them experience, through the example of a dialogue which the reader has the illusion of overhearing, the demands of reason, and eventually the norm of the good.[48]

The work of formation required a knowledge of the nature of the soul and its true good, for without this knowledge all forms of persuasion and attempts to lead it would be an artless practice, like trying to treat a body with medicine while not understanding the nature of the body.[49] The soul was to be led into knowledge of what is truly Real and this required an initiation from one who was himself at the highest and most perfect level.[50] One must have knowledge of what one is seeking to hand on and explain: otherwise it would be as though one were explaining the value of fighting on horseback while all the time one had a donkey in mind.[51] Plato is here making sure that rhetoric is placed firmly below philosophy: the art of communication has value only to the extent that it is an expression of the true. This leading into truth must also be one that knows the state of the person being led: it is akin to spiritual direction, the gradual leading of a soul according to its current state and propensity. The teacher needs to know what kind of speech is needed for a *particular* soul, what will lead it on further towards the truth.[52]

In the light of these points, Plato now considers the value of written and oral means of communication. Although the written form appears to be efficient and therefore able to convey wisdom and truth to others easily, it is a blunt instrument, he argues, as regards the leading of souls. The written word is open to all and wanders about "indiscriminately," getting into the hands of both those who understand it and those who do not. It has in itself no ability to teach

---

[47] Jaeger, *Aristotle*, 24–25.
[48] Hadot, *What is Ancient Philosophy?*, 73.
[49] *Phaedrus* 245c, 270b–271d.
[50] *Phaedrus* 249c–250a, 277b.
[51] *Phaedrus* 260b.
[52] *Phaedrus* 271d–272b, 277b–c.

souls as they need to be guided. And so a reader can merely imagine that he knows something. Texts cannot respond to questions nor defend themselves when attacked. A text, therefore, needs a person alongside it to support and explain it, for it is merely an image of the discourse between souls, mirroring the spiritual reality of that primary dialogue.[53]

Plato makes a comparison with planting and sowing. Just as a farmer plants in the correct season in order to care properly for his crops and their growth, so also one concerned for the formation of another must know when and how to sow. And so while he may sow seeds in writing—"gardens of letters," of "dream-images"—this is really a pleasure for his old age, to remind himself of the growth that takes place through dialogue:

> The dialectician chooses a proper soul and plants and sows within it discourse accompanied by knowledge—discourse capable of helping itself as well as the man who planted it, which is not barren but produces a seed from which more discourse grows in the character of others. Such discourse makes the seed forever immortal and renders the man who has it as happy as any human being can be.[54]

The "text" of truth and of all that is good, noble and just must be written in the *soul* of the other person and this requires personal engagement. The true teacher is the one who realizes that his writings are, if read in isolation from a living voice, of little worth since they need the author himself, or another in his stead, to be able to defend and explain the written word as well as to know the soul who needs to receive the truth given on the written page. The teacher himself, then, is the one who exercises a genuine paternity, and can truly engender new life in another.[55]

We find in Plato, therefore, a primacy of the personal in communication and a privileging of dialogue with another soul. The written word has its rightful place but is in service to this goal which can only be achieved in a dialogue of truth, of a mutual growth in relationship with that which is true and good. It is in dialogue that questions can be answered, that the desires and motivations of the other can be uncovered and discussed, that truth can be differentiated from error, and that limited perspectives can be broadened. Dialogue allows for questions to be asked and for personally applicable answers to be given.

---

[53] *Phaedrus* 275a–276a.
[54] *Phaedrus* 276e–277a, and see 276a–e.
[55] *Phaedrus* 277e–278d.

Plato's philosophy was attractive to the Alexandrian school in part due to this interest in the transformative nature made possible by this kind of personal encounter. The Socratic dialogical style was another *preparatio* for the coming of Christ. For Clement and Origen, the process of dialogue is intended to help the person engage with the *Logos*, the person of Christ, the supreme Good. In the previous chapter we saw the central place given to the role of modeling in the development of character, through the relationship of the growing "child" to the pedagogue with an emphasis on educational development through individual relationships, and this understanding carries over into the way in which teaching is developed in the Alexandrian tradition. It is not that one does not give lectures or speak with groups, but that these need to be accompanied whenever possible by an attention to individuals so that a secure "planting" and "sowing" of the Christian word can take place.

A characteristic of the school that was noted by Eusebius, therefore, was the importance it accorded to the place of Christ-centered friendships between teachers and pupils, the faith taught and handed down in the context of friendships grounded in a mutual pursuit of holiness. Eusebius quotes from a letter from Alexander, then bishop of Jerusalem, to Origen, in which Alexander writes of his own experience of friendship at the school:

> For this also has proved to be the will of God, as thou knowest, that the friendship that comes to us from our forefathers should remain unshaken, nay rather grow warmer and more steadfast. For we know as fathers those blessed ones who went before us, with whom we shall be ere long: Pantaenus, truly blessed and my master, and the holy Clement, who was my master and profited me, and all others like them. Through these I came to know thee, who art the best in all things, and my master and brother.[56]

Alexander sees the relationship of indebtedness he has to Pantaenus, Clement, and Origen as one of friendship and warmth, the teacher being both master and brother. This theme of friendship between those who give and receive the faith has a rich background in classical thought: members of the philosophical schools, for example, would often refer to each other as "friends."[57] Aristotle clearly saw the collaboration among the members of his philosophical school in this way,[58] while in the Roman world Cicero's *De Amicitia* later

---

[56] H. E. VI.14.8-9. See also H. E. VI.8.7.
[57] Cf. Plato, *Seventh Letter* 347e and Diogenes Laertius V, 52-53; X, 11.
[58] *Nicomachean Ethics* 1164b3; 1171b29-1172a9.

provided a framework for Aelred of Rievaulx's classic work, *Spiritual Friendship*, discussing friendship in the monastic life. A famous witness to Origen's capacity for developing a close friendship with his pupils is Gregory Thaumaturgus who, on leaving Origen's school in Caesarea, wrote a thanksgiving address, speaking of how Origen's friendship led Gregory and his brother to study with him:

> ... the stimulus of friendship was also brought to bear upon us—a stimulus, indeed, not easily withstood, but keen and most effective—the argument of a kind and affectionate disposition, which showed itself benignantly in his words when he spoke with us and associated with us.[59]

Gregory was to live in Origen's household for the next five years. The friendship manifested itself especially in Origen's concern for the care of his disciples' souls, for the focus was always on the primary question, "How should I live?," the friendship in service to this end.[60] Origen sought to uncover with Gregory and Athenodorus what manner of persons they were, and then "the things that are truly good, which man ought to strive after, and then the things that are really evil, from which men ought to flee."[61] It was Origen's dedication to these personal and universal truths that captured Gregory, so that he learned to love both philosophy and the "master of philosophy, this inspired man."

The heart of this friendship, Gregory emphasized, was the person of Christ himself and within this mutual love for Christ "the soul of Jonathan was knit with the soul of David." The friendship that grew between them made them inseparable: "he holds us now, and has held us ever since that time." He was "truly a paradise for us."[62] It was a supreme act of freedom to be so knit, Gregory commented, to give oneself and receive another in this way, for a soul cannot be coerced. Nonetheless, Origen counseled them not to attach themselves to any human teachers, even if they were thought of as the wisest of all, but only "to God alone, and to the prophets,"[63] and so Gregory concedes that while he is tempted to speak of Origen as the exemplar of the wise man he will follow Origen's way of thinking in this matter as well:

---

[59] "The Oration and Panegyric Addressed to Origen" VI.
[60] As Aristotle notes, mutual affection can be disadvantageous if one does not love truth more than pleasing one's friend (see 1096a12-17).
[61] "The Oration and Panegyric Addressed to Origen" VI.
[62] "The Oration and Panegyric Addressed to Origen" XV.
[63] Ibid.

I shall not speak of him as a perfect pattern, but as one who vehemently desires to imitate the perfect pattern... and who labours to make us, who are so different, of like character with himself, not mere masters and apprehenders of the bald doctrines concerning the impulses of the soul, but masters and apprehenders of these impulses themselves.[64]

Origen taught them "the word of salvation" and wanted them to receive this word in such a way that it would govern their souls so that it "shall be itself the king of all." And it is this, Gregory said, that Origen truly achieved, so that the word, "like some spark lighting upon our inmost soul" burst into a flame of love and drew them towards Christ, the "unutterable Beauty."[65]

In addition to the theme of holy friendship, Clement also linked teaching to the notion of paternity or maternity.[66] Christ is the only-Begotten who in turn begets his spiritual children. Christ the Teacher receives his capacity to teach from his Father, and his teaching is life-giving, generative. The human teacher must assist the divine Teacher precisely by fostering new life in others. Clement ties the whole of *Stromateis*, Book 3, a defense of procreation in marriage, to his theme of the art of true Christian teaching: His ethics of marriage, rooted in his kerygmatic understanding of the goodness of the God who gives and sustains life, enabling the generation of a child as an act of cooperation with the good Creator,[67] Clement sees mirrored in the spirituality of teaching—"If a man produces children in obedience to the Logos, nurtures them, and educates them in the Lord, as with the man who fathers children following instruction in the truth, there is a reward in store for him, as for the elect seed too."[68] There is a reward both for the natural father and for the spiritual father, and for the children as well.

We have already noted Clement's description of those he had known who had faithfully handed down "the true tradition of the blessed teaching directly from Peter and James and John and Paul, the holy apostles," describing those who received this teaching as

---

[64] "The Oration and Panegyric Addressed to Origen" XI.
[65] "The Oration and Panegyric Addressed to Origen" VI.
[66] Thierry Maertens notes this as one of the distinctive points in Clement's understanding: *Histoire et Pastorale du Rituel du Catéchuménat et du Baptême* (Publications de Sanit-André, 1962), 76–77.
[67] See also *Paedagogus* 2.10.83; 91–97. For an analysis of Book 3 of the *Stromateis*, uniting Clement's marital ethics to his theology of reciprocity, see Osborn, *Clement on Alexandria*, 242–51.
[68] *Stromateis* 3.15.98.4.

"son receiving it from father."⁶⁹ It is significant, as Annewies van den Hoek has pointed out, that Clement almost never refers to himself as a teacher, but rather as a father.⁷⁰ And this, Clement tells his readers, is what Christians call their religious instructors because of their role in bringing about new life in others: "the sketch of a soul which yearns to preserve the blessed tradition without losing a single drop runs something like this: 'When a man loves wisdom, his father's heart will be warmed' (Prov. 29:3)."⁷¹ After all, what is wisdom for, except for sharing? "The Savior is always engaged in saving," and "What is the use of a wisdom which does not bring wisdom to the person who is capable of listening?"⁷²

This emphasis on the act of teaching as a work of paternity or maternity echoes the character of religious formation in the ancient world which, as we saw, was essentially family-based, with the key roles in education being taken by the parents. The principle of paternity in teaching was also one emphasized in Judaism: "He who teaches the son of his neighbor the Torah, Scripture ascribes it to him as if he had begotten him."⁷³ And we may also think of St. Paul's description of himself as a father. "For though you have countless guides (*paedagogus*) in Christ," he tells the Corinthian community, "you do not have many fathers. For I became your father in Christ Jesus through the gospel."⁷⁴ Paul identifies himself as a father because he has brought new life to them in Christ through the Gospel. Through the transmission of the Gospel new life had been generated. It is a fatherhood, of the highest kind, of new life in the Spirit.⁷⁵

This paternity was not only seen as the initial act of giving new life but also more broadly in the ongoing exercise of care and education: Annewies van den Hoek reminds us that *papas* was the common form of address of children to their pedagogues.⁷⁶ And it became the

---

[69] See the account in *H. E.* V.11.5.
[70] See the discussion in "The 'Catechetical' School of Early Christian Alexandria and Its Philonic Heritage," 64.
[71] See *Stromateis* 1.1.12.1.
[72] *Stromateis* 1.1.12.3.
[73] Babylonian Talmud, *Tractate Sanhedrin* 19b.
[74] *1 Cor.* 4:15.
[75] We should note, of course, how carefully Paul writes: he is not seeing himself as the source of the new life, which is rather one that is communicated "in" Christ and "through" the Gospel. The source of new life is divine. But Paul, nonetheless, is claiming a unique relationship with the believers as the one who communicated the Gospel of Christ to them. For a discussion, see C. K. Barrett, *A Commentary on the First Epistle to the Corinthians* (New York: Harper and Row Publishers, 1968), 115, 245–46.
[76] "The 'Catechetical' School of Early Christian Alexandria and Its Philonic Heritage," 64.

common way of speaking of the line of instructors in the school, as we have seen from that letter of Alexander.[77] By the third century this had also become the way of addressing a bishop, especially in Alexandria. This use of "father" for instructors in the faith, and then for Alexandrian bishops is interesting since it is especially from Alexandria and the surrounding area in Egypt that we see the emergence of the key role of the *abba* in monasticism which was to maintain a deeply personal passing on of the Christian heritage. Alexandria thus became the locus for the championing of this form of transmission of the faith—a point we can see confirmed from the fact that it was Athanasius, bishop of Alexandria, who wrote the life of Anthony, the founder of the spiritual way of life based on this understanding of the primary significance of fathering another person in the faith.[78] Indeed, the character of the bishop as *papas* is beautifully illustrated by Athanasius himself who was loved especially for his persistent pastoral care and teaching activity, often at great personal cost.[79] The typically close relationship between the monastic and the episcopal *abba*, as well as the importance of monasticism to the maintenance in Egypt of a Christian learning rooted in holiness, can be illustrated by the fact that St. Cyril chose Shenoute, the Abbot of the White Monastery, to accompany him to Ephesus.[80]

In this matter of spiritual paternity, then, the Egyptian monks excelled, and the *Apothegmata*, the sayings of the Desert Fathers in Egypt, Syria and Palestine show us very clearly the archetypal place of the spiritual father in Christian formation,[81] the *abba* so called because he was a spiritually life-giving figure: "The spiritual Father exercised a genuine 'paternity'—in the name of God—engendering

---

[77] "for we know *as fathers* those blessed ones..." (H. E. VI.14.9, our italics).
[78] Athanasius, *St Anthony of the Desert* (Charlotte, NC: TAN Books, 2014).
[79] For a thoughtful discussion of Athanasius as father see Gwynn, *Athanasius of Alexandria*, 131-58.
[80] Shenoute was renowned for his contribution to Coptic spiritual literature: we have around four thousand pages of his letters, homilies and treatises. Andrew Louth has properly noted that, while this desert tradition is primarily concerned with "spiritual" matters, "it was representatives of this tradition of seemingly undogmatic piety who played an important role in the defense of the Church's dogmatic tradition in the fourth century and thereafter" (*Discerning the Mystery*, 94). For Shenoute and his importance in Egyptian monasticism see Stephen Emmel, "Shenoute's Place in the History of Monasticism," in eds. G. Gabra and H. N. Takla, *Christianity and Monasticism in Upper Egypt* (Cairo: The American University in Cairo Press, 2008), 31-46.
[81] See E. A. Wallis Budge, *Paradise of the Fathers* (London: Chatto and Windus, 1907); Norman Russell, *Lives of the Desert Fathers, Historia Monachorum in Aegypto*, Cistercian Studies 34 (London: Mowbray, 1983).

the life of the Spirit in the disciple."[82] This paternity was effective precisely to the extent that the *abba* understood that his work of discipleship with another person was entirely subordinate to God's action. As a teacher, guide and counselor, he was able to assist because he trusted the spiritual life given in baptism, a life that could be nurtured and fostered but which he did not control. The key to fruitful paternity was to know that such paternity lay not within oneself but only in God, and to help others to find this fathering from him. As Clement noted, "There is only one teacher, whether of lecturer or student, and he is the source of understanding and of the word."[83]

The written word

Dialogue, undertaken in friendship, with the paternal or maternal giving of a personal word, was seen as crucial; but the school did not on this account downplay the necessity of other forms of communication. If the spiritual practice of dialogue was especially indebted to the Platonic tradition, other forms of instruction, including public lectures, and more attention to communication through the written word, have a clear background in Aristotle's school as well as in the Jewish tradition of the centrality of Sacred Scripture.[84] Neither Clement nor Origen wanted to set up an opposition between communicating with the oral and the written word: "If two people preach the word, one in writing, one orally, receive them both: they have made the faith operative by their love."[85] It will not do to place the oral and written elements in Christian teaching in opposition to each other. "Whichever method the Lord's worker uses to sow the good grain, to help the stalks grow, and to reap the harvest, he will be clearly seen as God's true farmer."[86] Both the written and the oral word can support the dialogue of salvation. We have already seen how the Alexandrian school recognized it as crucial to maintain, protect and develop a literary culture, through its library, its *scriptorium*, and the development of writings and scholarship by its leaders.[87] In addition to the written Revelation contained in the Scriptures of Israel which the Church, as the long-awaited Bride of God, claimed as her own and then added

---

[82] Thomas Merton, *Contemplation in a World of Action* (New York: Doubleday and Co., 1973), 283.
[83] *Stromateis* 1.1.12.3.
[84] For styles of learning and teaching in the Lyceum see Lynch, *Aristotle's School*, 88-92, and Jaeger, *Aristotle*, 324-41.
[85] *Stromateis*, 1.1.4.1.
[86] *Stromateis* 1.1.7.1.
[87] Thus Marrou: the Church knew that "there was an absolute minimum of literary culture" that she could not do without (*A History of Education in Antiquity*, 316).

her own Scriptures, this ever-growing literary heritage included the liturgies of the Church and writings of many kinds that shaped the mind and imagination of the Christian people.

Helping others to a discovery of the riches of the Scriptures has been undoubtedly one of the greatest contributions of the school to the development of Christian culture and one of its points of greatest emphasis. Thus, when Eusebius introduces Pantaenus it is as an interpreter of the Sacred Scriptures, both orally and in writing;[88] Clement's interest, as we have seen, lies in uniting the reading of the Scriptures to the philosophical approach of the schools, while for Origen, the master-exegete, interpreting the Scriptures was his lifetime's work (Didymus following in Origen's footsteps in this respect).

It is in the Alexandrian school that the understanding of the spiritual sense of the Scriptures was most fully developed in the early centuries of the Church, leaving in this area a heritage of inestimable value for catechesis. "So many meanings occur to us at once..." Origen wrote, "perhaps we should now ask which of them we should adopt for our text."[89] One of the most well-known facts about the Alexandrian school is this finding in the Scriptures of "so many meanings."[90] The school's awareness of the rich dimensions of the scriptural texts has been beautifully expressed in a well-known passage from Newman:

> It is in point to notice also the structure and style of Scripture, a structure so unsystematic and various, and a style so figurative and indirect, that no one would presume at first sight to say what is in it and what is not. It cannot, as it were, be mapped, or its contents catalogued; but after all our diligence, to the end of our lives and to the end of the Church, it must be an unexplored and unsubdued land, with heights and valleys, forests and streams, on the right and left of our path and close about us, full of concealed wonders and choice treasures.[91]

In this passage from Newman we are in the figurative world of Clement in the *Stromateis*, the faith as a place of pathways, wooded hills and valleys, of concealment and of eventual manifestation to the persistent explorer. Newman himself refers his readers to the parables

---

[88] H. E. V.10.4. Clement comments on this in *Eclogae Propheticae* 56. See also the comments by Clarke, *Higher Education in the Ancient World*, 128.
[89] Origen, *Commentary on John* 1:19.
[90] Augustine discusses this same question in a number of places in *De Doctrina Christiana* in terms of the relationship between the *signum* and the *res*, pointing out ways in which a sign can represent *several* different realities (e.g., 3:2–34).
[91] *An Essay on the Development of Christian Doctrine*, Part I, Chapter II, Section I, Paragraph 14 (6), 71.

in Mark of the mustard seed, of the leaven in the flour, and of the seed sown in the ground that springs up of itself as illustrations of the hidden riches in the Scriptures which have their "own innate power of expansion," their "active, engrossing, and interpenetrating power."[92] It is this active spiritual principle in the Scriptures which is the source of its "many meanings."

The single conviction that underlay this Alexandrian focus on the spiritual meaning was that in the reading of the Scriptures one always finds Christ if one seeks him there. And—inseparably—that for this finding of Christ one must be gradually putting on his life: only the one who has the mind of Christ can trace and uncover his presence in the Sacred Scriptures. To comprehend the Christocentric meaning of the Scriptures a virtuous circle must be pursued, of prayer, of reading according to the rule of faith, and of docility to the Spirit who provides the spiritual meaning of the text. The symbolic and metaphorical nature of the Scriptures are compared by Clement to the veil of the sanctuary.[93] Such an image reminds us that when we come to read the Scriptures we stand before God's holiness and that there is a purification that must take place, a consecration and dedication to God before we can enter. In this time of the Teacher's formation, therefore, the *disciplina arcani* that was so important for the catechumenate now found expression in the introduction of an allegorical exegesis of Scripture entailing a gradual unfolding of the spiritual meaning of the Scriptures while at the same time "trying the earnestness and patience of inquirers."[94] The meaning of the symbols would be gradually uncovered as God made the reader worthy to receive their meaning. Origen emphasizes this same truth: to understand the Scriptures, there must be an ongoing healing of our blindness, just as Jesus healed the man born blind, and we should understand this in the first place as a moral blindness.[95]

A recurring strength of the Alexandrian school is this recognition that all learning involves a series of implicit moral and spiritual commitments, commitments that are daily tested in the process of formation: a willingness to be open to reality, to receive and explore honestly and without distortion that which one finds, an attitude of humility before the truth, and a generosity with that which one

---

[92] *An Essay on the Development of Christian Doctrine*, Part I, Chapter II, Section I, Paragraph 16 (7), 73-74.
[93] See *Stromateis* 5.4.19.2–20.1
[94] *Arians of the Fourth Century*, 56, 59.
[95] Origen, *Commentary on John* 10.18, 25.

discovers. In all reading and truth-seeking, above all, one is seeking to find ways to allow that which *is* to show itself more truthfully and fully. When, as in the case of the Scriptures, the truth being sought is God's Revelation of himself, the commitment to ongoing conversion necessarily intensifies and the moral sense of the Scriptures helps us to attend to the requisite changes and enlargements required of us. Even so, the truths one seeks are beyond the capacity of the soul. And so one must beg for God's illumination of the soul.[96] Coming to a deeper knowledge and understanding of the Scriptures always entails entering more and more deeply into God's free Revelation of the mystery of his love.

As one learned to await the gradual unveiling of the mystery of Christ in the Scriptures, harnessing all expectant energies for each graced discovery, every reading was considered both a personal and an accompanied reading: one reads truly only within the community of faith which can interpret and assist in making present for each person the way in which the word "speaks" into each individual situation for that individual's transformation. In the school we always find the oral word—of teaching, guidance and homily, accompanying the written. We are fortunate to have detailed evidence from the latter stages of the school's existence of the ways in which Didymus saw his classroom as an entry point for this divine work of transformation as he encouraged his students to engage in this kind of reading. The struggles involved are communicated by a telling metaphor: the biblical text was to be approached as a divine arena into which one enters to learn how to live in Christ.[97] And the end point of each reading and teaching is always the anagogical sense, the eschatological. The mystery of Christ is to be realized *in* each person. The Bride is to be made ready and to find herself in Christ, united to him, and re-made in his likeness. Then Christ may at last hand her over to the Father. Adam Cooper expresses the point strikingly, in a passage describing the thought of Maximus the Confessor, but which applies equally to the Alexandrian school: "Scripture's purpose has been fulfilled when through ascesis the believer himself *becomes* Scripture—a living symbol of Christ."[98]

---

[96] Origen, *Commentary on John* 10.6, 18, 21, 23; 19.10.
[97] For a detailed discussion, see Layton, *Didymus the Blind and His Circle in Late-Antique Alexandria*, 36-55, analyzing Didymus's exposition of Psalms 20-44 (LXX numbering). For a discussion of a stenographer's notes of Didymus's teaching methodology in general, treating of the literal and then of the spiritual senses, see 26-35.
[98] Adam Cooper, *The Body in St Maximus the Confessor*, 42-43.

If the one sought in the reading is Christ, and oneself *in* Christ, what are the principles to be followed, and how does one support others in learning how to read and to teach in this way?

In the first place, a clear commitment of faithfulness to Tradition, to the *regula fidei,* marked the school in its investigation of the "many meanings" of the Scriptures, governing the spiritual exegesis that it undertook. In his Preface to *De Principiis,* Origen emphasized the importance of this faithfulness: while there were "many who think they hold the doctrine of Christ, some of them differing in their beliefs from the Christians of earlier times... we maintain that that only is to be believed as the truth which in no way conflicts with the tradition of the church and the apostles."[99] The spiritual reading of the Scriptures is not for Origen, then, an occasion for indulging a spirit of originality and experimentation in exegesis but is undertaken rather for the deeper and more worthwhile penetration of the text before one, bringing out its spiritual essence for the sake of the journey of the soul into the mystery of Christ.

In the second place, a hermeneutic of the mystery of love governs the interpretation of the text. In the journey of ongoing formation, one always seeks to move beyond literal or wooden readings of the Scriptures that might hide this ultimate truth that needs to be discovered. From the beginning, one of the driving points behind the quest for these spiritual meanings was undoubtedly also an apologetic one, and especially the need to correct anthropomorphic conceptions of God that the Scriptures might seem to imply. Clement and Origen are representative of early Christians as a whole in attacking popular pagan religious conceptions and myths that implied that God has a body or feels emotions. But the Scriptures were open to this kind of accusation, also, and so in his (unfortunately lost) *Stromateis,* Origen discussed a series of "difficult" passages in the Scriptures—difficult in the main because they contained such crude anthropomorphisms.[100] Origen's method of interpreting each of these passages—and also passages in the Scriptures that seemed to contradict one another—was to uncover their spiritual meanings and to emphasize

---

[99] *De Principiis,* Preface, 2.
[100] So thoroughly did Origen undertake this task that Robert Grant comments that when Porphyry, the third-century critic of Christianity, read Origen's work, "he presumably found that a good deal of his anti-Christian task had been done for him. All he had to do was accept Origen's negative statements... and reject the deeper spiritual meanings which Origen had sought to find" ("The *Stromateis* of Origen," in *Épektasis. Mélanges Patristiques offerts au Cardinal Jean Daniélou,* eds. J. Fontaine and C. Kannengiesser [Paris: Beauchesne, 1972], 292).

God's transcendence.[101] God, he explains, accommodates us in the language he uses of himself; we should think of this as part of his condescension. Origen compares this to the way parents use baby-talk, giving special names and terms to things. If someone were to hear us speaking in these ways to a baby, he would realize that we had not lost our mind by talking like this but were speaking the child's language.[102] So with all instances in which God presents himself in human terms—for example, when he appears to change his mind, or to become angry, or to be ignorant of the future. He is speaking with us as his children who cannot yet understand a more adult language.

There were, then, apologetic reasons for a spiritual reading of the Scriptures. But such a rationale was of diminishing importance by the time Clement and Origen were writing, for to a considerable extent, Jews and Christians had fought these battles and the ground gained now simply had to be held. Now, then, the use of a spiritual reading could be turned over in another, and more positive and schematic, direction: to find and to present a greater sense of the one mystery of Christ that characterizes the whole of the Scriptures as a single organic work. The mystery of Christ could be uncovered as *the* meaning of the entire text, as "the whole exegesis."[103] The spiritual reading of the Scriptures was a way of speaking of its Christocentric reality. And this Christocentric reading, we can remind ourselves, included the reader (and the whole of Christ's Body as reader): it is the *Christus totus* that was to be discovered in the reading. The Alexandrian exegesis is interested in how the spiritual meanings can assist in the journey of the members of Christ's Body towards the holiness of God's love. Origen returns often to the use of apparently harsh language in the Scriptures and typically discusses these passages in medical terms: when God appears to act or speak in this way he is really working with us as a surgeon who knows what is needed to heal us.[104] And so in general when the Scriptures speak of God's anger, of his discipline, and of his punishment, this is to be understood in the context of God's salvific mercy and restoration, as elements of the one healing plan. Discipline is united with wisdom within a hermeneutic of God's

---

[101] For example, see Origen's comments in *Contra Celsum* IV:13,71,72. See the discussion of this apologetically-motivated work of Origen in Richard P. C. Hanson, *Allegory and Event: A Study of the Sources and Significance of Origen's Interpretation of Scripture* (London: SCM Press, 1959), 218–31.
[102] *Homilies on Jeremiah* 18.6.4–7.
[103] Henri de Lubac, SJ, *Medieval Exegesis: The Four Senses of Scripture*, I (Edinburgh: T&T Clark, 1998), 237.
[104] *Homilies on Ezekiel* III.8.2; V.1.2–4.

love. Thus, commenting on Exodus 8:5, for example, Origen explains the meaning of God's "jealousy" and "chastisement":

> Therefore, if this "jealous God" asks for you and wishes your soul to cleave to him, if he keeps you from sin, if he corrects and chastises you, if he is indignant, if he is angry and uses a kind of jealousy against you, know that this is your hope of salvation.... See the compassion and loyalty of the good God. When he wishes to have mercy, he says he is indignant and angry.[105]

Scriptural language about God's "anger" and "jealousy" is really a way of speaking about his love. God's "anger" is to be understood as metaphorical, not literal. Only the language of the love of the Lord is to be taken literally—as is confirmed by Origen's approach to the Song of Songs in which the literal level of the text of this divine love song is taken by him to be identical with the spiritual sense.[106]

Just as the discovery of the spiritual meaning of the Scriptures was to serve this spiritual development of the reader, so the ordering of the scriptural *curriculum* also—the scriptural reading program Origen proposed was that which he judged best served the care and development of the soul. This echoes the way in which philosophical schools of the period would read and provide exegesis on the classic texts of their founders: texts were studied, not simply because of their canonical status in the school, but also for their spiritual value to members of the school. Hadot argues that the texts were often selected because they corresponded to the desired "stages of spiritual progress"[107] that needed to be undertaken, following whatever was the preferred order of curricula in the different schools—ethics, physics and logic, or sometimes these in a different order. He draws our attention to Origen's Prologue to his *Commentary on the Song of Songs*, in which Origen comments on the position of the Song of Songs within the Wisdom writings. Why, asks Origen, is the Book of Proverbs placed first, Ecclesiastes second, and the Song of Songs third? He argues that it is because Proverbs deals with moral matters (ethics), Ecclesiastes with the nature of things (physics), and the Song of Songs with mystical or theological matters (what he calls here the "inspective" matters,

---

[105] *Homilies on Exodus*, VIII.5.
[106] See J. Christopher King, *Origen on the Song of Songs as the Spirit of Scripture*, 56–59. This, of course, is why both the *Roman Catechism* and the *Catechism of the Catholic Church* offer as the fundamental pastoral principle of catechesis that the love of the Lord be "made accessible" to the learner through whatever teaching is being provided (*Roman Catechism*, Preface, 10; *CCC* 25). Only the language of love is to be taken literally.
[107] *What is Ancient Philosophy?*, 239.

learning the art of viewing things so as to discover the heavenly realities behind them). Origen also relates this order to God's naming of himself as "the God of Abraham, the God of Isaac, and the God of Jacob," for Abraham is the exemplar of moral philosophy through obedience, Isaac of natural philosophy for his seeking out the roots of things[108] and Jacob of the inspective science, for he saw the angels' paths reaching to heaven.[109] The ordering of the reading of biblical texts, then, is for the sake of leading the reader by steps and stages, like the angels on Jacob's ladder, towards the heaven of God's love.

Within this overall hermeneutical stance of seeking to enter more deeply into the mystery of Christ and of his love, holding oneself ready to receive and act upon the promptings of grace, two particular ways of reading the Scriptures were brought together in the school, typology and allegory.

The school maintained, with the Christian exegetical tradition up to this point, the important place it accorded to *typology* — of people, events and institutions anticipating and pre-figuring Christ and his Church and the culmination of God's plan in heaven. A typological reading of the Scriptures thus enables one to discern God's progressive Revelation and action, the story of God's one work of salvation.[110] The drama of salvation is played out in history, at the center of which stands Christ in the flesh. It is always from the historical and the particular that one begins. Understanding the literal meaning is the starting point for a true appreciation of the spiritual, and mistakes at the literal level, they knew, must be corrected for they will point one away from that deeper engagement with the power of the Scriptures.[111] Moreover, the literal is to be honored, for what is of nature and history is destined to be transfigured, not left behind.[112]

---

[108] Cf. *Gen.* 21:12ff.
[109] See his *Commentary on the Song of Songs* Prologue, 3, and for a discussion Christopher King, *Origen on the Song of Songs as the Spirit of Scripture*, 222-40.
[110] Cf. *Protrepticus* 9.87.3.
[111] For example, in a discussion of the ritual instructions in Exodus 12, Origen stressed the need for an accurate etymology of *pascha*. Melito of Sardis had mistakenly proposed that it was linked to the Greek verb "to suffer," *paschein*. This led to a focus on the historical Jesus's suffering as a key to understanding the meaning of the Paschal requirements. Clement and Origen knew that the term was derived from a Hebrew word meaning "passage" and emphasized that Exodus was not only to be seen as a prefiguring of Jesus's passion but referred directly to us and to our lives in Christ. The Paschal instructions speak to Christ's passage from death to eternal life, but also to our passage at baptism, from the old lives of sin to our rebirth in Christ. See the discussion in Trigg, *Origen*, 188-91.
[112] At the same time, the way in which the literal level could lead into the spiritual could also be by provocation, the Holy Spirit allowing apparently useless

Thus, everything in the Old Testament points forward to the New. And yet Christ is not absent from the Old but hidden in it. All the epiphanies of God in the Old are of the Logos, who is thus in dialogue with God's people, preparing them for his coming in the flesh at the Incarnation. Origen, in fact, sees the relation of the literal and spiritual senses of the Scriptures by analogy with the Incarnation in which the divine is joined to history and creation.[113] The New Testament thus records the center of God's design as the unsurpassable grace of the enfleshing of the divine Logos. As the converging point of all signs, he is the spiritual sense *made* literal.

The typological relationship between the literal and spiritual meanings of the Scriptures are the movement, then, from the Old Covenant to the New, from prophecy to fulfillment, from the hints and shadows of the Old to the fullness and glory of the New. The central moment of the Incarnation is itself thought of as dynamic, leading onwards to the time of the "whole Christ," of Christ sacramentally present in his people, and of the Spirit who gives the mind of Christ to the Church, making this understanding of the Scriptures possible. As we have noted, such a reading is a supernatural one, requiring an ascetical commitment on the part of the reader: the Spirit is given in order to transform the Church and all who read the Scriptures as her members so that they can gain this understanding, and this work of graced transformation is in fact the *telos* of the reading—the Spirit unveiling Christ's work of gathering all to himself and handing all things over to his Father.

A second way of reading is inseparably united to this, the *allegorical*. Alongside the dynamic of this typological, historical reading, the school proposed a sacramental dynamic of symbol and sign, of nature and history participating, through grace, in the "eternal Gospel" of heaven.

While some patristic scholarship has been hesitant about the value of this allegorical reading, with a concern that it can be too unmoored from its literal foundation,[114] this kind of reading of the Scriptures was understood by the Alexandrians to enable one rather to penetrate to the *depth* of the literal, the depth of nature and history. An allegorical

---

detail in the text in order to push the reader to search for a deeper meaning. When the Scriptures appear obscure it may be the signal to dig more deeply and energetically, especially by hunting for "similar expressions" elsewhere in the Scriptures for clues (cf. *De Principiis* IV.3.5).

[113] Cf. *De Principiis* IV.1.1; IV.1.7. See also J. H. Crehan, "The Analogy between *Verbum Dei Incarnatum* and *Verbum Dei Scriptum* in the Fathers," *Journal of Theological Studies* 6 (1995), 87–90.

[114] Cf. Jean Daniélou SJ, *From Shadows to Reality: Studies in the Biblical Typology of the Fathers* (London: Burns & Oates, 1960), 57–65, although he makes some concessions.

reading of the Scriptures was also in line with how Philo and the Hellenizing Jews in Alexandria had already interpreted the Torah, their allegorization of the Law making it easy for Jewish Christians in due course to find in the Church a natural continuation of that heritage.[115]

This way of reading the Scriptures is part of the wider understanding of the school that we have already seen, in which Clement and Origen "'baptized' the Platonic dualism of the world on two planes," providing a sacramental understanding of the world.[116] It was also tied into anthropology, which is typically presented as a simple account of the person as made up of body and soul, paralleling the literal and the spiritual.[117] The allegorical reading of the Scriptures for the Alexandrian school was part, then, of their sacramental understanding of the cosmos, with everything on the natural and historical level being mirrored on the spiritual. If the Old Testament found its fulfillment in the New, the New Testament is itself a shadow of the "eternal Gospel" in which it participates.[118] All that is unfolded in history finds its meaning in the light of this deeper and eternal reality. The Scriptures, like the sacraments, are thus signs of, and participations in, a spiritual and eschatological Reality. The eschatological and the spiritual come together, for the Eschaton is but the final creaturely participation in That which eternally *Is*. The sacrament of baptism both anticipates and participates in the purification which continues after death, as well as the illumination of heaven when we

---

[115] That heritage would be continued in and through the work of the Cappadocians in the East and Ambrose in the West. See also the comments on the relationship between Origen and Ambrose in their understanding of mystagogy in Enrico Mazza, *Mystagogy: A Theology of Liturgy in the Patristic Age* (New York: Pueblo Publishing Co., 1989), 14-15, 24-25, 33. In terms of the heritage the school had received, allegorical exegesis also had a place in the way in which the philosophical schools read the Greek myths, and especially Homer, as a means of finding significant universal truths in these stories. Origen was familiar with this work, and in his reply to Celsus, he points to many such examples—thus, Zeus's punishment of Hera is "really" God's ordering of matter. The passage in Homer is the *Iliad* XV.18-24 and Origen's comments are in *Contra Celsum* III.43, IV.48 and VI.42. See also Origen's comments on allegory and the Greek myths (VIII.66-68) and the mysteries of Dionysius (III.23). For a recent discussion, see William Stanford's analysis of the way the *Odyssey* was treated by Stoic philosophers so that it becomes an extended metaphor for spiritual and philosophical progress: *The Ulysses Theme: A study in the Adaptability of a Traditional Hero* (Oxford: Oxford University Press, 1954).
[116] The phrase is from Blosser, *Become Like the Angels*, 236, as a comment on Origen's approach.
[117] Origen at times also tied his understanding of reading according to the threefold senses of Scripture to a threefold anthropology of body, soul and spirit (*De Principiis* IV.2.4).
[118] See *De Principiis* IV.3.13 for this phrase which Origen takes from *Revelation* 14:6.

will finally see God face to face, while the new life of the Christian after baptism is also a "first resurrection," anticipating and sharing in the final resurrection and transformation of the body.[119] The Scriptures are the key for "reading" the world in this way. Newman sums up this unified understanding in the Alexandrian tradition of nature and history ordered towards a final unveiling at the end of time of all that is eternally present, with the Scriptures offering deeper glimpses of this fuller truth:

> ... room was made for the anticipation of further and deeper disclosures, of truths still under the veil of the letter, and in their season to be revealed. The visible world still remains without its divine interpretation; Holy Church in her sacraments and her hierarchical appointments, will remain, even to the end of the world, after all but a symbol of those heavenly facts which fill eternity.[120]

AND TODAY

In its remarkable vision of a mystagogical period focusing on a deepening in holiness and a formation for teaching, the Alexandrian school was seeking to establish a pathway for long-term, sustained growth in the Christian life. It saw this as being achieved through a union of spiritual accompaniment and support with a concentration on a learning of the Scriptures which constantly challenged one to go deeper and to be clothed in the truths and mysteries one was uncovering there. When John Paul II introduced the goal of catechesis he did so precisely by focusing on the concept of the mystery of Christ that lies at the center of this Alexandrian account:

> The primary and essential object of catechesis is, to use an expression dear to St. Paul and also to contemporary theology, "the mystery of Christ." Catechizing is in a way to lead a person to study this mystery in all its dimensions: "to make all men see what is the plan of the mystery... comprehend with all the saints what is the breadth and length and height and depth... know the love of Christ which surpasses knowledge... (and be filled) with all the fullness of God." It is therefore to reveal in the Person of Christ the whole of God's eternal design reaching fulfillment in that Person. It is to seek to understand the meaning of Christ's actions and words and of the signs worked by Him, for they simultaneously hide and reveal His mystery.[121]

---

[119] Origen, *Commentary on John* 10, 35, 232.
[120] *Apologia Pro Vita Sua*, 37.
[121] *CT* 5, citing *Eph.* 3:9, 18–19.

The *Directory for Catechesis* therefore appropriately identifies the catechist as a "mystagogue" — i.e., one who leads others into the Mystery — describing the catechist as one "who introduces others to the mystery of God, revealed in the Paschal mystery of Christ; as an icon of Jesus the teacher, the catechist has the twofold task of transmitting the content of the faith and leading others into the mystery of the faith itself."[122]

The contemporary tool for this entry into mystery, Christocentric in focus, is undoubtedly the *Catechism of the Catholic Church*. It offers a hermeneutic of reading the Scriptures and doctrine in the light of the mystery of Christ, gathering up all that is historical and natural to find in Christ the whole of God's economy of salvation. The *Catechism* asks for a reading attentive to the unity of the Scriptures, and to the unity of Scripture and Tradition, noting how the truths of the faith are mutually coherent, to be understood within the single plan of God.[123] In its "practical directions" for reading the *Catechism*, the authors have placed the brief instruction: "This catechism is conceived as *an organic presentation* of the Catholic faith in its entirety. It should be seen therefore as a unified whole. Numerous cross-references in the margin of the text (numbers found at the end of a sentence referring to other paragraphs that deal with the same theme), as well as the analytical index at the end of the volume, allow the reader to view each theme in its relationship with the entirety of the faith."[124]

An "organic reading," undertaken with the help of these tools informing the *Catechism*'s presentation, unites the mysteries of the faith around Christ as one makes connections between Christian life, belief, liturgy and prayer. A personal journey of transformation necessarily accompanies this pathway of discovery: as one encounters the unity of the Scriptures and mysteries of the faith and their harmony, one is aroused to seek the recovery of such integrity in one's own life. One helpful aspect of such a reading as facilitated in the *Catechism* — and one that is deeply coherent with the convictions of the Alexandrians — is that different starting points in such a reading can be respected. Because of the cross-references, one can *begin* at any place in the *Catechism*, in any of its parts or sections, with a point of departure in a particular dogma, a specific event in one's life, or one's reflections on certain scriptural passages or sacramental signs. These function as the many tributaries leading into the great river of Christ,

---

[122] DC 113b.
[123] See CCC 112-14.
[124] CCC 18.

leading the reader to penetrate the *nexus mysteriorum*,[125] the "net of mysteries," in an orderly way. In and through such an organic reading of the Deposit, one enters into a Christocentric understanding of the unity of the faith, finding Christ and the truth of his salvific love at the heart of this reading. The personal organic reading of the faith in the *Catechism* by means of these cross-references is thus never an arbitrarily associative one; the interpretative work undertaken in such a reading is always undertaken with reference to the mystery of Christ: "The mutual connections between the dogmas, and their coherence, can be found in the whole of the Revelation of the mystery of Christ."[126]

A second element from the Alexandrian account that the contemporary Church will want to benefit from is surely the place it accords to a personal transmission of the faith. In the modern catechetical Magisterium, John Paul has reminded bishops of the necessary expression of this personal concern for their people through the provision of catechesis: "A thousand duties call you: from the training of new priests to being actively present within the lay communities, from the living, worthy celebration of the sacraments and acts of worship to concern for human advancement and the defense of human rights. But let the concern to foster active and effective catechesis yield to no other care whatever in any way. *This concern will lead you to transmit personally to your faithful the doctrine of life.*"[127] In this exhortation to personal engagement, John Paul was echoing Paul VI's passionate uniting of the meaning of "witness" to its etymological roots in the reality of martyrdom: the Christian message "merits having the apostle consecrate to it all his time and all his energies, and to sacrifice for it, if necessary, his own life"[128] for "modern man listens more willingly to witnesses than to teachers, and if he does listen to teachers, it is because they are witnesses."[129] This theme of the catechist-witness-martyr is also highlighted in the opening pages of the *Directory for Catechesis*: "The Church, in every part of the world, can present models of catechists who have attained holiness and even martyrdom in living their ministry every day. Their witness is fruitful and makes it still thinkable in our time that each of us can persevere in this adventure even in the silent, laborious, and sometimes thankless work of being a catechist."[130]

---

[125] See *CCC* 90.
[126] Ibid.
[127] *CT* 63 (my italics).
[128] *EN* 5.
[129] *EN* 41.
[130] Salvatore Fisichella and Octavio Ruiz Arenas, *DC* "Preface."

This unexpectedly ascetical message to catechists finds a softer, but no less demanding image in Paul VI's reminder of the tradition of paternity and maternity in the transmission of the faith which we saw was prominent in Alexandria and the spiritual and pastoral traditions that it inspired. Speaking of the love that an evangelizer must have for those to whom the Gospel is handed on, he asks: "What is this love? It is much more than that of a teacher; it is the love of a father; and again, it is the love of a mother. It is this love that the Lord expects from every preacher of the Gospel, from every builder of the Church."[131]

The primacy accorded to a personal transmission of the faith finds its natural corollary in the *Directory for Catechesis*'s preference for a strongly relational style of catechesis, especially for the sake of the dialogue and guidance that can be provided within such an approach.[132] The commitment of witness is united to dialogue as one learns a "pastoral dialogue without relativism, which does not negotiate one's Christian identity."[133] In the *Directory* dialogue is proposed widely as a pedagogy helpful for the Church—in her relationship to science, culture, politics, with other religions, and with various academic disciplines—because in part through such dialogue the personal character of the transformation called for by the Gospel, which might otherwise go unnoticed, is highlighted.[134] A dialogical style, moreover, seems particularly appropriate for a catechesis in the context of the new evangelization since here the teacher seeks from the learner a *recognition* of what has already been culturally received but now needs to be seen anew, newly encountered—in Platonic terms, "remembered." In this situation, writings (and beautiful art, Plato says) can "remind" one of the truth, but they remain only poorly audible without the living voice of another soul who can genuinely help a person "remember"—that is, call to mind in a way that restores integrity to life and so is authentically transformative.[135] Plato made clear that this was the purpose of Socrates's dialogues with others—he was a midwife of the truth already present in the other

---

[131] EN 79.
[132] DC 53-54.
[133] DC 54.
[134] See DC 333, 358, 360, 391, 398. In addition to these general areas of dialogue, the *Directory* points to the obvious importance of such a "style" in the area of individual discipleship also: "In the time of the new evangelization, the Church desires that catechesis as well should accentuate this dialogical style, to make more easily visible the face of the Son who, as with the Samaritan woman at the well, stops to begin a dialogue with every human being in order to lead him or her with gentleness to the discovery of the living water (cf. John 4:5-42)" (DC 54).
[135] See *Phaedrus* 275a-e.

person, but forgotten. And Socrates's midwifery can be compared to Jesus's use of parables which, uniting the familiar with the unexpected, were able to shock the listener into a different perspective so that what was common and "known" in one respect could now be seen for what it *really* is, a sign of something spiritual, a word from the Lord. All sacramental catechesis is of this nature, of course, not necessarily providing an easy transition of perspective, but seeking to jolt the person from the concrete sign to what is spiritually signified, lifting the other into a sacramental vision.[136]

A recovery of the spiritual reading of the Scriptures is the essential companion to this renewed sacramental vision. Newman's commentary on the school in this area, with which we have already engaged, is both helpful and provocative and can assist us in moving beyond an exegetical landscape in which a desultory, horizontal reading of the literal meaning alone has for so long dominated academic scripture scholarship, largely leaving any formational implications of the Scriptures to be received as private devotional exercises disassociated from their ecclesial and dogmatic environment. In his 1833 *Arians of the Fourth Century*, Newman's commendation of the catechetical school, "founded (it is said) by the Evangelist himself" as a "pattern to other Churches in its diligent and systematic preparation of candidates for baptism"[137] was connected precisely to the value he saw in its tradition of scriptural interpretation. In this regard, he compared the Alexandrian Church favorably over and against the Antiochene tradition, arguing that the Syrian school of theology was responsible for the rise and threat of the heretic Arius, especially in the persons of the Antiochene Paul of Samosata and Lucian.[138] The Antiochene school was at fault precisely for devoting its attention too narrowly to the "literal and critical interpretation of Scripture," ignoring the "mystical sense" which is the Church's "most subtle and powerful method of proof."[139] "It may almost be laid down," Newman asserts, "that the

---

[136] Romano Guardini issued a clarion call for a restoration of such a catechesis, asking for the Church to help people to recapture the reality of "the liturgical act," a recapturing that entails "a spiritual inwardness . . . so that an 'epiphany' may take place" ("A Letter from Romano Guardini," *Herder Correspondence*, August 1964, 237–38).
[137] *Arians of the Fourth Century*, 41.
[138] The theological rivalry between Alexandria and Antioch is well known and it is worth noting the long-standing political antagonism that preceded this: for example, under the Ptolemies two Syrian wars were fought with Antiochus I over the possession of Coele-Syria.
[139] *Arians of the Fourth Century*, 404.

mystical interpretation and orthodoxy will stand or fall together."[140]

Newman here links the question of heterodoxy or orthodoxy to biblical styles of exegesis, and he continues by implicating the entire spiritual quest of Christianity in this question of scriptural interpretation. What Newman saw in the school's practices for reading the Scriptures was an instinct and hunger for *fullness*, for finding the richest possible meaning—and that reading was always to be preferred since it was the meaning that most reflects the capacity of creatures to receive, in their own mode of being, the inexhaustible riches of God's own life that he seeks to share.[141] Teachers formed in this tradition of scriptural discovery would know that it is therefore only in transmitting the faith in its fullness that ecclesial communion is made possible. Catechesis, supporting this unity in communion, as well as the spiritual progress of each of the Church's members, will not be content with a minimalist principle of commonality but will always seek to unveil and hand on an account of the faith that sacrifices none of its integrity. It is precisely the catholicity of fullness that enables the catholicity of universality.[142]

Ultimately, Newman saw remaining with the literal sense as a refusal to take seriously the symbolic dimensions of reality, an unwillingness to enter the mystery, to seek holiness. It meant that the engagement with "the scope of Divine Intelligence" was muted and merely human modes of perception and thinking were allowed to enter into questions of formation and Christian maturity. Every "refinement of thought, subtle versatility of feeling, and delicate reserve or revenant suggestiveness" was inclined to be excluded in favor of a narrow rationalistic temper.[143] Ultimately it was the holiness of the Alexandrians that attracted Newman and he saw this as inseparable from their commitment to certain ways of learning and teaching the faith, a dogmatic spirituality grounded in the allegorical reading of the Scripture and of the world.[144]

---

[140] Ibid., 405.
[141] Cf. *DC* 397e.
[142] Cf. *DC* 177-178.
[143] *Arians of the Fourth Century*, 409.
[144] Cf. Benjamin King, *Newman and the Alexandrian Fathers: Shaping Doctrine in Nineteenth-Century England* (Oxford: Oxford University Press, 2009), 13-14, 79-83. Peter Nockles, *The Oxford Movement in Context: Anglican High Churchmanship 1760-1857* (Cambridge: Cambridge University Press, 1994), 319ff., and Williams, *Arius*, 2-6, both point to the Tractarian context of Newman's picture as a background to these points. Newman's understanding of the Antiochene tradition and its relationship to Arius is a compilation and tapestry with an eye to making a contemporary argument. But while some of Newman's contrasts between Antiochene

A Christocentric typological reading is thus needed as a standard approach to the Scriptures, together with the kind of allegorical exegesis that we find in the Alexandrian tradition. The preferred personal pedagogy so carefully developed at the school, united to such a diligent reading of the Scriptures, acts as a continual reminder that the Real and the Good which are the object of the spiritual journey are not "principles" or ideals, or even the great Forms, but the Person of Christ whose image must grow in the soul until it achieves its full likeness to him.

---

and Alexandrian theology may be historically questionable, the crucial point is that the Alexandrian school held together doctrine and spirituality and saw these as in turn united to an allegorical reading of Scripture.

CODA

Mark's Gospel as Catechumenal Icon in Miniature

AS WE CONCLUDE OUR STUDY OF THE ALEXANdrian school, I would like to return to the question of the relevance of the Gospel of Mark to the themes we have been exploring. With our knowledge of the catechumenal project that was developed in so visionary a fashion in Alexandria in the second to early fifth centuries, how far can we discover foundational architectural features for this catechetical venture in the Gospel of Mark, the Gospel that tradition has judged to be an apostolic gift, through the teaching of St Peter, for the Alexandrian church?

John Paul II described Mark's as a catechumenal Gospel, paralleling Matthew as a catechist's Gospel. The close links between Mark and Matthew are not a modern discovery. Augustine, as we noted earlier, saw Mark as a summary of Matthew's Gospel. In fact, while this judgment undoubtedly increased the neglect of Mark in the Church, Augustine's position was both interesting and nuanced. He variously described Mark's relationship to Matthew as that of a companion or attendant (*pedissequus*), epitomizer (*breviator*), and follower (*sequeretur*). What stands out clearly is Augustine's sense of a natural pairing of Matthew and Mark. Mark is "preferentially the companion of Matthew."[1] John Paul's identification of Mark as a catechumenal Gospel, paralleling Matthew as a catechist's Gospel, is to that extent one in line with tradition, even though the character of Mark as "catechumenal" was not explicitly given by the school itself, nor by any of the Fathers. Matthew's privileged position as a Gospel from which to teach, however, is certainly reflected in the number of episcopal patristic commentaries that have survived and is also strikingly confirmed by its prominence in Clement's *Stromateis*, his mystagogical volume dedicated to the formation of teachers.[2] If Mark is indeed

---

[1] *De consensu evangelistarum* 4.10.11.
[2] Black helpfully provides the numbers: approximately 281, compared to 127 references to Luke, 111 to John, and only 29 to Mark (*Mark*, 174, n.20). Black also points to the manuscript evidence demonstrating the popularity of Matthew in Alexandrian Christianity of this period, again reinforcing our sense of the commitment of the church there to the importance of teaching.

the "preferential companion" to Matthew's catechetical Gospel, then it is not unreasonable to enquire as to whether it might indeed be as a catechumenal figure.

Taking this dual characterization seriously can offer insights into the language used by Papias to describe the two Gospels. As Eusebius records him,[3] Papias says that Mark wrote "without order" (*ou mentoi taxei*), "without arrangement" (*ouch... syntaxin*), in comparison to Matthew who wrote in an "orderly" way (*synetaxato*). Mark, rather, followed Peter in writing "as necessity demanded" (*pros tas chreias*). That comparative description has typically been taken as a simple derogation of Mark's style, but Black draws attention to the scholarship of Josef Kürzinger[4] who argued that Papias was using "the standard rhetorical terminology of his day."[5] The judgment that Mark wrote *ou mentoi taxei* signified, not that he was writing without a chronological sense, or without attention to the coherent structure of the narrative, but without "literary artistry." The phrase *pros tas chreias* was a reference by Papias to the tradition of *chreiai* in rhetorical instruction, the use of sayings and personal stories as illustrative material to help train pupils in the early stages of written composition and speeches.[6]

Kürzinger's work can help us see that discerning in Mark a number of thematic strands is not incompatible with Papias's comment, and that we perhaps discern rightly if we find in Mark's Gospel something "preliminary," serving an early training in the faith, especially in its focus on the immediacy of narrative action and the drama of an ever-present sense of conflict and misunderstanding. While not offering the orderly arrangement needed by the teacher provided by Matthew with his clear structure of five blocks of catechetical material, Mark's Gospel serves the precise function of an initial leading into faith, providing exactly what is needed for an understanding of the radical nature of conversion.[7]

---

[3] See H. E. III.39.15–16.
[4] *Papias von Hierapolis und die Evangelein des Neuen Testaments: Gesammelte Aufsätze, Neuausgabe und Übersetzung der Fragmente, Kommentierte Bibliographie* (Regensburg: Friedrich Pustet, 1983).
[5] Black, *Mark*, 89.
[6] Black himself believes that Papias may have been less interested in the comparative judgement about Mark and Matthew than in wanting to defend Mark's Gospel as a written account of Peter's teaching, emphasizing that Mark made no false statements in doing so and left out nothing significant from Peter's preaching (*Mark*, 88–93).
[7] So Georges Dabrincourt, arguing for a strong catechumenal model in Mark, does not in fact need to oppose Papias on this point: "Sans doute il faut reviser

STRUCTURE AND THEMES

Some commentators have indeed offered a maximal catechumenal reading of Mark. Two very different examples can be offered. Georges Dabricourt in his *L'initiation chrétienne selon saint Marc* argues that the sacraments of initiation provide the framework for understanding the order and presentation of Mark's material, the Gospel composed to assist the leading of converts into the Church. Following the generally agreed view that the central pivotal section of Mark, from 8:22-10:52, is crucial for the right interpretation of the Gospel—the sequence beginning and concluding with the healing of a blind man through faith, and within which we find, as "the great dividing line"[8] of the Gospel, Peter's acclamation of faith in Jesus as the Christ and the subsequent announcement of the Paschal mystery—Dabricourt proposes that three great opening themes lead into this center and that the same three are mirrored on the other side of the center, completing the cycle. The themes are sacramental and Trinitarian, inviting a progressive meditation upon the sacraments of initiation leading to the overcoming of blindness, a culmination expressed in the gradual healing of the first blind man and in Peter's confession of faith. The Gospel leads with the person of the Father and the sacrament of baptism, is followed by a focus on the great works of the Holy Spirit and the sacrament of confirmation, and climaxes on the work of the Son and the Eucharistic miracles, feeding the Jews and the Gentiles.[9] The sacraments of initiation are thus presented as introducing one into the fullness of Trinitarian life: baptism making one a child of the Father, confirmation anointed with the Spirit, and the Eucharist receiving the divine Son as heavenly food.[10] More recently, Charles Bobertz has provided a fascinating reading of Mark's Gospel focusing on "the ways in which every aspect of Mark—characters, time, and places—reflects the realities of the ritual setting of the early house churches."[11] He proposes reading Mark from the perspective of an early Christian household, in a situation of pastoral pressure and the

---

la fameuse appreciation raportée par Papias: 'Marc écrivit san ordre'" (*L'initiation chrétienne selon saint Marc* [Paris: Apostolat des editions, 1970], 156).

[8] The phrase is from Lightfoot, *The Gospel Message of St. Mark*, 6.

[9] The location of each of these Eucharistic miracles and the terms used in each case for the baskets indicate the dual references to the Jews and the Gentiles (cf. the discussion in Augustine Stock, O.S.B., *Call to Discipleship: A Literary Study of Mark's Gospel* [Wilmington, DE: Michael Glazier, 1982], 124-28).

[10] Cf. Dabricourt, *L'initiation chrétienne selon saint Marc*, 19.

[11] Charles Bobertz, *The Gospel of Mark: A Liturgical Reading* (Grand Rapids: Baker Academic, 2016), 4, n.15.

threat of persecution, gathered around the Eucharist and reflecting especially upon questions concerned with the inclusion of Gentile Christians into the Church through faith and baptism.

Even if we do not find all elements of these catechumenal readings equally convincing, Dabricourt's and Bobertz's work have the merit of highlighting the presence of sacramental themes in Mark, especially the sacraments of initiation,[12] as well as the household context in which the Christian faith was practiced and transmitted. And certainly, scholarship today would in general share the view that the Gospel was composed with much care, the apparent naïveté, or obscurity, in Mark's style masking a more deliberate arrangement of material. Schildgen's characterization of the Gospel, for example, as one of "ambiguities, paradoxes, and 'open-endedness'"[13] is rightly seen not as accidental, but rather a chosen style that engages by inviting to a journey of discovery, with the ever-present theme of misunderstanding in Jesus's group of disciples providing for every new reader a travelling companion on that journey who points out the necessity of being open to a radical *metanoia*, a fundamental change of mind and heart.

Discipleship and conversion

The focus on formation in the Gospel is a point of common agreement.[14] As we saw earlier, Mark's Gospel claims the theme of Jesus as Wisdom instructing his foolish and obdurate disciples as a central focus. The Gospel highlights a pedagogy of discipleship and faith. Forming a kind of sub-text to the Gospel narrative is the habitual reticence on Jesus's part concerning his identity. Mark opens his

---

[12] Given the close relationship between Peter and Mark, it is interesting to note that some commentators have seen a baptismal catechesis, and perhaps even a liturgical guide to the Paschal vigil, in the *First Letter of Peter*: see F.L. Cross, *1 Peter, A Paschal Liturgy* (London: A.R. Mowbray and Co. Ltd., 1954) and E.G. Selwyn, *The First Epistle of St Peter* (London: MacMillan, 1946), especially 393-400. Even if such a view cannot be sustained as a whole (and for a critique of Cross's thesis see T.C.G. Thornton, "1 Peter, a Paschal Liturgy?" *Journal of Theological Studies*, New Series, 12, 1, April 1961, 14-26), it is undeniable that strong baptismal themes are present.

[13] Schildgen, *Power and Prejudice*, 21. The author herself it must be said would not necessarily be sympathetic to this work of seeking unity and coherence in the Tradition, inhabiting rather a post-modern scholarly world which is happy to accept a fragmenting of unity among the books of Scripture, accepting "multiple theologies rather than ... the single truth or story they were often made to represent" (126).

[14] An extended treatment of this theme is Augustine Stock's *Call to Discipleship*. He focuses on the narrative form of the Gospel as a journey fraught with struggle and incomprehension, pointing finally to what is needed for conversion and understanding. Stock also sees a parallel between the ordering of events in the Gospel and the *kerygmatic* summaries offered in *Acts* (see 31-39, 64-70).

Gospel with a clear proclamation of who Jesus is: "The beginning of the gospel of Jesus Christ, the Son of God."[15] Jesus is the Son of God. But as soon as we enter the narrative itself, we find Jesus's identity surrounded with "mystery and enigma,"[16] while time and again Jesus tells those with whom he engages not to reveal who he is.[17] Many know his true identity (God the Father declares it at his baptism and demons at his healings) but Jesus insists on it being veiled. Scholars have described this Markan theme as the "Messianic Secret."[18]

Morna Hooker has shown how pedagogically important this secrecy theme in the Gospel is: "If we ask how Mark makes use of the secret, then it is important to notice that *it functions in precisely the opposite way to what one expects*: it serves as a means of revelation to the hearers/readers of the gospel."[19] This Markan theme is therefore in service to the broader concern with the nature of discipleship. Richard Peace concurs: "the theme which plays the controlling part in the unfolding of the Gospel of Mark is the conversion of the Twelve."[20] While the reader of the Gospel—and the demons—know who Jesus is, his own disciples do not, until Peter makes his profession, illuminated by divine grace. Yet even after Peter's profession Jesus insists on secrecy and the disciples reveal their incomprehension of his actions over and again. Understanding Jesus's true identity, and especially how his messiahship is characterized by suffering, service and the kingship of love on the Cross will come about for the disciples only gradually. A mature faith is needed to embrace the truth of the suffering servant Messiah. The disciples will do so eventually, learning slowly and by stages by sharing in his life and eventually by sharing his destiny.[21] The material in this half of the Gospel following Peter's

---

[15] Mk. 1:1.
[16] Lightfoot, *The Gospel Message of St. Mark*, 5.
[17] For example, see Mk. 1:24-25, 34; 3:11-12; 8:30.
[18] The phrase originates from William Wrede's work of 1901 which appeared in an English translation, *The Messianic Secret* (Cambridge: James Clarke & Co., 1971). James L. Blevins discusses the history of research into this theme in the greater part of the twentieth century in *The Messianic Secret in Markan Research 1901-1976* (Washington, D.C.: University Press of America, 1981).
[19] Morna Hooker, *The Gospel According to Saint Mark*, Black's New Testament Commentaries (Peabody, MA: Hendrickson, 1991), 67.
[20] Richard V. Peace, *Conversion in the New Testament: Paul and the Twelve* (Grand Rapids: William B. Eerdmans, 1999), 112, and see 105-25 for the argument.
[21] Wrede's own conclusion was that Jesus claimed neither to be Messiah nor divine and that these ascriptions were given only after the Resurrection (see *The Messianic Secret*, 211-52). The view of Vincent Taylor is closer to our own, that "Jesus imposed silence because of the nature of Messiahship as He conceived it to be. To Him it was not primarily a matter of status but of action.... The Messiah

confession bears, then, the marks of a deliberate focusing of material to illustrate what is involved in a close discipling aimed at the Paschal mystery. Through the insistence on secrecy, Jesus is inviting his disciples to share in the mystery of his life, in and through their discipleship. To know who he is and his work of redemption is to enter into the mystery of God's plan that will require a deep and ongoing conversion and a faith in him that is lived out in union with him in his Church.[22] For the disciples, knowing the Lord will come into view only through this sharing in his life, sacramentally by sharing in his baptism and then in living out the day to day realities of the baptismal vocation as a "life in Christ."[23]

Clearly, this Markan theme of conversion and discipleship resonates in many features of the Alexandrian school—in its understanding of faith as the gradual entering into mystery, in the emphasis on the stable presence of formators for the sake of discipleship, in the practice of the *disciplina arcani*, and then in its sacramental and allegorical understanding of both the Scriptures and of the cosmos, that at the heart of historical truth and its inspired scriptural record is the deeper spiritual truth that presents itself in paradox, in signs of contradiction.

Baptism and faith

A closely related theme in Mark is the presence of a *sacramental understanding* of this journey of discipleship. It can sharpen one's perspective on a theme to begin with a parody, and we find one offered in the "discovery" of the extract from the so-called *Secret Gospel of Mark* in the *Letter to Theodore*. With the support of this short extract, the author of that *Letter* claimed that it was necessary for the true Christian "gnostic," the one ready for advanced wisdom, to receive the teaching in this secret gospel. Moreover, this further, secret knowledge

---

already, He would not be the Messiah until His destiny was fulfilled" (*The Gospel According to St. Mark* [London, Macmillan, 1952], 123).

[22] N. T. Wright explains the conversion of understanding that was required of the disciples: "It was a claim to a Messiahship which redefined itself around Jesus' own kingdom-agenda, picking up several strands available within popular messianic expectation but weaving them into a striking new pattern, corresponding to none of the options canvassed by others at the time. Jesus' style of Messiahship... was sufficiently dissimilar to mean that everyone, from his closest followers through to the chief priests, misinterpreted at least to some extent what he was really getting at; and that the movement which did come to birth after his Resurrection, though calling itself messianic, cherished agendas and adopted lifestyles quite unlike those of other movements with the same label. If Jesus was a Messiah, he was a Messiah with great difference" (*Jesus and the Victory of God: Christian Origins and the Question of God*, 2 [Minneapolis, Fortress, 1996], 539).

[23] Cf. *Phil.* 1:21.

must be kept from simple believers. In his discussion of the *Letter* and this extract, Morton Smith argues that it reveals Mark to be closer to gnostic groups in the early Church, reserving hidden wisdom for a mature, elite group of Christians: "Belief in and practice of mysteries allegedly greater than baptism and the eucharist were, of course, frequent in gnostic circles."[24] He goes on to suggest on the basis of its supposed authenticity: "Clement's Church may have practiced a second baptism by which the believer achieved true gnosis."[25] If the *Letter*, purporting to be from Clement, were to be judged authentic then the school itself would indeed need to be placed closer in its thinking to gnostic Alexandrian schools and a significant gap would be placed between ordinary Christian believers and "advanced" Christians, and between faith and knowledge. If, as I have argued, the *Letter* is not from Clement then we have no reason to believe that this second "secret Gospel," as a development of the canonical Gospel of Mark, is relevant for our understanding of either the school or Mark himself. A strict differentiation between simple and mature believers is not the correct hermeneutical key for understanding either Mark's or the school's adoption of a formation that, as we know, proceeds by stages into deeper knowledge of the mystery of Christ. Rather, as one advances in the faith one uncovers further depths of insight into texts and teachings that are available in principle to all.

Tradition has clearly read both Mark's Gospel and the school in this latter sense.[26] The reading of canonical Mark and of the school that we find in the Tradition unites the deepening journey of faith in Christ's mystery to the sacramental illumination of baptism—hence the light that suffuses the portrait of John Paul, beckoning the entire Church. It is with this authentic sacramental emphasis that Clement, especially in the *Paedagogus*, was responding to one-sided Gnostic understandings of the Gospel and the nature of discipleship. For Gnostic Christians Jesus is primarily the imparter of intellectual truth; he is the transcendent Revealer, but not so much the *actor*, and certainly not the *suffering* Messiah.[27] Clement's holistic guidance for formation and Mark's Gospel, on

---

[24] Smith, *Clement of Alexandria and a Secret Gospel of Mark*, 44.
[25] Ibid., 168.
[26] For a good discussion of Clement and his understanding of allegory which would support the more traditional position see David Dawson, *Allegorical Readers and Cultural Revision in Ancient Alexandria* (Berkeley: University of California Press, 1992), 183-98.
[27] So Rowan Williams, who stresses that, by comparison with the authentic Christ of Mark's Gospel, the Gnostic Jesus "gives to his disciples the *information* which they will require in their ascent to God" (*The Wound of Knowledge*, 26).

the contrary, emphasize the unity of actions and words. Indeed, in the Gospel of Mark, Jesus's unique authority lay not merely in knowledge he came to communicate, in words of truth, but rather in what Mark calls Jesus's "new teaching" of word and act together.[28]

Even if we reject the Clementine source of Morton Smith's *Letter*, however, we can accept Smith's judgment that the canonical Gospel of Mark should be read as deeply "catechumenal" i.e., concerned with initiation into the mystery of Christ through baptism, so as to receive and live from him eucharistically.[29] This understanding of the catechumenal character of Mark would seem to be indicated by its early liturgical use. Mark was generally neglected in early lectionaries, but early Coptic lectionaries read Mark during Lent,[30] the period of immediate preparation for the Easter liturgy which was normally also associated with baptism, while Mark played a significant role in the early Roman Easter liturgy, with Mark's account of the curing of the deaf man, 7:32-37, being used when candidates for baptism were touched as part of that Easter liturgy.[31]

In further support of this identification of the catechumenal character of the Gospel, it is interesting to note that the *Catechism of the Catholic Church* has received the Gospel in this way, referring to Mark's Gospel proportionately more than any other in its second part, its teaching on the liturgy and sacraments. By comparison, the *Catechism* uses Matthew proportionately more in its part on the moral life, Luke in its part on prayer and John in the creedal part. Thus we find in the pages of the *Catechism* a certain character of each Gospel highlighted in relation to its four parts. As a gathering of the catechetical tradition of the Church, the *Catechism* has found Mark's Gospel especially helpful in providing for readers an appreciation of the Church's understanding of the sacraments of initiation and the liturgy.

---

[28] Mk. 1:27. The "new teaching" of word and mighty work in the first half of the Gospel, prior to the confession of faith by Peter in chapter 8, is followed by a new emphasis in the second half of the Gospel, of an equally "new teaching," this time of word and suffering (cf. Lightfoot, *The Gospel Message of St. Mark*, 36-38). For the leaders of the school, as we have seen, emphasis is laid on countering this Gnostic understanding of Christ, affirming instead the importance of a holistic formation in the faith. In line with this we see Origen in his Scripture commentaries, for example, consistently separating himself from, and responding to, Gnostic versions of the faith such as those associated with Basilides and Heracleon (for a discussion of Origen's Alexandrian work on John see Heine, *Origen: Scholarship in the Service of the Church*, 86-103).
[29] See Smith, *Clement of Alexandria and a Secret Gospel of Mark*, 168-88.
[30] Schildgen, *Power and Prejudice*, 41.
[31] See Geoffrey G. Willis, *A History of the Early Roman Liturgy: To the Death of Pope Gregory the Great* (London: Boydell and Brewer, 1994), 78, 126-27.

Baptism is clearly central to the Gospel. The first chapter might be seen as the presaging of the great theme of gathering and redemption: set in the wilderness, we can see there his portrait of Christ the Logos healing the cosmos in his own person. The call to holiness that was unfolded in the Old Covenant is first presented to the reader in the person of John the Baptist who announces the coming of the one who will baptize in the Holy Spirit, bringing God's people definitively from their death in sin to new life. Jesus is then baptized in the wilderness, offering the point of identification with all of those in need of redemption, including—as Clement made explicit—with all who will thereafter be baptized in him, as well as foreshadowing the baptism of his death and resurrection, the climactic event by which renewal will occur.[32] The promise of this renewal is then immediately set forth: the transformation of the wilderness into paradise: "The Spirit immediately drove him out into the wilderness. And he was in the wilderness forty days, tempted by Satan; and he was with the wild beasts; and the angels ministered to him."[33] In the wilderness Christ the incarnate Logos draws the spiritual and natural *logoi* to himself in harmony. The realms of the visible and invisible dwell with him in peace. Here the struggle of the first Adam is reenacted and the final victory over Satan prefigured. The Good News of this renewal is then straightaway announced by Jesus, the Good News of the Kingdom which is "at hand" in him.[34]

That promised harmony, the reconciliation of a fallen cosmos, can make its gradual appearance in the life of those who seek to follow Christ only through a conflicted process of transcendent understanding, sacrificial action in love, and a Spirit-led work of *metanoia*. As the formation of the disciples intensifies after Peter's declaration of faith, Jesus makes the link between his Paschal mystery and baptism clear. On the way to Jerusalem, as he is preparing for his death and Resurrection, when James and John ask him for the right to sit at his right hand in the kingdom, Jesus replies, "You do not know what you are asking. Are you able to drink the cup that I drink, or to be baptized with the baptism with which I am baptized?"[35] Jesus's entry into the mystery of his dying and rising is described as his baptism, a reality into which the disciples are invited as their pathway to the kingdom which he had come to proclaim and to bring.

---

[32] See the discussion in Ernest Best, *The Temptation and the Passion: The Markan Soteriology*, 2nd ed. (Cambridge: Cambridge University Press, 1965), 153–56.
[33] Mk. 1:12–13.
[34] Mk. 1:14–15.
[35] Mk. 10:38.

A small incident recorded in Mark (and also in this form in Luke) when Jesus and his disciples entered Jerusalem "on the first day of Unleavened Bread," might invite a sacramental reading, uniting baptism again to the coming passion.[36] Jesus sent two of his disciples ahead of him to prepare the Passover meal, telling them to follow a man carrying a jar of water and make the preparations in the house he enters—the householder will show them "a large upper room furnished and ready."[37] Coptic tradition has identified the man carrying the jar of water as Mark himself leading the disciples to his home,[38] and of course if the water-carrier was Mark then the slightly odd feature of the guide would be simpler to explain, for in first-century Palestine carrying water would have been a work undertaken by women. Whether or not Mark has placed a figure of himself personally leading the two disciples, we might see a sacramental imagery being developed here, the reader being led to understand that through the water of baptism one is led to the mystery of the Eucharist, the definitive sacramental presentation of the Paschal offering.

The last supper is followed by a tiny incident, uniquely recorded in Mark's Gospel, that may be a further image of baptism as an entry into Christ's dying and rising in the figure of a young man in the Garden of Gethsemane who runs away naked. After Jesus's arrest, it is said of the disciples, "they all forsook him, and fled." Mark's text then adds, "And a young man followed him, with nothing but a linen cloth about his body; and they seized him, but he left the

---

[36] Cf. Bobertz, *The Gospel of Mark*, 161, n.3.
[37] Mk. 14:12–16.
[38] The Monastery of St Mark in Jerusalem, with the offices of the Syriac Orthodox patriarch, is today on the site where Mark's house was thought to be located. The identity of the house with the upper room as that belonging to Mark's family finds some support from references in *Acts*. In *Acts* 12, we are given the story of Peter escaping from prison through the miraculous intervention of an angel. As soon as he left prison, "he went to the house of Mary, the mother of John whose other name was Mark, where many were gathered together and were praying" (*Acts* 12:12). Mary was clearly a prominent member of the Church in Jerusalem in the earliest days, providing hospitality for the apostles, a point that also correlates with the fact that Mark and Barnabus were cousins (*Col.* 4:10) and that Barnabus made his wealth available to the apostles (*Acts* 4:36–37). It is a plausible step from here to identify this home, clearly familiar to Peter and the apostles, as the upper room of Acts chapters 1–2 and the place of hospitality identified by Jesus on entering into Jerusalem. Moreover, since Barnabus was of a Levitical family (Acts 4:36–37), and given that he and Mark were cousins, it is possible that Mark's family was also of the tribe of Levi. In manuscripts of the *Vulgate*, in the Preface to Mark's Gospel, he is identified as "Mark the Evangelist, who exercised the priestly office in Israel, a Levite by race" (see Joseph MacRory, "St. Mark," *The Catholic Encyclopedia*, 9 [New York: Robert Appleton Co., 1910]).

linen cloth and ran away naked."[39] A figure of a nameless young man is picked up again at the Resurrection of Christ: "And entering the tomb, they saw a young man sitting on the right side, dressed in a white robe."[40] A young man flees naked at the beginning of the passion and a young man is clothed in white, an evangelist of the Resurrection, at the conclusion of the Gospel.

The mysterious figure of the young man in the Garden, naked and in flight, has been viewed by commentators in both literal and symbolic ways,[41] with some commentators seeing in this anonymous figure Mark's depiction of himself, fearful but finally sitting at the right side of Christ, saved through his death and Resurrection.[42] In his commentary on the extract from the "secret Gospel" of Mark in the *Letter to Theodore*, Morton Smith interprets the fact of the young man's appearing in the Garden at night as a baptismal reference,[43] pointing to Hippolytus for support,[44] as well as the fact that in John's Gospel it is at night that Nicodemus comes to Jesus and receives a baptismal instruction.[45] We can appreciate the possible baptismal imagery in this small incident, however, independently of any judgment on the authenticity of the Mar Saba *Letter* for others have proposed an identification of the two figures of the "young man," seeing an image of baptism in the rehabilitation of the young man, now clothed in Christ and united to him through the Paschal mystery, an image with which every catechumen being presented for baptism would have been able to identify since the ancient practice of the Church was for the candidate to stand naked for baptism and then to be dressed in white, "putting on Christ" as a garment. The Markan text, it is pointed out, may indicate this sacramental reference in that the term used twice for the young man's garment, *sindona*, a linen cloth, is only employed in one other place, to refer to the linen cloth in which Christ's body is wrapped and laid in the tomb.[46]

---

[39] Mk. 14:50-52.
[40] Mk. 16:5.
[41] For a reasonably comprehensive discussion of the range of proposals see Raymond E. Brown, S.S., *The Death of the Messiah: From Gethsemane to the Grave* (New York: Doubleday, 1994), I. 294-304, and it is worth noting the variety present in St Thomas's *Catena Aurea* (*Catena Aurea: A Commentary on the four Gospels Collected out of the Works of the Fathers* [Southampton: St. Austin Press, 1997], II: 299).
[42] Cf. Donald English, *The Message of Mark* (Downer's Grove, IL: InterVarsity Press Academic, 1992), 222-23.
[43] *Clement of Alexandria and a Secret Gospel of Mark*, 115, see the Letter III.6-11.
[44] *Apostolic Tradition* XXI.1.
[45] Jn. 3:1-10.
[46] Mk. 14:51-52; 15:46. For the image of baptismal clothing see Gal. 3:27; 2 Cor. 5:4; Rev. 3:4-5, 18; 4:4; 16:15, and see also Hippolytus, *Apostolic Tradition* 21:11-20.

Julian Haas, for example, in his catechumenal reading of the Gospel, regards it as a pivotal event in this way.[47]

The most penetrating account of this incident is that of Austin Farrer who, confirming the general direction of these baptismal readings, also uses it to bring us back to the broader question of the style of the Gospel. Opening his discussion with a disingenuous comment that "there is surely some symbolic motif here, if we could only hit upon it," Farrer offers a lengthy unpacking of the incident in the context of the passion narrative, weaving together the sacramental and Joseph themes present.[48] Farrer's understanding of the poetical and symbolic dimension of Mark's Gospel as a whole is particularly pertinent: "The further we go into the question, the more clearly we see that St. Mark's words are shaped by a play of images and allusions of a subtle and allusive kind which belongs to imagination rather than to rational construction." These images and allusions are not themselves "the substance of revealed truth," but it is through such images that the force of substantial truth is brought out by Mark in the Gospel.[49] It is an awareness that Helen Gardner shared, that Mark was writing "something nearer a poem than a treatise."[50] Mark's Gospel offers us the Good News in all of the mystery with which Newman describes the Christian life given in sacramental form:

> At times we seem to catch a glimpse of a Form which we will hereafter see face to face. We approach, and in spite of the darkness, our hands, or our head, or our brow, or our lips become, as it were, sensible of the contact of something more than earthly. We know not where we are, but we have been bathing in water, and a voice tells us that it is blood. Or we have a mark signed upon our foreheads, and it spake of Calvary. Or we recollect a hand laid upon our heads, and surely it had the print of nails in it, and resembled His who with a touch gave sight to the blind and raised the dead. Or we have been eating and drinking; and it was not a dream surely, that One fed us from His wounded side, and renewed our nature by the heavenly meat He gave.[51]

There is a debate concerning the ending of Mark's Gospel. Many manuscripts conclude at 16:8, and the apparent abruptness and

---

[47] Julian Haas, *Mark's Gospel: Catechumenal Way of the Lord to the Father* (Delhi: Media House, 2008), 14-16.
[48] Austin Farrer, *The Glass of Vision* (Glasgow: The University Press, 1948), 136-46.
[49] Ibid., 145-46.
[50] Helen Gardner, *The Business of Criticism* (Oxford: Clarendon Press, 1959), 102-3.
[51] John Henry Newman, "Worship, a Preparation for Christ's Coming," *Plain and Parochial Sermons*, 5, 1 (London: Longman, Green, and Co., 1901), 10-11.

obscurity of the final verse have led many to propose that Mark's conclusion was originally more extended and well-rounded. I am convinced by commentators who see this enigmatic ending as in fact the original conclusion of the Gospel, perfectly fitting the allusive style of the text, its quality of being, as Gardner said, "something nearer a poem."[52] But the longer conclusion of Mark's Gospel, which the Church affirmed in due course to be part of the inspired Scriptures, does provide a fitting return to the theme of the healing of the cosmos through Christ the new Adam, as he gives his Great Commission to the apostles: "And he said to them, "Go into all the world and preach the gospel to the whole creation. He who believes and is baptized will be saved; but he who does not believe will be condemned."[53] The Gospel is for the "whole creation." The Greek word for "creation" here, *ktesis*, is that which is used by Jesus when he refers to the "beginning of the creation which God created."[54] The creation to which the Gospel is to be announced for the sake of its transfiguration by the redeeming Logos is the entirety of the visible and invisible orders.[55]

---

[52] On this question of the ending of the Gospel Lightfoot's comments are particularly incisive: *Studies in the Gospel of Mark*, 80–97.
[53] Mk. 16:15–16.
[54] Mk. 13:19.
[55] Cf. Col. 1:15, 23; 2 Cor. 5:17.

POSTSCRIPT

E.M. FORSTER, IN A SHORT ESSAY ON "HAPPINESS," described what he saw as a fundamental human desire: for a "magical island"—that place of peace dwelling in the heart, but exteriorized "in the past or the future for safety."[1] Forster found his island in Alexandria, where he served with the Red Cross during the First World War. He wrote *A History and a Guide* to the city as well as a collection of essays, *Pharos and Pharillon*, recreating the life of the city both in antiquity and in later times.[2] Forster's own relationship to Christian Alexandria was largely ironic and detached, his philosophical and religious preferences skeptical, and increasingly looking towards oriental thought.[3] His sense of a certain kinship with Clement of Alexandria, though, stands out in his often irreverent and mocking commentary on the Christian period. While Clement is not spared, Forster does note that in his conciliatory personality and sensitive writings we see perhaps that "the graciousness of Greece" is "not quite incompatible with the Grace of God."[4]

In modern Alexandria, the "dominant memory in the chaos is now British," as Forster puts it, "for here are some large holes, made by Admiral Seymour when he bombarded the fort in 1882,"[5] and in the mid-twentieth century British rule in Egypt led to Alexandria occupying a key position in the allied defense of North Africa during the Second World War. This is where my mother, in fact, spent most of her war years and she, like Forster, found it a place of enchantment. She remembered her war years there as some of her best, offering opportunities—in between the raids and attacks—for seeking and finding common wartime cause between Egyptian Christians and Moslems.

In his writings on Alexandria, Forster had sought to evoke "an entire city from the dead."[6] The portrait of John Paul offering the Alexandrian school's contribution as light for our present work of catechesis expresses something of this same desire, though John

---

[1] E. M. Forster, "Happiness," in *Abinger Harvest* (London: Edward Arnold and Co., 1942), 38.
[2] *Alexandria: A History and a Guide* (Whitehead Morris: Alexandria, 1922); *Pharos and Pharillon* (London: Hogarth Press, 1923).
[3] Forster described himself as belonging to "the fag-end of Victorian liberalism" (John Colmer, *E. M. Forster: The Personal Voice* [London: Routledge, Kegan and Paul, 1975], vii). For a discussion of his Alexandrian writings see 142–51.
[4] *Pharos and Pharillon*, 42
[5] Ibid., 23.
[6] See Colmer, *E. M. Forster*, 147.

Paul is conscious of drawing upon a *living* Tradition to serve a *living* Magisterium.[7] In the Victorian period, Newman had also sought to evoke for us the glory of the Christian Alexandria and, as we have seen, he wrote warmly and extensively of the Alexandrian Church and of its catechetical school. As Benjamin King puts it, "the Greek Fathers, especially those from Egypt, became his lifelong companions."[8] We can therefore conclude by returning to Newman, who offered a stirring call to courage and trust for the work of new evangelization in his famous "Second Spring" sermon.[9] Preached in the middle of the nineteenth century in an England from which the Catholic institutional presence had been expelled three hundred years before, Newman explored the possibility of a second "moment" for the Church, a second spring.

His sermon is both realistic in its assessment of the difficulties that could be anticipated while also full of hope. And the two are united for him, the difficulties and the hope. The winter of discontent and the new springtime he saw as belonging together.[10] Through his insight that the seeds for the new spring are sown precisely in a period of apparent barrenness, Newman points to the authentic response needed for this call to a new evangelization. Certain trees are planted in winter, not in the spring, because it is in the winter that their roots strike deep into the ground to seek the nourishment and water they need. The best planting takes place in harsh conditions. Their capacity for growth in the spring depends upon this period of winter. Fair-weather planting yields weak growth. Newman's acknowledgement of winter is a kind of *felix culpa*. Like Origen's intuition that an apparently arid scriptural passage is an invitation to dig more deeply, so Newman saw his wintery environment pointing to the necessity to push down roots for nourishment from sources that lie deep within the earth and to find in and through that spreading of roots sustenance that will sustain, enlarge, and strengthen the growth of the tree until it can stretch and flower for the sake of all that

---

[7] For Forster, on the other hand, we must lend solidity to our magical island which can only in the end be "part of a dream from which humanity will never awake" ("Happiness," 38).

[8] *Newman and the Alexandrian Fathers*, 2.

[9] See John Henry Newman, *The Second Spring: A Sermon by John Henry Newman*, with introduction, notes and exercises by Francis P. Donnelly, SJ (Longmans, 1934).

[10] In a somewhat different context, that of possible martyrdom, Origen reminded his readers of the verses in the Song of Songs that Christians should not be surprised by wintry weather for it is precisely "in the winter's storm that the blessed must first show how they have mastered their pilotage" (*Exhortation to Martyrdom* V.30) – a perhaps fondly-recalled Alexandrian image of the ship coming into harbor.

need to find life within its scope. Christians seeking renewal press down deep into nature and into history and find Revelation in both, since both are held in the Logos who unites all things. Newman had learned just such a truth, perhaps, from his companions in the Alexandrian Church, from a soil which can now plentifully nourish our own age.

WORKS CITED

Abd-el-Ghani, Mohammed. "Alexandria and Middle Egypt: Some Aspects of Social and Economic Contracts under Roman Rule." In W.V. Harris and G. Ruffini (eds.) *Ancient Alexandria between Egypt and Greece*. Columbia Studies in the Classical Tradition 26. Leiden: Brill, 2004, 161–78.

Africa, Thomas. *Science and the State in Greece and Rome*. Chichester: John Wiley and Sons, 1968.

Agus, Jacob B. *The Meaning of Jewish History*. London: Abelard-Schuman, 1963.

Alcinous. *The Handbook of Platonism (Didaskalikos)*. Tr. and ed. with commentary by J. Dillon. Oxford: Clarendon Press, 1995.

Aquinas. *Catena Aurea: A Commentary on the four Gospels Collected out of the Works of the Fathers*. Southampton: St Austin Press, 1997.

Aristotle. *Complete Works*. J. Barnes (ed.). Princeton: Princeton University Press, 1984.

Armstrong, Arthur H. (ed.). *The Cambridge History of Later Greek and Early Medieval Philosophy*. Cambridge: Cambridge University Press, 1967.

Athanasius. *St Anthony of the Desert*. Tr. J.B. McLaughlin. Charlotte: TAN Books, 2014.

——. *De Incarnatione*. Tr. and ed. by a religious of C.S.M.V. New York: St. Vladimir's Seminary Press, 1993.

Athenaeus. *The Diepnosophists*. Tr. C.B. Gulick. Loeb Classical Library. Cambridge, MA: Harvard University Press, 1927.

Atiya, Aziz S. *History of Eastern Christianity*. Notre Dame: University of Notre Dame Press, 1967.

Augustine. *Confessions*. Tr. W. Watts. Loeb Classical Library. London: William Heinemann, 1960.

——. *De consensu evangelistarum*. In M.B. Riddle (ed.), *Saint Augustine: Sermon on the Mount, Harmony of the Gospels, Homilies on the Gospels*. Tr. S.D.F. Salmond. Nicene and Post-Nicene Fathers. Grand Rapids: William B. Eerdmans Publishing, 1974: 65–236.

——. *De Catechizandis Rudibus*. Tr. The Rev. Joseph P. Christopher. Ancient Christian Writers. Westminster: The Newman Bookshop, 1946.

Babylonian Talmud: Tractate Sanhedrin. I. Epstein (ed.). London: Soncino Press, 1987.

Bagnell, Roger S. *Egypt in Late Antiquity*. Princeton: Princeton University Press, 1993.

Barnard, Leslie W. "St. Mark and Alexandria." *Harvard Theological Review* 57, 2 (1964): 145–50.

——. *Athenagoras: A Study in Second Century Christian Apologetic*. Paris: Beauchesne, 1972.

Barnes, Timothy D. "The Edition of Eusebius' Ecclesiastical History." *Greek, Roman and Byzantine Studies*, 21 (1980): 191–201.

Barrett, C.K. *A Commentary on the First Epistle to the Corinthians*. New York: Harper and Row Publishers, 1968.

Bauer, Walter. *Orthodoxy and Heresy in Earliest Christianity*. Translated by R.A. Kraft and G. Kroedel. Philadelphia: Fortress Press, 1971.

Bayliss, Grant D. *The Vision of Didymus the Blind: A Fourth-Century Virtue Origenism*. Oxford: Oxford University Press, 2015.

Beeson, Trevor. *Discretion and Valour: Religious Conditions in Russia and Eastern Europe*. London: Fount Paperbacks, 1974.

Behr, John. *Asceticism and Anthropology in Irenaeus and Clement*. Oxford: Oxford University Press, 2000.

——. Introduction. *Origen: On First Principles*, Vol. 1. Oxford: Oxford University Press, 2017.

Benedict XVI. Apostolic Letter, *Ubicumque et Semper*. Vatican City: Libreria Vaticana Editrice, 2010.

——. Apostolic Letter, *Fides per Doctrinum*. Vatican City: Libreria Vaticana Editrice, 2013.

Best, Ernest. *The Temptation and the Passion: The Markan Soteriology*. 2nd ed. Cambridge: Cambridge University Press, 1965.

Bevan, Edwyn. *A History of Egypt under the Ptolemaic Dynasty*. London: Methuen and Co., 1927.

Bigg, Charles. *The Christian Platonists of Alexandria*. Oxford: The Clarendon Press, 1913.

Bingham, D. Jeffrey. "Paideia and Polemic in Second-Century Lyons: Irenaeus on Education." In K.M. Hogan, M. Goff and E. Wasserman (eds.) *Pedagogy in Ancient Judaism and Early Christianity*. Atlanta: SBL Press, 2017: 323-58.

Black, C. Clifton. *Mark: Images of an Apostolic Interpreter*. Minneapolis: Fortress Press, 2001.

Blevins, James L. *The Messianic Secret in Markan Research 1901-1976*. Washington, D.C.: University Press of America, 1981.

Blosser, Benjamin P. *Become Like the Angels: Origen's Doctrine of the Soul*. Washington, D.C.: The Catholic University of America Press, 2012.

Bobertz, Charles A. *The Gospel of Mark: A Liturgical Reading*. Grand Rapids: Baker Academic, 2016.

Boersma, Gerard. *Heavenly Participation: The Weaving of a Sacramental Tapestry*. Grand Rapids: William B. Eerdmans Publishing, 2011.

Brehier, Emile. *The Hellenistic and Roman Age*. Tr. W. Baskin. Chicago: The University of Chicago Press, 1965.

Bremmer, Jan M. "The Family and other Centres of Religious Learning in Antiquity." In J.W. Drijvers and A.A. MacDonald (eds.) *Centers of Learning: Learning and Location in Pre-Modern Europe and the Near East*. Leiden: Brill, 1995: 29-38.

——. *Greek Religion*. 2nd ed. Cambridge: Cambridge University Press, 2021.

Brock, Sebastian P. "The Phenomenon of the Septuagint," *Old Testament Studies*, 17 (1972): 11-36.

Brown, Blanche. *Ptolemaic Paintings and Mosaics and the Alexandrian Style*. Cambridge, MA: Archeological Institute of American, 1957.

Brown, Peter. *The Body and Society*. London: Faber and Faber, 1988.

———. *Power and Persuasion in Late Antiquity: Towards a Christian Empire.* Madison: University of Wisconsin Press, 1992.
Brown, Raymond E., SS. *The Death of the Messiah: From Gethsemane to the Grave.* New York: Doubleday, 1994.
Bruce, F. F. *The Epistle to the Hebrews.* Grand Rapids: William B. Eerdmans, 1964.
Brumbaugh, Robert S. *Plato for the Modern Age.* New York: Crowell-Collier, 1962.
———. and N. M. Lawrence, *Philosophers on Education: Six Essays on the Foundations of Western Thought.* Boston: Houghton Mifflin Co., 1963.
Budge, E. A. Wallis. *The Contendings of the Apostles II,* London: Henry Frowde, 1901.
———. *Paradise of the Fathers.* London: Chatto and Windus, 1907.
Butler, Alfred J. *The Arab Conquest of Egypt and the Last Thirty Years of the Roman Dominion.* 2nd ed. Oxford: Oxford University Press, 1978.
Camilletti, Fabio A. *The Portrait of Beatrice: Dante, D. G. Rosetti, and the Imaginary Lady.* Notre Dame: University of Notre Dame Press, 2019.
Cannuyer, Christian. *Coptic Egypt: The Christians of the Nile.* New York: Harry M. Abrams, 2001.
Carrington, Philip. *The Early Christian Church, Vol. II.* Cambridge: Cambridge University Press, 1957.
Casel, Odo, OSB. *The Mystery of Christian Worship.* New York: The Crossroad Publishing Company, 1999.
Catechism of the Catholic Church. Vatican City: Libreria Vaticana Editrice, 1997.
Chadwick, Henry. "Faith and Order at the Council of Nicaea: A Note on the Background of the Sixth Canon." *Harvard Theological Review* 53, 3 (1960): 171–95.
———. "Philo." In A. H. Armstrong (ed.), *Cambridge History of Later Greek and Early Medieval Philosophy.* Cambridge: Cambridge University Press, 1970.
———. *Early Christian Thought and the Classical Tradition.* 2nd ed. Oxford: Clarendon Press, 1987.
———. "Philosophical Tradition and the Self." In G. W. Bowertock, P. Brown and O. Grabar (eds.) *Late Antiquity: A Guide to the Postclassical World.* Cambridge, MA: The Belknap Press of Harvard University Press, 1999: 60–81.
———. *The Making of a Rift in the Church: From Apostolic Times until the Council of Florence.* Oxford: Oxford University Press, 2003.
Chadwick, Henry and J. E. L. Oulton. *Alexandrian Christianity.* Philadelphia: Westminster Press, 1954.
Cherniss, Harold F. *The Riddle of the Early Academy.* Berkeley: University of California Press, 1945.
Chesterton, G. K. *Orthodoxy.* Peabody, MA: Hendrickson Publishers, Inc., 2006.
Cicero. *De Finibus.* Tr. H. Rackham. Loeb Classical Library, London: William Heinemann, 1967.
Clark, Gillian. *Monica. An Ordinary Saint.* Oxford: Oxford University Press, 2015.
Clark, Stephen R. L. "The Use of 'Man's Function' in Aristotle." *Ethics* 82 (1972): 269–83.
———. *Aristotle's Man: Speculations on Aristotelian Anthropology.* Oxford: Clarendon Press, 1975.

——. *Plotinus: Myth, Metaphor, and Philosophical Practice*. Chicago: The University of Chicago Press, 2016.

——. *From Athens to Jerusalem: the Love of Wisdom and the Love of God*. Brooklyn, NY: Angelico Press, 2019.

Clarke, Martin L. *Higher Education in the Ancient World*. London: Routledge and Kegan Paul, 1971.

Clarke, W. Norris, SJ. *Explorations in Metaphysics*. Indiana: University of Notre Dame Press, 1994.

Clement of Alexandria. *Protrepticus*. Tr. G.W. Butterworth. Loeb Classical Library. Cambridge, MA: Harvard University Press, 1919.

——. *The Rich Man's Salvation*. Tr. G.W. Butterworth. Loeb Classical Library. Cambridge, MA: Harvard University Press, 1919.

——. *To the Newly Baptized*. Tr. G.W. Butterworth. Loeb Classical Library. Cambridge, MA: Harvard University Press, 1919.

——. *Paedagogus (Christ the Educator)*. Tr. S. Wood. Washington D.C.: Catholic University of America Press, 1954.

——. *Stromateis Books 1-3*. Tr. J. Ferguson. Washington D.C.: Catholic University of America Press, 1991.

——. *Paedagogus* and *Stromateis*. In A. Roberts and J. Donaldson (eds.) *The Ante-Nicene Fathers, Vol II*. American Edition. Edinburgh: T&T Clark, reprinted 1994: 207-567.

——. *Eclogae Propheticae*. https://catholiclibrary.org/library/view?docId=Fathers-OR/Clement_of_Alexandria__Eclogae_propheticae.gr.html.

Clement of Rome. "The First Epistle of Clement to the Corinthians." *The Apostolic Fathers I*. Tr. K. Lake. Loeb Classical Library. Cambridge, MA: Harvard University Press, 1985.

Cointet, Pierre de, Barbara Morgan, and Petroc Willey. *The Catechism of the Catholic Church and the Craft of Catechesis*. San Francisco: Ignatius Press, 2008.

Cole, Basil, OP. *Music and Morals: A Theological Appraisal of the Moral and Psychological Effects of Music*. New York: Alba House, 1993.

Coleridge, Samuel T. *The Friend*. B.E. Rooke (ed.). London: Routledge and Kegan Paul, 1969.

Collins, John J. "Wisdom and Torah." In K.M. Hogan, M. Goff and E. Wasserman (eds.) *Pedagogy in Ancient Judaism and Early Christianity*. Atlanta: SBL Press, 2017: 59-79.

Colmer, John. *E.M. Forster: The Personal Voice*. London: Routledge, Kegan and Paul, 1975.

Congregation for the Clergy. *General Directory for Catechesis*. Vatican City: Libreria Vaticana Editrice, 1997.

Cooper, Adam. *The Body in St Maximus the Confessor: Holy Flesh, Wholly Deified*. Oxford: Oxford University Press, 2005.

Cornford, F.M. *Plato's Theory of Knowledge*. London: Routledge & Kegan Paul Ltd, 1935.

Cranz, F. Edward. "Kingdom and Polity in Eusebius of Caesarea." *Harvard Theological Review* 45 (1952): 47-66.

Cranshaw, James L. *Education in Ancient Israel: Across the Deadening Silence.* New York: Doubleday, 1998.
Crehan, Joseph H., SJ. "The Analogy between *Verbum Dei Incarnatum* and *Verbum Dei Scriptum* in the Fathers." *Journal of Theological Studies* 6 (1995): 87-90.
Cribiore, Raffaella. *Writing, Teaching and Students.* Atlanta: Scholars Press, 1996.
—. "Why did Christians Compete with Pagans for Greek Paideia?" In K.M. Hogan, M. Goff and E. Wasserman (eds.) *Pedagogy in Ancient Judaism and Early Christianity.* Atlanta: SBL Press, 2017: 359-74.
Criddle, A.H. "On the Mar Saba Letter Attributed to Clement of Alexandria." *Journal of Early Christian Studies.* 3, 2 (1995): 215-20.
Cross, F.L. *1 Peter, A Paschal Liturgy.* London: A.R. Mowbray and Co. Ltd., 1954.
Crouzel, Henri, SJ. "L'imitation et la 'suite' de Dieu et du Christ dans le premiers siècles chrétiens, ainsi que leurs sources gréco-romaines et hébraïques." *Jahrbuch für Antike und Christentum.* 21 (1978): 7-41.
—. "Current Theology: The Literature on Origen 1970-1988." *Theological Studies.* 49 (1988): 499-516.
Dabricourt, Georges. *L'initiation chrétienne selon saint Marc.* Paris: Apostolat des Éditions, 1970.
Daniélou, Jean, SJ. *The Bible and the Liturgy.* Notre Dame: University of Notre Dame Press, 1956.
—. *From Shadows to Reality: Studies in the Biblical Typology of the Fathers.* London: Burns & Oates, 1960.
—. *La Catéchèse aux Premiers Siècles.* Paris: Fayard-Mame, 1968.
—. *Gospel Message and Hellenistic Culture.* Tr. John A. Baker. London: Darton, Longman and Todd, 1973.
Davis, Harrold T. *Alexandria the Golden City.* Evanston: The Principia Press Illinois, Inc., 1957.
Davis, Stephen J. *The Early Coptic Papacy: The Egyptian Church and its Leadership in Late Antiquity: The Popes of Egypt.* New York: The American University in Cairo Press, 2004.
Dawson, David. *Allegorical Readers and Cultural Revision in Ancient Alexandria.* Berkeley: University of California Press, 1992.
Delia, Diana. "The Population of Roman Alexandria." *Transactions of the American Philological Association* 118 (1988): 275-92.
de Lubac, Henri, SJ. *The Motherhood of the Church: Followed by Particular Churches in the Universal Church.* Tr. Sr. S. Englund. San Francisco: Ignatius Press, 1982.
—. *Theology in History.* Tr. A.E. Nash. San Francisco: Ignatius Press, 1996.
—. *Medieval Exegesis: The Four Senses of Scripture.* Tr. M. Sebanc. Edinburgh: T&T Clark, 1998.
—. *History and Spirit: The Understanding of Scripture According to Origen.* Tr. A.E. Nash. San Francisco: Ignatius Press, 2007.
de Margerie, Bertrand, SJ. *The Christian Trinity in History.* Tr. E.J. Fortman. Still River: St Bede's Publications, 1982.

de Vleeschauwer, Herman J. "Les bibliotheques ptolemeennes d'Alexandrie." *Mousaion* 1 (1955): 1-40.

Dillon, John. *The Middle Platonists: 80 B.C. to A.D. 220*. Ithaca, NY: Cornell University Press, 1977.

Dio Chrysostom. *The Thirty-Second Discourse*. Tr. J.W. Cohoon and H.L. Crosby. Loeb Classical Library. London: William Heinemann, 1951.

Diodorus Siculus. *History* Tr. C. Bradford Welles. Loeb Classical Library. Cambridge, MA: Harvard University Press, 1963.

Diogenes Laertius. *Lives of Eminent Philosophers*. Tr. R.D. Hicks. Loeb Classical Library. London: William Heinemann, 1925.

Dix, Gregory, OSB. *The Shape of the Liturgy*. London: A & C Black, 1945.

Drijvers, Han J.W. "The School of Edessa: Greek Learning and Local Culture." in J.W. Drijvers and A.A. MacDonald (eds.) *Centers of Learning: Learning and Location in Pre-Modern Europe and the Near East*. Leiden: Brill, 1995: 49-59.

Dujarier, Michel. *A History of the Catechumenate: The First Six Centuries*. Tr. Edward J. Haasl. New York: Sadlier, 1979.

——. *The Rites of Christian Initiation: Historical and Pastoral Reflections*. Tr. and ed. Kevin Hart. New York: Sadlier, 1979.

Dulles, Avery. "From Images to Truth: Newman on Revelation and Faith." *Theological Studies* 51 (1990): 252-67.

Dunn, James D.G. *Christology in the Making*, 2nd ed. Grand Rapids: William B. Eerdmans, 1996.

——. *Jesus and the Spirit: A Study of the Religious and Charismatic Experience of Jesus and the First Christians as Reflected in the New Testament*. Grand Rapids: William B. Eerdmans, 1997.

Dzielska, Maria. *Hypatia of Alexandria*. Tr. F. Lyra. Cambridge, MA: Harvard University Press, 1995.

Echle, Harry A. *Terminology of the Sacrament of Regeneration, according to Clement of Alexandria*. Washington, D.C.: Catholic University of America, 1949.

Edwards, Mark. *Origen against Plato*. Aldershot: Ashgate Publishing Ltd., 2002.

Ellens, J. Harrold. *The Ancient Library of Alexandria and Early Christian Theological Development*. Claremont, CA: The Institute for Antiquity and Christianity, 1993.

Elliott, James K. *The Apocryphal New Testament: A Collection of Apocryphal Christian Literature in an English Translation*. Oxford: Clarendon Press, 1993.

Eliot, T.S. *The Four Quartets*. London: Faber and Faber, 1944.

El Masri, Iris Habib. *The Story of the Copts: The True Story of Christianity in Egypt, I: From the Foundation of the Church to the Arab Invasion*. California: St Anthony Coptic Orthodox Monastery, 1982.

Emmel, Stephen. "Shenoute's Place in the History of Monasticism." In G. Gabra and H.N. Takla (eds.) *Christianity and Monasticism in Upper Egypt*. Cairo: The American University in Cairo Press, 2008: 31-46.

Emmett, Laurence. "Clement of Alexandria's *Protrepticus* and Dio Chrysostom's Alexandrian Oration." *Studia Patristica* 36 (2001): 409-14.

Empereur, Jean-Yves. *Alexandria Rediscovered*. London: British Museum Press, 1988.

English, Donald. *The Message of Mark.* Downer's Grove: InterVarsity Press Academic, 1992.
Epictetus. *The Discourses.* C. Gill (ed.). London: Everyman, 1995.
Eusebius. *The Ecclesiastical History.* Tr. K. Lake and J.E.L. Oulton. Loeb Classical Library. Cambridge, MA: Harvard University Press, 1926 and 1932.
———. *Praeparatio evangelica.* Greek text in *Die Praeparatio evangelica.* Karl Mras (ed.) et al. Berlin: Akadamie-Verlag, 2 Vols. 1982-83.
Farrer, Austin. *The Glass of Vision.* Glasgow: The University Press, 1948.
Ferguson, Everett, ed. *Conversion, Catechumenate, and Baptism in the Early Church.* New York: Garland, 1993.
———. *Baptism in the Early Church: History, Theology and Liturgy in the First Five Centuries.* Grand Rapids: William B. Eerdmans, 2009.
Ferguson, John. *Clement of Alexandria.* New York: Twayne Publishers, 1974.
Field, Anne. *From Darkness to Light: How One became a Christian in the Early Church.* Ben Lomand: Conciliar Press, 1997.
Finn, Thomas M. *The Liturgy of Baptism in the Baptismal Instructions of St John Chrysostom.* Washington D.C.: Catholic University of America Press, 1967.
———. *Early Christian Baptism and the Catechumenate: Italy, North Africa, and Egypt.* Collegeville: The Liturgical Press, 1992.
Fisichella, Rino and Octavio Ruiz Arenas. "Preface." *Directory for Catechesis.* Vatican City: Libreria Vaticana Editrice, 2020.
———. Introduction. In Pontifical Council for the Promotion of New Evangelization. *Enchiridion della nuova evangelizzazione.* Vatican City: Libreria Editrice Vaticana, 2014: v-xi.
Forster, E.M. *Alexandria: A History and a Guide.* Whitehead Morris: Alexandria, 1922.
———. *Pharos and Pharillon.* London: Hogarth Press, 1923.
Francis. *Praedicate Evangelium.* Vatican City: Libreria Vaticana Editrice, 2022.
Frankfurter, David. *Religion in Roman Egypt: Assimilation and Resistance.* Princeton, NJ: Princeton University Press, 1988.
———. *Christianizing Egypt: Syncretism and Local Worlds in Late Antiquity.* Princeton, NJ: Princeton University Press, 2018.
Frend, W.H.C. *The Early Church: from the Beginnings to AD 461.* Worcester: Billing and Sons Ltd., 1992.
Gabra, Gawdat, W. Lyster and C. Hulsman (eds.). *Be Thou There: The Holy Family's Journey in Egypt.* Cairo: American University in Cairo Press, 2001.
Gadamer, Hans-Georg. *Truth and Method.* London: Sheed and Ward, 1975.
Gardiner, Alan H. "The House of Life." *Journal of Egyptian Archaeology* 24 (1938): 157-79.
Gardner, Helen. *The Business of Criticism.* Oxford: Clarendon Press, 1959.
Garrett, Duane. *Proverbs, Ecclesiastes, Song of Solomon.* Nashville: Broadman, 1993.
Girgis, Samir Fawzy. *A Chronology of St Mark.* Cairo: St John the Beloved Publishing House, 2002.
Glad, Clarence E. "The Rhetoric of Moral Exhortation in Clement's *Pedagogue.*" In J. Starr and T. Engberg-Pedersen (eds.), *Early Christian Paraenesis in Context.* New York: Walter de Gruyter, 2004: 433-66.

Glucker, John. *Antiochus and the Late Academy*. Gottingham: Vandenhoeck and Ruprecht, 1978.
Goehring, James E. *Ascetics, Society, and the Desert: Studies in Early Egyptian Monasticism*. Harrisburg, PA: Trinity Press International, 1999.
Grant, Robert M. "The *Stromateis* of Origen." In J. Fontaine and C. Kannengiesser (eds.), *Épektasis. Mélanges Patristiques offerts au Cardinal Jean Daniélou*. Paris: Beauchesne, 1972: 285-92.
——. *Early Christianity and Society*. London: Collins, 1978.
——. *Eusebius as Church Historian*. Oxford: Clarendon Press, 1980.
——. "Theological Education at Alexandria." In B.A. Pearson and J.E. Goehring (eds.), *The Roots of Egyptian Christianity*. Studies in Antiquity and Christianity. Philadelphia, 1986: 178-89.
Green, Henry. "The Socio-Economic Background of Christianity in Egypt." In B.A. Pearson and J.E. Goehring (eds.), *The Roots of Egyptian Christianity*. Studies in Antiquity and Christianity. Philadelphia, 1986: 100-113.
Gregory Thaumaturgus. "The Oration and Panegyric Addressed to Origen." In A. Donaldson and J. Donaldson (eds.), *Ante-Nicene Fathers, Volume VI*. Grand Rapids: William B. Eerdmans, 1971: 21-39.
Sidney H. Griffith. "Asceticism in the Church of Syria: The Hermeneutics of Early Syrian Monasticism." In V.L. Wimbush and R. Valantasis (eds.), *Asceticism*. New York: Oxford University Press, 1995: 220-45.
Griggs, C. Wilfred. *Early Egyptian Christianity from its Origins to 451 CE*. Leiden: Brill, 1990.
Grindheim, Siguard. "Direct Dependence on Philo in the Epistle to the Hebrews." *Novum Testamentum* 65 (2023): 517-43.
Guardini, Romano. "A Letter from Romano Guardini." *Herder Correspondence* (August 1964): 237-38.
Guillaumont, Antoine. *Aux origines du monachisme chrétien: Pour une phénoménologie du monachisme*. Bégrolles-en-Mauges: Abbaye de Bellefontaine, 1979.
Guthrie, W.K.C. *A History of Greek Philosophy, Vol. III*. Cambridge: Cambridge University Press, 1969.
Gwynn, David M. *Athanasius of Alexandria: Bishop, Theologian, Ascetic, Father*. Oxford: Oxford University Press, 2012.
Haas, Christopher. *Alexandria in Late Antiquity: Topography and Social Conflict*. Baltimore: Johns Hopkins, 1997.
Haas, Julian, OFM Cap. *Mark's Gospel: Catechumenal Way of the Lord to the Father*. Delhi: Media House, 2008.
Hadot, Pierre. *Plotinus or The Simplicity of Vision*. Chicago: The University of Chicago Press, 1993.
——. *Philosophy as a Way of Life: Spiritual Exercises from Socrates to Foucault*. Oxford: Blackwell Publishing, 1995.
——. *What is Ancient Philosophy?* Tr. M. Chase. Cambridge, MA: The Belknap Press of Harvard University Press, 2002.
Hanson, Richard P.C. *Allegory and Event: A Study of the Sources and Significance of Origen's Interpretation of Scripture*. London: SCM Press, 1959.
Hardie, W.F.R. *Aristotle's Ethical Theory*. Oxford: Oxford University Press, 1968.

Harmless, William. *Augustine and the Catechumenate*. Collegeville: Liturgical Press, rev. ed., 2014.
Hedstrom, Darlene L. Brooks. "Archeology in Early Christian Egypt." In D.K. Pettegrew, W.R. Caraher and T.W. Davis (eds.), *The Oxford Handbook of Early Christian Archeology*. Oxford: Oxford University Press, 2019: 665-84.
Heine, Ronald E. *Origen: Scholarship in the Service of the Church*. Oxford: Oxford University Press, 2010.
———. *Origen: An Introduction to His Life and Thought*, Eugene, OR: Cascade Books, 2019.
Hengel, Martin. *Judaism and Hellenism: Studies in their Encounter in Palestine during the Early Hellenistic Period*. Philadelphia: Fortress Press, 1974.
———. *The Charismatic Leader and His Followers*. Tr. J.C.G. Greig. Edinburgh: T&T Clark, 1981.
———. *Studies in the Gospel of Mark*, London: SCM Press, 1985.
Hippolytus. *The Apostolic Tradition*. Gregory Dix (ed.), Rev. ed. London: SPCK, 1968.
Hogan, Karina Martin. "Would Philo Have Recognized Qumran *Musar* as *Paideia*?" In K.M. Hogan, M. Goff and E. Wasserman (eds.), *Pedagogy in Ancient Judaism and Early Christianity*. Atlanta: SBL Press, 2017: 81-100.
Hofinger, Johannes and Francis Buckley. *The Good News and its Proclamation*. Notre Dame: University of Notre Dame Press, 1968.
Holte, Ragnar. "Monica, 'the Philosopher.'" In P. Merino and J.M. Torrecilla (eds.), *Charisteria Augustiniana Ioseph Oroz Reta dicta*. Madrid, 1994: 2. 293-316.
Homer. *The Iliad*. Tr. A.T. Murray. London, William Heinemann, 1965.
Honigman, Sylvie. *The Septuagint and Homeric Scholarship in Alexandria: A Study in the Narrative of the Letter of Aristeas*. London: Routledge, 2003.
Honigmann, Ernest. "Philippus of Side and his 'Christian History' (written about 434-439)." *Patristic Studies, Studi e testi* 173 (1953): 82-91.
Hooker, Morna. *The Gospel According to Saint Mark*. Black's New Testament Commentaries. Peabody, MA: Hendrickson, 1991.
Horace. *Satires, Epistles, Ars Poetica*. Tr. H.R. Flairclough. Loeb Classical Library. London: William Heinemann, 1926.
Hurtado, Larry W. *The Earliest Christian Artefacts: Manuscripts and Christian Origins*. Grand Rapids: William B. Eerdmans, 2006.
Inowlocki, Sabrina. "Eusebius of Caesarea's 'Interpretatio Christiana' of Philo's De via contemplativa." *Harvard Theological Review* 97, 3 (July 2004): 305-28.
Irenaeus. *Adversus haereses*. In A. Roberts and J. Donaldson (eds.), *The Ante-Nicene Fathers, Vol I*. American Edition. Grand Rapids: Wm. B. Eerdmans, reprinted 1994: 309-567.
Isichei, Elizabeth. *A History of Christianity in Africa*. London: SPCK, 1995.
Isocrates, *Panegyricus*. Tr. G. Norlin. Loeb Classical Library. London: William Heinemann, 1980.
Jaeger, Werner. *Paideia: The Ideals of Greek Culture*. Tr. G. Highet. 2nd ed. Oxford: Oxford University Press, 1939.
———. *Aristotle: Fundamentals of the History of his Development*. Tr. R. Robinson. 2nd ed. Oxford: Oxford University Press, 1948.

—. *Two Rediscovered Works of Ancient Christian Literature: Gregory of Nyssa and Macarius*. Leiden: Brill, 1954.

—. *Early Christianity and Greek Paideia*. Oxford: Oxford University Press, 1969.

Jerome. *De Viris Illustribus. On Illustrious Men*. Tr. T. P. Halton. Fathers of the Church Series. Washington D.C.: Catholic University of America Press, 1999.

—. *Epistles*. Tr. W. H. Fremantle, G. Lewis and W. G. Martley. *Nicene and Post-Nicene Fathers, Second Series*, Vol. 6. Philip Schaff and Henry Wace (eds.). Buffalo, NY: Christian Literature Publishing Co., 1893.

John XXIII. Address for the Solemn Opening of the Second Vatican Ecumenical Council, Thursday 11 October, 1962. AAS 54 (1962): 785-95.

John Paul II. *Catechesi tradendae*. Vatican City: Libreria Vaticana Editrice, 1979.

—. Homily during Holy Mass in the Sanctuary of the Holy Cross, Mogila. AAS 71 (1979): 864-69.

—. *Familiaris consortio*. Vatican City: Libreria Vaticana Editrice, 1981.

—. *Fides et ratio*. Vatican City: Libreria Vaticana Editrice, 1988.

—. *Christifidelis laici*. Vatican City: Libreria Vaticana Editrice, 1988.

—. *Fidei Depositum*. Vatican City: Libreria Vaticana Editrice, 1992.

—. *Ecclesia in Africa*. Vatican City: Libreria Vaticana Editrice, 1995.

—. *Ecclesia in Eucharistia*. Vatican City: Libreria Vaticana Editrice, 2003.

Johnson, Aaron P. *Ethnicity and Argument in Eusebius'* Praeparatio Evangelica. Oxford: Oxford University Press, 2006.

Jonas, Hans. *The Gnostic Religion: The Message of the Alien God and the Beginnings of Christianity*. 2nd rev. ed. Boston: Beacon Press, 1963.

Jones, A. H. M. "The Social Background of the Struggle between Paganism and Christianity." In A. Momigliano, *The Conflict Between Paganism and Christianity in the Fourth Century*. Oxford: The Clarendon Press, 1963: 17-37.

Jones, H. Stuart. "Claudius and the Jewish Question at Alexandria." *The Journal of Roman Studies* 16 (1926): 17-35.

Josephus, *Antiquities of the Jews*, Tr. H. St. J. Thackery. Loeb Classical Library. London: William Heinemann, 1967.

—. *The Life Against Apion*. Tr. H. St. J. Thackery. Loeb Classical Library. London: William Heinemann, 1976.

—. *The Jewish War*, Tr. H. St .J. Thackery. Loeb Classical Library. London: William Heinemann, 1997.

Jungmann, Josef A., SJ. *MA of the Roman Rite: its Origins and Development*. Tr. Francis Brunner, CSsR. New York: Benzinger Brothers, 1955.

—. *Handing on the Faith: A Manual of Catechetics*, New York: Herder and Herder, 1959.

—. *The Early Liturgy: To the Time of Gregory the Great*. Tr. F. A. Brunner, CSSR. London: Darton, Longman and Todd, 1960.

—. *The Good News: Yesterday and Today*, New York: W. H. Sadlier, 1962 (Abridged version of *Die frohbotschaft und unsere glaubensvenkundigung*, 1936).

Justin Martyr. *The First and Second Apologies*. Tr. Leslie William Barnard. Ancient Christian Writers. New York: Paulist Press, 1997.

Kavanagh, Aidan. *The Shape of Baptism: The Rite of Christian Initiation*. Collegeville: The Liturgical Press, 1978.

Kees, Hermann. *Ancient Egypt: A Cultural Topography*. Tr. Ian F. D. Morrow. T. G. H. James (ed.). Chicago: University of Chicago Press, 1962.
Kelly, J. N. D. *Early Christian Creeds*. 3rd ed., London: Longman Group Ltd, 1972.
Kevane, Eugene. "*De Doctrina Christiana*: A Treatise on Christian Education." *Recherches Augustiniennes* 4 (1966): 97-133.
—. "*Translatio imperii*: Augustine's *De Doctrina Christiana* and the Classical *Paideia*." *Studia Patristica* XIV (1976): 446-60.
—. *Jesus the Divine Teacher*. Bloomington: AuthorHouse, 2005.
King, Benjamin John. *Newman and the Alexandrian Fathers: Shaping Doctrine in Nineteenth-Century England*. Oxford: Oxford University Press, 2009.
King, J. Christopher. *Origen on the Song of Songs as the Spirit of Scripture: The Bridegroom's Perfect Marriage Song*. Oxford: Oxford University Press, 2005.
Kittel G. (ed.). *Theological Dictionary of the New Testament*. Grand Rapids: William B. Eerdmans, 1967.
Klijn, F. J. "Jewish Christianity in Egypt." *The Roots of Egyptian Christianity*. B. A. Pearson and J. E. Goehring (eds.). Minneapolis: Fortress, 1986: 161-75.
Koester, Helmut. "Egypt." *Introduction to the New Testament, Volume II: History and Literature of Early Christianity*. 2nd ed. Berlin: de Gruyter, 2000: 225-30.
Kramarz, Andreas, LC. "Christian Reception of the 'New Music' Debate in the Church Fathers and Clement of Alexandria." *Greek and Roman Musical Studies* 6 (2018): 359-78.
—. "A Call for Universal Harmony: The 'New Song' in Scripture, Patristic Commentary, and Liturgy." *Antiphon* 26, 2 (2022): 105-33.
Lamberton, Robert. *Homer the Theologian: Neoplatonist Allegorical Reading and the Growth of the Epic Tradition*. Berkeley: University of California Press, 1989.
Langer, Rudolf E. "Alexandria – Shrine of Mathematics." *American Mathematical Monthly* 48, 2 (February 1941): 109-25.
Layton, Richard. *Didymus the Blind and His Circle in Late-Antique Alexandria: Virtue and Narrative in Biblical Scholarship*. Urbana: University of Illinois Press, 2004.
Leaney, Alfred R. C. *The Jewish and Christian World 200 BC to AD 200*. Cambridge: Cambridge University Press, 1984.
Leo XIII. *Aeterni Patris*. Vatican City: Libreria Vaticana Editrice, 1879.
Letter of Aristeas. Tr. H. St. J. Thackeray. London: SPCK, 1918.
Lewis, C. S. *An Experiment in Criticism*. Cambridge: Cambridge University Press, 1969.
—. "Myth Became Fact." In *God in the Dock: Essays on Theology and Ethics*. Grand Rapids: William B. Eerdmans, 2014: 54-60.
—. *The Abolition of Man*, London: Fount Paperbacks, 1978.
Lightfoot, Robert Henry. *The Gospel Message of St Mark*. Oxford: Oxford University Press, 1950.
Lilla, Salvatore R. C. *Clement of Alexandria: A Study in Christian Platonism and Gnosticism*. Oxford: Oxford University Press, 1971.
Liturgy of St Mark. G. J. Cumming (ed.). Rome: Pontificum Institutum Studiorem Orientalium, 1990.

Lodge, R.C. *Plato's Theory of Education*. New York: Harcourt, Brace, 1947.
Louth, Andrew. *Discerning the Mystery: An Essay on the Nature of Theology*. Oxford: Clarendon Press, 1984.
Lovejoy, A.O. *The Great Chain of Being*. New York: Harvard University Press, 1936.
Ludwig, Emil. *The Nile*. New York: The Viking Press, 1937.
Lynch, John. *Aristotle's School*. Berkeley: University of California Press, 1972.
J.G.M., "Review of E. Bevan, A History of Egypt under the Ptolemaic Dynasty." *The Journal of Hellenic Studies* 48, 1 (1928): 106-8.
Maertens, Thierry. *Histoire et Pastorale du Rituel du Catéchuménat et du Baptême*. Publications de Sanit-André, 1962.
Maier, Harry O. "Clement of Alexandria and the Care of the Self." *Journal of American Academy of Religion* 62.3 (1994): 719-45.
Markus, Robert A. *Saeculum: History and Society in the Theology of St Augustine*. Cambridge: Cambridge University Press, 1970.
———. "Church History and Early Church Historians." In D. Baker (ed.), *The Materials, Sources and Methods of Ecclesiastical History*. New York: Barnes and Noble Books, 1975: 1-17.
Marlowe, John. *The Golden Age of Alexandria*. London: Victor Gollancz, 1971.
Marrou, Henri. *A History of Education in Antiquity*. Tr. G. Lamb. London: Sheed and Ward, 1956 (Original French text published in 1948, as *Histoire de l'Education dans l'Antiquité*, Paris: Editions du Seuil).
———. *Saint Augustin et la fin de la culture antique*, 4th ed. Paris: E. de Boccard, 1958.
Mazza, Enrico. *Mystagogy: A Theology of Liturgy in the Patristic Age*. Tr. M. O'Connell. New York: Pueblo Publishing Company, 1989.
McDonald, James I. *Kerygma and Didache: The Articulation and Structure of the Earliest Christian Message*. Cambridge: Cambridge University Press, 1980.
McGuckin, John A. *St Cyril of Alexandria: the Christological Controversy, its History, Theology and Texts*. Leiden: E.J. Brill, 1994.
———. *At the Lighting of the Lamps: Hymns of the Ancient Church*. Harrisburg: Morehouse Publishing, 1995.
———. (ed.) *The Westminster Handbook to Origen*. Louisville, KY: Westminster John Knox Press, 2004.
Seeing the Glory: Studies in Patristic Theology. Yonkers, NY: St Vladimir's Seminary Press, 2017.
MacIntyre, Alasdair. *After Virtue*, London: Duckworth, 1985.
———. *Three Rival Theories of Moral Enquiry*. London: Duckworth, 1990.
Manetho. Tr. William G. Waddell. Loeb Classical Library. London: William Heinemann, 1940.
Méhat, André. *Étude sur les 'Stromates' de Clément d'Alexandrie*. Patristica Sorbonensia 7. Paris: du Seuil, 1966.
Mendelson, Alan. *Secular Education in Philo of Alexandria*. Cincinnati: Hebrew Union College Press, 1982.
Merton, Thomas. *Contemplation in a World of Action*. New York: Doubleday, 1973.
Miller, J.B. "The Role of Education in Jewish History." In L. Finklestein (ed.), *The Jews: Their History, Culture and Religion*. New York: Harper and Row, 1960.
Milne, Joseph G. *A History of Egypt Under Roman Rule*. London, 1898.

Momigliano, Arnaldo. "Pagan and Christian Historiography in the Fourth Century A.D." In A. Momigliano (ed.), *The Conflict Between Paganism and Christianity in the Fourth Century*. Oxford: The Clarendon Press, 1963: 79-99.

Monson, Andrew. "Late Ptolemaic Capitulation Taxes and the Poll Tax in Roman Egypt." *Bulletin of the American Society of Papyrologists* 51 (2014): 127-60.

Morello, Sebastian. *The World as God's Icon: Creator and Creation in the Platonic Thought of Thomas Aquinas*. Brooklyn, NY: Angelico Press, 2020.

Mortley, Raoul. *The Idea of Universal History from Hellenistic Philosophy to Early Christian Historiography*. Lewiston, Queenston and Lampeter: Edwin Mellen Press, 1996.

Noshy, Ibrahim. *The Arts in Ptolemaic Egypt*. Oxford: Oxford University Press, 1937.

Nautin, Pierre. *Origène: Sa vie et son œuvre*. Paris: Éditions Beauchesne, 1977.

Newman, John Henry. *Historical Sketches, Volume III*. London: Longmans, Green and Co. Ltd, 1885.

—. "Worship, a Preparation for Christ's Coming." *Plain and Parochial Sermons*, Vol. 5, no.1. London: Longman, Green, and Co., 1901.

—. *The Second Spring*. Introduction, notes and exercises by F.P. Donnelly SJ. Longmans, 1934.

—. *The Idea of a University*. London: Longmans Green, 1947.

—. *Apologia Pro Vita Sua*. M. Svaglic (ed.). Oxford: Oxford University Press, 1967.

—. *An Essay on the Development of Christian Doctrine*. Westminster, MD.: Christian Classics, Inc., 1968.

—. *Arians of the Fourth Century*. Introduction and notes by Rowan D. Williams. Notre Dame, IN: University of Notre Dame, 2001.

—. *Fifteen sermons preached before the University of Oxford between A.D. 1826 and 1843*. J.D. Earnest and G. Tracey (eds.). Oxford: Oxford University Press, 2006.

Nock, Arthur D. *Conversion, The Old and the New in Religion from Alexander the Great to Augustine of Hippo*. Baltimore: The John Hopkins University Press, 1998.

Nockles, Peter B. *The Oxford Movement in Context: Anglican High Churchmanship 1760-1857*. Cambridge: Cambridge University Press, 1994.

Nongbri, Brent. *God's Library: The Archeology of the Earliest Christian Manuscripts*. New Haven: Yale University Press, 2018.

O'Brien, Carl Séan and Sarah Klitenic Wear. "The Figure of the *Diadochos*, from Socrates to the Late Antique Athenian School of Neoplatonism." In J.F. Finamore and S.K. Wear (eds.), *Defining Platonism: Essays in Honor of the 75th Birthday of John M. Dillon*. Steubenville: Franciscan University Press, 2017: 253-70.

Oden, Thomas C. *How Africa Shaped the Christian Mind: Rediscovering the African Seedbed of Western Christianity*. Downers Grove, IL: IVP Academic, 2007.

—. *Early Libyan Christianity*. Downers Grove, IL: IVP Academic, 2011.

—. *The African Memory of Mark: Reassessing Early Church Tradition*. Downers Grove, IL: IVP Academic, 2011.

—. *A Change of Heart: A Personal and Theological Memoir*. Downers Grove, IL: IVP Academic, 2014.

———. *The Rebirth of African Orthodoxy: Return to Foundations*. Nashville: Abingdon Press, 2016.

Oesterley, William O.E. "Egypt and Israel." In S.R.K. Glanville (ed.), *The Legacy of Egypt*. Oxford: The Clarendon Press, 1942: 218-48.

O'Leary, De Lacy. "The Egyptian Contribution to Christianity." In S.R.K. Glanville (ed.), *The Legacy of Egypt*. Oxford: The Clarendon Press, 1942: 300-331.

Oliver, Willem H. "The Heads of the Catechetical School in Alexandria." *Verbum et Ecclesia* 36, 1 (2015): Art. #1386, 14 pages. http://dx.doi.org/10.4102/ve.v36i1/1386.

Origen. *Commentary on the Gospel of John*. Introduction and notes A.E. Brooke. Cambridge: Cambridge University Press, 1896.

———. *Exhortation to Martyrdom*. Tr. H. Chadwick. Library of Christian Classics, Vol. 2: Alexandrian Christianity. Philadelphia: The Westminster Press, 1954.

———. *On Prayer*. Tr. J.J. O'Meara. Ancient Christian Writers, Vol. 19. London: Longmans, Green and Co., 1954.

———. *The Song of Songs: Commentary and Homilies*. Tr. and notes R.P. Lawson. Ancient Christian Writers, Vol. 26. New York: The Newman Press, 1956.

———. *Contra Celsum*. Tr. H. Chadwick. Cambridge: Cambridge University Press, 1965.

———. *Homilies on Genesis and Exodus*. Tr. R.E. Heine. Washington, D.C.: Catholic University of America Press, 1982.

———. *Homilies on Numbers*. Tr. Thomas P. Scheck. Ancient Christian Texts. Downers Grove, IL: InterVarsity Press, 2009.

———. *Homilies on Jeremiah*. Tr. John Clark Smith. Washington, D.C.: Catholic University of America Press, 1998.

———. *Homilies on Ezekiel*. In *Origen of Alexandria: Exegetical Works on Ezekiel*. Roger Peace (ed.), Tr. Mischa Hooker. Ipswich: Chieftain Publishing, 2014.

———. *On First Principles*. Tr. G.W. Butterworth. Notre Dame: Christian Classics, 2013.

Osborn, Eric. "Teaching and Writing in the First Chapter of the *Stromateis* of Clement of Alexandria." *Journal of Theological Studies*. New Series, 10, 2 (1959): 335-43.

———. *The Beginning of Christian Philosophy*. Cambridge: Cambridge University Press, 1981.

———. *Clement of Alexandria*. Cambridge: Cambridge University Press, 2005.

———. "One Hundred Years of Books on Clement." *Vigiliae Christianae* 60, 4 (2006): 367-88.

Parker, Charles P. "Musonius in Clement." *Harvard Studies in Classical Philology* 12 (1901): 191-200.

Parsons, Edward A. *The Alexandrian Library: Glory of the Hellenic World*. London: The Elsevier Press, 1952.

Pater, Walter. *Imaginary Portraits*. London: MacMillan and Co., 1914.

Patterson, L.G. "The divine became human: Irenaean themes in Clement of Alexandria." *Studia Patristica* 31 (1997): 497-516.

Patterson, Stephen. "The Secret Gospel of Mark: An Introduction." In R.J. Miller (ed.), *The Complete Gospels: Annotated Scholars Version*. Santa Rosa: Polebridge Press, 1994: 408-11.

Paul VI. *Africae terrarium*. AAS 59 (1967): 1074-5.
—. *Evangelii nuntiandi*. Vatican City: Libreria Vaticana Editrice, 1975.
Peace, Richard V. *Conversion in the New Testament: Paul and the Twelve*. Grand Rapids: William B. Eerdmans, 1999.
Pearson, Birger A. "Friedlander Revisited: Alexandrian Judaism and Gnostic Origins." *Studia Philonica* 2 (1973): 23-29.
—. "Christians and Jews in First Century Alexandria." *Harvard Theological Review* 79 (1986): 206-16.
—. "Earliest Christianity in Egypt: Some Observations." In B.A. Pearson and J. E Goehring (eds.), *The Roots of Egyptian Christianity*. Philadelphia: Fortress Press, 1986: 132-60.
—. *Gnosticism, Judaism, and Egyptian Christianity*. Philadelphia: Fortress Press, 1990.
—. "The Problem of 'Jewish Gnostic' Literature." In *The Emergence of the Christian Religion: Essays in Early Christianity*. Harrisburg: Trinity Press International, 1997: 122-46.
—. "Ancient Alexandria in the 'Acts of Mark.'" In *Gnosticism and Christianity in Roman and Coptic Egypt*. London: T&T Clark International, 2004: 100-113.
—. "Egypt." In M.M. Mitchell and F.M. Young (eds.). *The Cambridge History of Christianity, Vol.1: Origins to Constantine*. Cambridge: Cambridge University Press, 2006: 331-50.
—. "Earliest Christianity in Egypt: Further Observations." In J.E. Goehring and J.A. Timbie (eds.), *The World of Early Egyptian Christianity: Language Literature and Social Context*. Washington, D.C.: Catholic University of America Press, 2007: 97-112.
Philo. *Complete Works*. Tr. C.F.H. Colson. Loeb Classical Library. Cambridge, MA: Harvard University Press, 1985.
Photius. *Bibliotheca*. Codex 118. R. Henry (ed.). Paris, 1969.
Pieper, Josef. "The Philosophical Act." In *Leisure: The Basis of Culture*. London: Faber and Faber, 1952.
—. "Corporeal Memory: the Concrete Things of History as Living Reminders." *Communio* XLVIII, 2 (Summer 2021): 405-19.
Pius XII. "Address to Groups of 'Christian Rebirth.'" AAS 39 (1947): 58-63.
Plato. *Complete Works*. Edited with introduction and notes by John M. Cooper. Indianapolis: Hackett, 1997.
Pliny. *Natural History*. Tr. H. Rackham. Loeb Classical Library. London: William Heinemann, 1952.
Plotinus. *Enneads*. Tr. S. McKenna. London: Faber, 1956.
Plutarch. *Lives*. Tr. B. Perrin. Loeb Classical Library. London: William Heinemann, 1959.
—. *Moralia*. Tr. F.C. Babbitt. Loeb Classical Library. London: William Heinemann, 1962.
Polybius. *Histories*. Tr. W.R. Paton. Loeb Classical Library. London: William Heinemann, 1922-68.
Pompa, Klaas Jan. "Patristic Evaluation of Culture." *Philosophia Reformata* 38 (1973): 97-113.

Porphyry. *Vita Plotini*. In *Plotini Opera*, I.P. Henry and H. Schwyzer (eds.) Oxford Classical Texts. Oxford: Clarendon Press, 1964.

Pontifical Council for the Promotion of New Evangelization. *Compendium on the New Evangelization*. Vatican City: Libreria Editrice Vaticana, 2014.

——. *The Directory for Catechesis*. Vatican City: Libreria Editrice Vaticana, 2020.

Potts, Daniel T. "Before Alexandria: Libraries in the Ancient Near East." In R. MacLeod *The Library of Alexandria: Centre of Learning in the Ancient World*. London: I.B. Tauris, 2000: 19-34.

Pouchelle, Patrick. "*Kyropaideia* versus *Paideia Kyriou*: The Semantic Transformation of Paideia and Cognates in the Translated Books of the Septuagint." In K.M. Hogan, M. Goff and E. Wasserman (eds.), *Pedagogy in Ancient Judaism and Early Christianity*. Atlanta: SBL Press, 2017: 101-34.

Pouderon, Bernard. *D'Athènes à Alexandrie: études sur Athénagore et les origines de la philosophie chrétienne*. Louvain: Editions Peeters, 1997.

Ratzinger, Joseph. "Introductory article and Chapter 1: The Dignity of the Human Person." In H. Vorgrimler (ed.), *Commentary on the Documents of Vatican II*, Vol. 5. New York: Herder and Herder, 1969: 115-63.

——. "Sources and Transmission of the Faith", *Communio*, X, 1 (Spring 1983): 17-34.

——. *The Ratzinger Report: An Exclusive Interview on the State of the Church*, with Vittorio Messori. Tr. S. Attanasio and G. Harrison. San Francisco: Ignatius Press, 1985.

——. *Principles of Catholic Theology: Building Stones for a Fundamental Theology*. Tr. Sr. Mary Frances McCarthy, SND. San Francisco: Ignatius Press, 1987.

——. *Introduction to Christianity*. Tr. J.R. Foster. San Francisco: Ignatius Press, 2004.

——. *The Unity of the Nations*. Tr. B. Ramsey. Washington, D.C.: Catholic University of America Press, 2015.

Rétif, André. "Qu'est-ce que le Kérygme?" *Nouvelle Revue Théologique* LXXI (1949): 910-22.

Reumann, John Henry. *The Use of Oikonomia and Related Terms in Greek Sources to about 100 A.D. as a Background for Patristic Applications*. Dissertation. University of Pennsylvania, 1957. http://repository.upenn.edu/dissertations/AAI0023631.

Rich, Audrey N.M. "The Platonic Ideas as the Thoughts of God." *Mnemosyne* 7, Fasc. 2 (1954): 123-33.

Ritter, A.M. "De Polycarpe à Clément: aux origins d'Alexandrie chrétienne." In ΑΛΕΞΑΝΔΡΙΝΑ: *Hellénisme, judaïsme et chirstianisme à Alexandrie. Mélanges offers au P. Claude Mondésart*. Paris: Éditions du Cerf, 1987.

Ritter, Heinrich. "The Christian Schools of Alexandria." *The Dublin Review* III, 6 (July-Oct 1864): 278-310.

Rius-Camps, Josep and Jenny Reid-Heimerdinger. *The Message of the Codex Bezae: A Comparison with the Alexandrian Tradition: Volume 4: Acts 18:24-28:31*. London: T&T Clark, 2009.

Roberts, Colin H. "The Greek Papyri." In S.R.K. Glanville (ed.), *The Legacy of Egypt*. Oxford: The Clarendon Press, 1942: 249-82.

——. *Manuscript, Society and Belief in Early Christian Egypt*. Oxford: Oxford University Press, 1979.

Roman Martyrology. Baltimore: John Murphy and Co., 1898.
Robinson, John A.T. *Redating the New Testament*. Philadelphia: Westminster Press, 1976.
Rubenson, Samuel. "From School to Patriarchate: Aspects on the Christianisation of Alexandria." In G. Hinge and J.A. Krasilnikov (eds.), *Alexandria: A Cultural and Religious Melting Pot*. Aarhus: Aarhus University Press, 2009: 144-57.
Rudolph, Conrad. "Macro/Microcosm at Vézelay: the Narthax Portal and Non-elite Participation in Elite Spirituality." *Speculum* 96, 3 (July 2021): 601-61.
Rufinus. *The Church History of Rufinus of Aquileia, Books 10 and 11*. Tr. P.R. Amidon. Oxford: Oxford University Press, 1997.
Runia, David T. *Philo in Early Christian Literature*. Von Gorcum, Assen: Fortress Press, 1993.
Russell, Norman. *Lives of the Desert Fathers, Historia Monachorum in Aegypto*. Cistercian Studies No. 34. London: Mowbray, 1983.
Saghy, M. "Monica, the ascetic." *Studia Patristica* XCI (2017): 363-76.
Sayers, Dorothy. "Charles Williams: A Poet's Critic." In *The Poetry of Search and the Poetry of Statement*. London: Victor Gollancz, 1963: 69-90.
Schefer, Christina. "Rhetoric as Part of an Initiation into the Mysteries: A New Interpretation of the Platonic *Phaedrus*." In A.N. Michelini (ed.), *Plato as Author: The Rhetoric of Philosophy*. Leiden: Brill, 2003: 175-96.
Schildgen, Brenda Dean. *Power and Prejudice: The Reception of the Gospel of Mark*. Detroit: Wayne State University Press, 1999.
Schliesser, Benjamin. "Why Did Paul Skip Alexandria? Paul's Missionary Strategy and the Rise of Christianity in Alexandria." *New Testament Studies* 67, 2 (April 2021): 260-83.
Selwyn, E.G. *The First Epistle of St Peter*. London: MacMillan, 1946.
Seneca. *Epistulae Morales*. Tr. R.M. Gunmere. Loeb Classical Library. London: William Heinemann, 1967.
Sextus Empiricus. *Outlines of Scepticism*. Tr. J. Annas and J. Barnes. Cambridge: Cambridge University Press, 1994.
Shepherd of Hermas. In M.W. Holmes (ed. and tr.), *The Apostolic Fathers*. 3rd ed. Grand Rapids: Baker Academic, 2007.
Shubert, Stephen Blake. "The Oriental Origins of the Alexandrian Library." *Libri* 43, 2 (1993): 142-72.
Simon, Marcel. *Verus Israel: a study of the relations between Jews and Christians in the Roman Empire AD 135-425*. Oxford: Oxford University Press, 1996.
Smith, Morton. *Clement of Alexandria and a Secret Gospel of Mark*. Cambridge MA, 1973.
—. "Clement of Alexandria and Secret Mark: The Score at the End of the First Decade." *Harvard Theological Review* 75, 4 (October 1982): 449-61.
Snyder, H. Gregory. *Teachers and Texts in the Ancient World: Philosophers, Jews and Christians*. London: Routledge, 2000.
Socrates. *History of the Church*. London: Henry G. Bohn, 1853.
Sozomen. *Ecclesiastical History*. Tr. C.D. Hartranft. *Nicene and Post-Nicene Fathers, Second Series*, Vol. 2. P. Schaff and H. Wace (eds.). Buffalo: Christian Literature Publishing Co., 1890.

Stanford, William B. *The Ulysses Theme: A Study in the Adaptability of a Traditional Hero.* Oxford: Oxford University Press, 1954.

Stapert, Calvin. *A New Song for an Old World: Musical Thought in the Early Church.* Grand Rapids: William B. Eerdmans, 2007.

Starr, James and Troels Engberg-Pederson (eds.). *Early Christian Paraenesis in Context.* Berlin, 2004.

Stanton, Graham N. *A Gospel for a New People: Studies in Matthew.* Louisville: Westminster Press, 1993.

Steiner, George. "On Difficulty." In *On Difficulty and Other Essays.* Oxford: Oxford University Press, 1978: 18–47.

Sterling, Gregory. "The School of Sacred Laws: The Social Setting of Philo's Treatises." *Virgiliae Christianae* 53 (1999): 148–64.

——. "'Philo Has Not Been Used Half Enough': The Significance of Philo of Alexandria for the Study of the New Testament." *Perspectives in Religious Studies* 30 (2003): 251–69.

——. "Philo's School: The Social Setting of Ancient Commentaries." In B. Wyss, et al. (eds.), *Sophisten im Hellenismus und Kaiserzeit.* Tubingen: Mohr Siebeck, 2017.

Stewart, Columba, OSB. "Rethinking the History of Monasticism East and West: A Modest *tour d'horizon*." In S. Bhattacharji, R. Williams and D. Mattos (eds.), *Prayer and Thought in Monastic Tradition: Essays in Honour of Benedicta Ward, SLG.* London: Bloomsbury, 2014: 3–16.

Stock, Augustine, OSB. *Call to Discipleship: A Literary Study of Mark's Gospel.* Wilmington, DE: Michael Glazier, 1982.

Strabo. *Geography.* Tr. H. L. Jones. Loeb Classical Library. Cambridge, MA: Harvard University Press, 1932.

Strousma, Guy G. *The End of Sacrifice: Religious Transformation in Late Antiquity.* Tr. S. Emmanuel. Chicago: University of Chicago Press, 2009.

Swancutt, Diana M. "Paraenesis in Light of Protrepsis." in J. Starr and T. Engberg-Pedersen (eds.), *Early Christian Paraenesis in Context.* New York: Walter de Gruyter, 2004: 113–55.

Tanner, Norman P., SJ (ed.). *Decrees of the Ecumenical Councils, Volume One: Nicea I to Lateran V.* London: Sheed and Ward, 1990.

Tatius. *Clitophon and Leucippe.* Tr. S. Gaselee. Loeb Classical Library. London: William Heinemann, 1917.

Taylor, Vincent. *The Gospel According to St. Mark.* London, Macmillan, 1952.

Tertullian. *Adversus Marcionem.* In A. Roberts and J. Donaldson (eds.), *The Ante-Nicene Fathers, Vol III.* American Edition. Grand Rapids: Wm. B. Eerdmans, reprinted 1978: 269–476.

Thomson, Stuart Rowley. "Apostolic Authority: Reading and Writing Legitimacy in Clement of Alexandria." *Studia Patristica* LXVI, M. Vinzent (ed.). Leuven: Peeters, 2013: 19–32.

Thornton, T.C.G. "1 Peter, a Paschal Liturgy?" *Journal of Theological Studies.* New Series 12, 1 (April 1961): 14–26.

Tollinton, Richard. *Clement of Alexandria: A Study in Christian Liberalism.* London: Williams and Norgate, 1914.

Trigg, Joseph W. *Origen: The Bible and Philosophy in the Third Century*. Atlanta: John Knox Press, 1983.
Tolan, Daniel J. "The Flight of the All-One to the All-One: The φυγὴ μόνου πρὸς μόνον as the Basis of Plotinian Altruism." *Harvard Theological Review* 114, 4 (Oct 2021): 469–90.
Tuccinardi, E. "A Stylometric Analysis of the Mar Saba Letter Attributed to Clement of Alexandria," *Vigiliae Christianae*, 74, 3 (2020): 265–88.
Turck, André. "Aux Origines de Catéchuménat," *Revues des Sciences philosophiques et théologiques* 48, 1 (January 1964): 20–31.
Tzamalikos, Panayiotis. *Origen: Cosmology and Ontology of Time*. Leiden: Brill, 2006.
Van den Broek, Roelof. "The Christian 'School' of Alexandria in the Second and Third Centuries." In J.W. Drijvers and A.A. MacDonald (eds.), *Centers of Learning: Learning and Location in Pre-Modern Europe and the Near East*. Leiden: Brill, 1995: 39–47.
———. *Studies in Gnosticism and Alexandrian Christianity*, Leiden: Brill, 1996.
Van den Hoek, Annewies. *Clement of Alexandria and his Use of Philo in the "Stromateis": an Early Christian Shaping of a Jewish Model*. Leiden: Brill, 1988.
———. "How Alexandrian was Clement of Alexandria? Reflections on Clement and his Alexandrian Background." *Heythrop Journal* 31 (1990): 179–94.
———. "The 'Catechetical' School of Early Christian Alexandria and Its Philonic Heritage." *The Harvard Theological Review* 90, 1 (January 1997): 59–87.
———. "Origen and the Intellectual Heritage of Alexandria: Continuity or Disjunction?" *Origeniana Quarta*. R.J. Daly (ed.). Leuven: Peeters, 1992: 40–50.
van Iersel, Bas E.F. *Mark: A Reader-Response Commentary*. Tr. W.H. Bisscheroux. Sheffield: Sheffield Academic Press, 1998.
Vatican Council II. *Ad Gentes*. Vatican City: Libreria Vaticana Editrice, 1965.
———. *Christus Dominus*. Vatican City: Libreria Vaticana Editrice, 1965.
———. *Lumen gentium*. Vatican City: Libreria Vaticana Editrice, 1964.
———. *Presbyterorum ordinis*. Vatican City: Libreria Vaticana Editrice, 1965.
———. *Sacrosanctum Concilium*. Vatican City: Libreria Vaticana Editrice, 1963.
Verdoner, Marie. *Narrated Reality: The Historia Ecclesiastica of Eusebius of Caesarea*. Frankfurt am Main: Peter Lang, 2011.
Versnel, Henk S. *Coping with the Gods*. Leiden: Brill, 2011.
Watson, Francis. "Beyond Suspicion: On the Authorship of the Mar Saba Letter and the Secret Gospel of Mark." *Journal of Theological Studies*, New Series 61, 1 (April 2010): 128–70.
Watts, Edward J. *Riots in Alexandria: Tradition and Group Dynamics in Late Antique Pagan and Christian Communities*. Berkeley: University of California Press, 2010.
Wheeler, Mortimer. *Rome Beyond the Imperial Frontiers*. New York: Philosophical Library, Inc., 1955.
Weil, Simone. *Gravity and Grace*. New York: G.P. Putnam's Sons, 1952.
———. *Lectures on Philosophy*. London: Routledge, Keagan and Paul, 1978.
Widdicombe, Peter. *The Fatherhood of God from Origen to Athanasius*. Rev. ed. Oxford: Clarendon Press, 2004.

Wilkins, Michael J. *Discipleship in the Ancient World and Matthew's Gospel*. 2nd ed. Eugene: Wipf & Stock Publishers, 2015.
Willey, Petroc. "The *Catechism* and the New Evangelization." In P. Grogan and K. Kim (eds.), *The New Evangelization: Faith, People, Context and Practice*. London: Bloomsbury T&T Clark, 2015: 209-20.
—. and Scott Sollom. "The *Catechism of the Catholic Church*: Some Anniversary Considerations." *International Journal for Catechesis and Evangelization* 3, 1 (2022): 49-64.
Williams, Rowan D. *The Wound of Knowledge*. London: Darton, Longman and Todd, 1979.
—. "Introduction." J. H. Newman, *Arians of the Fourth Century*. Notre Dame: University of Notre Dame, 2001.
—. *Arius: Heresy and Tradition*, Rev. ed. Grand Rapids: William B. Eerdmans, 2001.
Willis, Geoffrey G. *A History of the Early Roman Liturgy: To the Death of Pope Gregory the Great*. London: Boydell and Brewer, 1994.
Wilken, Robert L. "Alexandria: A School for Training in Virtue." In P. Henry (ed.), *Schools of Thought in the Christian Tradition*. Philadelphia: Fortress, 1984: 15-30.
Witt, R. E. *Albinus and the History of Middle Platonism*. Cambridge: Cambridge University Press, 1937.
Wood, Simon P. "Introduction." *Clement of Alexandria: Christ the Educator*. Washington D.C.: Catholic University of America Press, 1954.
Wrede, William. *The Messianic Secret*. Tr. J.C.G. Grieg. Cambridge: James Clarke & Co., 1971.
Wright, N.T. *Jesus and the Victory of God: Christian Origins and the Question of God*, Vol. 2. Minneapolis: Fortress Press, 1996.
Yarnold, Edward, SJ. *The Awe-inspiring Rites of Initiation*. 2nd ed. Edinburgh: T&T Clark, 1994.
Young, Frances M. "The God of the Greeks and the Nature of Religious Language." In W.R. Schoedel and R.L. Wilken (eds.), *Early Christian Literature and the Classical Intellectual Tradition*. Paris: Editions Beauchesne, 1979: 45-74.
—. *From Nicaea to Chalcedon: A Guide to the Literature and its Background*. London: SCM, 1983.
—. *Biblical Exegesis and the Formation of Christian Culture*. Cambridge: Cambridge University Press, 1997.
—. "Towards a Christian *paideia*." In M.M. Mitchell and F.M. Young (eds.), *From Origins to Constantine: Cambridge History of Christianity Vol. 1*. Cambridge, 2006: 485-500.
Young, N.H. "παιδαγωγός: The Social Setting of a Pauline Metaphor." *Novum Testamentum* 29 (1987): 150-76.
Zuntz, G. *The Text of the Epistles: A Disquisition Upon the Corpus Paulinum*. London, 1953.
Zurawski, Jason M. "Mosaic Torah as Encyclical Paideia: Reading Paul's Allegory of Hagar and Sarah in Light of Philo of Alexandria." In K.M. Hogan, M. Goff and E. Wasserman (eds.), *Pedagogy in Ancient Judaism and Early Christianity*. Atlanta: SBL Press, 2017: 283-307.

INDEX OF NAMES AND SELECTED SUBJECTS

Abd-el-Ghani, Mohammed, 56n82
Africa, African, xv, 2, 9–10, 21–23, 31, 35n13, 81–82, 304
Africa, Thomas, 95n23
Agus, Jacob B, 48n56, 53
Alcinous, 95n26
Alexander the Great, 4, 31–35, 42, 45, 47, 54, 167–68
Alexander, bishop, 109n79, 269, 273
Anthony of the Desert, 70, 81, 273
Anthropology, Christian anthropology, 169–70, 183–84, 189–93, 235–45, 283
Antioch, Antiochene, 86, 103, 288n138
Apostolic, apostolic succession, apostolic Tradition, 20, 64, 72, 78, 87, 97–102, 106–11, 159, 264
Aquinas, Thomas, 26, 192–93, 301n41
Aristeas, 39–40, 49–50
Aristotle, Aristotelianism, Peripatetic, 25, 33n4, 50n61, 91–96, 125–26, 129n167, 147–48, 156n86, 167–70, 174, 179–80, 193, 201, 237–43, 249, 269–70, 274
Arius, 73n40, 107, 288–89
Asceticism, ascetical practice, virtue, 69–72, 91, 96–97, 122, 134–35, 140–42, 155–56, 161, 182, 186, 196, 201, 211, 213–17, 220–22, 227–41, 243n103, 286–87
Athanasius, 3, 70, 73n40, 81–82, 102–3, 108, 187–88, 273
Athenaeus, 43n37, 46, 168n14
Athenagoras, 101–2, 111n87
Augustine, 6n10, 9–10, 26, 45n42, 77, 80, 151, 161n107, 166n5, 200–1, 275n90, 291

Bagnell, Roger S., 46
Baptism, baptism and faith, 2, 9–10, 13–14, 24, 62, 79, 111, 123–24, 188, 198–99, 212–17, 220–26, 228–29, 244, 246, 251, 253–54, 296–303
Barnard, Leslie W., 79n59, 85, 87n97, 102n48
Barnes, Timothy D., 73n40
Barrett, C.K., 272n75
Basilides, 67, 298n28

Bauer, Walter, 66
Bayliss, Grant D., 121n132, 122
Beauty, via pulchritudinis, 16–17, 26–27, 31–32, 34, 50n61, 113–14, 157–58, 186–87, 208–12, 218–20, 261–62, 271, 287
Beeson, Trevor, 11n28
Behr, John, 100, 181n74, 223–24, 236n72, 245n115, 250n139
Benedict XVI, Ratzinger, Joseph, xvii, 8, 12, 21n53, 22, 45n42, 59, 164, 166, 184n79, 195, 219, 221
Best, Ernest, 299n32
Bevan, Edwyn, 44n38, 55n79
Bigg, Charles, 198n13
Bingham, D. Jeffrey, 155n83
Black, C. Clifton, 80, 85–88, 291–92
Blevins, James L., 295n18
Blosser, Benjamin P., 244n106, 283
Bobertz, Charles A., 293–94, 300n36
Boersma, Gerard, 173n35
Bremmer, Jan M., 258n7
Brock, Sebastian P., 40n25, 138n23
Brown, Blanche, 34n9
Brown, Peter, 164n2, 239n87, 244n105
Brown, Raymond E., SS, 301n41
Bruce, F.F., 64n4
Brumbaugh, Robert S., 208n57
Budge, E.A. Wallis, 82n71, 167n12, 273n81
Butler, Alfred J., 46n44

Caesarea, 74–76, 91, 103–5, 118–19, 127–28, 198n10, 212, 215, 221–22, 270
Camilletti, Fabio A., xvin2
Cannuyer, Christian, 120n125
Carrington, Philip, 113
Casel, Odo, OSB, 258
Catechism of the Catholic Church, 5n8, 6–8, 19n48, 218n105, 219, 250n140, 254, 256, 280n106, 285–86, 298
Catechumenate, catechumenal, xiii–xiv, xv, 4, 6n10, 8–14, 22–23, 26–28, 62, 78–80, 88–89, 106, 109–11, 126, 194, 197, 200–20, 221–56

Celsus, 153, 166, 199, 210, 215, 229n38, 244, 283n115
Chadwick, Henry, 86, 106n65, 125, 160n105, 170n22, 180n65, 199n16, 223n14, 243n103, 260n18
Cherniss, Harold F., 93n19
Chesterton, G.K., 249
Christ
   All-Beautiful, 208-12, 261
   Bridegroom, 245-46, 257, 264-65
   Child, 142n37, 218, 236, 246, 250-52, 260, 271
   Image, 185-86, 188, 211-14
   Logos, Word, xiii, 24, 62, 81, 91, 114-16, 148, 153-55, 159-60, 177-82, 183-88, 205-9, 211-12, 219, 224-25, 227, 236, 244, 249, 253, 259, 269, 271, 282, 299, 303, 306
   Mystery of Love, 198, 217, 229-34, 257-84
   New Adam, 214, 299
   Pedagogue, 26n71, 28, 142, 144-60, 204-5, 221-53
   Redeemer and Savior, 24, 73, 142, 157, 173, 197-98, 212, 231, 272
   Son of the Father, 114, 142, 156-57, 181, 236, 246-48, 260-61
   Teacher, 7, 26n71, 28, 109, 115-16, 148, 204-5, 227-28, 252-53, 257, 265-84
   Wisdom, 177-82
Cicero, 43n37, 92, 201, 269
Cleopatra, 4, 41, 43n37, 45, 55-56
Clark, Gillian, 166n5
Clark, Stephen R.L., xi, 97n33, 147n50, 170n20, 173n32, 241n94
Clarke, Martin L., 200n20, 276n88
Clarke, W. Norris, SJ, 192n102, 193n107
Clement of Alexandria: life and writings, 109-10, 111-16, 194; leadership of school, 3, 89-90, 97-103
Clement of Rome, 146
Cointet, Pierre de, 189n95
Cole, Basil, OP, 239n84
Coleridge, Samuel T., 15
Collins, John J., 143n41, 152n71
Colmer, John, 304nn3,6
Constantinople, 10n21, 44n37, 72n35, 81n68, 87n95, 99
Cooper, Adam, 184n79, 277

Cornford, F.M., 170n19
Cranz, F. Edward, 76n51
Crehan, Joseph H., SJ, 282n113
Cribiore, Raffaella, 145n45
Criddle, A.H., 112n92
Cross, F.L., 294n12
Crouzel, Henri, SJ, 116n108, 125n150
Culture, Christian culture, inculturation, custom, xiii, xvii, 2, 5-6, 11-13, 17-20, 21n57, 24-28, 31-33, 37-44, 49-52, 56, 59-61, 68-72, 76-77, 89, 123-25, 134-37, 144, 149-50, 152-53, 160-62, 172-73, 189-92, 206, 211, 255-56, 265, 274-75, 287
Curriculum, liberal arts, 1, 25, 61, 93, 118, 126-29, 133-38, 140-44, 155-56, 161, 280-81
Cyril of Alexandria, xvi, 3, 19, 81, 165n4, 273
Cyril of Jerusalem, 9, 10n21, 230n43

Dabricourt, Georges, 292n7
Daniélou, Jean, SJ, 5n7, 9, 20n51, 118n115, 282n114
Darius, 32
Davis, Harrold T., 37n19
Davis, Stephen J., 104n57
Dawson, David, 297n26
Delia, Diana, 46n44, 48n55
Demetrius, bishop, 75, 90, 103-7, 127
Demetrius of Phalarium, 37, 38n21, 49n60, 147n49, 168
Didymus the Blind, xv-xvi, 3, 54, 70, 73n39, 98, 101, 103, 111, 121-22, 164, 184n79, 212n85, 214, 245, 275, 277
Dillon, John, 92n16, 129n167, 151n64, 168-70
Dio Chrysostom, 35, 36n14
Diodorus Siculus, 46, 48n57, 78n58
Diogenes Laertius, 33n4, 126n152, 269n57
Directory for Catechesis (2020), 6-12, 17-19, 24-25, 28n81, 59, 162-63, 192, 217-20, 248n129, 253, 256, 285-87, 289nn141, 142
Disciplina arcani, 227-34
Dix, Gregory, OSB, 81
Drijvers, Han J.W., 67n16
Dujarier, Michel, 10n20, 23n63, 27n76, 257n2

Index of Names and Selected Subjects 329

Dulles, Avery, 2 n2
Dunn, James D. G., 100 n41, 258 n3
Dzielska, Maria, 165 n4

Echle, Harry A,, 222 n11
Edwards, Mark, 174 n42, 181 nn72,74, 201 n23
Egypt, Egyptian, Copt, Coptic, 4, 9, 21-23, 31-48, 54-58, 62-72, 73 n40, 78-88, 99, 102, 104, 116, 120, 138 n20, 140 n33, 142 n37, 145 n45, 151-53, 167-68, 171 n24, 196 n5, 212, 215, 229, 231 n53, 243 n103, 258, 265 n44, 273, 298, 300, 304-5
Ellens, J. H., 39 n23
Elliott, James K., 86 n92
Eliot, T. S., 18
El Masri, Iris Habib, 102 n49
Emmel, Stephen, 273 n80
Emmett, Laurence, 200 n22
Empereur, Jean-Yves, 16 n37
Epictetus, 228 n36, 236
Epicurus, Epicurean, 1, 91-93, 95-96, 174
Eusebius of Caesarea, 33 n5, 45, 52 n67, 54 n76, 63, 71-78, 81-88, 90-91, 98-110, 117-28, 153-54, 181, 201-2, 262, 269, 275
Evangelization, new evangelization, xiii, xvii, 1,6, 8-14, 17-20, 22-24, 70, 79, 89, 123-24, 160, 189, 202-3, 217-20, 255, 287, 305

Farrer, Austin, 302
Ferguson, Everett, 10 n20, 223 n13
Ferguson, John, 60 n97, 205-6
Field, Anne, 10 n20
Finn, Thomas M., 10 n20, 123 n140
Fisichella, Rino, 11, 18 n42, 286
Forster, E. M., 304-5
Frankfurter, David, 69 n20, 152
Frend, W. H. C., 65 n7

Gadamer, Hans-Georg, 14
Gardiner, Alan H., 40 n28
Gardner, Helen, 302-3
Garrett, Duane, 139 n28
General Catechetical Directory (1971), 256
General Directory for Catechesis (1997), 162 n109, 253, 256

Girgis, Samir Fawzy, 86 n90
Glad, Clarence E., 227 n30
Glucker, John, 93 n18, 94 n20
Gnostic, Gnosticism, 52, 65-68, 71, 98, 111, 114, 116, 119, 155-56, 160, 194-200, 213, 229, 243-44, 253, 296-98
Goehring, James E., 70 n25
Grant, Robert M., 74 n45, 107 n69, 278 n100
Green, Henry, 57
Gregory of Nazianzus, 121
Gregory of Nyssa, 108
Gregory Thaumaturgus, 91, 128-29, 174-75, 178, 182, 270-71
Griffith, Sidney H., 69 n24
Griggs, C. Wilfred, 104 n57, 112 n89
Grindheim, Siguard, 64 n4
Guardini, Romano, 288 n136
Guillaumont, Antoine, 71 n31
Guthrie, W. K. C., 95 n23, 135 nn9,10
Gwynn, David M., 70 n27, 103 n54, 107 n69, 273 n79

Haas, Christopher, 35 n11, 46 n45
Haas, Julian, OFM Cap, 302
Hadot, Pierre, 94, 96-97, 108 n71, 164 n2, 186 n85, 267, 280
Hanson, Richard P. C., 279 n101
Hardie, W. F. R., 241 n95
Harmless, William, 6 n10, 10 n20
Hedstrom, Darlene L. Brooks, 70 n25
Heine Ronald E., 5, 37 n18, 50 n62, 65 n8, 66 n11, 67 n15, 100 n40, 106 n54, 107 n68, 108 n72, 117 n112, 118, 165 n3, 182 n74, 198 n10, 298 n28
Hengel, Martin, 49 n58, 85, 88 n102, 128 n162, 178 n52
Hippolytus, 9, 77, 91 n10, 126, 215, 221, 254 n165, 301
Hofinger, Johannes, 218
Hogan, Karina Martin, 142 n37
Holiness, 11, 28, 71, 83, 116, 188, 194, 199, 230, 257, 269, 276, 289
Holte, Ragnar, 166 n5
Homer, 39, 51 n65, 119, 136, 138, 148, 152, 182-83, 190, 223 n16, 240 n90, 283 n115
Honigman, Sylvie, 39-40, 50 n60
Honigmann, Ernest, 78 n58
Hooker, Morna, 295

Horace, 133
Hurtado, Larry W., 64n3

Iersel, Bas E. F, van, 85n85
India, 33, 36, 39, 45, 201-2
Inowlocki, Sabriana, 71
Irenaeus, 87n96, 88, 110n82, 155-58, 161n107, 199
Isichei, Elizabeth, 21n56
Isocrates, 60, 91n11, 133

Jaeger, Werner, 33, 133-36, 146-47, 150-51, 154n77, 158, 169, 238, 245n115, 248, 255-57, 274n84
Jerome, 54n76, 81-83, 88, 101-2, 107, 109, 113, 121, 126
Jerusalem, heavenly Jerusalem, 9, 10n21, 18n42, 50n61, 52, 58, 62-63, 65-66, 74n45, 76n50, 83, 103, 105, 109n79, 161n107, 173, 188, 200, 212, 230n43, 269, 299-300
Jews, Judaism, Jewish education, Jewish understanding of *paideia*, 39, 47-54, 58-59, 64-66, 71nn30,31, 106, 137-44, 167-68
John XXIII, 18-19
John Paul II, xv-xvi, 6-7, 12, 19n48, 22, 24-28, 63, 79, 88, 123n144, 128, 164n1, 167n9, 189, 192, 255, 284-86, 291, 297, 304
Johnson, Aaron P., 154n76
Jonas, Hans, 195n4, 196n6
Jones, A.H.M., 68n18, 166n6
Jones, H. Stuart, 47n50
Josephus, 40n26, 47nn49,51,52, 50n60, 53n73
Jungmann, Josef A., SJ, 9, 81n68, 215, 218, 258n7
Justin Martyr, 91, 149n58

Kavanagh, Aidan, 13-14
Kees, Hermann, 32n3, 55n81
Kelly, J.N.D., 122n138
Kerygma, kerygmatic, proclamation, 7-8, 12n32, 25-27, 65, 86, 113, 118n115, 120, 122, 124, 153-62, 184, 194-95, 200-14, 217-20, 225-26, 246-48, 253, 271, 294n13
Kevane, Eugene, 138n21, 161n107
King, Benjamin John, 289n144, 305

Klijn, F.J., 65n9, 82n74
Koester, Helmut, 64n1
Kramarz, Andreas, LC, 209nn60,66

Lamberton, Robert, 51n65
Langer, Rudolf E., 37n19
Layton, Richard, 70, 103n55, 121n129, 122, 184n79, 212n85, 214, 245, 277n97
Leaney, Alfred R.C., 47n53, 55n81, 58nn88,89
Leo XIII, 164n137
Letter of Aristeas, 39-40, 49, 50n60
Letter to Theodore, Mar Saba, 112, 296-98, 301
Lewis, C.S., 15, 148
Libraries, scholarship, research, 18-19, 37-43, 49-50, 73-75, 92-93, 96n27, 104-5, 113, 123-28, 146-47, 274-75
Lightfoot, Robert Henry, 80, 293, 295, 298n28, 303n52
Lilla, Salvatore R.C., 153, 174n41
Lodge, R.C., 237n79
Louth, Andrew, 14n34, 17, 25n69, 265, 273n80
Lovejoy, A.O., 183n77
Lubac, Henri de, SJ, 5n7, 6, 125n150, 159n100, 279n103
Ludwig, Emil, 56
Lynch, John, 47n48, 92nn14,15, 93n17, 95n24, 96n27, 126n152, 134n7, 161n108, 168n14, 274n84

Macarius Politicus, 101
Maertens, Thierry, 271n66
Maier, Harry O., 165n3
Margerie, Bertrand de, SJ, 144n42
Mark, Evangelist, 22, 31, 54n76, 63, 78-88, 92, 102, 107, 112, 300-2
  Gospel, xv, 22-23, 28, 63, 78-88, 97, 111, 262, 276, 291-303
  Liturgy, 81
Markus Robert A., 73-77
Marlowe, John, 31n1, 42, 198n13
Marriage, parents, family, home, 62n109, 137-38, 140-41, 144-45, 158, 223, 248, 254-55, 265, 271-72, 279
Marrou, Henri, 26n75, 69, 106, 133n1,3, 134nn5,7, 138n22, 161n108, 201, 223n16, 250, 255, 258, 274n87

Mazza, Enrico, 283 n115
McDonald, James I, 12 n32
McGuckin, John A., 4 n5, 18 n47, 43 n37, 91 n10, 105, 117, 119-20, 121 n127, 127, 149 n58, 154 n77, 159-60, 206 n48, 211 n76, 225 n25
MacIntyre, Alasdair, 8 n14, 189-92
Manetho, 40, 42
Martyrdom, persecution, 11, 13, 81-82, 85, 88, 101, 117, 120, 165 n4, 204, 286, 305 n10
Méhat, André, 108, 123 n139, 198 n12, 221 n4, 246 n120
Merton, Thomas, 273-74
Miller, J. B., 137 n17
Milne, Joseph G., 57 n85
Momigliano, Arnaldo, 76 n52, 77 n54
Monasticism, consecrated religious life, 27, 69-72, 94, 97, 108, 120 n120, 145, 273-74
Monson, Andrew, 57 n86
Morello, Sebastian, 192 n102, 193 n107
Mortley, Raoul, 33 n5
Moses, 49 n59, 51, 69, 142 n37, 151, 153-54, 171, 212 n86, 241, 252
Mystagogy, post-baptismal formation, 28, 124, 203, 222, 235, 242, 245 n115, 252-53, 257-90

Noshy, Ibrahim, 34 n9
Nautin, Pierre, 129 n166, 221 n6, 222 n10
Nietzsche, 190-91
Newman, John Henry, xi, 2, 44 n37, 59, 149, 161 n107, 228 n37, 231, 233-41, 255, 275, 284, 288-89, 302, 305-6
Nock, Arthur D., 42 n34, 45 n41, 178 n52
Nockles, Peter B., 289 n144
Nongbri, Brent, 65 n10, 121 n133

O'Brien Carl Séan, 165 n2
Oden, Thomas C., 20-23, 81-82, 86 n90
Oesterley, William O. E., 152 n71
O'Leary, De Lacy, 69 n23
Oliver, Willem H., 102
Origen: life and writings, 116-20, 122-23, 126-29; leadership of school, 3, 88-90, 97-111
Osborn, Eric, 26 n72, 22 nn82,83, 60 n95, 112, 113 n96, 115 n103, 155, 208, 227, 236, 247 n122, 266 n46, 271 n67

Pantaenus, 3, 45, 74 n45, 90, 98-102, 109-11, 125, 127-28, 201-2, 269, 275
Parker, Charles P., 236 n71
Parsons, Edward A., 34, 38 n21, 39 nn23,24, 40 n29, 41 n31, 42, 43 n37
Pater, Walter, xvi
Patterson, L. G., 155 n82
Patterson, Stephen, 112 n89
Paul VI, 5-6, 22, 82 n73, 287
Peace, Richard V., 295
Pearson, Birger A., 52 n71, 67 n14, 70 n25, 79, 82 nn71,72, 107 n69
Peter, Apostle, 54 n76, 65, 83-88, 97, 99, 210, 264, 271, 291-95, 298 n28, 299, 300 n38
Peter, bishop of Alexandria, 101-3
Philip of Side, 78, 101-2, 111 n87
Philo of Alexandria, xi, 9 n18, 44, 48 n54, 51-54, 60, 71, 83, 113, 122, 128, 129 n167, 140-44, 150-51, 164, 170-71, 180-81, 196 n7, 241-43, 283
Philo of Larissa, 94
Photius, 99
Pieper, Josef, 16, 114
Pius XII, 10
Plato, Platonism, Middle Platonism, Neo-Platonism, xi, 1, 26, 50 n61, 51, 91-97, 114, 117, 119, 125, 129 n167, 133-37, 139 nn24,25, 140 n32, 141 n35, 151-53, 164-71, 174-75, 179-88, 189, 192 n102, 193, 195, 201, 206 n46, 208 n57, 209, 212 n84, 216 n102, 236 n73, 237-45, 248, 259 n11, 261, 265-69, 283, 287-88
Pliny the Elder, 45 n40, 167 n11
Plotinus, 26, 97, 193, 195 n1, 265 n45
Plutarch, 33 n5, 43 n37, 133 n2, 152, 168 n15, 248, 258 n7, 259, 261 n21
Polis, political, 10, 33 n4, 39, 41-42, 44-45, 50 n61, 60-61, 81 n68, 102-3, 136-37, 143, 145-46, 151, 167-68, 173, 255, 266, 287, 288 n138
Polybius, 74 n44
Pompa, Klaas Jan, 32 n2
Porphyry, 92, 117, 278 n100
Pontifical Council for Culture, 219 n108
Pontifical Council for the Promotion of New Evangelization, 7 n11, 11 n26, 12
Potts, Daniel T., 40 n27

Pouchelle, Patrick, 142n37, 155
Pouderon, Bernard, 90n4, 101
Proclus, 166, 193
Pseudo-Dionysius, 193
Pythagoras, Pythagorean, 1, 94-95, 151-52, 169-70, 229n38, 232n56

Rétif, André, 124n145
Rhodon, 4, 78, 101, 104
Rich, Audrey N.M., 181n71
Ritter, A.M., 65n6
Ritter, Heinrich, 113, 228n36
Rius-Camps, Josep, 68n12
Roberts, Colin H., 41n30, 65-66, 85
Robinson, John A.T., 80
Rome, xvii, 2-3, 9, 19, 31, 36n16, 44-46, 54n76, 56-58, 63, 76n50, 77, 83-87, 103, 109, 112, 120n125, 133, 146, 161n107, 199n16, 215, 221
Rubenson, Samuel, 3n4
Rudolph, Conrad, 37n19
Rufinus, 73n39, 103, 109, 121
Runia, David T., 53n75, 54, 64n4, 65n8, 113n97, 122, 128, 265
Russell, Norman, 273n81

Saghy, Monica, 166n5
Sayers, Dorothy, 231n50
Schefer, Christina, 261n20
Schildgen, Brenda Dean, 80, 85n84, 86n93, 294, 298n30
Schliesser, Benjamin, 66n11
Scripture versions, exegesis, interpretation, place in formation, 3, 5, 9, 21, 28, 50-53, 69, 78-88, 99n37, 112-13, 117-21, 124-27, 140-44, 148, 152n71, 154, 159, 171, 173n36, 176-77, 179, 184-88, 198, 206n48, 218, 222-24, 236, 241, 246, 252, 257, 265, 274-84, 288-90
Selwyn, E.G., 294n12
Septuagint, 39-40, 50, 140-44, 155, 252n151
Seneca, 95
Sextus Empiricus, 172n31, 173
Shenoute, 273
Shepherd of Hermas, 106
Shubert, Stephen Blake, 40n27
Simon, Marcel, 53n74
Smith, Morton, 112, 297-98, 301

Snyder, H. Gregory, 92n13
Socrates, philosopher of Athens, 91, 135-36, 145, 170n19, 201, 208n57, 261, 266, 269, 287-88
Socrates, Church historian, 72n35, 74, 78, 165n4, 222n10
Sollom, Scott, 187n88
Sozomen, 72n35, 74, 102n51
Spirituality, spiritual guidance, spirituality of learning, xvii, 8, 89, 96-97, 116, 119-20, 184-88, 195, 231-34, 250-51, 265-74, 284-90
Stanford, William B., 283n115
Stapert, Calvin, 209n67
Steiner, George, 59
Sterling, Gregory, 54n77
Stewart, Columba, OSB, 69n22, 108n71
Stock, Augustine, OSB, 293n9, 294n14
Stoic, Stoicism, 1, 51n45, 93n17, 94n26, 97, 125, 129n167, 148, 169-70, 174, 204, 228n36, 236-38, 241n95, 244, 283n115
Strabo, 34n7, 35, 41n32, 43n37, 47, 96n27, 201n28
Strousma, Guy G., 200
Swancutt, Diana M., 227n29

Tatius, 35n10
Taylor, Vincent, 295n21
Tertullian, xv, 9, 87n96, 91nn8, 10, 221n3
Thomson, Stuart Rowley, 111n85
Thornton, T.C.G., 294n12
Tollinton, Richard, 203
Trigg, Joseph W., 120, 281n111
Tolan, Daniel J., 265n45
Tuccinardi, E., 112n92
Turck, André, 221n3
Tzamalikos, Panayiotis, 181

Valentinus, 67, 155
Van den Broek, Roelof, 65n5, 72, 75n48, 104, 106, 108n72, 265n44
Van den Hoek, Annewies, 1, 72n36, 106n66, 109, 128, 272
Vatican Council II, 5, 8, 9n17, 184n79
Verdoner, Marie, 54n76, 75, 76n49
Versnel, Henk S., 167n10
Vleeschauwer, Herman J. de, 40n27

Watson, Francis, 112
Watts, Edward J., 46n46
Wear, Sarah Klitenic, 165n2
Weil, Simone, 16
Wheeler, Mortimer, 45n40
Widdicombe, Peter, 181n72, 230n46, 247nn124,128
Wilken, Robert L., 90n4, 125, 129
Wilkins, Michael J., 139nn24,26,27
Willey, Petroc, 7n13, 187n88, 189n95
Williams, Charles, 231n50
Williams, Rowan D., 107-8, 186n86, 229, 289n144, 297n27
Willis, Geoffrey G., 298n31

Witt, R.E., 95n26
Wood, Simon P., 111, 113n96
Wrede, William, 295nn18,21
Wright, N.T., 296n22

Yarnold, Edward, SJ, 10n20
Young, Frances M., 2n2, 103n56, 119n118, 230n42
Young, N.H., 223n15

Zeno, 91-93
Zenobia, 43n37, 57n84
Zuntz, G., 128n162
Zurawski, Jason M., 140n31

ABOUT THE AUTHOR

PETROC WILLEY was appointed by Pope Benedict XVI a Consultor for the Pontifical Council for the Promotion of the New Evangelization, and is currently a Consultor to the Dicastery for Evangelization in the Section for Fundamental Questions regarding Evangelization in the World. A Professor of Theology and Catechetics at Franciscan University, Steubenville, in Ohio, he has authored numerous books and scholarly articles on the catechetical *ressourcement*, including *The Catechism of the Catholic Church and the Craft of Catechesis*. He studied theology and philosophy in London, Liverpool, Maynooth, and Rome, and before his move to the United States in 2015 taught in England, in Catholic institutions in Oxford and Birmingham. He is married to Katherine and has four children and a growing number of grandchildren.